Studying and working in France

MANCHESTER
1824

Manchester University Press

Studying and working in France

A student guide
Second Edition

Russell Cousins,
Ron Hallmark and Ian Pickup

Manchester University Press
Manchester and New York

Distributed exclusively in the USA by Palgrave

First edition published 1994 by Manchester University Press
Reprinted 1994

This edition published 2007 by
Manchester University Press
Oxford Road, Manchester M13 9NR, UK
and Room 400, 175 Fifth Avenue, New York, NY 10010, USA
www.manchesteruniversitypress.co.uk

Distributed exclusively in the USA by
Palgrave, 175 Fifth Avenue, New York, NY 10010, USA

Distributed exclusively in Canada by
UBC Press, University of British Columbia, 2029 West Mall,
Vancouver, BC, Canada V6T 1Z2

British Library Cataloguing-in-Publication Data
A catalogue record for this book is available from the British Library

Library of Congress Cataloging-in-Publication Data applied for

ISBN 978 0 7190 5548 5 paperback

This edition first published 2007

16 15 14 13 12 11 10 09 08 07   10 9 8 7 6 5 4 3 2 1

Typeset in Ehrhardt and News Gothic
by Koinonia Ltd, Manchester
Printed in Great Britain
by Bell & Bain Ltd, Glasgow

Contents

To Jenny, Joan and Anne

Introduction

Since the publication of the first edition of *Studying and Working in France* in 1994, much has changed both in the French higher education system and in student attitudes and expectations. The present edition is a newly researched, revised and expanded version of the original volume, informed by this two-fold evolution. In its revised form the *Guide* provides an up-to-date account of higher-education structures and seeks to answer often-expressed student and parental concerns about adapting to a French lifestyle, finding accommodation and coping financially.

Though primarily geared towards Anglophone EU students, the text addresses a number of administrative concerns particular to students from North America and Australasia. Practical advice is also offered to all those who wish to spend a formative period in France, but not necessarily as full-time students: those who have elected to be language assistants in a school, college or university, or who have opted for a work-experience placement. Successive chapters provide essential information and everyday advice for those setting out on a gap year, for undergraduates fulfilling course requirements or for students acquiring experience in the workplace or engaged in teaching. In its general advice, the volume seeks to address the needs of all those planning an extended formative stay in France.

Mobility schemes such as ERASMUS or SOCRATES have successfully increased student movement between EU member states, and there are now several thousands of non-indigenous students in France either on exchanges or as individual 'free-movers'. For these visiting foreign students, particularly those on inter-university exchanges, there are sections dealing with study-contracts, the French pedagogic and assessment systems, and the workings of the European Credit Transfer System.

Although institutional student-exchange programmes are much more commonplace than a decade or so ago, there are still many aspects of life in French higher-educational institutions (and, indeed, in French society in general) for which many visiting students seem ill-prepared. To remedy this situation, individual chapters seek to facilitate preparation and integration by providing advice on planning the intended stay, dealing with the necessary administrative and academic procedures and how to adapt to the host French community.

The *Guide* may be used in various ways. Firstly, as a source of general information on French institutions (their courses and administrative procedures), work-experience placements and assistantships; secondly, as a source of answers to concerns about accommodation and financial matters; and, thirdly, to clarify the meaning of common academic acronyms or abbreviations, or those used in advertisements. Part I provides background information for the student new to French higher education. After an explanation of the pattern of higher education institutions in Chapter 1, Chapter 2 examines course structures and academic awards. Chapter 3 is an account of accommodation and welfare services, and explains how the various offices of the CROUS can play a key role. Part II reviews a series of practical steps to ensure a successful formative period in France. Chapter 4 outlines employment opportunities in France such as work-experience placements, assistantships and vacation jobs. For those engaged in full-time study, Chapters 5 and 6 focus on steps to be taken both before departure and then on arrival in France, with practical guidance relating to administrative and registration procedures, securing accommodation, making financial arrangements and becoming a member of the student community. Chapter 7 prepares all Anglophones for their return home and for their reintegration in the home-based study programme. Part III provides an alphabetical list of principal French institutions of higher education, together with brief descriptions of the relevant major towns, and incorporates tourist information such as leisure facilities, accommodation options and travel connections.

Finally, the Glossary and abbreviations list (including acronyms) embraces the academic, administrative, practical and everyday expressions which are likely to be encountered both before and during the period in France. When first introduced in the main body of the text, these key French terms are italicized alongside their English equivalents.

The institutions included in Part III are, for the most part, the ones about which the authors are most knowledgeable. Their combined experience as Year Abroad tutors for BA, BCom, BSocSc, BSc and LLB students spending one month, six months or, more normally, a full academic year at a French institution of higher education is at the core of the *Guide*. However, the authors would like to acknowledge the invaluable contribution of many students – past and present – in updating and reviewing local information, as well as the generous co-operation of French colleagues and friends who, over the years, have advised so expertly.

This new version of the *Guide* will have served its purpose if it helps the many – sometimes doubtless apprehensive – students *en route* to *la belle France*, to enjoy more completely their unrivalled opportunity to experience another culture. Whether setting out to pursue their academic studies, to undertake a work-experience placement, or simply to improve their knowledge and understanding of the language, people or way of life of their adopted country, both committed and wavering francophiles will undoubtedly benefit from their period in France. As individuals, they will return not only better informed, but with an enhanced breadth of perspective and an increased depth of maturity. Not least of all, through their diverse cultural experiences and contacts they will have been personally enriched, and through their achievements they will enjoy greater self-esteem and self-confidence. In the years ahead they will come to savour, and continue to benefit from, this formative French period. Their future employers will have no doubt about these accumulated benefits.

Part 1
Background information

1
The pattern of higher-education provision in France

Students choosing to study or work in France will have a better understanding of their French counterparts if they know about their educational background and the choices they have already made.

French eighteen-year-old secondary-school pupils (*lycéens*), armed with their school-leaving certificate (*baccalauréat*) and intending to pursue their studies to a higher level, have a number of possibilities. Some will attempt to secure a place in the advanced technical-training departments of the *lycées* (*sections de techniciens supérieurs*) or brave the selection procedure for one of the much sought-after *Instituts universitaires de technologie* (IUTs). Others will stay on at the *lycée* and enrol for courses (*classes préparatoires*) which lead to the highly competitive and selective alternative system of the *grandes écoles* and the *écoles spécialisées*. But the vast majority (over 60%) of those taking the *bac général*, a significant proportion (almost 20%) of those taking the *bac technologique*, and even a few with the *bac professionnel* will decide to take up their automatic right to register at a university.

Since the majority of foreign students will also probably register in French universities, this *Guide* will focus first on those institutions, whilst placing them in the broader context of higher education in France.

1.1 The universities

French universities have a long and venerable history. The earliest amongst them date from the thirteenth century: Paris (1211), Toulouse (1229) and Montpellier (1289). The church, of course, exercised a virtual monopoly on education more or less to the time of the Revolution. As with so many other aspects of French society, however, the framework of the present educational system was established by Napoleon. For administrative purposes, France was divided into *académies*, each one headed by a representative of the central authority, the *recteur*. This administrative structure still persists today. However, Napoleon's concept of the University – l'Université Impériale – is no longer valid. Whereas the Emperor defined the University as the education system in its totality, incorporating the *écoles primaires*, the *lycées* and the *facultés*, subsequent changes have narrowed the use of the term to post-*baccalauréat* institutions of higher education.

For all practical purposes, the present university structures can be traced back to the education reform act (*loi d'orientation*) which emerged from the social and political upheavals of 1968 (*les événements de mai '68*). It was the untenable situation in the *facultés* that was a major determining factor in the events of that year. Overcrowding had reached unprecedented levels: in many instances, the lecture rooms could come nowhere near to accommodating the numbers of students enrolled. At Nanterre, for example, the university, built to cater for some 2,000 students, was faced with some 20,000 registering in October 1967. Staffing provision was manifestly inadequate. The hopelessly adverse staff–student ratios exacerbated even further the endemic impersonal relations between teacher and taught. A new generation of students began to question fundamental issues concerning the nature of the curriculum, the functioning of the various *facultés*, and indeed the very relationship between the universities and society at large.

Out of all this unrest emerged the parliamentary legislation on higher education which was passed in November of that year and which, viewed retrospectively, is to be seen as a watershed in the history of French universities. The *loi d'orientation*, initiated by Général de Gaulle and the then Ministre de l'Education Nationale, Edgar Faure, led to a radical reorganization of the French university system. The hundred or so faculties, loosely grouped together as universities (usually one for each of the twenty-three *académies*) were abolished and replaced by seventy-one new-style universities and a small number of outposts (*centres universitaires*). The various *facultés* and their constituent departments therefore ceased to exist (though the term *faculté*, or *fac* for short, still has currency) and were replaced, as the main subdivisions of a university, by *unités d'enseignement et de recherche* (UER). The latter could correspond in their focus either to a traditional discipline (UER d'Anglais) or to a faculty (UER de Médecine et de Pharmacie) or even to a grouping of related disciplines (*thème d'études*) – for example, UER des Sciences de l'Environnement. The underlying aim of the UER – as the name suggests – was the symbiotic linking of teaching and research in higher education, two of the three basic functions (*missions*) of the universities, as laid down in the Act. The third, *la formation de l'homme* (the development of human potential), also marked a radically new departure in its extension of interest beyond the purely intellectual side of the personality.

The fundamental principles informing the *loi d'orientation* were autonomy, participation and *pluridisciplinarité* (multi-disciplinary structures). Autonomy, as enshrined in the Act, in theory gave the universities and their constituent *unités d'enseignement et de recherche* the power to determine their own internal structures. They were to be run by committees or councils (*conseils*) composed of elected representatives from the student body, and the administrative and ancillary staff, in addition to the teaching and research staff. The highest elected body – the *Conseil d'Université* – incorporated a number of distinguished outside members who were prominent in the life of the region. Autonomy also applied to academic matters: the *conseil* of each UER was given the power to lay down its own programme of studies, research activities, teaching methods and modes of assessment. Decisions on these various matters had, however, to respect predetermined criteria (*règles communes*) to meet the requirements of standard national diplomas (see pp. 11–12). Autonomy extended to financial matters: monies and other resources provided centrally were placed under the budgetary control of individual establishments, but, again, within limits and guidelines imposed nationally.

The second fundamental principle – participation – is already evident in the existence of the various *conseils* referred to above, and is to be seen as a direct consequence of the events of May 1968. For the first time, students were given the right to vote their own representatives onto the relevant *conseils*. Elections amongst the teaching and research staff encouraged self-determination at every level. Members of the *conseils d'université* held ballots to elect their own representatives at regional and national level.

The third principle underpinning the *loi d'orientation* – *pluridisciplinarité* – was designed to break down the rigid, historically based, faculty distinctions between individual areas of study. It was also intended to diminish the formidable power of senior faculty *professeurs* (referred to in derogatory terms as *les mandarins*), who controlled all aspects of their own academic subjects. The new universities, though they might well have a dominant focus, were to be established as multi-disciplinary structures, combining, wherever possible, arts and letters with science and technology.

Since 1968, French universities have been in a constant state of change and evolution: successive Ministers of Education have seemed determined to leave as their legacy their own *loi* with its new initiative or focus.

But despite subsequent legislation, the determining principles and global structures of the *loi d'orientation* subsist, along with the democratization which is such a salient feature of this Act.

There have been significant changes. The number of universities has now expanded to about eighty in mainland France, and the number of outposts (*antennes*) has massively increased to meet the exceptional growth in student numbers and to provide some elements of university study in virtually all towns of any real size. Concerns to emphasize the career function of higher education led to a major change of nomenclature: the *unités d'enseignement et de recherche* were replaced with *unités de formation et de recherche* (UFR), thereby placing much more emphasis on training (*formation*).

More recent measures have sought to address the vexed problem of reconciling university autonomy, and the consequences of decentralization, with the need for national coordination. The priority was to promote research excellence and a reasonably fair distribution of course provision. Since the system, however, steers students towards their local or regional universities, some measure of supra-regional planning had to persist. The upshot was the introduction in 1989 of a system of quadrennial contracts between the universities and the Ministry of Education, whereby the institutions set out their plans and objectives, and the Ministry confirms their entitlement to confer the relevant diplomas and allocates funds for the agreed activities.

Plans have been mooted – and hotly contested too – to introduce a new style of university management which will diminish the power of the councils and place more authority in the hands of the presidents.

But, on the whole, subsequent reforms have sought to address two main concerns: to reduce the worrying drop-out rate, particularly during the first *cycle*, and to make qualifications, and the studies that lead to them, more appropriate to the world of work and career outlets. The measures that have emerged from the latter concern will be considered in Chapter 2, when we come to examine courses as they evolved on the classical pattern. In terms of the wastage rate, various remedies have been tried, and, while they have had some effect, it is clear that much still remains to be done. Estimates produced some twenty years ago (in the early 1980s) suggested that, depending on disciplines and locations, somewhere between 30 and 60 per cent of students embarking on first-year courses did not reach the *deuxième cycle*. The picture became even blacker when it was suggested that these figures took no account of those who just 'disappeared' and did not, for whatever reason, register for the second year. However, more recent figures for 2002–03 suggest that the overall success rate for transfer between *cycles* is now about 56 per cent, and is above 50 per cent for all disciplines, a figure that both demonstrates the improvement and highlights the ongoing problem.

Measures that have been tried to reduce the dropout rate include: greater liaison between institutions of secondary and higher education, with university open days for final-year *lycée* pupils; better briefing of students over pathways, with induction weeks on arrival, to avoid misunderstandings over the nature of courses, their demands and possible career outlets; greater flexibility to allow course changes without penalty at the end of the first semester, in the event of a wrong initial choice of strand; better support mechanisms, with senior students (from the *deuxième* and *troisième cycles*) taking on the role of academic and welfare tutors; greater compensation between different components of a course, rather than a blanket requirement to pass every contributory *unité de valeur* (UV). It remains to be seen how successful such initiatives can be as long as entry to the universities remains open to all.

The French university system differs in many respects from that of the UK and the USA, for example, perhaps most fundamentally in terms of access: whereas in the Anglo–Saxon tradition, entry is selective and, in some cases, fiercely competitive, French universities are open to all holders of the *baccalauréat* (*bacheliers*) and equivalent qualifications; even if this right of automatic entry, particularly for the most popular disciplines, in practice applies only to the local university, and even then only for the year in which the *baccalauréat* is achieved.

The second great attraction of a university education is that such study is free – or virtually so. Only administration fees of some €350 a year are charged. These two features are regarded as basic republican rights that, over the years, have been constantly reaffirmed by legislation, confirmed by the Conseil Constitutionnel, and hotly defended, by direct student action if necessary, when appearing to be under threat.

Last, but not least, the modern universities cover the full range of disciplines, and offer a wide variety of courses and qualifications. For anyone intending to enter the professions – and become a teacher, lawyer or doctor – university study remains the only route possible. What is more, they – and only they – award the national diplomas: at *bac +2* (the *diplôme d'études universitaires générales* (DEUG)), *bac +3* (*licence*), *bac +4* (*maîtrise*) and *bac +7/8* (*doctorat*). Whichever university students attend, they receive the same national diploma, whose status is guaranteed by the criteria laid down by Ministry of Education. This universality of standard is yet another 'public service' principle, ensuring parity of esteem for a *licence* from a fledgling provincial foundation and the same degree from

Paris I Panthéon-Sorbonne.

However, the fact remains that, despite their attractions, the universities have for decades been subject to major problems. Their staff–student ratios remain very high, and relations between teachers and taught are distant and impersonal in consequence. Figures show that while the university student population increased between 1968 and 1995 from just over 300,000 to over one and a half million, the staff–student ratio actually declined between 1970 and 1990 from 1:20.8 to 1:24.7, and this average hides many gross disparities: in Medicine and Science, the figure was about 1:15, while in *Lettres* it was 1:34.6 and in Law 1:55!

The universities, then, remain overcrowded and badly under-funded, more so than other sectors of HE. Figures produced for 2002 showed that over €11,000 was spent per student in STS or *classes préparatoires* (see 1.2 below), but only an average of about €7,000 on a university student (except for students in an IUT or in the engineering sector). Moreover, given that the universities are mainly state-funded, and that the main item of expenditure is the salaries of tenured staff, rapid solutions appear unlikely. Whenever money has been provided to redress the balance somewhat, as in the early 90s, under Jospin as Minister of Education, circumstances have overtaken good intentions. In the event, with the university student population increasing rapidly at about 7 per cent a year between 1990 and 1993, the extra cash did little more than match expansion.

The universities are, then, the work-horses of the French higher-education system and also the poor relation. They have had to cope with a forty-year period of expansion which has seen their student numbers increase by a factor of 5, while struggling for the resources to cope. With the Plan Université 2000, designed to prepare for 2 million HE students by the early twenty-first century, the combined efforts of the State and local authorities succeeded in injecting capital investment into the universities. Major building works were undertaken that helped to cope with the increase in student numbers during the crucial years, but did little to improve the general living and working conditions of students. It remains to be seen whether the Plan U3M (Université du Troisième Millénaire) with its different priorities can make a significant impact in this respect.

1.2 *Etudes courtes*: the STS and IUT

Over the years, many attempts have been made to adapt the content of the 'classical' two-cycle, four-year strand to the perceived needs of society. In particular, some forty years ago there surfaced a general apprehension that the 'classical' pattern of study, into which a student was locked before coming onto the job market, was too long and too theoretical to cater for the requirements of an increasingly fast-moving technological society. The need was not for theorists but for practitioners who could be trained rapidly in the range of skills required to plug the holes developing in the job market. Hence, there was the development of shorter courses in both the already existing advanced technical-training departments of the *lycées* (*sections de techniciens supérieurs* – STS), and in new establishments that were set up, as from 1966, in conjunction with the universities, the *instituts universitaires de technologie* (IUTs).

Both sorts of establishment have seen massive expansion over the last thirty years. There are now more than 2,100 STS and well over 100 IUT throughout mainland France, with at least one IUT in almost every medium-sized town. Moreover, the numbers attending them have increased dramatically: between 1980 and 2002, students in the STS went up by 275 per cent, from just under 61,000 to 169,000, while during the same period the population of the IUT increased by 108 per cent, from over 52,000 to 109,000.

The two types of establishment have much in common. Both run two-year courses leading to a diploma that is designed specifically to secure immediate employment: the *brevet de technicien supérieur* (BTS) in the case of the STS, and the *diplôme universitaire de technologie* (DUT) in the case of the IUT. Both select students on academic record, or by interview seeking to test motivation or general knowledge. Sometimes, in the case of the more demanding IUT, there are written tests. Both types of establishment have been popular with students and widely welcomed by employers.

But there are differences between them, too. In the STS, some two-thirds of the places are filled by those who have taken the *bac technologique*, while those from the general and professional strands represent one-fifth and one-tenth respectively. Since the STS are to be found in the *lycées*, to attend them does not entail the kind of upheaval and change of scene that an IUT course does. Classes are fairly small, and consist of about 30 students. Courses are intensive, comprising about thirty hours' classes per week, with work in addition to be done at home. Staff supervision and support is more in evidence. There is, however, little assessed coursework, and the award of the diploma depends upon performance in examinations. Progress is checked by results in the first-year examination, which are crucial, prior to the award of the diploma after successful completion of second-year tests. In fact, the experience feels very much like a continuation of the final years of *baccalauréat* study, apart, that is, from the periods of direct professional training that fill two-thirds of the time. The focus tends to be highly specialized, often in relation to the needs of the local economy, though all in all there are syllabuses covering virtually the whole spectrum of activity. These can be personalized and narrowed by the options available. The level of employment is more restricted than with an IUT qualification – intermediate management, perhaps, at best – but the success rate is high.

The IUT differs in its surroundings, its recruitment and its focus. Since each IUT is part of a larger university – though not necessarily located on the same site – students can enjoy the infrastructure benefits this entails, such as library resources and language laboratories. Two-fifths of the places are filled by students from the *bac général*, and only one-third and 1 per cent respectively from the technological and professional strands. Cohorts are larger than in the STS, and total between 50 and 100 students, unlike the crowds overflowing from lecture halls found in the *filières classiques*. There is work in smaller groups in support of lectures, however, in the form of seminars (*travaux dirigés* – TD) and practical classes (*travaux pratiques* – TP), and the level of staff support in both academic and methodological terms is significant, especially for tutored projects. The workload is heavy, and incorporates a large measure of assessed coursework, which, for most DUT, dispenses with the need for a final examination.

The focus of a DUT is always wider than a BTS, and the approach is more theoretical. That remains true despite the practical training that occupies half of the course. What is more, there are areas of professional activity that are not covered by the various special fields of the DUT: the visual arts, applied arts or textiles, for example. Nonetheless, the diploma is highly valued, and job sights can be set a little higher than for the holders of a BTS.

Employment prospects are generally considered to be excellent for holders of both the BTS and the DUT, certainly in any of the industrial fields, but they do vary somewhat according to sector. It is more difficult to find a contract in the service industries, for example. Nevertheless, however much these two diplomas were designed to turn out practitioners quickly, rampant diploma inflation has led at least half the students (two-thirds of DUT and one-third of BTS) to go on to further studies, either to one of the new *licences professionnalisées*, or, after an introductory certificate (*certificat préparatoire*), an MSG or MST. These courses will be discussed in Chapter 2.

To round off this account of two-year, post-*baccalauréat* courses, some mention should be made of another similar, professionally orientated diploma, the *diplôme d'études universitaires scientifiques et techniques*

(DEUST). It was introduced in 1984 within the universities, in parallel to the DEUG and acceptable as its equivalent for purposes of further study. The DEUST was, however, specifically set up to provide a practical qualification to reflect the needs of local and regional specialities in terms of industry, commerce, leisure activities and the arts; indeed, the various DEUST licensed by the Ministry called upon the active participation in the teaching process of personnel from the relevant professional sectors. Examples of such courses were *formation aux métiers de l'eau* (Lyon I), *droit des assurances* (Poitiers) or *profession immobilière* (Toulon).

The new development represented by the DEUST does not appear to have burgeoned in any major way. However, its future is assured, as it is to be continued by some universities under the new dispensation, with entry possible after a general first semester.

1.3   The *grandes écoles* and *écoles spécialisées*

Alongside the universities, the *grandes écoles* train senior personnel for the public and private sectors, industry and commerce. These establishments already admit foreign students and the numbers of such students spending a period of study-residence in them will no doubt increase, given the proliferation of exchange agreements, both within the EU and beyond.

The *grandes écoles* have an extremely important role to play in France and one which marks them out as radically different from institutions of higher education elsewhere. Their role is to train top civil servants, researchers, engineers, senior administrative and management personnel for the public and private sectors, the teaching profession, industry, commerce and the armed forces.

To give a precise definition of the *écoles* is almost impossible because of their diverse nature and function. Whilst some are attached to universities and share their teaching staff, others are separate entities with their own specialist teachers. Some are private, and charge high fees, some are State-run and offer bursaries or other forms of financial assistance. Some are highly specialized in one field of activity (telecommunications, for example), while others are generalist within a broad scientific or commercial area. In entry level and course duration, a survey of practice rapidly reveals that virtually all formulae are possible: entry can be post-*baccalauréat*, at *bac +2*, *+3* or *+4* etc, while courses can last three years or four years or more.

It is thus very difficult to make generalizations about them. But, before going further, it is wise to clarify the term *grandes écoles*, as there is always a danger of its being abused. There are many specialist schools and colleges, especially in the scientific, engineering and commercial fields, but the only ones allowed to call themselves *'grandes'*, strictly speaking, are those who have been admitted to the Conférence des Grandes Ecoles, and appear on its membership list. Even with that restricted definition, there are about 300 of them. While they cover all fields of activity, most fall into two main groups, the commerce schools and the engineering schools.

A high proportion of the *écoles supérieures de commerce* are sponsored by local Chambres de Commerce et d'Industrie, and are therefore called *consulaires*. The *grandes écoles d'ingénieurs* contain many of the oldest foundations (Ecole des Mines, Ecole des Ponts et Chaussées, Ecole Polytechnique), which these days fall under the aegis of various ministries. The curriculum in the different *écoles* is to a large extent determined by the exigencies of the relevant outside professional bodies. Admission is competitive and highly selective, and is achieved either by success in special examinations, followed by interviews, or through existing high-level qualifications. Access to the *écoles normales supérieures* and to most of the big engineering and commerce schools, for example, follows two years of intensive, post-*baccalauréat* study in the *classes préparatoires aux grandes écoles* in the *lycées*.

The number of students enrolled (fewer than 200,000) is small by comparison with the million and a half in universities. The influence exercised by the *écoles*, however, is enormous. The distinguished Ecole Nationale d'Administration (ENA), for instance, admits only about a hundred students per year, but from amongst its ranks have come a whole galaxy of prominent figures in French public life: three Presidents of the Fifth Republic (Pompidou, Giscard d'Estaing and Chirac), seven Prime Ministers of the Fifth Republic (Chirac (twice), Fabius, Rocard, Balladur, Juppé, Jospin, and Dominique de Villepin) were all former students (*énarques*), as were a large number of government ministers during the same period, and a large cohort of their senior civil servants.

In historical terms, the notion of the specialist *grandes écoles* dates from the aftermath of the Revolution of 1789 and was reinforced in the nineteenth century by the needs created by the industrial revolution. The Convention (1792–95) established the Ecole Polytechnique, the Ecole Normale Supérieure, the Conservatoire des Arts et Métiers and the Conservatoire de Musique. The Ecole Polytechnique, for example, remains semi-military in character and is a major training ground for the upper echelons of the Armed Forces, as well as for senior engineering personnel employed in government service. It also has a formidable record for producing captains of industry. It provides an intensive two-year scientific programme, conducted at a very high level, which enables its students to further their studies at a prestigious *grande école d'application* in their chosen field of study (for example, l'Ecole Nationale Supérieure des Mines, l'Ecole Nationale Supérieure des Ponts et Chaussées (Civil Engineering) or l'Ecole Nationale Supérieure des Télécommunications). The *grandes écoles* are primarily associated with commerce or with science and engineering (there are in excess of 200 such establishments that are empowered to award the highly prized and very remunerative engineering diploma (*diplôme d'ingénieur*)). Others specialize in the Humanities (for example, l'Ecole des Chartes or l'Ecole Nationale Supérieure des Bibliothécaires, which train archivists, palaeographers and librarians for the major state libraries), while still others specialize in administration, such as l'Ecole Nationale d'Administration referred to above, l'Institut National d'Administration Publique and the various Instituts d'Etudes Politiques; not to mention the many establishments which provide training for their students in the different agricultural disciplines or prepare them for research careers in various public or private bodies. The list is very long indeed.

Special mention should, however, be made of the *écoles normales supérieures* (ENS), which are four in number, and whose primary function is to train scientific researchers, university teachers, a limited number of senior secondary teachers and, more generally, top civil servants, local-government officials and management personnel for the public sector. All candidates for one of the ENS are obliged to sign an undertaking to work for the State for a minimum of ten years; once admitted, they assume the status of trainee civil servants (*fonctionnaires stagiaires*) and receive a salary (€1,500 per month) throughout their four years in the establishment.

The above *grandes écoles* award their own *diplômes*. The status of the award reflects the reputation of the institution, which is a function of the competition for entry, the level and duration of study (usually three years after the two years of intensive preparation), and the posts and salaries offered to their graduates, factors which are constantly analysed in the media and especially by the relevant professional bodies.

Alongside the *grandes écoles*, the *écoles spécialisées* provide training for entry into certain careers: to become, for example, paramedics of various kinds (nurses, physiotherapists, opticians, etc.), social workers (including specialists in education or activity leaders), artists and architects, musicians, dancers, actors and theatre technicians, communicators (including journalists), paralegals and estate agents, or non-commissioned officers in the armed forces. There are many such establishments – and of variable quality. As with the *grandes écoles*, the value of the qualification depends upon the reputation and standing of the individual institution with the relevant professional body. Entry often requires some form of post-*baccalauréat* preparation, is invariably selective, and, for the best of them, highly competitive. Some form of work experience may be preferred, or even required. Studies can last for between two and six years, with little chance of re-orientation in the event of a student not making the grade. The qualification obtained at the end may be a *diplôme d'état* (DE) or an award of the individual establishment.

In this chapter, we have placed French universities in the broader spectrum of higher education in France. The diversity of provision should not blind us to the fact that only a minority of *bacheliers* (or, colloquially, *bachots*) attend the *grandes écoles*, or even the STS and IUT; it is the university system which caters for the majority of post-*baccalauréat* students. It is to courses there that we shall now turn our attention.

2
Courses in French universities

This chapter examines French universities in terms of their course patterns, grouping of disciplines, the duration of studies and the qualifications that are awarded.

Academic programmes in French universities are organized somewhat differently from those in the UK and the USA, for example. It is therefore important to be familiar with course structures and with the level required.

Those Anglophones following courses for foreign students (many of which take place during vacations) will find the last section of the chapter most useful. However, they will still profit from the general overview provided for students registering for the whole, or an integral part, of a national diploma.

The universities' national diplomas mark them out as being different from the *grandes écoles*, each of which, as explained in the previous chapter, confers its own diploma. Universities have the right to offer, in addition to the *diplômes nationaux*, their own *diplômes d'université* – awards which are not sanctioned by the Ministry centrally but which have been created to satisfy a specific need. The Université Stendhal (Grenoble III), for example, registered students from its foreign ERASMUS partners for the *diplôme d'université d'études européennes intégrées (ERASME) premier ou deuxième cycle*. It is the phrase *diplôme d'université* which immediately signals the 'localized' nature of the award. The word *cycle* takes us on to one of the main functions of this chapter: an analysis of the organization of courses into their various groupings and levels.

However, the presentation of course patterns is complicated by the fact that, since 2002, French universities have been living through what was trumpeted by the Minister of Education as 'the biggest reform since 1984', which involves a basic reorganization of courses and diplomas. The necessary modifications were perceived as being so far-reaching that a phased

Schéma des études supérieures

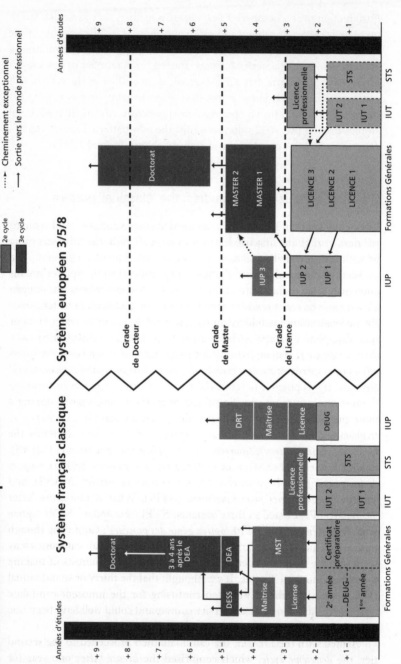

introduction over a number of years is envisaged, as they are extended to
more and more institutions and more and more disciplines within those
institutions. In the meantime, traditional study patterns will continue to
co-exist alongside the newer formats. Indeed, for a number of years, even
intermediate diplomas that will eventually be abolished by the reform will
continue to be awarded in response to student demand. Consequently, it is
necessary to present the two patterns independently: first of all, traditional
studies in their pre-2002 state; secondly, the new pattern *Licence-Master-
Doctorat*, which is known by the shorthand abbreviation of LMD.

2.1 The organization of studies: the 'classical' pattern

University study in France was organized in three successive and sequen-
tial tiers (*cycles*): the first two lasted for two years each, the third was more
or less open-ended. The *premier cycle* was designed to offer a grounding in
university study and an introduction to the individual disciplines' meth-
odologies. It led to the award of the first-level national diploma, the *diplôme
d'études universitaires générales* (the DEUG) – a qualification which, since
the rationalization introduced in the early 1990s, could be taken in some
nine discipline clusters: *administration économique et sociale* (AES); *arts*;
droit; *économie et gestion*; *lettres et langues*; *sciences et techniques des activités
physiques et sportives*; *sciences et technologies*; *sciences humaines et sociales*; and
théologie. It was possible to refine these rather broad categories by breaking
them down into more specific subject areas (*mentions*), thereby giving a
more precise indication of the specialisms. Hence the DEUG *sciences et
technologies*, breathtakingly all-encompassing at first sight, contains the
mentions: *mathématiques, informatique et applications aux sciences* (MIAS),
sciences de la matière (SM), *sciences de la terre et de l'univers* (STU), *sciences
de la vie* (SV), *mathématiques appliquées et sciences sociales* (MASS), and
sciences et technologies pour l'ingénieur (STPI). What is more, the latter
mention (STPI) existed in three variants: STPI *'sans option'*, STPI *'option
génie des systèmes'*, and STPI *'option génie des procédés'*. Confusing though
this arrangement of categories, sub-categories and sub-sub-categories may
seem initially to an outsider, it was introduced in the interests of making
the system more intelligible. It was thought that the thirty or so individual
DEUG that it replaced were too confusing for the innocent candidate
trying to make a choice of university course, and could well have been one
of the causes of costly errors and high wastage rates.

    Armed with the DEUG, the candidate then proceeded to the second
tier, the *deuxième cycle*, which comprised the *licence* (after one year (or

two semesters) of further study (*bac* +*3*)) and the *maîtrise* (after two years (*bac* +*4*)). The underlying aim was to offer a progressively more focussed degree of specialization in a subject area, while maintaining elements of choice, as in the *premier cycle*. The *licence* corresponded roughly to the Bachelor's degree in the UK or the USA, and the *maîtrise* to the Master's, though these analogies are somewhat misleading, given differences of course organization and the nature of study. The *maîtrise* looked forward to the third tier, the research tier, in that it always included a mini-dissertation (*mémoire*) on a specialist topic, which the student researched and documented independently.

The *troisième cycle* corresponded to the postgraduate area in the UK and the USA. The first year of study led to the award of the *diplôme d'études approfondies* (DEA), itself an essential methodological preparation and qualification for those wishing to embark upon a doctoral thesis (*doctorat*). Traditionally in France, particularly in the Humanities, the *doctorat d'état* was a *magnum opus*, a definitive statement on a subject area, which could take up to twenty years to complete. This was replaced by a somewhat more modest thesis, whose main function was to demonstrate research capability. The creation of a single pattern for the *doctorat* was intended to bring France's requirements more into line with the initial research qualifications of other countries, in particular her European partners and the USA.

Though the DEUG led towards specialization, it was always multi-disciplinary in nature, and composed of three blocks of subjects. In the first, introductory semester (*semestre d'orientation*) these were defined as one block that was basic to the discipline (*UE fondamental*) and was therefore compulsory; the second block was devoted to introducing a different discipline (*UE de découverte*), chosen from a restricted list, which could form the basis of a change of course without time penalty at the end of that semester, should the candidate have chosen wrongly in the first place. The third study block was given over to introducing candidates to the methodology involved in the discipline chosen (*UE de méthodologie*). At the end of the first semester, the candidate made a definitive choice of discipline, and continued for the following three semesters with three blocks of disciplines: basic, methodological and *culture générale*, which effectively meant optional elements designed to broaden and personalize the individual course pathway chosen, and could be taken from any such units available in any area of study taught in the university.

The units comprising the first two *cycles* of the 'classical pattern', known as *unités d'enseignement* (UE) were themselves groups of courses, clusters of what used to be referred to as *unités de valeur* (UV). To succeed in the DEUG, all UE must be passed, but not necessarily all their component parts. Measures of compensation were allowed between the constituent elements of any UE and a pass was achieved when an average mark of 10 out of 20 was reached for the UE as a whole. Within the structure of the diploma, not all UE carried the same weighting. They could be set against each other in terms of *coefficients* or, sometimes, *unités de compte* (UC); the basic UE (*fondamental*) had a weighting of 2, while the other two blocks counted 1 each. Assessment was generally by a variable mixture of coursework marks (*contrôle continu*), end-of-first-semester examinations and end-of-year examinations (*partiels* or *devoirs sur table* and *examens de fin d'année*). Once candidates had achieved 70 per cent of the weighted marks required for the first year of the DEUG, they were allowed to register provisionally in the second year, subject to making good the missing elements before any diploma could be awarded. Barring exceptional circumstances, the DEUG had to be completed in three years.

It is at this point that the picture becomes more complex. As was stated above, holders of the *baccalauréat* may register in the discipline of their choice in the university of their choice, without being subject to any process of selection on entry. Once in the university, however, it is a different matter: a marked feature of French universities over the last thirty or so years is the growing degree of selection that has faced students as they proceed through their university careers. It was always said that, in the open French system, selection was achieved by failure, so that the number of candidates proceeding from year to year automatically decreased, as some failed. This remains true. But in addition to this inherently random process, more and more deliberate selection found its way into the universities through the introduction of a growing number of highly sought-after, professionally orientated courses that were all competitive at the point of entry, and were located, in particular, in the *deuxième cycle*.

As was mentioned in Chapter 1, a lasting concern about French university studies over the last forty years has been that they were too abstract and insufficiently geared to subsequent employment. The response to this was to 'professionalize' them increasingly, and this process transformed significantly the *deuxième cycle* in particular. This occurred to the extent that it became possible to talk of a dual system from that stage onwards: the generalist strand, which all students who passed the DEUG could embark upon as of right, and the professional strand, where courses had a selective entry and only the best were accepted.

Candidates who chose the generalist route proceeded with their chosen discipline, which had to be related to the field of their DEUG. Their aim could have been to take a competitive examination at a later stage, or to go on into the *troisième cycle* with a career involving research in mind.

The CAPES (*certificat d'aptitude à l'enseignement secondaire*) – which can be prepared in the selective *instituts universitaires de formation des maîtres* (IUFM), accessed post-*licence* – or the highly competitive *agrégation*, prepared for post-*maîtrise* in the universities, both lead to the teaching profession, which continues to absorb some 20 per cent of university students. The distinction of a doctorate continued to attract many people. Alternatively, they may have been postponing selective study until the beginning of the *troisième cycle*, where they could follow one of the highly specialized and successful *diplômes d'études supérieures spécialisées* to provide a 'professionalized' qualification at *bac* +5, to cap what may have been generalist studies up to that point. It is true, too, that both generalist *licences* and *maîtrises*, while not very marketable in terms of employment, could serve as a solid base for a transfer route (*passerelle*) into a later year in a *grande école*, via the increasingly common opportunities made available for parallel access (*admissions parallèles*).

However, what revolutionized the *deuxième cycle* was the introduction of professional *maîtrises*. The earliest of these were the *maîtrise de sciences de gestion* (MSG), the *maîtrise d'informatique appliquée à la gestion* (MIAGE) and the *maîtrise de sciences et techniques* (MST). These two-year diplomas, developed alongside the more traditional and academic *licence/maîtrise* pattern, appear to have succeeded well in fulfilling their initial aim of bridging the gap between the universities and subsequent professional activity. From the outset, they attracted large numbers of highly qualified candidates, so that selection at entry proved to be severe. At Nancy II, for example, only 81 out of 368 candidates were admitted during the first three years of its MSG course. For the MST, on average, only one out of ten candidates was successful in obtaining a place. Applications could be made only by holders of the DEUG or its equivalent; candidates had also to be in possession of a *certificat préparatoire* before being allowed to register on the first year of the course.

Instruction on the above *maîtrises professionnalisées* was highly intensive and involved direct contact with industrialists and other outside specialists, both on the course and during industrial placements. The MST in particular offered a flexible formula covering a wide range of specialisms: there were more than seventy in Science and Computing, nearly fifty in Arts and Social Sciences and about the same number in Law, Economics and Business Studies.

Finally, some mention should be made of the *magistères*. These 'super-diplomas', introduced in 1985, fulfilled a similar function by means of three years of study for an even more stringently selected group of DEUG-holders. With the number of such courses initially increasing every year (in 1988 there were ten new MST and fifteen new *magistères* licensed by the Ministry), the diversification of opportunities at this level was further enhanced. At the time, the impression was that 'la professionnalisation des deuxièmes cycles va bon train'. The MSG, regarded as the Rolls-Royce of these qualifications, started to offer serious competition to the *grandes écoles de commerce*, a situation that was virtually unheard of before. All the more worrying for recruitment was that, within the universities, the diploma was 'free', and not subject to the high fees charged by most of the outside institutions. Even if the groups of students involved started off as being relatively small in comparison with total figures, they increased with time: in 1989, slightly over 3,000 MST and just over 3,000 MSG and MIAGE diplomas were awarded.

Having made an impression on the *deuxième cycle*, the powers that be determined to introduce the same process into the earlier years of the course. Two creations of the Jospin *régime* confirmed the determination of the Ministry to prepare university students in a more appropriate fashion for the world of work: the *instituts universitaires professionnalisés* (IUP), and the *instituts universitaires de formation des maîtres* (IUFM). The latter were part of the Minister's response to the need to raise the profile of the teaching profession and thereby meet the challenge of recruiting teachers in sufficient numbers for the end of the century. Intended to provide a common training for teachers of all levels, the IUFM were created in 1991 to take in students at the *bac +3* level and prepare them for the national competitive recruitment examinations, whilst enhancing their classroom experience. Financial inducements in the form of teaching allowances (*allocations d'enseignement*), paid over two years, were introduced to increase the numbers enrolling.

The IUP chose candidates at the end of the first year of university study – thereby pushing selection within universities back by a year – and conferred upon them an alternative executive qualification (*titre d'ingénieur-maître*) at the end of three further years. The number of students increased four-fold during the early years – from 2,000 to 8,000 between 1990 and 1991. Distinctive features of the programmes included the participation for 50 per cent of the teaching of industrial practitioners, and the encouragement of a large element of industrial experience for the students, on occasion extending to the creation of genuine sandwich courses. The portmanteau title of *ingénieur-maître* should not mislead Anglophones: it embraces, in addition to a standard range of scientific and technological specializations, various areas of general and special administration (such as *administration publique et privée*), commercial and general management (for example *commerce international*, *gestion hôtelière et touristique*), and communication studies (for example *sciences de l'information et communication, documentation dans l'entreprise*).

Finally, to complete the arsenal of professional qualifications awarded by the universities, a one-year *licence professionnelle* was created in 2000, with the accent placed very much on providing for industrial and commercial sectors that were having difficulty recruiting (information technology, large-scale distribution), concentrating particularly on skills shortages (electronics, new materials science, food safety). Recruiting candidates at *bac +2*, the courses were open not only to all DEUG-holders, but also to the increasing numbers of holders of the BTS or DUT, who persisted with further study and who found adaptation to the more theoretical generalist strand difficult and unpalatable.

It should not be thought, however, that attempts to nudge university 'long' courses in the direction of a greater awareness of the needs of an appropriately trained workforce have been largely restricted to the final years of study. As from the early 1980s, efforts were made to influence course content and structures at all levels and in all disciplines, by seeking to incorporate into the early years of all courses, as part of the reform of the *premier cycle*, elements of career counselling and, on occasion, of preliminary employment orientation (*préprofessionnalisation*). Even Arts students committed to the pursuit of as long-established an academic discipline as *lettres modernes* – the language and literature of France – were caught up in this trend and were required to follow courses which sensitized them to the potential career outlets of their chosen *filière*. This approach was later reinforced by the creation of induction courses for all students.

Moreover, new course patterns were instituted as variants of traditional strands. Multi-disciplinary, professionally orientated programmes were developed, such as *administration économique et sociale* (AES) and *mathématiques appliquées et sciences sociales* (MASS) and *langues étrangères appliquées* (LEA). 'Classical' courses for modern linguists, for example, essentially entailed, and still entail, the study of one foreign language and its civilization and culture (*langues et civilisations étrangères / langues vivantes étrangères* (LCE/LVE)). This was not ideal for the needs of the contemporary business world, hence the introduction of new applied modern languages courses, LEA, which combined, together with the study of two European languages, elements of Economics, Marketing, Accounting, Management and Business Studies. In common with the professionally orientated courses examined above, LEA programmes also created links with the business world and prescribed work placements. On occasion, a period of study-residence in the country of one of the target languages was also compulsory.

2.2 Reform: *Licence-Master-Doctorat* (LMD)

Announced in 2002, when the first legislation setting it up was passed in France, the LMD reform is the French response to what has become known as the Bologna process. Involving some thirty-odd countries from the greater Europe, these measures seek to bring about a harmonization of programmes between countries that will lead to greater standardization of qualifications, thereby promoting mobility for students and professionals alike. They are based upon a structure which incorporates three levels of diploma: L for *licence*, awarded after three years of post-*bac* study; M for *master*, which requires two more years; and D for *doctorat*, which will take a minimum of three years after award of the *master*. Hence the alternative way of referring to it as 3–5–8. Each of these levels will give access either to further study or to the job market.

Two other essential building blocks for the system are the semester, which will become the basic element of reference, and the system of credits known as ECTS (European Credit Transfer System). Whereas France had officially introduced the semester as a unit of teaching in the mid-1990s, the unit of reference for the purposes of progression remained on the whole the academic year. Now the semester is definitely to be the unit of reference, though the same ambiguity persists, since the six semesters required for the licence are organized into years known as L1, L2 and L3. Nevertheless, studies are now to be sanctioned at the end of each semester, with students having the automatic right to register for the next semester provided they have no more than one semester's credits outstanding. To pass a semester, it is necessary to acquire a total of thirty credits. Hence, 180 credits are required for the *licence*, a further 120 for a *master*, and a grand total of 480 to reach the *doctorat*.

Courses will continue to be organised into UE, as has been the case since 1996. Once passed, these course units remain realisable capital assets (*capitalisables*). They are also transferable: transferable between universities throughout France and countries abroad, in the first instance, thus promoting very positively student mobility; transferable, too, between course strands, so that students making an initial wrong choice of course may be helped by switching their acquired 'capital' of relevant credits to a new course, thereby avoiding having to start again. Once acquired, their value does not diminish, so that a student may, for example, decide to withdraw from study and then pick up again at a later date from the point reached. Flexibility, then, is the keynote in the promotion of the system.

The other advantage of the system is said to be the freedom it allows the student to design a more personalized pattern of study. Each of the first two levels will have its 'generalist' strand and its 'professional' strand,

and efforts are being made to ensure maximum opportunities to switch between one and the other at a number of different points. The generalist strand will lead to a *licence*, and then to a 'research' *master*, and perhaps to a *doctorat*. At the appropriate level, students will be able to take competitive examinations leading to the civil service or the teaching profession – or persist through to the end and aim at a career in research or in higher education. The 'professional' will continue to feed the outlets that have already been successfully exploited for the *licence pro* and the professionally orientated *maîtrises*.

Where studies are concerned, students must choose, within a coherent group or groups of courses, a programme that will provide the best preparation for the chosen career, finding a way through the compulsory and optional elements, and opting, perhaps, between a study semester or a practical placement. All pathways will contain core courses, complementary courses chosen to personalize the programme, and university-wide free electives (including sport, or a cultural activity, or a major role in a student society, for example). There will be theoretical elements, methodological elements and practical and applied elements. The chosen pathway may contain professional orientation modules (*préprofessionnalisation*), approached through individual or group projects, for example, and transferable skills (modern languages, computer skills, research skills, project skills, and so on) will be emphasized at all points. It is up to the student to juggle with these components and come up with an appropriate mix.

To help guide students through this potentially daunting maze, each institution will design a certain number of model pathways (*parcours-types*), where 20 of the 30 credits for a semester are suggested for each typical disciplinary field, leaving the individual to make up the rest by choosing from units in complementary disciplines, or from university-wide electives. It is also proposed that counselling arrangements be strengthened, so that students may have an opportunity to discuss their choices with those responsible for the course, or with senior students acting as tutors, or with counsellors (*conseillers d'orientation*). This freedom of choice is seen as bringing about a strengthening of commitment to the chosen course, and increased motivation, which will, in turn, help to reduce wastage rates. In addition, some institutions have already instigated remedial measures to help those in difficulty, with reduced workloads and increased personal support.

To take account of these freedoms and the inevitable divergences in courses, degree certificates will in future have an accompanying academic profile, listing courses taken and skills acquired, for the benefit of other institutions or employers alike.

Individual universities were asked to profit from their autonomy to apply the reform in their own ways and to stipulate their offerings for these new 'national' diplomas. Hence, the situation has been somewhat chaotic, as each institution has decided when to join the process, and which disciplines to trail, initially.

Old course patterns and new patterns have continued to exist side by side, and this makes it difficult to perceive a clear overall picture. During the period of conversion, the old intermediate diplomas that will eventually disappear – DEUG, *maîtrise* – have continued to be awarded, and look like being maintained for some time yet: hence a DEUG is available on demand to students who have successfully completed four semesters, or 120 credits, towards a *licence*, and a *maîtrise* to those who have completed the first 60 credits of a *master*. Transitional arrangements have been made to ensure that students do not lose out: the professionally orientated selected *maîtrises*, at present awarded at *bac +4*, will gradually be absorbed into the new system, and transformed into *masters professionnels* at *bac +5*. The DEA and DESS have already been replaced by a *master recherche* and a *master professionnel* respectively. Holders of the DUT and BTS will continue to be able to embark upon the third year of a *licence pro*, subject to recognition of their qualifications by the university concerned. What is more, the reform reaches further than the universities, and affects too the *grandes écoles* and the *écoles spécialisées*, some of which are being empowered for the first time to award a national diploma (*master*) at *bac +5*. Far from clear, however, is the fate of the DUT, an internal university diploma, whose syllabuses are currently being re-examined.

However much university autonomy may have been emphasized, with regard to national diplomas, national legislation has laid down the main underlying principles, so that the result is an odd compromise. For the *licence*, the student will have to choose between the generalist strand, and the professional strand, but considerable ingenuity has gone into devising patterns that allow this choice to be delayed until the end of the third semester, with as many elements as possible common to the two, and as many transfer routes as possible to other courses being left open. One difference between the two, once the choice has been made, is that only in exceptional circumstances will further study be allowable after a *licence pro*.

Students choose a *licence* within a general field of study (*domaine*), covering several disciplines, which is related to those followed in their *bac*. However, emphasis is placed upon studies being multi-disciplinary – at least at the outset – so that the choice within that general field is narrowed as late as possible. However, since courses are deemed to proceed along the lines of progressive specialization, students subsequently choose a narrower subject area (*mention*) to give the degree coherence, and ultimately an optional specialist field to particularize it. But at what point? Normally the *mention* will be selected at the end of the first semester; but in some institutions this choice may be delayed until the end of the third or even the fourth semester. Meanwhile, the maximum number of opportunities for change of course is maintained, and as many transfer routes out as possible are left open. Some institutions operate a major–minor system, a major being a discipline which corresponds to at least half the total of credits, and a minor to one that amounts to less than half. The objective remains the same, however: multi-disciplinarity and the acquisition of a solid base of knowledge in each of the constituent disciplines.

The *master* is regarded as the keystone of the new system. It is at this point that real specialization comes into play. All holders of a *licence générale* may embark as of right upon the open first year, choosing sooner or later between a research or a professional orientation (*master R* or *master P*). But entry into the second year is selective, based upon academic record and also an interview to examine the proposed professional project. Those who have passed the 60 credits from the first year, but are unsuccessful in securing a place in the second, will for the time being be awarded a *maîtrise* and may use this qualification for the same range of options and transfers that were discussed above under the classical pattern.

Most *licences* will lead to a range of *masters*, so once again a narrower discipline area (*mention*) must be chosen, which will ultimately be refined, usually at the end of the second semester, through an even narrower specialism (*spécialité*). Those who choose the research bias are obviously destined for a doctorate and a career in the research area. Those who gain access to professionally orientated courses will enter the job market and take advantage of the opportunities and success rate of the current *bac +4* and *bac +5* professional diplomas. Whichever of the two is chosen, there will be a mix of theoretical, methodological and practical skills courses: one very important innovation with the *masters* is that all students must pass at least one foreign language at the appropriate level before the diploma can be awarded.

Doctoral studies are similar the world over, and represent the peak of excellence in individual achievement. In France, as elsewhere, schools of doctoral studies are being organized, and candidates will complement their own high-level research projects and theses with multi-disciplinary skills courses designed to smooth their transition to subsequent employment.

These ambitious plans have, in recent years, progressively involved more and more institutions. The process will, in theory, be extended to all universities by 2007. But what, one may ask, will be the outcome? There are undoubtedly resource implications here, and the current financial climate in France is not propitious for a massive increase in investment through public spending. It is also true that there are pockets of resistance – sometimes very vocal pockets of resistance – to these reforms in principle and to what they may imply in terms of the 'globalization' of education and its transformation from a national public service to a market commodity. In addition, traditional forces of reaction and apathy within the system, the vested interests that have seen off earlier attempts at transformation, or at least reduced them to empty shells and purely cosmetic measures, are far from moribund. Will the same happen this time? The jury is out...

2.3 Courses for foreign students/vacation courses

So far the focus has been on the French educational system and its provision for French nationals – or for those students from abroad who are suitably qualified and of sufficient level in their mastery of the French language, to be assimilated into the same courses. However, it should be made clear that universities in France have always seen it as part of their mission to provide courses in French language and civilization for non-French speakers. As distinct from the UK, for example, where such provision is for the most part firmly in the hands of the private sector, state education in France has always assumed responsibility for the dissemination to non-Francophones of the national language and culture. There are many reasons for this: some are historical, and are to do with nostalgia over the status of French as a major diplomatic and commercial language; others relate to coordinated efforts to protect the French language against the hegemony of English. At all events, the extent of the provision is impressive in terms of both level and variety of formulae.

There are short courses (four weeks, six weeks, eight weeks and so on) run during Easter and, more commonly, summer vacations. In addition, universities, through their specialist units (Centre International d'Etudes Françaises (CIEF), Département d'Enseignement du Français Langue Etrangère (DEFLE), or Institut International d'Etudes Françaises (IIEF) for instance) provide courses throughout the academic year designed to accommodate a range of needs at a variety of levels. There are courses for complete beginners (*débutants*) as there are for advanced learners; courses for students with a special interest in Commerce, Economics or Law and refresher courses for foreign nationals who teach French; short, intensive courses to enable those whose French is limited or rusty to follow standard courses in French universities and year-long programmes leading to the award of nationally recognized diplomas.

The three main university diplomas concerned are: the *certificat pratique de langue française* (*premier degré*), the *diplôme d'études françaises* (*deuxième degré*) and the *diplôme supérieur d'études françaises* (*troisième degré*). These state-approved awards were created by decree in 1961; they entail increasing levels of difficulty, though there are no academic prerequisites in the case of the first two listed. A good basic knowledge of language and culture is required for entry to the *certificat* course. The diploma comprises an introduction to the methodology of courses in higher education and offers various options dealing with the cultural, economic and political life of France. To qualify to take the advanced diploma, candidates must already be in possession of the *diplôme d'études françaises* and have the *baccalauréat* or its equivalent. The course presupposes knowledge of the exercises and working practices of the French university system; holders of this award were able to apply for exemption from the first year of the *premier cycle* in *lettres modernes* or LCE/LVE, for example.

Alongside these awards, there exist two *diplômes nationaux* created by decree in 1985; the *diplôme élémentaire de langue française* (DELF) and the *diplôme approfondi de langue française* (DALF). These two diplomas operate on a modular basis. Candidates may follow the course in its entirety or take as little as one module at a time. There is no academic prerequisite for the DELF, but candidates for the DALF must be in possession of the DELF or provide evidence that they have reached a standard which corresponds to its sixth and final unit. The DELF is designed to give candidates a level of linguistic and cultural competence which will allow them to live successfully in a French-speaking environment. The level specified for the DALF is that which will enable candidates to cope adequately with the demands of a university course.

It would be wrong to omit from this review of qualifications for foreign students the highly reputed diplomas awarded by the Chambre de Commerce et d'Industrie de Paris (CCIP), which sanction various areas of French for special purposes, and are available, too, in some university departments teaching foreign students. The most obvious, perhaps, are: the *certificat de français juridique*, the *certificat pratique du français commercial et économique*, and the *diplôme de français des affaires*, which exists at two levels – *premier degré* and *deuxième degré*.

Whereas, in general, higher education in France is 'free', courses for foreign students are more commercially priced (typically anything between €500 and €800 for a semester, or €1,000 and €1,800 for a year). For further information on courses for foreign students, see the detailed university entries in Part III.

So far we have concentrated in our examination on academic provision. It is time now to turn to other services that affect the lives of anyone who may be involved in study of any kind: accommodation and welfare services, understood in their broadest sense.

3
Accommodation and welfare services

British students in particular are accustomed to their home institution providing for a wide range of non-academic needs. Each university, or college, runs its own accommodation service for halls of residence, self-catering flats or private-sector housing, and provides catering, sports facilities and general welfare services. Additionally, in each academic institution there is a Students' Union, which often duplicates this 'official' provision (for eating and welfare, for instance) as well as promoting a vast array of clubs and societies to meet a wide spectrum of political, cultural, sporting and leisure interests.

This is by no means the situation in French universities. They remain, very definitely, institutions of learning, devoted to the pursuit of teaching and research. Historically, there has been no equivalent in France of Students' Unions with their own premises and their general social and leisure commitments. Those student organizations which do exist under this name tend to be national and political, concerned with educational policy and practice, as their representation on governing bodies within universities and associated institutions testifies; or, on the other hand, local and specialized, formed for the promotion of a single activity (*associations sportives*, *associations culturelles* and so on). Hence, provision for the practical needs of student living is vested in a national government-funded body, the Oeuvres Universitaires.

3.1 The role of the CNOUS and CROUS in student life

The Oeuvres are administered through a national centre in Paris, 28 regional centres (each serving an *académie*), and further local centres. The Centre National des Oeuvres Universitaires et Scolaires (CNOUS) defines general policy, allocates government funding to the regional centres, and performs a general supervisory, coordinating and facilitating function. The Centres Régionaux des Oeuvres Universitaires et Scolaires (CROUS), located in the main academic centre of each *académie*, provide the various student services, while the Centres Locaux des Oeuvres Universitaires et Scolaires (CLOUS) fulfil the same function in other university towns. Though a CLOUS is always dependent upon its tutelary CROUS, it may well enjoy a definite measure of independence, including control of its own allocation of funds. Finally, to bring their services more directly to a widely dispersed student body, the CROUS also operate a system of sub-offices or outposts in other academic centres (*antennes*).

From the outset, the Oeuvres were entrusted with the mission of 'improving living and working conditions for students'. Whereas the *aides directes* help the most needy students with grants, the *aides indirectes* provide subsidized meals, cheap accommodation and a range of other social and cultural services throughout France and her *Départements d'Outre-Mer* (DOM). The Oeuvres are proud of their democratic structures and ensure that the governing bodies (*conseils d'administration*) of both the CNOUS and the CROUS reflect the views of students. Elected representatives of student para-political organizations sit alongside academics, administrators, other grades of staff and outside personalities. The *Conseil d'administration* of the CNOUS is chaired by a direct nominee of the higher-education minister, while the regional equivalent is chaired by the relevant *recteur d'académie*, who also rejoices in the title of *chancelier des universités*.

The clientele of the Oeuvres Universitaires et Scolaires is by no means restricted to those studying in the universities or the *grandes écoles*. It embraces groups from many other sorts of institutions (*écoles d'infirmières* or *classes préparatoires aux grandes écoles*, for example). In fact, the condition of entitlement to its services is that the beneficiary should 'be registered in an institution (or a section of an institution) of higher education recognized as qualifying for the system of *sécurité sociale étudiante*'. The student card issued by the academic institution acts as the passport to the various services.

3.2 **Student restaurants**

It is through the subsidized meals in the Resto-U and Cafés that the CROUS makes its biggest impact on the student body, as the crowds that throng the restaurants at lunchtime (and to a lesser extent, in the evening) or sit over coffee in the adjoining *cafétéria* will testify. Apart from convenience, this popularity undoubtedly lies in the state subsidy which in 2004–05 kept the price of a meal ticket (*ticket de repas*) down to €2.65. On this basis alone, the Resto-U is central to student living.

The range of food varies from the 'traditional' three-course meal to simple fast food, such as pizzas, and light snacks. The restaurants are self-service, with the advantage that students can choose dishes to suit their own tastes. Those with particular dietary needs are catered for in the *restaurants médico-sociaux*. Meal tickets are available to student cardholders in books of ten (*un carnet*), obtainable at the restaurants. Access to the Resto-U is not restricted to those registered locally and entitled to eat at the cheap rate. Other groups may be authorized to use the facilities if they pay a higher, non-subsidized rate (the *tarif passager*), which is determined by the *conseil d'administration* of the CROUS concerned, and may therefore vary from one *académie* to the next. In addition to these directly operated facilities, there is a system of *restaurants agréés* which provide for students who may study or work in establishments some distance from University-orientated facilities – 18+ *sections* in *lycées*, for example (*classes préparatoires*, STS and so on – see Chapter 1), hospitals or *grandes écoles*.

Inevitably, opinions vary about the food served but the Resto-U is certainly good value. It would be impossible to cater for oneself at the same price. For foreign students there is the added attraction that the Resto-U is one of the few places where French students congregate in large numbers, thus providing the chance for contact and the beginnings of integration.

3.3 **CROUS accommodation**

The second major concern of the Oeuvres is to assist students with their accommodation. This entails, in the main, providing places in their own halls of residence (or in hostels with which they have an agreement (*foyers agréés*)), allocating rooms in cheap municipal flats (*habitations à loyer modéré*) or bed-sitters (*studios*) or acting as honest broker for private landlords. Unless your university has a specific agreement for accommodation with your host university, or you are studying in France as a *boursier* or *érasmien*, it is by no means certain that you will be able to obtain a place in CROUS-controlled accommodation. A proportion of rooms are, however, reserved for foreign students, including, in particular those on inter-university or European exchange and mobility schemes. Even 'free movers' will find that rooms do occasionally become available, especially in the less-populated university towns.

Eligibility criteria are strict. Normally, applications from 'free movers' (those from the EU) will only be considered if they can satisfy one of the following conditions:

- They have worked full-time or part-time in France in the year of their application. Both paid and unpaid employment qualifies, but must be *bona fide*.
- Their parents or guardian have paid taxes in France for the year in question.
- They have lived in France for at least two years and their parents or guardian have been domiciled in France for two years and paid taxes during that period.

For those who are eligible, or who are fortunate, there may be a choice of different types of accommodation. Each type is categorised by the living area (expressed in square metres) and the provision of facilities. All contain the basic items of furniture, and these are the most common:

- A furnished room in a traditional hall of residence, with roughly 9 or 10 square metres of living space, hand basin and perhaps a bidet. Showers, cooking facilities and toilets are shared facilities.
- New-style, refurbished rooms in halls with perhaps slightly more space, and incorporating a private toilet, shower and washing facilities.
- Flatlets (*studios*) having up to 15 square metres of living space with shower, toilet, refrigerator and microwave.
- Flats categorised as T1, with about 20 square metres of living space with cooking facilities and a separate bathroom incorporating a private shower and toilet.
- Flats categorized as T1 bis, which are similar to T1 except that the cooking area can be screened off.
- Larger flats, styled as T2, which means that there is an additional bedroom, or two bedrooms (T3). This will give a surface area of between 30 and 50 square metres of living space. It is unlikely that you would be allowed to occupy such accommodation alone; rather you would be required to share with others. Indeed, the larger flats are in such short supply in the CROUS housing stock that they are often reserved for student families (*jeunes ménages*).

The monthly rental for each of these types of accommodation varies according to the category and facilities provided. For a room in a traditional hall you should allow €130 per month, payable for 9 months, but for the flatlets (*studios*) or flats between €200 and €350 payable obligatorily for 12 months. There are additional expenses to bear in mind. A reservation deposit (*dépôt de garantie*) of between €150 and €250 will be required, again depending on the nature of the accommodation, as well as compulsory insurance. Policies start at about €20 for a traditional room, but increase with the size of the accommodation, and mature students (over 28) may well have to pay more. However, students can apply for housing benefit, of which there are two kinds: *aide personnalisée au logement* (APL) and *allocation logement à caractère social* (ALS).

In both cases, for the benefit to be available the accommodation must meet certain standards of size and salubrity. In both cases, too, your personal circumstances and the level of your resources are taken into account. However, APL is only available if the landlord has signed an appropriate agreement with the state. This often applies to the newer CROUS residences, as well as to private-sector accommodation. It is obviously possible, therefore, to determine in advance whether this allowance might be available. On the other hand, ALS is a general benefit for all citizens on low incomes, impoverished students included, and is payable however inexpensive the accommodation (rooms in traditional halls, for example). If awarded (and you are likely to receive one or other subsidy), APL is paid direct to the landlord, leaving the tenant to settle the outstanding balance; ALS is paid to the individual claimant, and the French state much prefers to do this via direct transfer into a French bank account.

In some towns, the CROUS can offer places in low-cost flats (*habitations à loyer modéré* – HLM). These can take the form of individual bed-sitters, or, more probably, flats with up to four or five bedrooms. Single students are each allocated a room, while the lounge, kitchen and bathroom facilities are shared. The CROUS is responsible for providing essential furniture, and for urgent day-to-day maintenance. The monthly charges reflect the basic rent plus, perhaps, any supplementary service costs payable to the owners of the HLM (often the town council). It is more usual for this form of accommodation to be allocated to students with their own families. However, in some towns, flats are assigned to groups of individuals. The application and admissions procedure is the same as for rooms in halls. However, students who are in HLM would be well advised to establish exactly what costs are covered by their monthly payments, and whether there are any other bills for which they are liable, such as heating, lighting or indeed the local residence tax (*taxe d'habitation*), which is levied on all residents on 1 January.

3.4 **Private-sector accommodation**

Given the above restrictions, a fair number of students will seek accommodation in the private sector. If the International Relations office (Service de Relations Internationales – SRI) of your host institution is unable to suggest possibilities, various other bodies exist to help you locate suitable accommodation, and these are listed in section 6.2, pp. 81–2, and Appendix 6.1. However, in recent years, it has become more and more difficult to find student accommodation in the larger urban centres, particularly those densely populated with students (for example, Paris and Toulouse) and this in itself is a good reason for avoiding these localities if you have a choice.

The range of accommodation on offer is wide and disparate, going from individual rooms in private households (*chambres chez l'habitant*) to *studios* and big independent flats that can be shared between groups of like-minded students. The terminology used to describe these dwellings is the same as outlined above, with units being referred to according to their size and the number of rooms involved. A *studio* or F1/T1 amounts to very much the same kind of place as already described, except that if the unit is referred to as a T1 or T2, rather than an F1/F2, it is most likely to be in a more modern property rather than an older conversion. When dealing with private accommodation, there is also the important consideration of whether it is furnished or unfurnished.

In the private sector, you will have to accept higher costs: between €200 and €500 a month for a single room with a family (depending on the services offered); €300 and €450 for a *studio*/T1/T1 bis, and up to €850 for a T3/F3 in the provinces. In Paris, these sums will be between 50 per cent and 100 per cent higher. Remember, too, that on top of the basic rent you will be required to pay towards the upkeep of communal areas, rubbish removal, water and, in some cases, heating. In addition, all tenants in France are required by law to take out insurance to cover the risks involved (*assurances multirisques habitation*). Policies of this kind are available from the student insurance services (*mutuelles*) and will be good value, but such extras all add to the costs of accommodation.

An alternative, though more expensive, possibility is the private-sector student flats that have mushroomed all over France in recent years. Developers were attracted both by the growing dearth of student accommodation and also, perhaps, by the advent of housing subsidies, which encouraged students to spend more on their living quarters. As a result, several chains of studio-type furnished residences for students have appeared in most university towns – Eurostudiome, Fac-Habitat, Campus Habitat, Les Lauréades – but at a price. Their rents are in the upper bracket, even for the private sector, ranging from €500 to €700. They have nevertheless proved popular, and therefore tend to fill up by May or June for the following year. Those interested can find details by trying the chain websites, or by using something like the Guide ADELE du Logement Etudiant, which is also available online at www.adele.org.

Occasionally, the opportunity may arise of living with a French family as a paying guest. This opportunity to experience such total immersion from a linguistic and cultural point of view may suit some students, at the expense, perhaps, of a certain amount of independence. It may also be possible to find offers whereby a family will reduce or even waive rent in exchange for duties round the house (looking after children for a certain number of specified hours a day, or offering English lessons to members of the household, for example). Females, in particular, are popular as *au pairs*, and if this appeals to you it may be an economic solution to a difficult problem. However, in such circumstances, the relationship can often change, and there remains the problem of reconciling domestic duties with the demands of the courses.

3.5 **Other CROUS services**

It is also to the CROUS that students are wont to turn for advice and help with many other, non-academic aspects of student life. Its information services, for example, act as a useful complement to the universities' own Services Communs (Inter)Universitaires d'Information et d'Orientation (SC(I)UIO). Questions may relate to administrative procedures (academic and civil), financial aid, career outlets, part-time jobs or leisure activities in the area. All the CROUS have some links with OTU Voyages, which offers cheap travel facilities by rail, sea and air (see section 6.8(b), pp. 95–6), not to mention the holiday packages and excursions which OTU organizes each year for students individually or in groups. In addition, each CROUS helps students find temporary part-time employment through a dedicated service: Emplois Temporaires Etudiants (ETE).

Three facets of the work of the CROUS deserve special mention: their role as a cultural stimulus, their social welfare facilities, and their provision for foreign scholarship-holders. Each CROUS receives a budget specifically for cultural activities. These include the dissemination of information on theatre, concert and sporting programmes, the funding of clubs in student residences, and the promotion of local and national competitions. Student clubs and societies usually come under the aegis of a joint committee in each residence made up of CROUS officials and student representatives (*conseil de résidence paritaire*). Facilities and activities vary considerably, but you may well find book and CD libraries, internet-access clubs, cine- and video-clubs, photographic dark-rooms, theatre groups and so on. Sometimes, too, there are sports facilities (for example tennis courts) in the proximity of the halls. In a number of university centres, there are Cultural Centres (*maisons d'activités culturelles*), which have special funding and offer a broad range of activities (cinema, theatre, fine arts, music, dance and so on).

Many CROUS also arrange low-cost trips and excursions, usually at weekends, or during holiday periods, to explore some aspect of the local region, or the country at large. They are particularly popular with foreign students, as are the 'international' evenings, when national student communities can make a contribution in terms of their own cultural heritage, or when some French festival can be celebrated in traditional style.

Student counselling is equally an important task of the Oeuvres. Each regional centre has its team of 'social workers' (*assistant(e)s de service social*) who are available for consultation, not only at the CROUS headquarters but also, on a less frequent basis, in residences and other student workplaces and premises. Obviously, to be able to address the problems that arise, the social counsellors have to work closely with a wide range of outside bodies in the field of general health and welfare. Individual cases, however, often involve colleagues in other departments of the CROUS, particularly over matters of accommodation, employment or financial hardship.

Financial help in an emergency can be obtained, in the form of either a grant or a repayable, interest-free loan, from the Fonds de Solidarité Universitaire (FSU). Applications for help from the fund are processed by the social service team, and submitted for approval to a CROUS committee. To deal with emergencies, however, each *assistant(e) social(e)* is empowered to make available limited funds immediately. Such help is intended to meet a given crisis and cannot be seen as a contribution to regular funding. Nevertheless, in a system where a significant number of students are not supported by grants, applications are numerous, particularly at the beginning of the academic year, when the outlay involved in preparing for the session – or the late receipt of monies from other sources – may cause particular problems.

3.6 CROUS provision for scholarship holders

The Oeuvres have for some considerable time been responsible for foreign students holding French government awards (*boursiers du gouvernement français*) and certain other foreign nationals whose governments have agreements with France (*boursiers des états étrangers*). This role begins before the *boursiers* arrive in France. Officials of the CNOUS help place the students in appropriate establishments of higher education, informing them of the terms and conditions of the award, and organizing any language or other preliminary training necessary to ensure maximum benefit from the French educational experience. Provision is made for their reception in Paris and onward travel to their ultimate destination. Groups of such students are often given short induction courses in the capital.

Once the *boursiers* arrive in their university towns, it falls to the local CROUS to ensure they are 'successful in integrating academically, socially and culturally in France'. This means far more than the automatic provision of student accommodation, induction, payment of the grant, and help with administrative arrangements and formalities. Throughout the course of study, contact is maintained with appropriate academic supervisors, and reports on progress are issued at regular intervals. Information is sent back via the CNOUS to the relevant grant-awarding ministry or foreign government, together with any special recommendations for action to overcome difficulties encountered, or to modify or enhance the original academic programme. Moreover, with the financial backing of the Ministère des Affaires Etrangères, each CROUS organizes for the benefit of such students a full programme of activities, designed to introduce them to different aspects of the business, social and cultural life of France. Here, the Service d'Accueil des Etudiants Etrangers (SAEE) at the CROUS has a crucial role to play.

3.7 Sport and medical facilities

It would be wrong to give the impression that student welfare is the exclusive preserve of the Oeuvres Universitaires. As laid down in the *loi d'orientation*, each university has its Service des Relations Internationales (SRI), its Service (Inter)Universitaire de Médecine Préventive (et de Promotion de la Santé) (SUMP, SIUMP or SUMPPS) and its Service Universitaire des Activités Physiques, Sportives et de Plein Air (SUAPS).

The SRI (under whatever guise it appears locally – Direction des Affaires Internationales, or Bureau de ...) is an obvious starting point for new arrivals from abroad, for help with registration and administrative procedures. It is the body that oversees and administers exchange arrangements with foreign partners, and liaises with national and supra-national agencies (SOCRATES, for example).

The S(I)UMPPS oversees the compulsory medical check for those registering at university for the first time, offers free medical care in some circumstances, usually by appointment, and has social workers who provide counselling. For those suffering from serious depression or requiring psychiatric help there is a dedicated service: the Bureau d'Aide Psychologique Universitaire (BAPU). Advice and contact services are also readily available in terms of HIV and AIDS (*le sida*), alcoholism, drug addiction, dietary needs, contraception and so on. It also disseminates the information coming out of government campaigns relating to current and on-going health problems in the population (such as measures to reduce smoking).

The SUAPS is responsible for organizing and publicizing programmes of activities. Its role has increased significantly in recent years, as it has become possible to attempt a sport module as an optional element in more and more courses. In the case of university sport, however, the principal motive force remains, in general, the long-standing student organizations, the *associations sportives*, which exist within individual institutions. A governing body in Paris, the Fédération Française du Sport Universitaire (FFSU), operating through regional offices, coordinates local, regional, national and even international fixtures in some thirty sports.

As is evident from the above, the CROUS and other student bodies, with their many services, are likely to play an important part in any successful stay in France. These key services will facilitate your integration into a French way of life, from cultural visits to cheap travel arrangements and ski trips. At all events, they are such as to help make your stay a happy one. Do not miss out on the opportunities offered.

Part 2
Practical advice

4
Working in France

Many foreign students spending time in France will not enrol full-time on university courses but will seek some form of employment. Some will work for short periods during vacations; others will take a gap year; a small number of graduates will be appointed as a *lecteur/lectrice* in higher education. But the most common alternatives to study will come in the form of a work placement or an assistantship. Each option involves its own procedures but there are steps common to all of them.

If your work experience in France is organized through an established scheme or exchange, some of the obvious formalities will be completed for you. But in order to work in France you will in all cases need to acquire various documents and to consider how best to present yourself to potential employers.

4.1 Documentation

The essential document required by all foreigners is a passport which is valid beyond the full duration of your stay. Proof of student status will, in addition, bring many benefits. It can be provided either through possession of a current student card from your home institution or an International Student Identity Card (ISIC card). The latter is available from local student travel offices at a cost of £7 [US $22] on production of evidence of student status and a passport-size photograph. For EU nationals, a work permit (*carte de travail*) is not necessary; other foreign nationals are required, in theory, to have obtained a job, an entry visa (*visa de [long] séjour*) and a work permit before leaving for France. American students with adequate French can, however, take advantage of a scheme organized by CIEE, New York, which enables them to seek employment in France for up to three months, once they are armed with a temporary permit (*autori-sation provisoire de travail*).

Once you are in France, it will be necessary to obtain a residence permit (*carte de séjour*) from the local authorities. This is particularly important if you intend to stay and work for more than three months. Initial application should be made either to the *préfecture* or to the police station (*commissariat*), where you will be asked to provide evidence that you can support yourself (an indication of solvency via a bank account or valid credit card). There will probably be a compulsory medical examination, certainly if you come from outside the EU. Once your application has been accepted, you will be presented with an interim acknowledgement of your application (*attestation de demande de résidence*), prior to being granted the actual document at a later appointment. Most agencies and employers will be happy to take you on under these conditions. As part of the documentation process, you may well have to acquire certification of your civil status (*fiche d'état civil*), which is available from the local town hall (*mairie*). An essential document for this – and other purposes – is the original of the long form of your birth certificate, plus a certified copy and translation (*copie et traduction certifiées conformes*). Section 5.1, pp. 64–5 contains suggestions as to how these may be most economically obtained. You will also need your work contract, three passport photographs, and proof of accommodation.

4.2 Making an application

Approaches to potential employers should be made in terms of a CV, or *résumé*, and covering letter.

The CV should, if possible, be typed and fitted onto a single sheet. Neatness and clarity of layout are of paramount importance. As qualifications are regarded as hyper-important in France, care should be taken to include dates and full titles of all diplomas already obtained and of any further awards in the pipeline. While hobbies and leisure activities might be considered as less important, all skills and experience relevant to work activities (driving licence and so on) should be included. Be careful to ensure the absolute accuracy of the information you provide; subsequent corroboration may be sought.

Covering letters – or indeed letters of acceptance of any post – should, however, be handwritten (*lettres manuscrites*). It will be considered more polite, and is often requested in advertisements because French employers commonly have recourse to graphologists when recruiting staff. The covering letter (*lettre de motivation*) is your opportunity to orientate the information given in the CV towards the requirements of the particular job. You will find in Appendix 2 a model CV in French and a covering letter, and in Appendix 3 a letter of acceptance.

The question of the language to be used in these communications is, however, a delicate one. Specialists in French will quite naturally make their applications in that language, couched in the appropriate formal French terminology (for example, *je me permets de poser ma candidature*). It is, however, recommended that even advanced learners have them checked by a native speaker. This might be the ideal opportunity to seek the help and advice of a French exchange student or colloquial assistant in your own institution. You might offer the same favour in return. Non-specialists should not raise false expectations of their competence in French and might be better advised to apply in English; this at least demonstrates proficiency in their native tongue, which may well be the key to some jobs.

4.3 Tax and health insurance

You will need to investigate the tax position carefully. If you are appointed as a language assistant in a school or university, for instance, you will probably be exempt from tax in France and your home country for up to two years in the job. A Double Taxation Agreement between the United Kingdom and France, for example, means that British assistants are exempt from French income tax for this period; and while sums earned abroad are in general liable for UK income tax, normally a 100 per cent deduction is allowed to returning assistants so that no UK tax will be levied.

If you discover that you are liable for French income tax, you should be aware that the financial year is the calendar year, and that tax is paid a year in arrears; that is to say that French employees pay off their tax bill in the course of the following year, either in three instalments, or monthly. If you take up a job in France for the first time, therefore, you will not be required to pay tax immediately. You should, however, register with the local tax office (*centre des impôts*) soon after arrival, and will be asked to submit a tax return for each year (*feuille de déclaration de revenus*).

Anyone working in France will, in all probability, be affiliated automatically to the French health and welfare scheme (*sécurité sociale*) for which contributions will be deducted from salary. This will qualify you for medical care only in terms of the French system, which needs to be supplemented to give 100 per cent cover (see section 5.3, pp. 69–71). The most obvious way of obtaining full cover is to take out a 'top-up' policy with a private insurance company (a *mutuelle*, for example), for which you will be eligible through your employment. Ultimately, it is up to you to check your health-care status with your employer. It is also important to remember that you will not be insured for health risks during your move to France, or during the period while you are looking for work, or during the first month or so of your employment. Independent arrangements are, therefore, to be recommended (see section 5.4, p. 71). Further information on Social Security arrangements for those moving within the EU is to be found in leaflet SA29 (*Your social security insurance benefits and healthcare rights in the European Economic Area*). This is available online at www.dwp. gov.uk/publications/dwp/2004/sa29_oct04.pdf.

4.4 Vacation work

Though there has traditionally been a range of casual jobs available to students during the summer months in France, the continuing high level of unemployment, particularly among young people, has reduced the number of opportunities. For the well-organized and persistent, however, there are still possibilities which will enable you to experience French life while eking out a basic existence. The service industry offers perhaps the most openings: there is a regular demand for hall or night porters, waiting staff, receptionists, chambermaids or kitchen helps in hotels. Bar work is also a fairly common, if not particularly remunerative, form of vacation work. Positions are more readily available for those who already have two years' experience in hotel and catering work (see Appendix 1.6 for useful addresses). Other popular options include jobs as supervisors, entertainers or couriers on campsites; as support staff on activity holidays or courses (*moniteurs,-trices* in *colonies de vacances*, or *animateurs,-trices* on vacation study courses). French employers require applicants to have good French and to acquire the appropriate qualification (the *brevet d'aptitude aux fonctions d'animateur* [BAFA]), which will entail attendance at an appropriate training programme organized and validated by the Direction Départementale de la Jeunesse et des Sports (see Appendix 1.8). It will involve some outlay but, as a qualified monitor, you will certainly recoup this investment in subsequent years.

Many female students work as an *au pair* (most employers prefer them to males) and this particular form of work can be arranged in advance through a specialist agency in the UK, which will, however, charge a fee for its services. There are also agencies in France (see Appendix 1.4). Work is for a minimum of three months and for a maximum of twelve (or possibly eighteen). Employers are required to obtain a work permit or contract (*accord de placement au pair d'un stagiaire aide-familial* or *contrat de travail de stagiaire professionnel*). Non-EU nationals will need the contract, together with a certificate of enrolment in a language course for foreign students, when they apply for the long-stay visa. There are many websites which give information on *au pair* posts and list agencies which offer work in France. Typical of these are: www.intransit-international.com/directory/ children_nannies.html; and www.europa-pages.com/au_pair/france.html.

For the United States, there is a website maintained by the Cultural Services of the French Embassy at www.frenchculture.org/education/ france/go/pair.html.

Casual summer work can still be found in labour-intensive farmwork, though modern methods have greatly reduced the need for unskilled labour. Fruit-picking, haymaking or grape harvesting (*les vendanges*) may prove to be attractive propositions, especially since it is possible to move from region to region as the various crops need to be harvested throughout the summer months. This type of work is, however, physically demanding and often involves long hours or exposure to variable weather conditions. Seasonal workers should receive the national minimum wage (the *salaire minimum interprofessionnel de croissance* or SMIC), which in the summer of 2005 was €8.03 per hour (gross).

Charity and voluntary work (such as archaeological digs and conservation projects) can also be arranged through the British Council (Learning) under the aegis of the European Voluntary Service scheme. Whilst this is aimed primarily at organizations in the UK, individuals may also apply. The relevant website is www.britishcouncil.org/connectyouth-programmes-european-voluntary-service. An SOS volunteer helpdesk may be accessed through this site.

Non-EU students anxious to find vacation work in France must do so under the aegis of a government-approved organization, and are required to have a work visa. Full-time North American students who are US citizens, are at least 18 years of age and have a minimum of two years' French at college may take advantage of the CIEE scheme referred to on pp. 47–8.

If you are already a student in an affiliated institution, it may be possible to find a placement through specialist organizations such as the International Association for the Exchange of Students for Technical Experience (IAESTE) or the Association Internationale des Etudiants en Sciences Economiques et Commerciales (AIESEC). In the UK, the relevant websites are: www.iaeste.org.uk and www.aiesec.co.uk. The United States has its own sites: www.aipt.org (on the home page, click on AIPT Programs) and www. aiesecus.org. IAESTE is devoted to finding placements in the technical and managerial fields, whilst AIESEC is more business orientated. Posts are difficult to obtain and are exchanged internationally; as reciprocity is the key factor, you stand a better chance of finding employment if you yourself are able to locate a job offer for someone from France. Remuneration will take the form of living expenses rather than salary. Most placements are for a maximum period of twelve weeks' duration, though exceptionally they may be for a whole year or more.

4.5 The gap year

It is very common for British school-leavers to intercalate a year abroad between the end of sixth-form study and their entry into higher education. This has many advantages: the broadening of horizons, the cultivation of a sense of independence and personal responsibility, perhaps even the opportunity to accumulate savings for the expensive years ahead.

Provided that it is spent in a constructive manner, the gap year is usually appreciated by university admissions tutors, who welcome the greater maturity the experience brings. Even in the case of non-linguists, a prolonged stay in France opens up new linguistic and cultural perspectives.

The idea of finding paid employment may initially seem daunting. There are, however, a number of options available to the adventurous, as can be explored, for example, by contacting the Espace Emploi International or the European Employment Service (see Appendix 1.6). It may be possible to organize a placement for yourself, especially if you have contacts in France – say, through a previous school exchange or pen-friend. Be aware, however, that French employers prefer to recruit applicants whom they can interview. For those who are unable to make use of contacts, it is possible to place advertisements in national and regional newspapers, or to write letters of application by the hundred. This method is, however, unlikely to produce a high rate of return. If you have no obvious way of breaking into French networks, it is probably wise to look to one of the professional organizations which specialize in finding temporary work in France.

An easier, if somewhat more expensive way of arranging your stay is to go through one of the many agencies which cater specifically for students intercalating a year between school and university. This may involve paying fees for registration and, again, on acceptance of a position. An obvious example in the UK is the GAP scheme (www.gap.org.uk). To register for this, you must normally be aged between 17 and 19 but not all posts are available to those under eighteen years of age. You can apply straight after taking your GCSEs but, in any event, as soon as possible in your final year of study at school (preferably before Christmas). Details of how to apply, interviews and fees payable are to be found on the website given above. Appointees must find their own travel expenses, and organize their insurance and medical cover. GAP will, however, arrange your flight so that you can travel out with other volunteers.

Placements in France are limited. Some idea of the range can be gleaned by consulting *The Gap Guidebook*, published annually by Peridot Press (see Bibliography). Work is challenging and good spoken French is essential. Full board and accommodation are provided, together with pocket money.

For those looking to spend only part of the year working abroad, seasonal opportunities exist. The Jobs in the Alps Agency (www.jobs-in-the-alps. com/jobs.htm), for example, organizes hotel work in Europe for German or French speakers. Winter season placements are from December to April; summer placements are from June/July to September. There are no inter-season placements in the Alps (May, October, November). Applicants must have A level French or its equivalent.

4.6 Teaching assistantships in secondary education

The assistantship scheme is long established, and many students look to it as a way of enhancing their command of the French language and their familiarity with the target culture. Particularly for those intending to pursue a career in teaching, a year in a French secondary school environment offers an unique opportunity to gain classroom experience. Being an English Language Assistant forms a recommended part of many British degree programmes in which French is a major component. For those undergraduates who choose to, or are asked to, spend a year in France as an *assistant(e)*, there are several steps which need to be taken. UK students of French who are in course will receive the appropriate form from their Year Abroad Tutor or Director of Studies, and should return their duly completed applications, together with any fee payable, via their academic sponsor. All candidates should normally be under 30, must be native speakers of English and must have completed at least two years in higher education. The scheme is administered by the British Council, whose 1 December deadline for submission (England and Wales) must be respected; the deadline for Scotland and Northern Ireland is 31 January (the relevant website is: www.britishcouncil.org/languageassistants-ela-how-do-i-apply.

htm). This website enables you to download the application form (and application guidelines), the medical form and the reference form (three copies of which will be needed with one passport photo attached to each). US candidates who are interested in participating in the scheme should contact the Institute of International Education, US Student Program Division, and request the current edition of *Fulbright and Other Grants for Graduate Study Abroad* (website: www.iie.org/TemplateFulbright. cfm?section=Fulbright). Further details can be obtained by contacting assistant.washington-amba@diplomatie.gouv.fr.

Most postings will inevitably be in the provinces. Although candidates may express a preference for a specific region of France, and for a particular type of school, it is not always the case that these can be accommodated. Successful applicants are appointed to serve from the beginning of October to the end of April or June; notification of posting will be sent direct from France, usually some time between June and August, though the certificate of appointment (*arrêté d'affectation*) may not arrive until late September. However, once you have learned in April that your application has been forwarded to France (and this means that you are virtually certain to be offered an assistantship), you should plan ahead and assemble administrative documents essential to your stay abroad, together with material you will wish to draw upon for your classes.

The essential documents you will require are those covered above in 4.1 (valid full passport, equipped with visa in the case of non-EU nationals, a certified copy and translation of the full form of your birth certificate, ISIC card and, once established in France, a *carte de séjour*; non-EU nationals may also need a work permit). Given your new status in the French educational system, you will be entitled to the *carte professionnelle*, which offers various advantages.

As you will be responsible – in the school or schools in which you will be working – for classes in conversational English, with pupils with a wide range of ability, motivation and attainment, pedagogical material will take different forms. In order to help you to prepare for your new post, you will receive a detailed information pack in the summer, approximately four to six weeks prior to your departure. Your pack will be specifically related to France and will give information concerning teaching ideas and induction courses in France. You are also strongly advised to download, from the British Council website, the Teaching Manual available at www. britishcouncil.org/languageassistant-manual.htm. Prior to your departure, it is also highly desirable that you assemble everyday written and visual material relating to your personal background: maps, posters, notices, timetables, advertisements, postcards, slides, photographs, newspaper cuttings, comics and magazines, mail order catalogues and so forth. Such material is easily collected with a little forethought and for little or no outlay. Tapes and CDs of popular and folk music are a particularly valuable resource. Learning the rules of a few verbal games will stand you in good stead and lead to stimulating classes in which all can be encouraged to participate. Once you are in post, you can also draw on the material made available by the British Council (see Part III, 8.20 under Useful addresses), particularly when you have ascertained what gaps there are in the local resources. Contacting your predecessor, where possible, either through your school(s) or national agency, will enable you to acquire further insights and practical advice based on first-hand experience. You should, however, remain open-minded until you are in a position to judge for yourself; preconceptions or false expectations can militate against your own integration into a new society and this society's acceptance of you.

You may well be offered accommodation by the school or through a member of staff, in which case this should become clear in the response to your letter confirming your acceptance of the appointment. If accommodation is not provided, and you are thrown back on your own resources, you should follow the procedures outlined in section 6.2, pp. 81–5. You should also remember that set-up costs are involved, and that not all assistants receive their first salary cheque at the end of October. You should, therefore, have access to enough money to see you through the first two months. You will, of course, need to open a bank account soon after your arrival, so that your salary can be paid by cheque or credit transfer (for advice on banking arrangements, see section 5.5, pp. 71–3). In order to make possible the automatic payment of your salary cheque, you will need to provide the school authorities with your banking details in the form of an individual identification number etc (*relevé d'identité bancaire* or RIB).

Experience shows that the transition from home or undergraduate life to what, in many instances, may well be a very different setting can be problematic on both personal and academic grounds. Finding yourself initially alone in a strange town, away from friends and a familiar environment, may be a new situation you will have to learn to cope with. Settling into a room or flat, building a new life, forming new acquaintances and establishing a working routine all take time. As a student, you will have been used to relating mainly to people of your own age. Now, as a language assistant, you have a somewhat ambiguous status: closer in age to your pupils but responsible to older colleagues. Though the teaching staff will doubtless welcome you, you should not expect to be treated immediately as an equal by them; nor should you expect automatic respect in the classroom. It would be wrong to assume that French schools are organized along the same lines as those you attended during your own secondary education, or, indeed, that they share the same ethos. Initially, you may well be perplexed by the internal hierarchy – the role of the *concierge* and of the school secretary, for example. Similarly, the awe in which are held the head of the *lycée* (*proviseur*) or the bursar (*intendant(e)*) may come as something of a surprise to you. You should also be aware that your French colleagues, like their university counterparts, will tend to be present in school only during their timetabled hours, and not at other times. Despite attempts by the Ministère de l'Education Nationale to promote a more rounded approach to personal development in schools, you may not necessarily find the same range of extra-curricular activities, or the same commitment to them, as at home.

Your predecessor may or may not have left a good impression, and your reception will undoubtedly be coloured by that. You may inherit a group of ready-made friends, or you may have to overcome negative preconceptions about *les anglophones*. A temptation which is to be resisted, in the long term, is to associate only with other English-speaking assistants. Although this is understandable for support in the early weeks, it will ultimately inhibit your language development and social integration. Your most likely peer group will probably consist of the young, part-time auxiliaries employed to maintain discipline, the *surveillant(e)s* (known familiarly as *pion(ne)s*). Under the control of the *surveillant(e) général(e)* – the *surgé* – they are often self-supporting students still in higher education. If you are in a *lycée*, you may well also encounter other groups of the same age, such as those engaged in post-*baccalauréat* studies: the STS (see Glossary and section 1.2, pp. 12–14) or *classes préparatoires* (see section 1.3, pp. 15–16).

While you are coming to terms with this new social environment, you will simultaneously be attempting to find your feet in an unfamiliar teaching situation. You may well have apprehensions about discipline, class sizes and being at a linguistic disadvantage, if it comes to having to explain in French points which might arise during your conversation classes in English. It is quite natural to experience self-doubt as to your abilities as a teacher. You may also be asked to carry out duties which go beyond those you had anticipated, such as correcting exercises, covering for absent colleagues and, as a native speaker of English, giving the language teachers the benefit of your 'authoritative' advice on usage. You will, quite naturally, be expected to be an expert on all matters relating to your own country, its civilization and culture. Documentation provided by such bodies as the British Council will be helpful in this respect. Above all, when drawn into cultural comparisons between France and your home country, do not cast yourself in the role of the superior foreigner, dismissive of indigenous practices and values.

As time goes by, you will grow in confidence and become more at ease in your French environment and, more specifically, with your various colleagues. In the classroom, your developing awareness of group dynamics will make you increasingly effective and respected as a teacher. You yourself will have to experiment with topics and adapt them to your individual style. Previous assistants have found that topics such as family life, food, housing, social relationships, national customs, pop music and travel lead to animated discussions. The British royal family, the American presidency and Hollywood seem to arouse endless curiosity!

At the end of the year, you will doubtless emerge with the impression that the gains far outweigh the losses: you will have learned much more about yourself and the way in which you interact with other people of all ages. You should certainly be a more resilient, self-sufficient person. You may even have had the opportunity to define more clearly your likely career path, certainly as regards the teaching profession. And, despite the apparent disadvantage of being paid to *be* Anglophone, you will have arrived at a much greater understanding of French society from within.

4.7 **Teaching assistantships in higher education**

As distinct from assistantships, where there are national schemes through which all individuals may apply, *lecteur/lectrice* appointments are, in the main, arranged on an annual or biennial exchange basis between universities in France and English-speaking universities. For those graduates appointed to lectureships, some of the initial difficulties of integration will be familiar, as a result of undergraduate experience. Colloquial assistants in higher education are, however, often in much the same quandary as school assistants *vis-à-vis* their new academic colleagues and duties, and will need some time to acclimatize to their responsibilities. As in any new teaching situation, you should clarify in advance the precise nature of your commitments. Within the academic department to which you are attached, there will certainly be a full-time colleague whose role will include supervision of *lecteurs/lectrices*, and whom you should consult.

Workloads will inevitably differ, from language laboratory supervision to the occasional lecture and marking of scripts. You may be given the opportunity to discuss preferences in the light of your perceived aptitudes. Be prepared to face very large classes in which it will be impossible to replicate the style of work you are used to in oral classes in your home institution. Although your contractual maximum number of contact hours is likely to be around twelve, you may be offered additional work (*heures supplémentaires*), perhaps even in a neighbouring institution, for which you will be paid extra. As classes can begin at eight in the morning and go on until nine in the evening, you may consider trying to achieve, by agreement, a certain grouping of hours, particularly if you wish to pursue your own studies in parallel. In many cases, you will be given a programme to follow, but not necessarily one which covers all your assignments. It is wise, therefore, to plan ahead and take with you the sort of easily collectable teaching materials described above. One particular point to bear in mind is that you may well be unaccustomed to presenting English grammar formally. Keen linguists in France will undoubtedly quiz you on moot points of English or American usage and you should be armed with a reputable English grammar book (see Bibliography for suggestions).

4.8 Work experience placements/internships

Work experience placements/internships (*stages*) are often arranged in one of two principal ways: either by your home institution, as the recognized format of the obligatory period of residence abroad specified for your study programme; or by the French educational institution to which you have been attached. You may, however, be required or encouraged to show initiative by finding your own placement and making your own detailed arrangements. Students who have already defined the kind of work they wish to undertake in terms of their career development may well achieve a better match in this way.

Obtaining employment independently will be an arduous and frustrating task. Given the French habit of operating through networks of relationships, it could be to your advantage to make use of any existing contacts you may have, or have available, through family, friends, or any educational establishments you have attended. If, of course, you have ever worked – even briefly during vacations – for a company which has links with France, you may be able to exploit this connection. Should none of these avenues be open to you, it will be a question of using standard reference sources to identify appropriate firms, and of writing speculatively. Do not neglect the resources of libraries, career services and those newspapers and periodicals which carry European advertisements. French friends may be able to help you through the information available on their Minitel system (see Glossary). The organizations IAESTE and AIESEC (see pp. 51–2) may be able to assist you within their respective specialist areas, if your institution is an affiliated member. In the US, CIEE is the major agency for internships. At all events, Appendix 6.1 will give you a series of useful internet addresses which will multiply as you follow through different links.

You should bear in mind that firms may be reluctant to employ students with little or no training in the job-specific skills. On the other hand, French companies do have a commitment to training and you may be fortunate enough to make contact with a firm that wishes to benefit from the presence of an Anglophone, or requires short-term technical input to a project. At all events, once you have secured an offer of employment, it will doubtless be necessary to seek the approval of your home institution before you finally commit yourself contractually.

If arrangements are made for you by your course administrator, it is likely that an appropriate contract will have been negotiated on your behalf. If left to your own resources, make sure the proposed terms of employment include the following: a detailed job description, an indication of place, duration, dates of employment, gross salary and benefits, including holiday entitlement, if appropriate. Your home institution will wish to be satisfied that the job proposals amount to more than an opportunity for linguistic immersion; they must also extend and hone the skills developed by the course you have been following. Your eventual contract should make provision for a supervisor within the firm and facilitate any required visits by your home tutors.

Once you begin your placement, you will need to be aware of the ethos that prevails in French firms. Though it is obviously dangerous to generalize, it is often the case that the hierarchy manifests itself in a more stringent fashion. Do not be surprised if the head of your company appears somewhat remote, with attitudes that oscillate between the patronizing and the authoritarian. Always use formal terms of address (for example, the *vous* form, *Monsieur*, *Madame*, and appropriate titles: *Monsieur le Directeur/Madame la Directrice*). At the beginning and end of the day – and not only when you are introduced for the first time, and on taking your leave at the end of your placement – remember to shake hands with fellow employees. Smart appearance is essential, as you will rapidly discover in the presence of your dress-conscious colleagues. In the office or workplace, keep relationships on a formal, business-like footing until exchanges of a more social or personal nature are initiated by others. Conversations which do not involve work are likely to centre, in the first instance, on the current state of health of the person speaking to you (the French equivalent of the British fixation with the weather). Within the firm, always deal with your immediate superior, unless instructed to do otherwise. When dealing with another organization, contact someone of equivalent status to

yourself. When entrusted with a specific task, discharge your duties punc-
tiliously, and then ensure, discreetly, that it is clear that you have fulfilled
your brief.

Your working day may be longer. Starting times may be earlier and you
could be expected to stay later than you anticipated at the end of the day.
Lunch breaks are, however, probably more flexible. It is important that you
keep good time and fit in with the working practices you observe during
the first few days of your placement. French firms attach a great deal of
importance to the notion of a harmonious working relationship among
their staff. When recruiting independently, they will regard this as one
of the most crucial factors in the selection of new personnel. You would
be well advised to avoid making classic mistakes such as: presuming, as
a degree student schooled in the latest theoretical approaches, that you
know better than long-standing practitioners; trying to foist on your
French colleagues the notion that your British or American methods are
innately superior; reacting insensitively to perceived cultural divergences
by assuming that 'we're all the same really'!

Whatever situation you find yourself in, you should not lose sight of
the fact that your placement is designed to benefit you in terms of career
development, both personal and academic. You should try to assess your
suitability, in the long term, for any of the styles and categories of work
with which you come into contact. Heightened self-evaluation and the
development of the ability to work with others are key by-products of work
experience. One way of charting your progress is to keep a written record
of your day-to-day experiences. This will, in any case, be invaluable when
you come to produce the report normally required at the end of trainee-
ships.

The work experiences outlined in the preceding pages vary greatly,
from a menial vacation job to full-time sandwich training with commercial or professional organizations. No matter what the nature and scope
of the employment you have undertaken, when the moment comes to say
goodbye, you will in all probability be reluctant to recognize that a unique
chapter in your life has come to an end. You must now resume your studies
in surroundings that are no longer as familiar as they were, having left
behind so many new-found friends. The real value of the benefits of this
experience will only be apparent in retrospect.

5
Studying in France: what to do before you go

Forward planning and careful preparation are essential for your study-residence, work placement or assistantship to have a successful outcome. Most of the preparatory steps for the latter have been outlined in Chapter 4 and we now turn to the needs of those students intending to follow full-time academic courses, though much of the advice will still hold good for those enrolling part-time alongside their other commitments.

Ill-prepared students arriving in France without the necessary paperwork, duly completed, are likely to fall foul of the relevant authorities and to have problems in finding accommodation. Even if your home institution has a written agreement simplifying registration procedures and incorporating concessions, you will still have to prepare the ground meticulously, while students not benefiting from an inter-university agreement will find that they have even more to do in advance to enrol correctly, obtain full student status, and find suitable accommodation.

The duration of your study-residence and the type of course envisaged will dictate the steps to be taken. Your own university or college may have already predetermined your host French institution, but for those with a 'free' choice, Part III is designed to help you decide: it complements what was said in Chapter 2 by giving you details of the principal French institutions and their urban setting. We recommend that you make this choice before embarking on any of the practical preparations set out below. Consult all available documentation provided by your institution, outlining academic courses and accommodation arrangements as well as tourist information about your chosen town. The advice of your year-abroad tutors can be supplemented by the views of students, reporting on their period in France, who will doubtless willingly provide a range of tips and insights not necessarily recorded in their reports. Like many a modern-day Emma Bovary, you may well have decided that Paris is the place to be, but studying in Paris as a foreigner has its undeniable drawbacks. As well as the minimum one year's pre-registration residence qualification for enrolment in the *premier cycle* of a national diploma, the cost of living in the capital is much higher than in the provinces and the cosmopolitan atmosphere is less representative of French life as a whole.

5.1 Pre-registration formalities

All foreign students intending to register in a university for the *premier cycle* for part (or even the whole) of a nationally recognized French qualification must demonstrate that (a) they have satisfied the requirements for university entrance in their own country and that (b) their competence in French is sufficient for their chosen discipline. Entry conditions to different French institutions, notably the *grandes écoles* or IUT, vary, but for most students looking to follow university courses from the first two years, DEUG or *licence*, the very first administrative document will be the *dossier de demande d'inscription préalable*, identified as the *formulaire blanc*. This is available from the Cultural Services Section of the French Embassy in your country during December, prior to the academic year of your application. Alternatively, these forms can also be downloaded from the following website: www.education.gouv.fr/prat/formul/familles. htm. The completed forms must be returned to the appropriate Cultural Services Section by *no later than* 31 January of the year in which you are applying. You will subsequently be required to sit a French language test (*test de connaissance du français*, or TCF) for which there is an administrative charge of approximately €60. Students from outside Europe should contact the French Embassy in their country of origin about local test centres and administrative arrangements.

However, certain categories of student are exempted from these requirements, principally those who live in countries belonging to the European Economic Area, and who are pursuing their studies in France under the aegis of a recognized inter-university agreement or mobility scheme. Equally, holders of scholarships, whether awarded by the French government or under the remit of CNOUS or EGIDE, qualify for this dispensation. These categories of student will apply directly to the university of their choice.

'Free-movers' (*étudiants hors programme d'échanges*) who wish to qualify directly for admission into a higher level that the first year of the course, must submit their previous qualifications and full transcripts of all assessments to a validating committee, which will also take into account linguistic proficiency. Each university has its own independent validation committee to approve or reject a candidate's record. Applications must include the following:

- A covering letter explaining your application (*lettre de motivation*).
- A certified copy of your birth certificate (long form) with a certified French translation.
- Copies of GCSE and A, AS or A2 level certificates, or equivalent secondary education qualifications, together with certified translations, which confirm your right to a place at a university in your home country.
- Your academic profile for the preceding two years (end-of-year results) duly translated.
- Five international reply coupons (*coupons-réponse internationaux*) and two large, self-addressed envelopes.

The *dossier* will, for most students, constitute the first encounter with a form to be completed in French. The experience can be a testing one, but it must be realized from the outset that, in the French system, often unexpected personal details are required every time you fill in a form (e.g. mother's maiden name, date of birth of siblings). You must take this and other forms seriously and provide all the information requested; if you do not, your application will either be returned to you or – and this is more likely – be consigned to the wastepaper basket. Form-filling is rather tiresome but in the long term the effort you put into it will be worthwhile; and, in any case, the information needed can be given painlessly, once you have mastered a few (recurring) terms and the abbreviations in common use in French university life (see Glossary).

The *dossier de demande d'inscription préalable* requires you to give details of your academic career to date, to state precisely the course for which you wish to register (diploma, *cycle*, year of study), and to list two French universities in order of preference. However, unless intending applicants, their parents or spouses can fulfil the stringent residential qualifications for the *académies* of the Paris region (Paris, Créteil, Versailles), they may not include any of the Paris universities in their list. With the *dossier* you will have received notification of the compulsory French language test, which forms an integral part of the application process. Providing you reached an acceptable standard, and your existing qualifications meet course requirements, there is a good chance that you will be accepted by your preferred university. If you were for any reason to be turned down by your first choice, your application would be forwarded to the university named as your second choice. Should you be rejected by both universities, you may appeal against this decision to the Ministère de l'Education Nationale.

If you are applying for a second registration, or to enter at a higher level than the first two years of the *premier cycle*, you should apply direct to your chosen university early in the New Year, *at the latest*, to seek admission and to establish registration requirements, since these will vary from university to university depending on the nature of the course. Exemption from the earlier years of the course will depend entirely upon whether the academic qualifications and detailed university transcript submitted satisfy the entrance requirements. Though the *dossier d'inscription préalable* (see above) is not a requirement in this instance, you are strongly advised to submit this *dossier*, in case entry into the higher level is refused.

It will take several months before you hear the outcome of your application. Once you have been notified of your place, the next stage will be to carry out the necessary registration procedures, and part of this process can sometimes be completed before you leave for France. Your first step will be to confirm the offer *by the deadline specified*. It is wise to send a photocopy of your French confirmation slip together with your own letter of acceptance (see Appendix 5.3 for a sample letter). Registration proper will then be completed either by correspondence or – as is more likely – once you arrive in France at the beginning of the academic year (see section 6.3, pp. 85–7).

This brings us on to the question of documentation. We have already mentioned the fact that details of your academic career will be deemed important throughout the registration process. You will also have to establish your nationality and civil status on more than one occasion. It is advisable, before you take leave of your home institution, to obtain more than one set of certified photocopies (*copies certifiées conformes*) and, where appropriate, similarly certified translations of the following documents: your academic qualifications to date (in the UK, for example, GCSE A, AS or A2 level certificates) and birth certificate (long form); your student card and passport; authentification of any higher education examination successes (first and/or second year of undergraduate study or first degree certificate); proof of your status as a grant-holder (e.g. SOCRATES/ERASMUS) or a scholarship-holder (e.g. AHRC funding).

Certification of your higher education examination results, together with details of all courses followed, will be particularly valuable where you wish to establish your entitlement to enter at a higher level of the course. The more complete this part of the documentation, the more detail given of course content, the easier you will find it to support your claim. In the past, many students failed to take with them such records of their academic achievements and it was often the case that they did not find registration as painless a process as those who were able to produce a fuller academic profile.

If you are to follow courses in France as part of an inter-university agreement, the registration process is usually simplified by prior institutional negotiation. In this case, a validated learning agreement (*contrat d'études*) sets out the courses to be followed in the host institution. Each specified course will carry a recognized value in terms of the European Credit Transfer System (ECTS), thus ensuring that, upon successful completion, you will have satisfied your home institution's requirements for the year. You will be required to sign this document which, in turn, will be countersigned by a representative of your own institution and, eventually, by a designated member of the host French institution. A sample document is provided in Appendix 5.4.

Two final points ought to be made regarding the documents you take with you. In the case of certified copies, the relevant French authorities may accept documentation provided by your home institution (stamped *copie certifiée conforme* and countersigned). In the case of certified translations, however, the official line is that only documents authorized by an approved French diplomatic or consular agent are acceptable. In practice, where regular contacts have been maintained between institutions over a period of years, certified translations provided by your year-abroad tutors under a recognized signature may suffice.

So much for the paperwork relating to your academic career. You will also need to obtain a medical certificate, with an appropriate French translation, dated less than three months prior to your departure. This should not entail a full medical examination, but will simply testify that you are medically fit to live in the student community and to participate in sporting activities (*apte aux sports*). However, it may not excuse you from the first-year medical examination which, in principle, French universities require after your arrival. If you are not an EEA national, you will, in any case, be required to undergo a medical examination when you apply for a *carte de séjour*. You will be notified where and when the examination is to be held and, to validate your certificate, you will need a fiscal stamp, which costs €55, from the local Office des Migrations Internationales (OMI).

Do not forget to take with you to France the originals of all the documents listed; your secondary education certificates are particularly important as they are *titres admis en équivalence du baccalauréat* and should therefore give you an automatic right to register. Some officials may need to check that they actually exist. *However, with all these documents, there is one golden rule: never surrender an original document (unless required to do so by the police); hand over to university officials only authenticated photocopies of documents.* Moreover, always keep one photocopy of everything listed above in reserve. Should you need additional copies while in France, it is worth remembering that main post offices have photocopying facilities.

For those of you who are to follow courses for foreign students (*cours pour étrangers*) or vacation courses (normally the *cours d'été* which take place in July, August or September – see section 2.3, pp. 31–3, and Part III), many of the above formalities will not apply. If you are to follow these courses, the chances are that your own institution has already established its own procedures; but even where this is the case, you will still have to justify your academic and civil status once in France. The more complete the paperwork you take with you, the easier registration formalities will be once you arrive.

Candidates for a *cours d'été* should ensure that their application form is completed and returned to the university in question in good time, and certainly well before the deadline set. Places on these courses are often limited and, once they are full, students will be turned away. Though registration procedures are greatly simplified, it is essential to plan ahead and to make sure that you are fully informed of requirements (e.g. compulsory language test on arrival) and of periods of study, which may last for only two or four weeks but which may clash with holiday plans. Check prior to your departure for France whether or not you are obliged to take the examinations which sanction your course and what certification, if any, is required by your home institution. In the UK, if such courses are compulsory, the costs incurred may be met, wholly or in part, by your university or college.

Vacation courses tend to be presented as packages that include accommodation and even trips to places of interest in the surrounding area. Accommodation for students spending part or the whole of an academic session in France presents greater difficulties.

5.2 **Accommodation matters**

Finding accommodation is, then, another exercise which has to be planned well in advance of your departure for France. As explained in Chapter 3, unless you are part of an exchange agreement, a French Government Scholarship holder, or a postgraduate student, it is by no means certain that you will qualify for a room in a CROUS-controlled hall of residence (*résidence universitaire*). A significant number of students, including 'free-movers', will, therefore, need to look for accommodation in the private sector.

If you are able to chose your own university town, consider very seriously avoiding the very large student centres – and especially Paris and

Toulouse – and aim instead for the more modest, but no less successful, welcoming or authentic towns and cities. Secondly, start early. You will find the whole process is quicker and less stressful, and the choice of accommodation greater in early rather than mid-to-late September, when hordes of French students back from their vacations start to make arrangements for the academic year ahead. Given the availability of cheap flights, in particular, some British students have taken to making exploratory visits at the end of their current academic session in June, or July, to make accommodation arrangements. Clearly, successful early exploration depends to some extent on proof (firm or provisional) of your student status in the host community, which may be essential for some contracts. However, the idea of an early start is to be applauded. Accommodation costs for such sorties can usually be made much cheaper by approaching the CROUS, which lets out some of its rooms from July to September at a special daily rate, the *tarif passager*, which is far less than that of any reasonable hotel room. Residence there might provide the additional opportunity of sounding out the local office over the possibility of longer-term accommodation. Over the summer, rooms sometimes become available through late withdrawals (*désistements*).

Groups of British students, in particular, tend to think in terms of sharing flats as they may have done at home. Before deciding on this option, do bear in mind the purpose of your residence in France. It is obviously true that to live together in a large monolingual group may well hinder, even prevent, the process of cultural integration and linguistic immersion so vital to the successful outcome of your study residence. Flat-sharing has so far not been a common practice among French students, but it is becoming more so, and there is even one major website dedicated to this purpose: www.appartager.fr. This may well provide the solution to those who like the idea of shared costs without the disadvantages of mono-culturalism. Students should arrive speedily at a mutually convenient arrangement over shared bills and charges, especially for utilities such as the telephone. This arrangement does not exclude students from claiming their individual housing benefit. If you opt for private-sector accommodation (see section 3.4, pp. 39–40), you must begin the process as soon as you are sure of your university place, or by May or June at the latest. The recommended websites (see Appendix 6.1) will allow you to examine flats through a virtual visit and to check availability.

Students who arrive in their chosen institutions at some later point in the academic year – for the second semester, for example – may find it easier to find accommodation. Some students will have left, some rooms will have been vacated, and landlords – state or other – anxious to avoid several months without rent coming in, may be more welcoming. However, the process of tracking down what is available will be the same. See section 3.4, pp. 39–40, for information about private-sector accommodation.

Many of the private hostels which form a viable alternative to a *résidence* are run under the aegis of religious denominations, though in principle they are open to students of all persuasions. Some in addition offer full- or half-board. Full lists of hostels in your area are available from the local CROUS or the Centre (Régional) d'Information (et de Documentation) Jeunesse (CIJ, CIDJ or CRIDJ). Individual university entries in Part III give the relevant addresses and telephone numbers, and list some hostels and private-sector accommodation.

Inter-university agreements often include designated help with accommodation, and in this case your residence application form will, in all probability, be sent to your home institution. If you are a 'free-mover', you will have to obtain a form (*dossier de demande d'admission en résidence universitaire*) direct from the relevant CROUS office, though in many cases it is possible to download the form from the appropriate internet site (see individual CROUS entries in Part III). This form, the Dossier Social Etudiant (DSE), becomes available at the end of the autumn semester and should be submitted early in the calendar year but, if you are a 'free mover', no later than 30 April, even though your place in the corresponding university has not been confirmed. Always remember to enclose an international reply coupon with any correspondence sent to the CROUS.

Application forms vary greatly – in layout and length – from one CROUS to another, but however long or short the form, always ensure that you give all the information required. Read the instructions carefully. Some sections will concern French nationals only and if a particular section, or part of a section, is not applicable, do not leave it blank but cross it out (*rayer les mentions inutiles*). It will also be occasionally necessary to adapt the form, designed for French students, to give an account of your academic record and personal circumstances as a foreign national. Rooms are allocated on a points system which takes into account factors such as your level of study, your family's financial situation and your period of study. Priority is given to students of modest means. As in the case of the *dossier d'inscription préalable*, forms which are returned to France incomplete may be ignored. It is particularly important to take note of the list of supporting documents (*pieces à joindre au dossier*), which are likely to include some – even all – of the certificates mentioned on p. 63, a number of passport photographs and self-addressed envelopes (your permanent home address with your country of origin in French), together with international reply coupons and a photocopy of your passport or student card.

Some CROUS authorities let their rooms to students who are staying only for a single semester rather than the full academic year, though sometimes at a higher rent. You will be required to put down a deposit (*caution*) against breakages or unpaid rent (normally equivalent to one month's rent) and to take out separate insurance, if it is not already included in the rent. Many authorities require that you give evidence of financial solvency and you will need the signature of a financial guarantor on a form headed *engagement de caution personnelle et solidaire*. The guarantor can in most cases be a parent or guardian. Further evidence of financial solvency is normally requested in the form of a statement of earned income of a parent or guardian; in the UK, Form P60 for employees, or a chartered accountant's statement for the self-employed, is perhaps the best means of providing this. You will also have to supply a certified translation together with an indication of the exchange rate used to arrive at the amounts quoted. Those applying for private-sector accommodation, in addition to all the above documentation, should have with them a letter from their parents or guardian agreeing to act as guarantor. This letter will also require a certified translation. Photocopies of the guarantor's recent salary slips are also desirable.

Some CROUS offices require you to send one month's rent before you arrive; if this is not the case, the sum in question – plus the *caution* mentioned above – is payable on arrival, before you are allowed to take possession of the room allocated to you. Rooms are available from either early September or October 1. If you intend to arrive before the date specified, you should ask for a *chambre passagère*, for which you will be charged as much as double the term-time rate on a *pro rata* basis. For further information on general procedures once you arrive in France, see section 6.1, pp. 78–81.

5.3   Health and personal insurance for visitors to France

It is absolutely essential that during your stay in France you have full accident and health insurance. The French health-care system (*sécurité sociale*) is very different from its British and American counterparts in a number of respects: standard cover is for up to approximately 65 per cent of allowable medical expenses only; the patient pays the sum involved and then reclaims it from the local Caisse Primaire d'Assurance Maladie (CPAM) (see section 6.7, pp. 93–4). Although there are reciprocal health-cover arrangements within the EU, students from non-EU countries should check their status before departure to France. Medical costs in France are high: if you had an accident and were covered for only 65 per cent of medical expenses, you could be faced with an impossibly large bill. UK students should make sure they have a valid European Community Health Insurance Card (EHIC), issued by the DSS in Newcastle (available from www.dh.gov.uk/travellers). In France this card is known as (la) Carte Européenne d'Assurance Maladie (CEAM).

Students following vacation courses or working for short periods in vacations have no other choice than to take out a private insurance policy prior to departure, as described in (*ii*) below. Those staying for more than three months need to consider making different arrangements. Anyone on a long-term employment contract in France, including language assistants, should expect to be covered by a combination of the French Health Care system and a 'top-up' policy from a relevant *mutuelle* (see section 4.3, pp. 49–50). It is worth comparing the following options.

(i) Sécurité sociale étudiante

Advantages: this is normally available on registration (though not usually for vacation courses) and, as it is the basis of French health care for students, it offers all the advantages of the local system. If you are eligible (i.e. a full-time student under 28), it costs €200 per year. If you are over 28 you must either produce a certificate of insurance taken out in your home country (with a translation certified by a French diplomatic or consular agent) or else subscribe to insurance in France, which may be considerably more expensive.

Disadvantages: *sécurité sociale étudiante* offers in the region of 65 per cent cover, depending on the nature of the claim, *for health care only, in terms of the French system.* It is therefore absolutely necessary to supplement it. Student policies such as those provided by LMDE or local equivalents affiliated to the Union Nationale des Sociétés Etudiantes Mutualistes Régionales (USEM) are designed specifically to do this. If you use this method, you must remember that it covers health care only; you may well consider taking out additional insurance for other risks (see p. 71 below).

(ii) Private insurance policies

Advantages: if you or your family already subscribe to a private health-care scheme, you may already be covered at no extra cost. If, on the other hand, you take out a policy with a private insurance company, such as Endsleigh in the UK, it will give you not only health insurance, but also cover for your journey to and from France, for your personal valuables, loss of cash and so on. Personal items are occasionally stolen or lost abroad, and should this happen, the Endsleigh – and other – policies are particularly helpful. If you choose an alternative method of health insurance, it is still possible to obtain from private insurance companies, or from travel agents and so on, an insurance policy which covers travel, cash, travellers cheques, credit and debit cards as well as personal valuables.

Disadvantages: private health-care schemes may have an unreasonably low ceiling for treatment abroad; do check the provisions carefully, including any restrictions concerning 'hazardous sports'. There is usually an excess on such policies, which means that you are liable for the first £45 (or so) of any claim, particularly if you fail to defray costs by drawing on the reciprocal cover provided by your EHIC/CEAM. You could find, therefore, that if you had a series of different minor illnesses, you would have to pay for all medications prescribed. Remember that an authenticated French translation of your insurance certificate will be essential.

Whatever you decide, make sure that you have 100 per cent cover for health care for the entire period of residence in France. For those of you staying for the whole, or even just part, of the academic year, the advantages of the French insurance system are compelling; but if you opt for this method of health-care insurance, it is advisable to take out additional travel insurance and cover for personal effects and cash while *en route*.

5.4 Other insurance

Once in France, you will be required to obtain insurance for your room and other liabilities. If you plan to take a car, you will, of course, need to consult your insurance broker or company about the extent of your cover, bearing in mind the length of your stay. If the expiry date of an existing policy occurs during the year, weigh up the relative advantages of renewal at home, or of taking out a French policy for the remainder of your stay. Try your local *mutuelle* for advice, though on all matters of insurance, information is available from the Centre de Documentation et d'Information de l'Assurance (CDIA). (See their website at www.cdia.fr). Car owners will also need to have with them their car registration document (*carte grise*).

5.5 Financial arrangements

Another area where advance planning is essential is that of finance. You will need money from the outset in order to complete registration formalities and to make the initial payments required for private accommodation, or by the local CROUS office. In the first few days you may choose to rely on a mixture of hard cash, travellers cheques, whether in paper or electronic card form, and money from a cash dispenser (*distributeur automatique de billets* (DAB)). However, the cost of these transactions can mount up. If you rely on a credit card for cash, remember that the money is treated as an advance and attracts high levels of transaction and debt-servicing charges.

The longer-term solution is to open a bank account and – for wage-earners, including *assistant(e)s* – this will be a necessity for the payment of their salary. Equally, un-waged students will find advantages in having a current account, cheque book and guarantee card. Student loans or other funds can be transferred from your home account to your French bank, while for any reimbursement of medical costs or the payment of ALS from the CAF, you will be required to give your French bank details. You will also find that various fees and deposits are often required to be settled by cheque and some landlords and service-providers insist on a monthly standing order (*virement automatique*) to cover bills. Your choice of bank is best left until after your arrival, so that you can establish which is the most convenient. Seek the advice of fellow students about the friendliness and efficiency of local banks as well as the types of account available, as these can vary considerably from bank to bank and from town to town. Before leaving home, obtain from your bank manager a letter, together with a certified translation, to confirm your credentials and financial status. Bear in mind that you can only open a bank account if you are to be resident in France for more than three months, otherwise you may apply to open an account with the Post Office or a savings bank (*caisse d'épargne*).

To open a bank account you will need the following documentation: your passport, some confirmation of your permanent address in France (*un justificatif de domicile*) and, if a non-EU national, a *carte de séjour*. After about ten days you should receive a cheque book and a bank card. Whereas there is usually no charge for the cheque book, the bank card, valid for two years, attracts a fee of between €15 and €40 depending on the type of card and issuing bank.

You may have become accustomed to free banking so it would be wise to check for potential service charges applied to your French account. These have been known to range from a few euros per month to €15 or more. Similarly, there are charges for closing an account or for stopping cheques. You should also be aware that there is often a double charge when monies are transferred between banks; your home bank as well as your French bank will apply a fixed fee and/or a percentage rate. One way to mininize this expense, and to speed up the process, is to use the French bank's DAB to draw money from your home account for imme-diate deposit. Though there will be the usual charges for this service, they will be less than the double fee outlined above and there is no delay. Do shop around – some banks even offer students an inducement (*un cadeau d'accueil*) to open an account. Whatever your choice, do remember that in France it is a civil offence to be overdrawn (*à découvert*) in a current bank account without the prior consent of your branch manager, and charges (*agios*) are extremely fierce. Some arrangement whereby, in an emergency, you can draw on funds at home is, therefore, to be recommended. Should your cheque book be lost or stolen, you must contact your branch immediately to stop all transactions (*faire opposition*). If the loss is outside banking hours, you should ring the Banque de France emergency number (08 36 68 32 08) with your account number to stop transactions. Finally, it is worth remembering that bank cards can be used in place of telephone cards in public booths, with the cost of the call debited directly to your account. Emergency numbers for international credit cards and French bank cards are to be found at the end of the *Guide*.

5.6 Travel arrangements

Before you leap on the first available low-cost flight to France, think more carefully about your travel arrangements. Make the journey, if you can, with fellow-students registering in the same French university: this can be more enjoyable and allows for mutual support in negotiating the journey, finding first-night accommodation and coping with registration. When making your travel plans, do take account of semester dates in France: you may need to be there in early September to register; the vacations between semesters may be only a couple of weeks, and, in addition, you will have a mid-year break in February to bear in mind. Check therefore the validity date of any return ticket. Equally, the end of the autumn semester and the beginning of the spring semester coincide with peak periods for travel, so that plans have to be made well in advance. Check that your passport will be valid beyond the duration of your stay and allow ample time for renewal if necessary. Do not forget your driving licence: even if you are not taking a car, you may wish to hire one during your stay; and, in any case, it is useful as an alternative form of identification.

For many UK students, the journey to France will be by either train or coach. Always seek the advice of more than one travel agent and, with proof of your student status, you should be able to obtain significant concessions through Eurotrain (rail) and Eurolines (coach). If you intend to travel regularly by train within France or in some cases move to a second European country, you may wish to consider the benefits of an Inter-rail pass, but this must be bought before you leave the UK (see section 6.8, pp. 95–6, for further details of discounted rail travel in France). If you can travel out by car (parents can be so useful!), it is worth planning your journey and possibly one or two overnight stays *en route*. Websites such as Mappy.com and those supported by the AA or RAC will provide route information, give the distance from home to destination and indicate the time you should allow. For overnight stays, you might like to consider one of the big hotel chains, such as the Accord group (Ibis, etc.), which usually have hotels on main routes, often conveniently located on the outskirts of big towns. Do not overlook, however, the possibilities of a stay at Logis de France hotels, which frequently have attractive rates for an evening meal, bed and breakfast, with the food cooked by the proprietor. For all chains, rooms can be reserved in advance by telephone or through the internet.

It is probable that you will need to take a considerable amount of luggage with you for your stay in France. In terms of clothing, for instance, it is worth bearing in mind that, although the weather may be extremely mild when you leave home, temperatures will drop significantly by the end of the first semester, particularly in the east and the north of France. A good supply of flexible, adaptable clothing, including several sweaters and appropriate waterproofs, is recommended.

Getting your belongings to France can also be a problem, since it is unlikely that everything will fit into a suitcase that you can reasonably manage by train or coach, or that will meet airline limits. There is no cheap solution. For UK nationals, companies such as the Excess Baggage Company will deliver luggage to an address in France from a number of mainline stations and London airports. As of 2005, a single suitcase or package (35 kilos) currently costs £90: for two the charge is £114 and for three £138. If two or three students are travelling together to the same address, the costs can clearly be shared. Delivery is between two and four weeks. Formalities include signing a security declaration. An alternative, cheaper, solution could be Parcel Force, which operates from main post offices. Charges are geared to guaranteed delivery times, so that the 24-hour service, for example, costs approximately £82 for a 15-kilo parcel or £95 for 20 kilos. For the same weights, but with delivery between two and three days, the respective costs are £59 and £66, while for delivery between one and four weeks, the costs fall to £45 and £48. These are indicative prices and you are advised to check current costs and conditions before proceeding. Those of you fortunate enough to travel by car will clearly have fewer problems.

The low-cost flight you may have so enthusiastically leapt on may be excellent for cheap passenger travel, but is often less attractive in terms of luggage allowances. Though highly suitable for an exploratory visit to arrange accommodation, or for return trips during your stay, these carriers may not fit the bill for your initial outward and final return journeys, when you are likely to have a considerable amount of baggage. Luggage restrictions – often as low as 15 kilos – and the accompanying high penalties for excess, should be borne in mind. Check before you book.

5.7 Things to take with you

Whilst it is to be hoped that you will adapt fully to the French way of life, and not act as the reluctant tourist scarcely tolerating all things foreign, you will almost certainly want to take a number of personal items with you. Indeed, some essentials, carefully selected, will save heartache and unnecessary expense. First consider your accommodation: if you are in halls, take posters, maps, photographs, postcards and so on to brighten up your room (with acceptable fixing materials). Bed-linen may be necessary, while a bed-cover, or even a simple rug, will make you feel more at home. At all events, it is a good idea to take a sleeping bag with you.

A personal radio/music system will provide entertainment; do not, however, bother to pack portable televisions or tv/video combis as the French system is incompatible with most others. If you are taking electrical appliances, such as hair dryers or travel irons, have them checked and if necessary re-plugged before you go. You will not be popular if a faulty appliance fuses all the lights in your corridor, flat or lodgings. Since standard French sockets differ, an international adaptor will be a useful investment. A torch may also come in handy. Tea- and coffee-making equipment is probably best left until arrival. Mini-boilers, for example, are inexpensive in France. Books are heavy, but you will be well advised to take with you your essential reference works and dictionaries. One final point: many students find a pack of cards, portable board games and so on a great source of comfort during the potentially difficult period of adaptation.

Check in advance what is provided in your CROUS and private-sector accommodation: you may need to supply full bedding and a wide range of kitchen utensils. Assess carefully what you can reasonably take with you and what you will have to buy after your arrival. If you are likely to be looking for private accommodation, it will be even more difficult to ascertain your needs.

Should you be accustomed to certain medicines or toiletries (e.g. creams or cosmetics), take a supply with you as they (or their equivalent) will undoubtedly be much more expensive in France. If you favour particular proprietary brands for common ailments, such as colds, headaches or stomach upsets, you may not find them in France. In some parts of France mosquitoes can be a problem and a suitable spray, cream or plug-in repellent will ensure a good night's sleep. Before leaving home, you might consider having your teeth checked and visiting the doctor, perhaps with a view to taking emergency or repeat prescriptions with you. It is sometimes helpful to have with you a list of vaccinations and inoculations, together with a record of a any commonly prescribed medicines you are allergic to – penicillin, for example. Note that tea, instant coffee and UK-produced confectionery are more expensive in France.

If you heed all the advice given in this chapter, you should encounter no major difficulties on arrival. You will, though, need time to adapt to life in a French community. For those on work placements, hints on how best to do this were given in Chapter 4; for those pursuing full-time academic courses, more detailed advice on registration procedures and on student life in general is given in the next chapter.

6
Studying in France: what to do when you get there

Chapter 5 outlined the advance planning process and procedures for applying to your preferred university, whether as a 'free mover', or as part of some exchange and mobility scheme. By early summer you will have heard whether or not you have been accepted and, if you have, whether it is by your preferred or second-choice university. After confirming in writing your acceptance of the place offered (see Appendix 5.3 for a sample letter) you must next take steps to reserve accommodation, if possible, and then to register. In some universities, the first stages of the registration process can be initiated by post – or even online – but in the majority of cases formal registration can only be completed in person during one of the periods specified, in July or, more conveniently for applicants from abroad, towards the end of September.

Once you arrive in your university town, what steps will you need to follow, and in what order? The answer to this question will again be determined by your status. As an exchange student of some kind, you will no doubt already have had contact with the appropriate administrative office in your host institution, and will be aware of where you are required to report. In this case, since accommodation arrangements are probably part and parcel of the agreement, you will wish to go straight to your accommodation (if already notified) or to that office and follow their advice. If you are a 'free mover', on the other hand, your first concern will no doubt be finding somewhere to live, as you will need a base while you complete the necessary time-consuming administrative and academic arrangements. Before you embark on this process, leave your heavier luggage at a convenient left luggage office (*consigne*) at the railway station (*gare SNCF*) or coach station (*gare routière*) near the centre of the town. Do remember, however, to keep all essential papers with you.

6.1 **Taking up CROUS-controlled accommodation**

If you have been allocated a room in a CROUS-controlled *résidence universitaire*, whether a traditional hall (renovated or not) or one of the more
recently constructed blocks of independent *studios* or flatlets, you may
well have received confirmation that a room has been reserved before your
departure. In this case, you will probably have been required to send a
letter of acceptance, usually together with a deposit (see section 5.2, p.
69). Even if you have been successful in obtaining such a room, you may
hear nothing further about your application until you arrive at your host
institution, where you will be informed by the office administering the
exchange which of the residences you are to be offered, and the procedures
for gaining access. At all events, you should plan your journey so that you
arrive during normal French office hours, preferably early in the morning,
since you may well find that local offices close for lunch, and are closed
again by 16.00 hours in many cases. Should you arrive after the office has
closed, then you will need to find an inexpensive hotel, or even a room in
the local youth hostel (*auberge de jeunesse*), for the first night, provided you
are already a member (see individual entries in Part III).

Once you have discovered in which residence you have been given a
place, you should go directly to the main office there (*secrétariat de direction*) to complete the necessary formalities, provide proof of the existence
of (or make satisfactory arrangements to take out) the obligatory insurance
(see section 3.3, p. 38), pay a month's rent and a *caution* (unless you have
already done so), and sign an agreed inventory of the contents of your
room. You will then receive the keys. You may be offered a choice of room.
In this case, though it may be tempting to live close to your own university
cohort, with whom you may have travelled, resist the temptation to stay as
a group: it will not assist integration. Equally, avoid, where possible, the
ground floor (which can be noisy and give rise to security problems) and
the proximity of communal facilities (potentially noisy and noisome).

If you arrive before 1 October, you may be required to pay either rent
for the whole of September (rent is payable by the month and in no other,
shorter instalments) or perhaps by the night at the temporary daily rate
(*tarif passager*), which can be as much as double the monthly rate *pro rata*.

French students' perceptions of hall are of a cheap base round which
they can organize their lives on an individual basis. More likely than not,
they live within the region and will return home on Thursday or Friday,
dirty washing in their bags, only to return for courses as late as the timetable
permits the following week. In other words, French halls are collections of
individual rooms that often have a deserted atmosphere at weekends, and
where there is little sense of community. There are communal facilities, but

even in traditional halls these are often minimal – a TV room, games room and, increasingly, internet access. Each floor usually has a kitchen with one or two hot-plates, but pots and pans must be provided by residents, and there may not be a fridge. Do not expect a laundry room, though there is sometimes a drying area, which may not be totally secure. An iron can often be borrowed from the *concierge*.

Though perfectly adequate and usually well heated, traditional individual study-bedrooms are small and fairly basic, and need decoration with personal belongings to brighten them and to make them more welcoming. Before you do this, however, check where you are allowed to fix materials to the wall and by what method. Unfortunately, it is also the case that standard British or American plugs will not fit French sockets, so you must either buy an international adaptor or have new plugs fitted to appliances, including razors, hair-dryers, radios, hi-fis, etc. Incidentally, hall regulations often forbid domestic electrical appliances in study-bedrooms, although the use of such appliances is very common. At all events, be careful not to overload the circuits; it is advisable to proceed with caution. Sheets may well not be provided, but you may be able to hire them if you have not brought your own. Rooms will be cleaned intermittently.

Acceptance of a place in official accommodation implies a readiness to abide by a number of basic rules concerning disturbances, the admission of guests, and the maintenance of your room in an acceptable condition. The area where foreign students most regularly find themselves at odds with their neighbours, or the authorities, is that of noise. Rules in this respect are strict, and visiting foreign students would be well advised to establish with their immediate neighbours (not forgetting those above and below) what is acceptable. The most common source of complaint relates to activities after 22.00 hours, when even relatively restrained conversation can give offence. In general, French students are in the habit of going to bed much earlier, and of getting up correspondingly earlier in the morning, than their counterparts from some other countries. Any disturbance after hours will almost certainly bring you into unpleasant confrontation with the night porter (*veilleur de nuit*), and may well be reported. This pattern is in part explained by classes starting at eight in the morning, an hour which is often purely hypothetical for British students used to a different routine.

Equally, the French are often shocked by the amount of alcohol consumed by their foreign visitors. In particular, drinking large quantities of table wine at improvised parties is frowned upon. Both discretion and moderation should be exercised in this respect. Taken together, the twin problems of noise and alcohol-related rowdiness generate most ill-feeling and often set back the process of integration. These aspects of behaviour give rise to mutual incomprehension and the strength of the reactions produced highlights cultural differences where least expected.

One final word of advice that relates, in particular, to traditional halls: in the interests of security, it is strongly recommended that you keep your door locked while you are inside your room, and relock it whenever you leave, even if you intend to go out only for a brief moment, to go down the corridor to the kitchen or elsewhere. Better safe than sorry!

Even if you are not successful with your application for a place in a traditional hall, you may be offered the possibility of alternative accommodation administered by the CROUS: either a *studio* in one of the more recently built new blocks (normally leased for twelve months only), or a room in an HLM, or in a private hostel with which the CROUS has an arrangement (see section 3.3, pp. 36–8). Such accommodation will be furnished, but you may well have to provide your own bedding. At all events, any one of these formulae will, in all probability, make you eligible for a housing subsidy, either the *aide personnalisée au logement* (APL) or the *allocation de logement à caractère social* (ALS) (see section 3.3, pp. 37–8).

Application for either ALS or APL should be made at your earliest convenience to the local Caisse d'Allocations Familiales (CAF). An application form can be downloaded from the national website (www.caf.fr), which will indicate what supporting documentation is required. This will include at least: a rent receipt (*quittance*) bearing your name; a copy of the tenancy agreement; proof of your student status in France, for example your student card (*carte d'étudiant*); a description of the accommodation from your landlord; and preferably a full-year residence permit (*carte de séjour*) (see section 6.3, pp. 86–7). The website also contains a facility to enable you to calculate the level of benefit you may be entitled to. Beware of counting on the sum you arrive at, however, as it is not guaranteed.

Once completed, the dossier should be submitted to the local CAF (see Part III for local addresses). There may then be a delay of two months or more before any reimbursement is forthcoming, during which period the rent will have to be paid in full from your own resources. Reimbursements will not cover the first month's rent, but may be backdated for up to three months. It is important, therefore, to keep accurate records of rent payments from day one.

Rent for CROUS-controlled accommodation other than rooms in traditional residences will be significantly more expensive but receipt of either of the above benefits will reduce the cost considerably. However, as explained in section 3.3, p. 38, students living in an HLM may be subject to the local residence tax (*taxe d'habitation*). You should therefore ask at the CROUS whether this charge has been incorporated into the monthly rental payments or is to be levied separately.

6.2 **Taking up private-sector accommodation**

Despite the acknowledged difficulty of finding *studios* and flats in the private sector, many visiting students will be obliged to do so. It is precisely these problems that have led to situations – not too unusual – whereby successive groups of students from the same home institution, attending courses in the same location, have come to agreements to hand down the same flat or flats from one cohort to the next. Provided you can come to some understanding as to how to cope with the potentially awkward gap in the summer, it is an arrangement which is obviously to the benefit of all concerned. Difficulties over student accommodation should always be borne in mind when decisions are made as to the location in France where any period of study residence may be spent, as we stressed in the planning section (Chapter 5). If you are part of a mobility scheme or regular inter-university exchange programme, then you are likely to receive serious help with accommodation. This will give you an edge in the market, if not guaranteed rooms. Should you prefer the greater independence – and perhaps comfort – of living in privately rented accommodation, or are obliged by force of circumstance to explore this market, you will probably have to accept considerably higher living costs, but you may still benefit from one of the housing subsidies described above.

Again the CROUS will offer advice and addresses, and this should be your first port of call. There is always the chance – if you arrive early enough in September – that there might have been a withdrawal, and that you happen to be in the right place at the right time to fill the vacancy. Even if this is wishful thinking, CROUS maintains a list of private landlords who are willing to let to students. No information of this kind will usually be given out at a distance, by telephone, fax or letter, so it is only on arrival that you can start to explore this resource. In any case, private landlords are normally anxious to have the opportunity of interviewing and assessing their prospective tenants. Be aware that lists are not always kept up-to-date – but then students who find accommodation through the lists do not always report back that they have done so.

CROUS is not the only source of information on student lets, however. The local CRIDJ performs a similar function, as do the local offices of the student *mutuelle* LMDE (if you are a subscriber). You will find offers either listed in a card system, or simply as notices pinned on boards. There is also the local Centre d'Information sur l'Habitat (address from the ANIL website – see Appendix 6.1) and the *service de logement* at the *mairie* in your host town. Do not neglect the local papers either, including the free press, which may have accommodation supplements appearing at regular intervals. The abbreviations used in advertisements may initially appear impenetrable; Appendix 6.2 will help you decipher the most common of these. While walking round the streets, keep your eyes open for notices in shop windows, or on casual notice boards, at the university or elsewhere. A local Anglophone cultural centre (whether British, American or Canadian) may well yield a range of offers from sympathetic Anglophiles. There are also websites that may be worth investigating; Appendix 6.1 refers you to some of the best-known of these.

One option you may come across, but which you are advised to avoid, is that of casual subletting (*la sous-location*). By paying rent to someone other than the landlord of the property, you may place yourself in a position whereby the proof of address you are able to provide is inadequate for administrative purposes, so you are unable to claim housing subsidy, and your insurance is void.

Once you have located offers, then you will need access to a telephone and a lot of patience. Again, the best advice is to start the process early: not only early in September, before the vast majority of French students start making their definitive arrangements for the academic year, but early in each cycle, the minute a newspaper comes out, or you see a notice go up, not a couple of hours later.

If all else fails, or if desperation sets in, you may have to resort to an agency. In the large towns, more than 50 per cent of lets are controlled by agencies. Be aware, however, that, to go through an agency, you will incur costs equivalent to between 10 per cent and 15 per cent of the eventual rent, costs which you will have to pay on signing the lease. An average working figure is a month's rent. In terms of choosing an agency, accepted advice is to avoid the smaller, independent outfits and look rather to those that are affiliated to the large professional organizations, such as the Fédération Nationale de l'Immobilier (FNAIM), which offer a better guarantee of service. In dealing with an agency, remember that, first and foremost, it is acting as the landlord's agent, and protecting his or her rights. But it has an obligation to protect your rights too, so do not be intimidated, and do not leap at the first offer made. When asked to specify your needs, be somewhat conservative, especially as regards the target rent. You can be sure that the tendency will be to show you flats towards the top of your range, and even just beyond, so you need to leave yourself room for manoeuvre.

Before entering into a tenancy, try to discover something of the neighbourhood. A seemingly quiet district may be a noisy commuter route first thing in the morning, or be frequented by dubious characters after dark. It is clearly essential that there should be convenient links with your place of work or study. In this respect, it is worth remembering that provincial bus services often stop as early as 20.30 hours, though tram routes, where available, continue for much longer. If your host institution is on the periphery of the town, and you decide to live nearby, this may pose problems for getting back if you wish to go out in the evenings. It may therefore be more sensible – and secure – to opt to live nearer the town centre and make the journey out for classes during the day, when public transport is more frequent. Use the website www.lindic.com as a starting-point in this discovery process.

Once you have located accommodation of your choice, there are a number of issues that it is advisable to clarify before you visit the property. How many rooms are there? Is it furnished or unfurnished? Is the heating specific (*individuel*) or communal (*collectif*)? Gas or electricity (gas is cheaper)? What is the rent and are there any charges to be paid over and above it? How far is it from the town centre, approximately (on foot, by car/public transport)? Are there agent's fees to be paid, or a deposit; and if so, how much?

Before you finally commit yourself, ensure that, in all cases, you obtain a tenancy agreement or lease (*bail*), which should contain: the name and address of the landlord; the starting date of the lease (which may differ from the date of signature) and its duration; a description of the property (number of rooms and so on), specifying which rooms and facilities are exclusive to the tenant and, where appropriate, which facilities are to be shared (a lift in a block of flats, for example); the rent payable and method of payment; and the amount of any deposit against breakages or unpaid rent (*dépôt de garantie*). Check, too, what notice is required to terminate your agreement (*la résiliation du bail*). Legally, this is specified as three months, notified by registered letter, but under certain circumstances it can be as short as one month.

Other conditions will vary according to the nature of the accommodation chosen. In a furnished room in a private house, for example, make sure that you have understood what facilities and services are included in the monthly rent, which is usually payable in advance, or what extra charges you may be liable for. Some landlords may make an additional levy for water, heating, lighting, clean linen and even for baths and showers. Others may allow you to share a kitchen, some may even provide breakfast. It is advisable to clarify the owner's attitude towards guests and whether there are particular rules about noise.

In an independent flat in a modern block, you should check what charges are made for maintenance of the common areas within the block, for waste removal and for heating (if it is communal), and whether the rent includes any allowance for these or for utilities (which is unlikely, so they must figure as extras in the budget). It is useful to know whether there is any allocated parking, or whether this might attract additional outlay.

In all cases, be punctilious in checking the inventory of your accommodation (*état des lieux*) in the presence of the landlord or landlord's agent. Ensure that note is taken formally of any discrepancies you find between what is listed and the actual state of the property. When you vacate the premises, you will be required to make good at your own expense any additional damage or deterioration that is noticed, and the landlord will not hesitate to deduct these charges from the deposit you left, and bill you for any excess. In these circumstances, even the smallest stain on the carpet or the furniture is worth noting. Equally, while you have witnesses, read the utility meters, so that there is a clear understanding of the point at which your billing should start.

Once in the property, you will have to arrange for connection of essential utilities. To do this, you should approach the agencies concerned (Electricité de France–Gaz de France (EDF–GDF), France Télécom and so on) and take advice on connection costs and billing rates and schemes. Unless you have all the home comforts (washing machine, dish-washer, microwave, music system and so on) and intend to use them regularly, you would obviously be advised to pitch your sights fairly low in terms of consumption. However, even if your mobile is going to be your main communications aid, you should consider activating your phone line. It will be cheaper than the mobile and you may need it for your computer. Incidentally, if you are sharing, consider one of the company's schemes for allowing you to identify your own calls in the bill, unless you can come to some mutually satisfactory internal arrangement. With respect to connection charges, you should think in terms of €15–20 for connection to each of EDF and GDF, and about €40 for the phone line. In the big university towns, there is usually a student accommodation forum in some central place throughout September and into October. All the above agencies are represented there, and it serves as a short-cut to contacting them all individually at their own premises. This will also be the place at which you can initiate your application for the appropriate housing benefit (see section 3.3, p. 38), for which the procedure is exactly the same as that described above in 6.1.

If the property is unfurnished – which it may be as such flats are less popular with students and therefore easier to find – you will need to acquire the essentials in terms of furniture and equipment. Enquiring of neighbours will reveal the location of the nearest flea market or second-hand dealer. Buy the barest essentials, and do not be afraid to improvise. Pots and pans, crockery and cutlery may be bought very inexpensively from the nearest supermarket or hypermarket.

In the event of dispute with your landlord, try negotiation first, having taken counsel from the advisors at CROUS, LMDE or any other agency to which you may subscribe. If the matter becomes serious and legal, you should contact, by registered letter, the Commission Départementale de Conciliation through the Préfecture of the *département* in which you are resident. The service is free, but should only be used as a last resort.

6.3 Registration (*inscription administrative*)

Once you have found yourself a base, whether temporary or permanent, you will be in a position to embark on the formalities involved in establishing your academic status. If you fall under an inter-university exchange arrangement, or mobility scheme of some kind, you will no doubt have started this process by returning documentation sent to you by coordinating offices. This, in turn, will have supplied you with essential dates for action. You may even have been in contact with a local academic or administrator responsible for overseeing your exchange, and already have a precise appointment. At all events, it is likely that you should first present yourself, if only as a courtesy visit, to the local Service des Relations Internationales (SRI), through which all such exchanges are coordinated. They may have further advice for you as to how to proceed. At all events, they may well issue you with a local document confirming your exchange status, and this will then smooth the path further along the route.

If you are a 'free mover', you will find that you have to take more initiative in making arrangements on your own behalf. Once again, a courtesy visit to the SRI may well be indicated, and this may enable you to short-circuit other procedures. Do not forget to take with you the response to your *dossier d'inscription préalable*, which establishes your right to register in the university concerned.

Attempts have been made in recent years to ease the registration process. French students now do the essentials online prior to arrival at the university and this has contributed to shortening queues. Nevertheless, it may well appear to you needlessly bureaucratic and frustratingly time-consuming. Some university towns have instituted giant beginning-of-year student fairs (Espace Rentrée Etudiant and so on) to initiate, if not complete, the multiple processes on one site. Sometimes student helpers (*tuteurs*) are employed to assist with the incomprehensible form-filling. This has also lessened some of the boredom and frustration. However, the corollary of the more open French system is the need to establish credentials, and you will consequently need a number of administrative and academic documents (see section 5.1, pp. 64–5), and a considerable degree of patience. Office staff may be over-stretched at peak periods, and temporary helpers drafted in may not always be completely familiar with every foreign student's qualifications. Time is needed to check carefully the academic, financial and legal status of each applicant, unless this has been done in advance. At all events, you should ensure that you have with you, on all occasions, your full sheaf of documents (including originals) provided by your home institution, together with the additions you yourself have made (see section 5.1, pp. 64–5). It is most annoying to be turned away and to be unable to complete part of your registration for want of a single piece of paper.

To minimize delays, the process is usually broken down into two stages, as you will soon discover. In the first instance you should seek out the registry specified (*bureau de scolarité*), if appropriate at the time indicated on the form confirming your place in your selected discipline, and collect a registration form. Arrive early in the day to avoid lengthy queues. You may be able to complete initial registration on the spot, or you may receive a provisional enrolment certificate and a dossier to complete, together with an appointment for full registration at a later date. Your provisional enrolment certificate will enable you to buy meal tickets from the CROUS and to qualify for student reductions. Unless there is an agreement with your home university to waive fees, you should allow about up to €350 for registration, and be prepared for additional library fees and other miscellaneous charges. Cheques are not usually accepted and you should have the amount needed in cash, though for security reasons some universities require payment by a money order (*mandat*) purchased from a post office. You should also have about a dozen black-and-white passport-size photographs, full-face, bare-headed, together with three large stamped, self-addressed envelopes. These will be used to inform you of examination dates, and possibly medical examinations.

In the case of students from outside the EU and the EEA, it may be that, before their registration can be completed, they are required to establish their residence status in France by obtaining from the Préfecture a document certifying that there is no obstacle to them being given a residence permit (*carte de séjour temporaire*) valid for the year. Since 2003, EU and EEA students are no longer required to obtain a *carte de séjour*, though it is still possible to find circumstances where it may be an advantage to have one (for example if it is envisaged that a temporary work permit may be sought).

In any case, students from outside the EU will already have armed them-selves with a *visa de long séjour D, mention étudiant*, prior to their arrival in France. This is indispensable for entry into France for any non-EU person proposing to stay for more than three months, and cannot be obtained once in the country. The *carte de séjour* is the next stage in this process. To obtain a residence permit, you will have to produce your passport with visa; your birth certificate and translation; your new student card or regis-tration certificate (or pre-registration certificate, if the visit is to obtain the temporary *récépissé de demande de carte* to allow registration); proof of financial status; evidence of Health Insurance in whatever form you have chosen (see section 5.3, pp. 69–71); proof of accommodation within the *département*; a written guarantee to attend a subsequent compulsory medical examination; at least four black-and-white passport-size photo-graphs; and a self-addressed envelope, bearing a €0.53 stamp, for a later appointment. You will also have to pay for the OMI fiscal stamp (€55).

The justification of adequate financial resources sometimes causes a certain amount of uncertainty. It means proving you have the ability to meet the requirements of a minimum student budget – as of 2006, about €700 per month in the provinces. This can be done by producing bank statements or other certificates of income (a student loan), or even a certi-fied guarantee from someone who is prepared to make you an adequate allowance. Similarly, for proof of address, you will require a statement from the CROUS, or from a private landlord, or a rent receipt clearly bearing the address and your name. Any documents or letters in English will need to be accompanied by appropriately certified translations, and you should ensure multiple photocopies of them all, so as to be in a posi-tion to show originals, and then leave a copy with the authorities. It is sometimes suggested that the compulsory medical process can be short-circuited by taking with you a medical certificate, dated not more than three months prior to departure, which has been provided by a doctor approved by the French consular officials in your country. This may be more trouble to arrange than it is worth. At all events, one suspects that the university authorities will probably insist that the compulsory SIUMP medical is taken.

As they now have no choice in the matter, non-EU students under 28 should be prepared to pay the compulsory subscription to the *sécurité sociale étudiante* scheme as part of the registration process, and then to take out the strongly advised supplementary policy with a student *mutuelle*, or other company, if they can manage to do so.

6.4 **Enrolment (*inscription pédagogique*)**

When you have completed formal registration, you will now need to confirm the courses you intend to follow by enrolling for them individually. Once again, the procedure followed here will differ, according to whether you are an exchange student or a 'free mover'. Exchange students will no doubt have received advice from their home institution on the general pattern of study, and perhaps even the specific units they are recommended to take. They may arrive in their host institution with a learning agreement (*contrat d'études* – see Appendix 5.4) already signed in their pocket – though there are always mechanisms to enable subsequent changes in the light of circumstances. Choice of courses on the spot may be facilitated through the advice of a local academic correspondent, or exchange coordinator.

If you are a 'free mover', it is more than likely that you will have to follow the pattern of study laid down for one year of the course, with its compulsory, optional and contrasting elements. You will need to establish the nature of this for whichever year of the course you may have been allowed to enter on the basis of your previous achievements. However, to determine this pattern of study, or the full range of courses available, it is advisable to obtain from the relevant *secrétariat*, or to buy if necessary, the current academic handbook (*Guide pédagogique*, *Guide de l'étudiant*, *plaquette* and so on). These are often published only at the last minute and may be hard to find. A more recent resource, if it has been updated, is the university website. If you have difficulty in obtaining access to this information – or, indeed, in understanding course structures and requirements – do not hesitate to consult the Services Communs (Inter)Universitaires d'Information et d'Orientation (SC(I)UIO). When you have acquired the relevant information, you may find that, by comparison with previous years, some courses have been withdrawn. If you are enrolled for a specific diploma, such as the *licence*, make sure you have understood the requirements, in particular the requisite number of UE, or *modules*, and the examination procedures.

You are likely to be required to follow a number of obligatory courses, others from a restricted range and yet others from an open list (for an outline of study programmes, see section 2.1, pp. 21–6). However, you will soon discover that popular courses fill up very quickly or that others have to be ruled out because of timetable problems. You should therefore always have in reserve a number of alternatives. In most universities, there are briefing meetings or induction courses for new students, to explain more fully course structures, the range of elements on offer and methods of assessment, such as *partiels*, *contrôle continu* and *examens de fin d'année*. These are very common for ERASMUS and other exchange students, and one suspects that 'free movers' may be allowed to sit in on them, with permission. Even if the full range of advantages or privileges does not apply in your case, the general information will be invaluable, so you should make every effort to attend such meetings. In order to do so, you will need to make regular visits to the UFR (Unité de Formation et de Recherche) concerned to consult notice-boards. It is also very useful to make contact with departmental secretaries, as they may well be able to speed up the operation. Use spare time to familiarize yourself with the layout of buildings.

Since you may well have to enrol for each course separately, and in person, you should be fully prepared beforehand. The process itself will doubtless appear chaotic, as it often works on a first-come-first-served basis and may well be completed for all courses in a single day. You should therefore arrive in good time at the designated rooms, have passport-size photographs ready to attach to the completed course form, and then move on quickly to other rooms to repeat the exercise for the other units you intend to follow.

Lectures and classes may not start for a further couple of weeks or so, and you should continue to check departmental notice-boards regularly to confirm the time and location of your chosen courses, as these may be altered for administrative or other reasons. During this period you can wisely begin your preparation by reading the prescribed works indicated in the handbook, and by testing out library resources both on campus and elsewhere in the town. Municipal libraries are often a useful additional resource (see Part III for local addresses).

6.5 **Adapting to French patterns of study**

(a) *Libraries*

University libraries in France are not organized on the same basis as those in the UK. One of the most obvious differences is that probably only a few dictionaries and general reference works (*usuels*) will be available on open shelves, and it is not possible to browse before making your final choice. If you wish to take out a book you must first note the reference in the library catalogues, fill in a request form, and hand this together with your library card to the librarian. Your request will be checked and the work, if available, will be fetched from the stacks. Borrowing time may be limited to hours or days rather than the whole term, and the number of volumes you may borrow at any one time will also be small. The amount of working space within the library is also likely to be restricted in comparison to that found in libraries back home. You will probably find, however, that depart-mental libraries give you easier access to essential works.

(b) *Lectures and seminars*

In the first few weeks, at least, lecture theatres (*amphithéâtres* or *amphis*) and seminar rooms are likely to be bursting at the seams, and you should arrive in good time to secure a reasonable place. Do not expect the indi-vidual attention and small group work which is a feature of some systems. For many students – unfamiliar with French pedagogical practice, and perhaps a little uncertain in their comprehension – following lectures and taking notes will initially be a bewildering experience. You should persist, however, as it is likely that most of the material required to pass the course – once properly analysed, understood and digested – will be covered in the lectures. This means that, apart from when it comes to preparing assignments, you may find somewhat less independent reading and input expected of you – certainly in the early years of university study. After all, students entering into the French university system are initially unselected. This is why you may also find that your French university friends, once you know them well enough to investigate such personal matters, spend a fair amount of time structuring and classifying their lecture notes – even to the extent of employing elaborate colour-coding systems to do so.

Equally, in the practical classes – *travaux dirigés* (TD) – the rigorous structures applied to essay work, or the strict methodology expected in an *exposé*, may appear dauntingly severe. A great deal of time and effort will be saved if students familiarize themselves as soon as possible with meth-odological approaches in French universities. There are two obvious ways of achieving this: attend the induction courses for new students referred to above, or sign up for a methodology module such as *techniques d'expression écrite et orale*, where available. One feature that may strike you is the widely varying quality of the student *exposés*. This, too, may be chalked up to the unselected entry, and the fact that French students themselves are learning the nature of these exercises 'on the hoof'.

Work required will vary from course to course. You should expect to produce for each unit up to two or three assessed pieces (essays, *exposés*) in the year, though for language classes there will be more regular amounts of work and possibly weekly exercises, most of which will be prescribed in the form of oral preparations for class discussion. Methods of assessment will differ. In France, all exercises are marked out of 20. Do not be surprised to find the full numerical mark range used uncompromisingly. Traditional French marking conventions (as distinct from the ECTS (European Credit Transfer Scheme) grades that will be used for international communication of results) are more or less as follows: *excellent*, 16+; *très bien*, 14+; *bien*, 12+; *passable*, 10+; and anything below this is *insuffisant* or worse! Formal assessment will be either by coursework (*contrôle continu*), half-year exams (*partiels*) in January or February and/or full examinations in May/June (*examens de fin d'année/devoirs sur table*). For the formal examination process, separate registration is usually necessary.

6.6 Settling down and making contacts

It is not unusual to feel a little homesick during the first few weeks, especially if you are experiencing life in a foreign country for the first time. There will even be occasions when you may begin to doubt the wisdom of committing yourself to an extended period of study in France. Such feelings are especially common when the initial excitement of discovering a different town has worn off and there is, as yet, no established pattern to your new life. Weekends in particular are likely to be low points, since so few French students remain in residence. You should seek to use the time positively by going out for the day, perhaps exploring the region, or visiting friends. The Tourist Office, the Centre d'Information Jeunesse (CIJ) or the Service des Activités Culturelles at the CROUS will provide useful information on local opportunities. If you do feel particularly low, you should arrange to consult an *assistant(e) social(e)* at the CROUS (see section 3.5, pp. 40–1), or in extreme circumstances there is a telephone helpline, SOS Amitié (see Part III for the local number).

Getting to know French people informally is not always easy and the means to achieve this goal are not particularly self-evident. In some universities, the Service d'Accueil des Etudiants Etrangers (SAEE) at the CROUS will provide contacts with welcoming French families, and, in a number of towns, organizations such as the Alliance Française or the municipal *accueil* exist to foster cultural links and the integration of foreign students. Outside these formal structures, you will find that shared interests in sport, religion or a cultural activity are often the way to establish a disinterested relationship with your French peer group, either in the university or, more especially perhaps, in the wider community. The Maisons des Jeunes et de la Culture (MJC), which still exist in some towns, provide such opportunities. If you enter 'loisirs' under your town in Yellow Pages (*pages jaunes*) online, you will discover a whole host of possibilities.

Do not expect French students, who will, in the majority of cases, already have a network of friends, to take to you without a reasonable effort on your part. Becoming involved with a drama group (French or English), a choir (religious or lay), a walking or rambling club, groups and associations in the town (*la vie associative*), a sports club, a church or a musical society will provide an arena where you can be seen to make your personal contribution. Eventually, your 'foreignness' will become secondary as mutual interest becomes the primary bond. If you simply hang around in groups, sentimentalizing about your friends back home and drifting into negative comparisons about French and English lifestyles, you are unlikely to endear yourself to the inhabitants of your (temporarily) adopted country. Rather, you will conform to the worst example of the stereotypical, inward-looking British exile regretting the loss of Empire.

Throw yourself into a French way of life. Read the local newspaper, listen to local radio stations, watch the local TV news, show an interest in the issues which concern your neighbours, provide yourself with topics of conversation. Check regularly the programme of activities at CROUS or at the University's Service des Activités Culturelles, or the Maison des Etudiants. These range from theatre trips and concerts – sometimes subsidized – through guided visits to local places of interests (*châteaux*, art galleries, vineyards and so forth) to more expensive excursions such as skiing weekends. It goes without saying that you will wish to sample the delights of your new town. You will naturally want to try cafés, restaurants and student bars for yourself, perhaps share the French love of the cinema, and you will be tempted by the potential pleasures of the nightclubs. But here a word of caution: French nightclubs/discotheques can be very expensive and, for females, occasionally little more than an arena for an exercise in self-defence.

For those of you living in self-catering accommodation, the local markets are a cheap source of fresh produce. As elsewhere, supermarkets and, much more particularly, hypermarkets on the outskirts of town are usually much better value than local corner shops. If you own a car, petrol is considerably cheaper at the hypermarket, and the savings you make will more than pay for the journey.

6.7 **Medical matters**

As we have outlined above, general medical insurance is compulsory and, if you intend to participate in sporting activities, further insurance will be required. If you have not already taken the precaution of providing yourself with full insurance cover, as described in section 5.3, pp. 69–71, you will have to take the necessary steps on arrival. If you are under 28, Sécurité Sociale Etudiante and an optional top-up scheme (LMDE for example) can be obtained at registration. Beyond 28, if you are not a student with an EU passport, you will have to take out private health cover.

(a) *Consulting a doctor or dentist*

Should you require medical advice or treatment, try in the first instance the University Health Centre (Service (Inter)Universitaire de Médecine Préventive et de Promotion de la Santé – S(I)UMPPS), if only because it is free. However, you may well encounter long delays and, because the service works primarily by appointment, you should not rely upon it in an emergency. You may prefer to consult a local doctor or dentist, in which case the recommendation of fellow students is often invaluable. Keep a record of the telephone number, in case you need to make contact urgently. Ensure that the practitioner of your choice is *conventionné*, that is to say that the work will be carried out according to the agreed scale of national charges within the French health insurance scheme. You will have to pay about €20 for a visit to a GP (*médecin généraliste*), €28 to see a specialist and even more for a psychiatric consultation. Higher charges apply for home visits and treatment on Sundays and public holidays, while emergency night calls carry a further supplement (the range is between €30 and €50). After your consultation, the doctor or dentist should provide you with a signed statement of the treatment carried out (*feuille de soins*). This will allow you to claim a refund on charges and on the medicines prescribed.

The system works in this way. The chemist will return your prescription with your medicines. The medicine containers have stamps (*vignettes*) which give the cost of the product. Stick these in the space reserved on the *feuille de soins*, which you sign and date. If you are operating in terms of E111, or the EHIC card, send or take this together with your prescription and *feuille de soins* to the local sickness benefits office (Caisse Primaire d'Assurance Maladie). You will first be given a statement itemising the refund to which you are entitled and subsequently the amount itself. You will receive about 70 per cent of the doctor's or dentist's fees and between 40 per cent and 70 per cent of most prescribed medicines. Some medicines marked with a triangle are not recognized for refunds. However, should you require regular repeat prescriptions for some chronic or on-going complaint, and take these to the same pharmacist, there is a scheme which spares you from having to pay up front each time.

If you are operating in terms of *sécurité sociale étudiante* (with or without a top-up policy), you should send to the Caisse Primaire or *mutuelle* office through which you agreed to be paid, documents establishing your entitlement to benefits (*sécurité sociale* and/or *mutuelle*), together with the *feuille de maladie* and/or the *feuille de soins*. If you have *sécurité sociale étudiante* cover with one of the top-up policies already mentioned, you can normally expect to be reimbursed 100 per cent. Private insurance policies will be subject to their own terms and conditions, but doubtless you will be required to present a full record of receipts and supporting documentation.

Remember to inform doctors you consult in France of any regular medication you are taking, including the contraceptive pill, since drugs prescribed for treatment may interact and produce unexpected and undesired side-effects.

(b) Hospital treatment

If you require out-patient treatment, you must pay and then claim a refund in the same way as when you visit a doctor. If your illness requires in-patient treatment, you will receive a certificate. The hospital authorities will forward the *avis d'admission-prise en charge* form, confirming you are undergoing treatment, to the appropriate local sickness benefits office. Provided you receive treatment in an approved hospital, 80 per cent or more of the costs, depending on the cover you have taken out, will be refunded directly to the hospital. You will have to find any balance and, if treatment lasts more than a day, a fixed daily hospital charge (*forfait hospitalier*) of €10.67.

(c) Contraception, AIDS and so on

Should you require contraception, discuss this with a member of the University Health Centre. Since the spread of AIDS (*le sida*), condoms (*préservatifs*) are now more readily available from street dispensers, often located outside chemists' shops (*pharmacies*). You should remember that there are other circumstances in which you might put yourself at risk: tattooing, ear-piercing and acupuncture are regarded with some suspicion by a number of US authorities. If you are in any doubt while you are in France, advice can be obtained from your local specialist centre, or local or national help-lines (such as Allo Sida – see Part III).

6.8 **Further practical advice**

(a) Personal safety

Regrettably, sexual harassment is not uncommon and many female students will decide to carry small defensive gas canisters (*bombes lacrymogènes*) or screech alarms for use against potential aggressors. Avoid dubious areas of the town or campus, and be particularly vigilant if returning after dark.

Poorly lit areas near telephone boxes are often the favourite haunt of 'flashers'. Mixed groups are less likely to receive unwanted approaches than one or two females together. In hall, it is a wise precaution always to lock your door, even if you are only away for a short time, and never advertise your absence by leaving notes for friends on the door. Before taking showers, you may consider it sensible to check that you are the only occupant, as Peeping Toms may be lurking. Invite into your room only people you are sure of, as the invitation may be misconstrued. Equally, advertisements on open notice-boards offering English lessons to paying clients may result in unwanted responses!

Sadly, hitchhiking has become a risky business and you would be well advised to think carefully before accepting a lift. Be on your guard against pickpockets and handbag snatchers. If you do lose personal papers, credit cards and so forth, register the fact immediately with the police, otherwise your insurance claim may be invalidated. Make a note of important details such as the numbers of your passport, *carte de séjour*, student registration card, insurance documents, credit cards and so on, in case of loss or theft (see inside front and back covers of this *Guide*). Another useful precaution, in any emergency, is to register with your nearest Consulate. The above advice may seem negative or unduly alarmist, but experience has shown that vigilance and common sense can eliminate potential threats to your personal safety in just about all the circumstances you are likely to encounter.

(b) *Travel*

During your period in France you may wish to visit friends, get to know other regions or perhaps, during holiday periods, cross into one of the adjoining countries. The organization OTU Voyages specializes in travel for students and young people. Branches may be found in or near the offices of the local CROUS, but it does not exist in all university towns. Part III gives details where available.

International rail travellers in Europe have a number of reduced-rate options. If you are planning to travel far enough and often enough, you might explore the various versions of the Inter-rail pass or the Eurodomino pass, which are available only to European residents. For North American and Australasian travellers, there is also a French Railpass, which offers unlimited travel for three or four days in a one-month period, with an option to extend it for up to six extra days. Similarly, it is worth investigating the advantages of the Billets BIJE, which are available from Agences Wasteels throughout Europe, and from some OTU agencies. In addition to reductions on train travel, they offer other benefits.

For travel within France, SNCF has a number of schemes offering substantial reductions to those under 26. Choice of the appropriate one will depend on the amount of travel envisaged, so plan carefully and estimate the potential savings. Casual, one-off excursions can be covered by a *Découverte 12–25* ticket, which offers 25 per cent off normal fares in off-peak periods – a saving which can sometimes be boosted to 50 per cent if the ticket is booked between 30 and 60 days in advance. However, if you intend to make several journeys over the length of your stay, it may be worth investing in a *Carte 12–25* for a year. For about €50, this will offer up to 25 per cent off normal fares for peak-time travel (*période blanche*) and 50 per cent off for off-peak travel (*période bleue*). If you are able to book your journey between 60 and 14 days in advance, you may qualify for a special heavily discounted ticket called PREM'S, where fares to a long list of destinations start as low as €20. There is even an offer whereby, if you book on line (www.voyages-sncf.com) in the week before departure, you may qualify for up to a 50 per cent reduction.

However, it is worth recalling that SNCF, like airlines, operates an allocation system on a first-come-first-served basis, with only a certain number of seats in each category available on many trains. It pays, therefore, to plan ahead and book as early as possible. Also remember to frank your ticket in one of the franking machines (*composteurs*) at the entrance to the platform. If you forget, you should seek out the ticket inspector (*contrôleur*) on the train as soon as possible, or risk being fined for being in breach of regulations (*en situation irrégulière*). It is also the case that all luggage on board must be labelled. You will see inspectors checking that this has been done as they make their way through the carriages.

The rail network in France is extensive and comfortable, and one of its delights is to travel by high-speed train, the TGV (*train à grande vitesse*). But do remember that you need a seat reservation as well as a ticket to do so. Alternatively, once you have settled and feel comfortable to look at other ways of travelling about the country, you might care to investigate one of the *bona fide* organizations for shared car travel (such as Allo Stop). There is usually an administration fee to be paid to the company, plus a mileage charge to the driver.

If you are planning a journey to France, between French cities or, even, simply need to find directions to a hotel or government service, such as the local CPAM or CAF office you will find the Mappy website (www.mappy.fr) extremely helpful and user-friendly. You will be able not only to download location maps or print off a detailed itinerary, but also to receive information on anticipated journey time and, where appropriate, the cost of motorway tolls.

(c) *Telephones*

To ring home from France, you dial: the French international access code (00); then the country code (for example, 44 for the UK, 1 for the USA or 61 for Australia); then your area code, which may vary slightly from its internal form (for example, Birmingham is 021 within the UK, and 21 from outside); and finally your domestic number. Thus to telephone Birmingham (UK), you dial: 00–44–21 followed by the subscriber's seven-digit number. If you are telephoning internally in France, from one province to another, dial the ten-figure number (the regional code plus the subscriber's number). To ring France from abroad, the country code is 33. Remember, too, to omit the 0 from the beginning of the area code.

An increasing number of telephone boxes take only phone cards (*télé-cartes*). Cards are sold in units of 50 or 120 at a cost of €7.40 or €14.75 respectively at post offices, railway stations and other outlets, including *tabacs* (which also sell postage stamps). It should be remembered that phone cards now carry an expiry date on the back. Cheap rates for all calls apply at certain periods; check your *télécarte* or the information sheet in the telephone box (*cabine*) for details. Equally, you may find numbers referred to by colour codes: *numéro vert, azur, indigo…* A *numéro vert* means the call is free anywhere in mainland France. Calls to a *numéro azur* are charged at local call rates, provided that the call is made on a landline within metropolitan France. A *numéro indigo* implies a special-rate call, but it is a complicated formula: there are three different charges, which vary according to the prefix, so it is best to be wary and to enquire in advance.

Using a mobile phone in France to stay in touch with home can prove to be expensive, whether you are making or, indeed, receiving the call. Those who have opted for pay-as- you-go will find tariffs particularly punitive, with basic provider connection charges as much as the call itself. Establish with your home-country provider whether there is a preferred local supplier and whether it would be in your interest to take out an international rate contract. Sending text messages will certainly prove less expensive than voice calls, since there is no charge to receive texts. If economy is required, leave your phone switched off and deal with any messages once a day. An alternative solution is to change your domestic SIM card for a French one. Original service providers should be prepared to do this for their customers, but if there is any difficulty, independent mobile phone retailers for a small charge can legally unlock the initial set-up to allow the installation of a French SIM, for which, of course, there will be some outlay, probably around €75 if purchased in France. However, once installed, the new SIM will allow you to receive calls for nothing and you will find that your outgoing calls both within France and to your home country will be considerably cheaper. Those spending short periods abroad (for vacation courses, for example) may consider investing in a travel SIM card, available, for example, from www.sim4travel.com. However, the maximum validity of such a card seems to be four weeks.

If you need to look for a French telephone number and have internet access, you will find two websites to be indispensable. For any commercial number, such as that of a restaurant or theatre, consult Pages Jaunes; for any domestic number you have forgotten, refer to Pages Blanches. Alternatively, if, from within France, you need to consult the telephone directory (*annuaire*) for any metropolitan area, this may be done at your local post office by using the Minitel system (*annuaire électronique*). The system provides its own instructions on the screen; you simply type in the information required.

Emergency numbers remain standard throughout France: Police 17, Fire 18, Medical Emergencies (SAMU) 15 from landlines; if you are using a mobile there is a single number for all emergencies: 112. Other numbers for the local ambulance services can be found in telephone boxes. Further local emergency numbers relating to individual university towns are given in Part III. It is a good idea to keep a list of these about your person.

One further word of advice: think carefully about the time at which you telephone French families. As a general rule, it is considered impolite to interrupt at meal times, and to intrude on privacy after 21.30. Your acquired appreciation of cultural mores will enable you to judge what is, or is not, acceptable. If phoning between countries, do not forget the differences in time zones: even your parents may not appreciate a well-meaning call at 3 am!

(d) Making the most of your student status

Although goods and services in France may cost more than in your own country, you can frequently make savings by virtue of your student status. Apart from the significant reductions to be obtained on public transport (local buses, coaches, trains and even air travel (see pp. 95–6)), there are usually special rates for cinemas, theatres, museums, concerts and nightclubs, though there may be restrictions as to days or times when these are available. Local leisure facilities – such as swimming pools, tennis courts, ice-skating rinks and so on – can be enjoyed at preferential rates, as well as many tourist attractions, including museums and art galleries (*musées*). *Remember, you must always produce your student card to prove your entitlement to these concessions.* Often local businesses, such as hairdressers, fashion shops and occasionally restaurants, will tempt you with discounts, though, of course, the reduction does not necessarily ensure good value for money. If you wish to hire sports or leisure equipment, such as skis or bicycles, always check first to see if there is a student rate. Finally, several major national newspapers and periodicals offer students discounts for a regular subscription.

7
Returning and reintegrating

Your study-residence, assistantship or work placement has come to an end. For many, particularly those who have spent a full academic year in France, it will be a moment of regret and apprehension: regret at leaving behind a lifestyle you have come to enjoy, friendships you have formed, another self in another place; apprehension, too, at starting a new course or returning to a university where former friends may have already graduated, where new accommodation will have to be found, where finals may loom. There are practical steps to be taken.

7.1 **Academic matters**

Your home university may well have required some form of certification that you have followed courses assiduously and have made progress in your chosen disciplines. The record of your performance in examinations during the year, whether in *partiels*, *examens de fin d'année*, or by *contrôle continu* (see section 6.4, pp. 88–9), will be available from the *scolarité* but do not assume that you will automatically receive results, particularly if you leave France before their publication. Take a stamped, self-addressed envelope (permanent address) to the appropriate *scolarité* with a request that your results should be forwarded to you. For those of you benefiting from a SOCRATES/ERASMUS award, for example, certification of a satisfactory performance is essential. Without such proof, you may be required to reimburse your grant. For students involved in exchange programmes, results may be communicated directly to the home institution in the form of ECTS credits, but do not rely solely on this arrangement. Ensure you have your own transcript before leaving.

Many universities also require report forms (*attestations*) to be completed by individual course tutors, and here again it is *your* responsibility to ensure that this happens. You should endeavour to see your tutors a couple of weeks before regular classes come to an end, and ask them to explain what is required of you. If you leave this step any later, you may find that your tutors are unavailable. When a course runs for only the first half of a year, you should ensure completion of certification at the equivalent period in the semester. There is no guarantee that you will be able to contact your tutor as the end of the year nears. You may at the same time need to remind your tutor tactfully that written exercises have not as yet been returned and that these are necessary for your portfolio. Should you be on a university exchange scheme, your contact in your host university might well be able to facilitate the process. If you have been required to write a dissertation, or a self-assessment report on your year, make sure you respect submission dates and keep photocopies of your work.

For those involved in a work placement there is often an end-of-year report (*rapport de stage*) to complete for your home university, which will complement the report to be forwarded by the company for which you have been working. Again, you should respect the submission dates given to you by your university.

7.2 Leaving your accommodation

Whether you have been living in a hall of residence, school flat or private accommodation, there are a number of formalities to complete and common sense courtesies to observe.

(a) CROUS-controlled accommodation

If you have spent your year in a hall, you should give the *directeur/directrice* and/or the CROUS proper notice of the date you intend to leave, especially if it is slightly earlier than anticipated. Make sure, too, that your rent has been fully paid for the agreed period. You may, of course, have a *caution* to reclaim, though often this is used to pay the last month's rent. If there is an inventory to be checked, ensure that this is carried out at the appropriate moment. It is very much in your interests to be there, otherwise you will not be in a position to challenge any charges presented to you. You may wish to stay on in the region beyond the end of the academic year, and in many cases it will be possible to retain your room, though this will probably be at the non-subsidized *tarif passager* rate. The CROUS often finds it administratively convenient to place successive years of students from particular universities in the same hall, provided that your own stay has been a harmonious one.

By the end of the year you will no doubt have acquired various domestic items, such as pots and pans. A helpful *femme de chambre* will usually agree to store them for the use of others – perhaps even students from your home institution. Politeness does matter in fostering relationships, and short notes to the *directeur/directrice* and *femme de chambre* marking your appreciation will not be out of place. Leave a good impression: it will help others next year. Sadly, students from a particular year, who have been less than reasonably behaved, have sometimes prejudiced the possibility of subsequent groups enjoying similar accommodation.

(b) Private-sector accommodation

If you have spent the year in privately rented accommodation, you will have many more formalities to complete. Apart from remembering to give appropriate notice for the termination of the lease, you will have to agree the inventory with your landlord or the agent. Similarly, due notice must be given for the final metering of utilities such as telephone, gas, electricity and water, and, before departure, the settling of accounts and any charges. If your accommodation has been unfurnished, you will have acquired furniture and essential domestic items. You will have to dispose of these, and the most convenient solution might be simply to re-sell everything to the original second-hand dealers. However, if your tenancy has been trouble-free – for you and your landlord – bear in mind students from your home institution coming out the following year. You may well be able to pass on your accommodation, including all your acquired domestic items, thus sparing them that stressful period of searching and, yourself, a return visit to the second-hand dealer.

7.3 Reporting back

During your stay in France you will have built up a considerable amount of invaluable local wisdom to pass on to future students. Doubtless those planning to come to 'your' French university, school – or even firm – will have already initiated contact but, even if this is not the case, you can still put your individual experiences down on paper. Your home institution may well have a system for doing this, but in any case, share with your peers your knowledge of, say, good cafés and nightclubs – and, more importantly, perhaps, those to avoid! Point out places of interest, offer basic information about how to get by, pass on the name of an especially friendly person at the *faculté* or at the CROUS, of a good doctor or dentist, indicate a helpful bank and convenient shops, while not forgetting any sports club or society you have found to be particularly welcoming. Send back to your home university town guides, a copy of the latest student guide, course booklets – indeed, any information that is more readily available on the spot – so that newcomers, facing choices for their year abroad, have the most up-to-date details possible. An honest evaluation of courses, in terms of content, organization, and quality of teaching will enable other students to make more informed decisions. Reflect, too, on how you think arrangements might have been improved for your own year. A report to your Year Abroad Tutor will be helpful for the planning of subsequent periods of study-residence or work placements.

There may well be French counterparts going to your home university or region the next academic year, although it is unlikely, perhaps, that the individuals concerned can be identified before your return home. However, if in the course of the year you have been approached by interested students, try to remain in contact so that you can welcome them on arrival and – perhaps – even offer them help over accommodation and integration into their new environment.

7.4 **Financial matters**

Occasionally students are tempted to retain their French bank accounts in the firm belief that they will return to France regularly or, indeed, permanently. However, even when the anticipated return takes place, it is not necessarily to the same part of the country and, given the parochial nature of some regional French banks, it is perhaps better to close your account and start again, should the need arise.

You must, of course, take the necessary steps to close your account, for which there is usually a charge. Do not let this prevent you from closing your account, however, as accounts which are left open, but which are not used, are also likely to attract unwelcome charges. The procedure for closing an account will vary from bank to bank and even branch to branch. It is important, however, to verify that all transactions have been completed; forgotten and unpresented cheques create problems once the account has been closed. You may well have to make alternative arrangements for the repayment of your deposits and the settlement of any outstanding charges.

For those in receipt of a salary, or of subsistence expenses, the account must not be closed until final payments have been received; or alternatively, arrangements should be made for money to be transferred to your home bank account. Do bear in mind that charges will be levied for any transaction.

7.5 **Travel arrangements**

As a student, you should be able to take advantage of special travel deals, but you may have to book well in advance. Without realizing it, you will have doubtless acquired a number of additional items – ski equipment, for example – which will now have to be transported back home. If your luggage has become too difficult to manage yourself, you can always send part of it by carrier, or perhaps through the post, especially if you are sending books (see section 5.6, p. 74). The charges, however, could be considerable. Customs arrangements within the European Union have become less restrictive, but you should remember that there are still a number of prohibited items: tear-gas canisters (*bombes lacrymogènes*), for example, are still illegal in the UK. Students returning to other countries – the USA or Australasia, for instance – should remember to check their own customs regulations

7.6 **The year ahead**

As with the careful planning for your period in France, it is now essential to prepare fully for the new academic year that awaits you at your home institution.

(a) *Academic matters*

At some point during your year in France, you will have been made aware that a fresh academic session awaits you on your return. A new set of reading lists will advise you of the books and materials you need, and it goes without saying that some books will not only be more readily available in France but considerably cheaper. Though paperback editions are usually stocked by UK university bookshops, critical editions and critical guides may have to be ordered. Similarly, if your field of study includes film, you will find a good range of DVDs and video cassettes in all FNAC outlets, though you will need a multi-standard player to reproduce French SECAM recordings in colour. Also, CDs recorded by French singers can be relatively expensive but often unavailable outside the country. A subscription (*abonnement*) to a favourite newspaper or magazine will keep you in contact with trends in French culture and developments in the contemporary language. Offering to exchange equivalent material with a keen Anglophile is clearly a cheaper way of doing this.

(b) *Accommodation*

Before the end of your year in France, it would be prudent to consider your accommodation arrangements for the following session. Remember there will be administrative deadlines for applications for a hall of residence or a university flat. Similarly, searching for private accommodation should not be left to the last moment. In recent years, the number of students accepted at UK institutions, in particular, has put severe pressure on accommodation resources, and in your year away that pressure may well have increased even more.

(c) *Financial matters*

If your lifestyle in France has exceeded your initial budgeting, and you are faced with the need to secure accommodation for the year ahead, a tactful communication with your bank manager about overdraft facilities may be in order. Remember, too, to make all the necessary arrangements with the Student Loans Company for further funding as you now enter your final year.

(d) *Reinsertion*

Settling down again – perhaps to the serious business of preparing for final examinations – may not be easy. Many students who have happily integrated into French student ways find that a period of rehabilitation is necessary. Fond memories of the home university may not match up to reality. Friends will have moved on, the campus may not look the same, freshers will doubtless seem like escapees from kindergarten. As you organize your own reinsertion into your home-based course, spare a thought for those students from France who may be joining your own department or another part of the university. A moment's reflection will recall the difficult, disorientating experiences of the first days at the French university, when a friendly face made a world of difference. You can now be that face for the new arrivals. Help them to settle in with practical advice. Now that you have first-hand knowledge of both educational systems and/or of work experience in both countries, you are in the privileged position of being able to explain the differences in practice and to give them the benefit of your wisdom. Encourage your visitors to join in the activities of one or more of the many campus-based social clubs, which are not so common in France; invite them out for the occasional meal or theatre trip; in short, unveil the mysteries of student sub-cultures. Why not invite them to speak in French on some aspect of life in France, where their personal experiences and reflections would no doubt be of interest and benefit to their hosts and make them feel more appreciated? Strange though it may seem, giving of your time to your opposite numbers will enable you to reintegrate more easily.

And soon the cycle will start again. As students who have already completed a period of study-residence or work in France, you may soon be placed in the position of advising inexperienced and potentially anxious students where they should spend *their* year abroad. Although the vast majority of students will have enjoyed a profitable year, your own experience may not have been perfect; indeed, it may have been less than you had hoped for. But, in your advice and assessment, try to distance yourself from purely negative reactions. Remember to temper your necessarily limited perceptions with those of others in order to provide a more rounded and balanced view of your period in France. Your perspectives on your stay will already have changed, and will go on changing; the perspectives and expectations of those following in your footsteps will, in the first instance, depend to a large degree on your briefing.

Part 3
French institutions of higher education and their towns

France: the metropolitan *académies* and major university towns

1. Aix-en-Provence	**11.** Limoges	**21.** Pau
2. Amiens	**12.** Lyon	**22.** Poitiers
3. Angers	**13.** Marseille	**23.** Reims
4. Besançon	**14.** Metz	**24.** Rennes
5. Bordeaux	**15.** Montpellier	**25.** Rouen
6. Caen	**16.** Nancy	**26.** Saint-Etienne
7. Clermont-Ferrand	**17.** Nantes	**27.** Strasbourg
8. Dijon	**18.** Nice	**28.** Toulouse
9. Grenoble	**19.** Orlèans	**29.** Tours
10. Lille	**20.** Paris et *la région parisienne*	

Introduction

The reasons for choosing a particular institution of higher education are many and varied. There is a wide range of options, but the student's ultimate choice is often determined as much by a town's geographical setting, and its leisure facilities as the academic programme on offer. This section, therefore, sets out to provide information on individual institutions, the disciplines taught, the town and the surrounding area.

The institutions

The list of institutions, though not exhaustive, offers the student a considerable choice. Universities are presented alphabetically under the more readily recognized town names, rather than according to their official nomenclature; hence, the Université Michel de Montaigne, for example, is to be found under Bordeaux. Paris and its region pose a special problem: it would be unrealistic to attempt to describe in detail the seventeen universities and other major institutions, or, indeed, to account for all the attractions and facilities of the French capital. The universities and their disciplines have all been listed but detailed descriptions are given only of the University of London Institute in Paris and the Cité Internationale de Paris.

Accommodation

Finding suitable accommodation usually comes a close second after deciding on a particular course of study and, for this reason, details of both CROUS-controlled and private-sector accommodation are provided for each university town.

Courses for foreign students

For those seeking to spend a short period of study-residence in France
– perhaps a vacation, a single semester, or some part of a gap year – the
information on the availability of courses for foreign students will be more
appropriate.

Useful addresses

Each entry contains a selection of useful addresses and telephone numbers
for those looking for the town's administrative offices: the Mairie, the
CAF, the Préfecture etc. Also given is general information on main
theatres, cinemas, museums and art galleries as well as sporting and other
leisure facilities. These listings are restricted to the most well-known,
and more complete information should be sought from the local Centre
d'Information Jeunesse (CIJ), the CROUS or the Tourist Office. Similarly
the hotels and restaurants given in the entry are no more than a convenient
first list for the student or visitor with no knowledge of the town. It should
be added that much of the information on restaurants, sporting and leisure
facilities has been provided by students of the University of Birmingham
who were spending a full academic year in the town concerned. The restaurants included were chosen for their value for money and ambiance. While
every attempt has been made to ensure that the information is correct, it
will be understood that changes can take place very quickly.

Glossary and appendices

It will quickly become apparent that familiarity with the acronyms given
and defined in the Glossary or explained even more fully in the text (see
Index) is essential. For reasons of space and ease of usage, the full title of
common administrative offices has not been spelled out in full, so that the
local Caisse Primaire d'Assurance Maladie or Caisse d'Allocations Familiales will be given respectively under their acronyms of CPAM and CAF.

The Appendices provide model letters for job and course applications along with application forms for CROUS accommodation, university courses and, for exchange students, a typical learning agreement. A
compendium of useful websites, newspaper abbreviations used in accommodation advertisements and details of embassies and consulates complete
this section. Finally, there is a list of emergency numbers and headings
which enable you to record personal information including contact telephone numbers.

1 Aix-en-Provence

Institutions of higher education and their disciplines

Académie d'Aix-Marseille
Université de Provence Aix-Marseille I
3 place Victor Hugo, 13331 Marseille Cedex 3. Tel: 04 91 10 60 00. www.
   up.univ-mrs.fr
SCUIO:
- 3 place Victor Hugo, 13331 Marseille. Tel: 04 91 10 60 58
- 29 av. Robert Schuman, 13621 Aix-en-Provence Cedex 1. Tel: 04 42 95
   32 23
SRI: 1 allée Bastide des Cyprès 13100 Aix-en-Provence. Tel: 04 42 17 14
   20
- **Aix-en-Provence**: sciences humaines, langues, lettres, arts, communication, musique
- **Marseille**: mathématiques, informatique, technologies, sciences,
   lettres, arts, communication
Antennes at Arles, Aubagne, Lambesc

Université de la Méditerrannée Aix-Marseille II
Jardin du Pharo, 58 bd Charles Livon, 13284 Marseille Cedex 07. Tel: 04
   91 39 65 00. www.mediterrannee.univ-mrs.fr
SCUIO:
- 58 bd Charles Livon, 13284 Marseille Cedex 07. Tel: 04 91 39 65 17
- 27 bd Jean Moulin 13385 Marseille Cedex 05. Tel: 04 91 32 43 57
SRI: 1 allée Bastide des Cyprès 13100 Aix-en-Provence. Tel: 04 42 17 14 20
- **Aix-en-Provence**: sciences économiques et gestion
- **Luminy**: sciences, sport
- **Marseille**: santé, mécaniques, sport, communication, sciences écono-
   miques et gestion
Antennes at La Ciotat, Gap

Université Paul Cézanne Aix-Marseille III
3 av. Robert Schuman, 13628 Aix-en-Provence Cedex 01. Tel: 04 42 17 28
   00. www.univ.u-3mrs.fr
SCUIO: 14 av. Jules Ferry, 13621 Aix-en-Provence Cedex. Tel: 04 42 21
   59 87
SRI: 1 allée Bastide des Cyprès, 13100 Aix-en-Provence. Tel: 04 42 21 59
   93
- **Aix-en-Provence**: droit et sciences politiques, études comptables,
   économie appliquée

- **Arles**: droit, sciences et techniques
- **Marseille**: droit et économique appliquée, sciences et techniques

Antennes at Puyricard, Salon de Provence

IUT:

- Aix-en-Provence. 413 av. Gaston Berger, 13625 Aix-en-Provence. Tel: 04 42 93 90 00
- Université de Provence. 3 place Victor Hugo, 13331 Marseille Cedex 03. Tel: 04 91 10 60 00

Other institution

Ecole Nationale Supérieur des Arts et Métiers (ENSAM)
Cours des Arts et Métiers, 13617. Tel: 04 42 93 81 81
Ingénieurs polyvalents à dominantes génie mécanique et génie industriel

University libraries

- Droit, Economie et Sciences, 3 av. Robert Schuman
- Lettres et Sciences Humaines, chemin Moulin de Testas
- Sciences Economiques, 14 av. Jules Ferry
- Section IEFEE, 25 rue Gaston de Saporta

Courses for foreign students

SCEFEE (Service Commun de l'Enseignement du Français aux Etudiants
  Etrangers)
Université de Provence, Centre Schuman, Bureau A145, 29 av. Robert
  Schuman, 13621 Aix-en-Provence Cedex 1. Tel: 04 42 95 32 17/18.
  www.up.univ-mrs.fr/wscefee
IEFEE: Institut d'Etudes Française pour Etudiants Etrangers
Université Paul Cézanne Aix-Marseille III, 23 rue Gaston de Saporta,
  13265 Aix-en-Provence Cedex 1. Tel: 04 42 21 70 90. www.iefee.com

CROUS

6 av. Benjamin Abram, 13621 Aix-en-Provence Cedex. Tel: 04 42 16 13 13.
  www.crous-aix-marseille.com.fr
ACEE (Accueil des Etudiants Etrangers): Cité Les Gazelles, av. Jules
  Ferry. Tel: 04 42 93 48 24

CILE (Centre d'Information de Logement Etudiant): 215 av. J. Villevielle. Tel: 04 42 38 79 52

CROUS-controlled accommodation

There is accommodation for approximately 3,000 students in halls close to the University campus. All halls are mixed. To apply for a room, you should write in the first instance to the ACEE (for address, see above).

- Cité les Gazelles, av. Jules Ferry
- Cité de Cuques, traverse de Cuques
- Cité l'Arc de Meyran, av. Gaston Berger
- Cité l'Estellan, av. du Maréchal Leclerc

CROUS restaurants

A traditional three-course meal is provided at all restaurants.

- Arts et Métiers (CRENSAM), 2 cours des Arts et Métiers
- Cuques, traverse de Cuques
- Les Fenouillères, av. Gaston Berger
- Les Gazelles, av. Jules Ferry. At Les Gazelles there is also a small cafeteria for pizzas, sandwiches, pastries etc.

Private-sector accommodation

- Résidence le Rossini, 4 rue de l'Esplanade de l'Arche. Tel: 04 42 26 51 50
- Le California, 21 rue Jean Adréani. Tel: 04 42 27 65 11
- Les Citadines, Aix Jas de Bouffan, 4 rue Achille Empéraire. Tel: 0800 970 117
- Les Jardins de Mozart, 540 av. Max Juvénal. Tel: 04 42 91 52 20
- Résidence James Chasseriaud, 19 rue du RICM. Tel: 04 42 17 30 10
- Les Estudines Mirabeau, 615 av. W.A. Mozart. Tel: 04 42 93 19 29
- Résidence Touraigue, 6 av. de St Jérôme. Tel: 04 42 38 07 37 (Females)

For accommodation offers look in the free Aix newspapers: *Aix Hebdo*, *Le Choc* and *Bonjour*.

The town and its surrounding area

A prosperous town of 140,000 inhabitants, Aix lies within easy reach of Marseille and the Mediterranean resorts. The University dates from 1413 and there are over 40,000 students registered at Aix campuses. As the historic capital of Provence, the town has a rich architectural heritage with fine civic buildings and a number of elegant seventeenth- and eighteenth-century town houses. Aix is justly famous for its old quarter and le Cours Mirabeau, a beautiful tree-lined avenue with attractive fountains. Buildings of note include the Cathédrale de Saint-Sauveur, the Bibliothèque Méjanes, the Pavillon Vendôme and the Palais de Justice. Among the artists and writers associated with Aix and its region are Paul Cézanne, Louise Colet, Emile Zola and St-John Perse. A culturally active town with several cinemas, theatres and a *conservatoire*, Aix hosts international film, dance and music festivals. The countryside around Aix, with its archaeological sites, is of particular interest and beauty. Areas to visit include the valley of the River Durance, the Luberon Mountains, Lake Bimont, the Sainte Victoire Mountain and the nearby Gorges du Verdon. There are several reputable local wines and the Côtes d'Aix-en-Provence now enjoys AOC status. Calissons d'Aix are a celebrated delicacy made from marzipan. The town can be reached by the A8 motorway and a local rail network links the town with Marseille. The TGV station which serves Aix is approximately ten minutes away at Arbois, while the nearest airport, Marseille-Provence, is about thirty minutes away by local bus.

Tourist information

Office Municipal de Tourisme, 2 place du Général de Gaulle, 13100. Tel: 04 42 16 11 61. www.aixenprovencetourisme.com

Hotels
The following are amongst the cheapest in the centre of Aix:
- Hôtel Paul, 10 av. Pasteur. Tel: 04 42 23 23 89
- Hôtel des Arts, 69 bd Carnot. Tel: 04 42 38 11 77
- Hôtel du Globe, 74 cours Sextius. Tel: 04 42 26 03 58
- Etap Hôtel (next to airport, with free shuttle). Tel: 04 42 79 31 79

Youth hostel
3 av. Marcel Pagnol. Tel: 04 42 20 15 99

Restaurants
There is a wide choice of restaurants and pizzerias. Here is a selection:
- Le Bistrot Aixois, 37 cours Sextius. Tel: 04 42 27 50 10
- Pizzeria le Rustique, 1 bd Aristide Briand. Tel: 04 42 96 35 76
- Le Palatino, 1 bis cours Mirabeau. Tel: 04 42 26 72 37
- Le Flunch, 2 av. des Belges. Tel: 04 42 27 25 22 (self-service)

Leisure facilities

For listings, consult *Guide Pratique* and *Le Mois à Aix* available in the tourist office.

Museums and art galleries
- Atelier Cézanne, 9 av. Paul Cézanne
- Musée Arbaud, rue du 4 Septembre
- Fondation Saint John Perse, Espace Méjanes, 8–10 rue des Allumettes
- Fondation Vasarely, av. Marcel Pagnol-Jas de Bouffan
- Musée Granet, 13 rue Cardinale
- Musée du Vieil Aix, 17 rue Gaston de Saporta

Theatre
- Théâtre des Ateliers, 29 place Miolis. Tel: 04 42 38 10 45
- Théâtre Ainsi de suite, 23 rue Gaston de Saporta. Tel: 04 42 21 60 08
- Théâtre Municipal Jeu de Paume, 17 rue de l'Opéra. Tel: 04 42 38 44 71
- Théâtre de la Fonderie, 14 cours St Louis. Tel: 04 42 63 10 11
- Théâtre Antoine Vitez, 29 av. Robert Schuman. Tel: 04 42 59 94 37
- Théâtre 108, 37 bd Aristide Briand. Tel: 04 42 21 06 70
- Théâtre des Musicomédies, 37 bd Aristide Briand. Tel: 04 42 96 65 09

Cinema
- Le Cézanne, 1 rue Marcel Guillaume. Tel: 04 42 26 04 06
- Le Mazarin, 6 rue Laroque. Tel: 04 42 38 91 16
- Le Renoir, 24 cours Mirabeau. Tel: 04 42 26 99 85
- L'Institut de l'Image, Cité du Livre, 8–10 rue des Allumettes. Tel: 04 42 26 81 82

Maisons des Jeunes et de la Culture
Fédération Régionale, 25 rue René Coty. Tel: 04 42 21 21 46
MJC Jacques Prévert, 24 bd de la République. Tel: 04 42 26 36 50

Sport
To obtain a university sports card, go to the Bureau des Sports with your student card, two photographs, and a medical certificate (translated into French if necessary) indicating your fitness for sport. There is a modest registration and insurance fee.
- Bureau des Sports, 3 av. Robert Schuman. Tel: 04 42 17 29 20
- CSU/SIUAPS, 35 av. Jules Ferry. Tel: 04 42 26 66 78
- FFSU: 16 rue Bernard du Bois, 13001 Marseille. Tel: 04 91 90 91 38

- Office Municipal des Sports, 33 chemin des Infirmeries. Tel: 04 42 91 54 40
- Complexe sportif de la Piolaine, 35 chemin A. Guijou. Tel: 04 42 59 15 42
- Piscine: 1455 chemin A. Guijou. Tel: 04 42 24 35 67
- Stade du centre sportif universitaire: 35 av. Jules Ferry. Tel: 04 42 26 66 78

Useful addresses

Main post office: 2 rue Lapierre. Tel: 04 42 16 01 50
Police: 10 av. de l'Europe. Tel: 04 42 93 97 00
Mairie: place de l'Hôtel de Ville. Tel: 04 42 91 90 00
Municipal libraries:
- Bibliothèque Méjanes, 8–10 rue des Allumettes. Tel: 04 42 91 98 88 (enrolment fee: €12,50)
- Bibliothèque La Halle aux Grains, place de l'Hôtel de Ville. Tel: 04 42 25 93 29
Internet cafés:
- Millenium, 6 rue Mazarine. Tel: 04 42 27 39 11
- Virtualis, 40 rue Cordeliers. Tel: 04 42 26 02 30
Bookshops:
- FNAC, 3 place Forbin. Tel: 04 42 38 54 20
- Librairie Goulard, 37 cours Mirabeau. Tel: 04 42 27 66 47
- Librairie de l'Université, 12a rue Nazareth. Tel: 04 42 26 18 08
- Librairie de Provence, 31 cours Mirabeau. Tel: 04 42 26 07 23
- Le Paradox, 15 rue du 4 Septembre. Tel: 04 42 26 47 99
- Librairie Ventes du Sud, 7 rue du Marechal Foch. Tel: 04 42 23 03 38
ANPE: 960 av. Pierre Brossolette. Tel: 04 42 93 84 00
Association Bienvenue aux Etudiants Etrangers: 56 cours Mirabeau. Tel: 06 09 62 88 07
BIJ: 37 bis bd Aristide Briand. Tel: 04 42 91 98 00
CAF: 135 chemin Roger Martin. Tel: 0 825 25 13 10
CILE: (Centre d'Information de Logement Etudiant), 215 av. J. Villevieille. Tel: 04 42 38 79 52
CIO: 39 rue Cardinale. Tel: 04 42 26 35 63
CPAM: 56 chemin Joseph Aiguier, 13297 Marseille. Tel: 0 820 01 3000
EDF-GDF: 68 av. St. Jérôme. Tel: 04 42 27 98 33
France Télécom, 6 rue Lapierre. Tel: 04 42 37 30 14
La MADE (Maison Aixoise de l'Etudiant): 215 av. J.Villevieille. Tel: 04 42 38 79 52
Service d'Accueil Hôtel de Ville, place de l'Hôtel de Ville. Tel: 04 42 91 93 10
Sous-Préfecture: 24 rue Mignet. Tel: 04 42 96 89 48 (*carte de séjour*)

Health care

BAPU: CU Les Gazelles, Pavillon 7, av. Jules Ferry. Tel: 04 42 38 29 06
SIUMPS (SMPI): 2ème étage RU les Fenouillères, av. G. Berger. Tel: 04 42 26 13 57
Espace Santé Jeunes, 5 rue des Allumettes. Tel: 04 42 93 64 05
Hospital: Centre Hospitalier, chemin des Tamaris. Tel: 04 42 35 50 00
Chemists: the late-night and weekend rota is published in the free guide, *Le Mois à Aix*:
- Pharmacie Rotonde Mirabeau. Tel: 04 42 23 34 73
- Pharmacie mutualiste de l'UMAR, 8 rue Espariat. Tel: 04 42 26 07 47
- Pharmacie des Nouvelles Facultés. 4 av. W. Churchill. Tel: 04 42 59 12 12
Local student insurance offices:
- LMDE, 6 rue Espariat. Tel: 0810 600 601
- MEP, 2 rue Reine-Jeanne. Tel: 0825 081 881
- La Mutuelle Provençale, 10 rue des Tanneurs. Tel: 04 42 26 58 46

Travel

Railway station
- av. Victor Hugo. Tel: 08 36 35 35 35
- TGV: Gare TGV de l' Arbois. Tel: 36 35

Coach station
av. de l'Europe. Tel: 04 42 27 17 91

Airport
Marseille-Provence. Tel: 04 42 14 14 14.

Taxis
- Aix Artisan Taxi, 855 chemin Lignane. Tel: 06 09 34 00 10
- Taxi Aixois, 1 cours Mirabeau. Tel: 06 09 53 75 56
- Taxi Radio Aixois, av. de l'Europe.Tel: 04 42 27 71 11

Buses
Aix-en-Bus. Tel: 04 42 93 36 36

Student travel
OTU, CU Les Gazelles, 31 av.Jules Ferry. Tel: 04 42 27 76 85

Emergencies

Ambulance. Tel: 04 42 26 40 40
All-night Chemist rota. Tel: 04 42 26 40 40
Police: 10 av. de l'Europe. Tel: 04 42 93 97 00
SOS Médecins. Tel: 04 42 26 24 00
SOS Dentistes. Tel: 17 (for duty dentist)
SOS Amitié. Tel: 04 91 76 10 10

2 Amiens

Institutions of higher education and their disciplines

Académie d'Amiens
Université de Picardie-Jules Verne Amiens
Chemin du Thil, 80025 Amiens Cedex 1. Tel: 03 22 82 72 72. www.u-picardie.fr
SCUIO: 11 rue des Francs-Mûriers, 80027 Cedex 1. Tel: 03 22 82 64 00
SRI: Direction des Affaires Internationales, Présidence, chemin du Thil, Cedex 1. Tel: 03 22 82 72 47
Lettres, sciences humaines, langues, droit, sciences politiques et sociales, économie et gestion, arts, mathématique, informatique, sciences, santé, sport
Antennes at Beauvais, Creil, Cuffles, Laon and Saint-Quentin
IUT: av. des Facultés, Le Bailly, 80025 Amiens Cedex 1. Tel: 03 22 53 40 40

Other institutions

Conservatoire National des Arts et Métiers (CNAM)
Av. des Facultés, 80000. Tel: 03 22 33 65 50. www.cnam.fr/cra/picardie
Ingénieur des techniques de l'industrie, spécialité mécanique. Deux options: maintenance ou production
Ingénieur des techniques de l'industrie, spécialité automatique et informatique industrielle

Ecole Supérieure de Commerce d'Amiens-Picardie (ESC Amiens-Picardie)
18 place St Michel, 80038 Cedex. Tel: 03 22 82 23 00. www.supco-amiens.fr
De nombreux modules spécialisés en troisième année.

University libraries

- Service Commun de la Documentation: Bibliothèque Universitaire, 15 placette Lafleur, BP 446, 80004 Cedex 1. Tel: 03 22 82 71 65
- Lettres, Sciences Humaines, chemin du Thil, 80025 Cedex 1. Tel: 03 22 82 72 99
- Droit, Economie et Sciences, 15 placette Lafleur, BP 446, 80004 Cedex 1. Tel: 03 22 82 71 65
- Sciences et Techniques (St-Quentin), 48 rue Raspail, 02109 St-Quentin Cedex. Tel: 03 23 62 89 39
- Santé, 12 rue Frédéric Petit, 80036 Cedex 1. Tel: 03 22 82 77 80

Courses for foreign students

Centre de Français Langue Etrangère (same address as Direction des Affaires Internationales above) provides intensive initiation and support courses in French for students from partner establishments. There are also year-long courses, and special courses, provided for certain groups on a fee-paying basis. For further information, see their web site www.u-picardie.fr/formations.

CROUS

25 rue Saint-Leu, BP 541, 80005 Amiens Cedex 1. Tel: 03 22 71 24 00. www.crous-amiens.fr
SAEE: Same address, same telephone number.
OTU: 53 rue du Don, 80000

CROUS-controlled accommodation
Some 4,000 places are available in traditional residences and self-contained flatlets, in and around town and on campus. The main ones are as follows. In town:
- Résidence Saint-Leu, 19 rue Tagault, 80039 (traditional rooms; females only, no male visitors)
- Résidence du Castillon, rue du Général Frère (traditional rooms, refurbished)
- Résidence des 4 Chênes, 54–58 square Friant, 80000 (*studios*)
- Résidence du Beffroi, 29 rue au Lin (flats and flatlets)
On campus:
- Résidence du Bailly A, B et C, av. P. Claudel, 80000 (traditional rooms)

- Résidence du Bailly D, av. P. Claudel, 80000 (traditional rooms, refurbished)
- Résidence du Thil, rue Albert Camus, 80025 (traditional rooms, refurbished)

In north Amiens:
- Nouvelle Résidence du Castillon, 15 rue du Général Frère (flats and flatlets)

CROUS restaurants

In town:
- Saint-Leu, rue de la Plumette (traditional self-service plus cafeteria service)
- La Veillère, rue Fernel (traditional self-service plus cafeteria service)
- Cafétéria Saint Charles, rue des Louvels (fast food and snacks)
- Cafétéria Pôle Cathédrale, 10 placette Lafleur (usual cafeteria food)
- Cafétéria de l'ISIEE, 14 quai de la Somme (snacks etc.)
- Cafétéria de la Faculté des Arts, 40 rue des Teinturiers (traditional self-service)

On campus:
- Le Bailly, av. des Facultés (traditional self-service plus cafeteria meals)
- Cafétéria La Rotonde, chemin du Thil (cafeteria service)

Private-sector residences

- Artémis, 327 boul. Bapaume, 80000. Tel: 06 30 09 58 60
- Campus Habitat, rue des Saintes Claires, 80000. Tel: 0820 830 820 (N° Indigo)
- Résidence Arc en Ciel, 115 rue des Tanneurs, 80000. www.les.sejours.com/arc_en_ciel

Privately run accommodation

- Société Régionale d'HLM, 13 rue Lesueur. Tel: 03 22 97 67 00
- SAP d'HLM, 6 bd de Belfort. Tel: 03 22 97 73 73
- Habitation Loyer Modéré, 4 allée Germaine Dulac. Tel: 03 22 46 20 46
- Foyer AFTAM, 181 rue du Faubourg de Hem. Tel: 03 22 69 60 10
- Centre d'Accueil APICAAF, Voie E, Campus Universitaire. Tel: 03 22 95 03 60
- Résidence des Teinturiers, rue des Teinturiers. Tel: 03 22 44 84 01

The town and its surrounding area

Amiens sits astride the River Somme, 150 kilometres north of the capital. A town of some 130,000 inhabitants, it is the *chef-lieu* of the Picardie region, and host to a university which expanded rapidly following its foundation in the late 1960s.

It has a long and venerable history. It occupies one of the most important prehistoric sites in Europe: the area of St Acheul has given its name to the palaeolithic period in question, the Acheulean, some 350,000 years BC. In Roman times, Samarobriva – the bridge on the Somme – in the territory of the Gallic tribe, the Ambiani, boasted an arena which could accommodate 15,000 people. The Middle Ages saw the town build its wealth, first on woad, and subsequently on velvet and corduroy. Thirteenth-century merchant prosperity provided the resources to build one of the largest and most impressive Gothic cathedrals in the West. As a bastion defending Paris to the North, Amiens has been the site of numerous conflicts over the ages, as well as providing the setting for the famous peace treaty between Napoleon and England in 1802. The infamous, bloody, First World War battlefield of the Somme was but a few miles away.

Today, Amien's main claim to historic fame is as the town of Jules Verne. The celebrated author moved there in 1871 and wrote most of his novels in the town, as well as becoming actively involved in local politics. His house, transformed into a Jules Verne documentation centre, and incorporating a reconstuction of his study, serves as a reminder of his association, as do the walks 'Sur les pas de Jules Verne' organized by the Centre. There are, however, other focuses of interest. The Cathedral deserves special mention, and not only because of its size: its rapid construction, over a period of barely sixty years, ensured a purity and homogeneity of style which it is difficult to match elsewhere.

The old quarter of St Leu, which has undergone much renovation in more recent years, offers picturesque views, and still sports the *marché sur l'eau*, to which was traditionally brought the produce from the market gardens (*hortillonnages*) established on the reclaimed marshy ground between the multiple branches of the Somme. The *hortillonnages*, now transformed largely into pleasure gardens, can still be viewed during trips in the same kind of flat-bottomed boats that originally plied the market trade.

Local delicacies include *pâté de canard*, already well known in the days of Rabelais, confectionery, such as macaroons made from almond paste, or the chocolate and almond *tuiles amiénoises*, and the stuffed *crêpe* known as *la ficelle picarde*, which has been introduced largely since the Second World War.

The town is host to a number of special events in the course of the year:

the *Réderie*, a kind of vast flea market, in October; an international film festival, *Festival des différences*, in November, when anglophone students are in demand as helpers; the *Carnæval* and *fête des hortillonnages* in May; an international jazz festival in April; and the *fête dans la ville* and *foire exposition de Picardie* in June.

With its mixture of the old and the new, its lively student population, and its proximity to Paris – barely an hour and a half away on a fast line, blessed with a frequent service – Amiens provides a welcome and a setting for study which have met with an enthusiastic response from foreign learners.

Tourist information

Tourist office: 6 bis rue Duseval. Tel: 03 22 71 60 50
Comité Départemental du Tourisme de la Somme: 21 rue Ernest Cauvin, 80000 Amiens. Tel: 03 22 71 22 71

Hotels
- Hôtel Victor Hugo, 2 rue de l'Oratoire. Tel: 03 22 92 74 02
- Hôtel Central Anzac, 17 rue Alexandre Fatton. Tel: 03 22 91 34 08

Restaurants
- Joséphine, 20 rue Sire Firmin Leroux. Tel: 03 22 91 47 38
- La Dent Creuse, 2 rue Cormont. Tel: 03 22 80 03 63
- La Table Picarde, 24 place Parmentier. Tel: 03 22 92 57 54

Leisure facilities

Museums
- Musée de Picardie, 48 rue de la République
- Musée de l'Hôtel de Berny, 36 rue Victor Hugo
- Maison Jules Vernes, 2 rue Charles Dubois

Theatre
- Maison du Théâtre, 8/10 rue des Majots. Tel: 03 22 91 10 14
- La Comédie de Picardie, 62 rue des Jacobins. Tel: 03 22 22 20 20
- Cirque Municipal, place Longueville. Tel: 03 22 95 08 90

Cinema
- Le Paris, 42 rue des Trois Cailloux. Tel: 03 22 91 54 47
- Le Picardy, 10 rue Ernest Cauvin. Tel: 0892 696 696

- Ciné St Leu, 5 rue Plumette. Tel: 03 22 91 61 23

Maison de la Culture
2 place Léon Gontier. Tel: 03 22 97 79 79

Sport
FFSU: IUT, av. des Facultés. Tel: 03 22 53 40 08
SUAPS: Campus Universitaire-Gymnase STAPS, allée Paul Grousset, 80025. Tel: 03 22 82 73 74
Direction Départementale de la Jeunesse et des Sports, 56 rue Jules Barni Tel: 03 22 91 53 41
Football: Stade de la Licorne
Swimming pools:
- Coliseum, rue Caumartin, 80027 Cedex 1. Tel: 03 22 71 12 12
- Le Nautilus, 1 rue Léo Lagrange, 80080. Tel: 03 22 44 44 66
Skating rink: Coliseum, rue Caumartin, 80027 Cedex 1. Tel: 03 22 71 12 12

Useful addresses

Post office: 7 rue des Vergeaux. Tel: 03 22 97 04 04
Municipal libraries:
- Louis Aragon, 50 rue de la République. Tel: 03 22 97 10 10
- Edouard David, 1 place du Pays d'Auge. Tel: 03 22 43 07 79
- Bernheim, 3 rue Georges Guynemer. Tel: 03 22 52 23 92
ANPE: Agence Jules Verne, 21 rue Millevoye, 80000. Tel: 03 22 33 82 00
CAF: 9 bd Maignan Larivière, 80022. Tel: 03 22 97 44 00
CRIJ: 56 rue du Vivier. Tel: 03 22 71 16 20
Mairie: place de l'Hôtel de ville. Tel: 03 22 97 40 40
Préfecture: 51 rue de la République. Tel: 03 22 97 80 80
Commissariat Central: 1 rue du Marché de Lanselles. Tel: 03 22 71 53 00
Bookshop: FNAC, 12 rue des Trois Cailloux, 80000. Tel: 03 22 22 48 50
Internet access: Neurogame Cybercafé, 16 rue des Chaudronniers. Tel: 03 22 72 68 79

Health care

Hospital: CHU, 2 place Victor Pauchet, 80080. Tel: 03 22 66 80 00
CPAM: 8 place Louis Sellier, 80012 Cedex 1. Tel: 0820 904 111
SUMPPS: rue du Campus, 80025. Tel: 03 22 82 72 33
LMDE: rue Duseval, 80004. Tel: 03 22 92 01 37
SMENO: 10 rue Jean Catelas, 80000. Tel: 03 22 91 02 81

Travel

Railway station
place Alphonse Fiquet. Tel: 08 36 35 35 35

Coach station
place Alphonse Fiquet. Tel: 03 22 92 27 03

Airport
The nearest international airport is Roissy-Charles de Gaulle which is 1 hour 30 minutes' drive from Amiens.

Taxis
Taxis Groupement Amiénois, 2 passage Alphonse Fiquet, 80000. Tel: 03 22 93 30 03

Buses
Local bus services: AMETIS, 10 place Alphonse Fiquet. Tel: 03 22 71 40 00

Emergencies

Local police. Tel: 03 22 22 25 50
Duty doctors: (24–hour service) 15
SOS Médecins. Tel: 03 22 52 00 00
All-night chemist. Tel: 03 22 44 72 60
Centre Anti-poison. Tel: 03 20 44 44 44
Urgences sociales. Tel: 115
Emergency dental treatment (Sundays and public holidays). Tel: 06 83 36 36 05

3 Angers

The institutions of higher education and their disciplines

Académie de Nantes: Universities
Université d'Angers
40 rue de Rennes, BP 3532, 49035 Angers Cedex 01. Tel: 02 41 96 23 23. www.univ-angers.fr
SCUIO: bd Beaussier, 49045 Cedex 01. Tel: 02 41 36 52 20
SRI: Présidence de l'Université, 40 rue de Rennes, BP 3532, 49035 Cedex. Tel: 02 41 96 23 02

Lettres, langues et sciences humaines, droit, économie et sciences sociales, sciences et techniques, santé
Antenne at Cholet
IUT: 4 bd Lavoisier, BP 2018, 49016 Cedex. Tel: 02 41 73 52 52

Université Catholique de l'Ouest
3 place André Leroy, 49100. Tel: 02 41 81 66 00. www.uco.fr
Théologie, lettres, langues, arts, musique, histoire, biologie, environnement, psycho, socio, informatique, math, communication, éducation
Antennes at Arradon Guingamp, La Roche-sur-Yon, Laval and Les Ponts-de-Cé

Other institution

Ecole Supérieure des Sciences Commerciales d'Angers (ESSCA)
1 rue Lakanal, BP 348, 49003 Cedex 01. Tel: 02 41 73 47 47. www.essca. asso.fr
Enseignements généralistes pendant les trois premières années, puis possibilité de se spécialiser en: management; marketing; marketing de la grande consommation; management de la relation client; finance/expertise conseil; activités bancaires; gestion/audit

University libraries

- Bibliothèque Montéclair (Médecine et Pharmacie), CHR, 3 allée du Pont, 49033 Cedex
- Bibliothèque Belle-Beille (Sciences et Lettres) 5 rue Lenôtre, 49045
- Bibliothèque Saint-Serge, 57 quai Félix Faure, 49100

Courses for foreign students

CIDEF, Université Catholique de l'Ouest, BP 808, 49008 Cedex 01. Tel: 02 41 88 30 15. Summer- and semester-long courses at various levels, with a variety of diplomas on offer.

CLOUS

(Comes under the Crous in Nantes)

35 bd du Roi René, BP 85128, 49051. Tel: 02 41 25 45 80. www.crous-nantes.fr

CROUS-controlled accommodation

The offer ranges from furnished rooms in traditional halls, some of which have been renovated to incorporate greater comfort, to flatlets in new or renovated blocks.

In town:

- Cité Bourgonnier, 19 rue Lainé Laroche, 49100 (122 renovated rooms)
- Cité Couffon-Pavot, 1 rue Léon Pavot, 49100 (200 traditional and 140 renovated rooms)
- Résidence La Madelaine, 21 rue Lainé Laroche, 49000 (43 T1)
- Résidence Célestin Port, 25 rue Célestin Port, 49000 (40 T1)
- Résidence Faidherbe, 4 rue Faidherbe, 49100 (57 T1)

On campus:

- Cité Belle Beille, 8–10 bd Victor Beaussier, 49045 Cedex (507 traditional and 108 renovated rooms)
- Cité Lakanal, 25 rue Lamark, 49045 Cedex (305 renovated en-suite rooms)
- Résidence Gaubert and Résidence Blandin, rue Gaubert and rue Blandin, 49000 (20 T1 and 12 T2)
- Résidence Flora Tristan, 1–5 square Flora Tristan, 49000 (100 T1 and 11 T1 bis)
- Résidence Dauversière 1, place de la Dauversière, 49000 (1 T1 bis, 20 T2 and 40 T3)
- Résidence Dauversière 2, rue Jeseph Wrezinski, 49000 (82 T1)
- Résidence René Rouchy, 3 rue René Rouchy, 49000 (108 T1 and 11 T1 bis)

CROUS restaurants

In town: RU Beaux Arts, 35 bd du Roi René (traditional meals, grills and Italian dishes; also has a cafeteria providing snacks)

On campus:

- RU Belle Beille, 3 bd Lavoisier (traditional meals, pizzas, grills, dishes of the day)
- Cafétéria de l'Astrolabe (snacks)
- Cafétéria de Médecine (in the CHU – traditional meals, sandwiches and snacks)
- RU La Gabare, 55 quai Félix Faure (traditional meals, dish of the day, grills and Italian dishes)

Private-sector residences

All are run by the same organization: Tel: 0820 830 830
- Saint-Serge, 5 place F. Mitterrand, 49000
- Les Carmes, 25 rue des Carmes, 49000
- Le Front de Maine, 42–44 av. Yolande d'Aragon, 49100
- Les Studiantes du Parc, 15 rue du Haut Pressoir, 49000

Private foyers
- Saint Aubin, 22 rue Don Puycharic, 49100. Tel: 02 41 88 85 32
- Foyer des Jeunes Travailleurs David d'Angers, 22 rue David d'Angers, 49100. Tel: 02 41 24 37 37
- Résidence Sonacotra, 43 bd Gaston Ramon, 49100. Tel: 02 41 43 76 31

The town and its surrounding area

Located some 300 kilometres south-west of Paris, *chef-lieu* of the *département* of Maine-et-Loire, Angers is a pleasant, lively town of 160,000 or so inhabitants, which sits astride the river Maine some 8 kilometres from its confluence with the Loire. It is an important centre for textiles, agricultural produce and and wine, as well as a significant educational forum, with its two universities, state and Catholic, and several high-ranking *grandes écoles*.

It is most famous as the former capital of the Counts – and later Dukes – of Anjou, who controlled vast areas of south-western France by the twelfth century; but its history did not start there. Founded by the Celtic tribe of the Andes, it became an important administrative centre in the time of the Romans, when it took the name of Juliomagus, and acquired a forum, baths and an amphitheatre. Subsequently it was occupied by the Franks, the Saxons, the Bretons and finally the Normans, before coming under the control of the Plantagenets. Restored to the French crown in the fifteenth century, it was granted municipal privileges by Louis XI. In the sixteenth century, its castle was the site of a significant diplomatic wedding: in 1598 Henri IV put an end to resistance by the Catholic League by marrying his son to the daughter of the duc de Mercoeur, the last serious hope of the Leaguers. Eight days later, the Edict of Nantes was signed. In this century, Angers was briefly the seat of the Polish government in exile in 1940, before becoming regional Gestapo headquarters in 1942. A certain economic decline during the nineteenth century was reversed in the final period of the twentieth.

What strikes the visitor immediately when approaching the city is the imposing castle, which sits on a promontory above the eastern bank of the river Maine, a magnificent example of a feudal fortress. Its massive curtain wall is supported by 17 dark grey circular towers standing 30 metres tall, the whole built from the black schist quarried locally. Tall and impregnable as the towers may still strike us as being today, but they are nothing like as awesome as they must have appeared in times gone by, surrounded by a moat, which has today been transformed into ornamental gardens, and then one or two storeys higher than they are now. The castle was begun in the ninth century, but rebuilt by St Louis betweeen 1228 and 1238; Henri III ordered its demolition during the wars of religion. Cunning delaying tactics by its governor ensured that, by the time of the King's death, only one or two storeys, plus machicolations and pepper-box roofs, had been removed, and the rest of the buiding was then reprieved.

The castle houses the breathtaking *Tapisserie de l'apocalypse*, woven between the fourteenth and sixteenth centuries, the biggest and oldest tapestry to have survived. Over 100 metres long and 5 metres high, displayed in special conditions of restrained illumination, it brings the last book of the Bible to life. It serves too to remind us how important a centre of tapestry-making Angers has always been – and remains today. On the other bank of the river, in the area known as La Doutre (lit. 'the other side'), a former eleventh-century hospital for the poor houses the Musée Jean Lurçat et de la Tapisserie Contemporaine, of which the centrepiece is the great tapestry *Le Chant du monde*, designed by Jean Lurçat in 1957 as a modern response to the *Apocalypse*. With four tapestry workshops still functioning, plus the existence here of the Centre Régional d'Art Textile, it is difficult to overestimate the contribution of this craft to the life of the city.

Angers has always been an important religious centre too. Christianity reached the town in the third century, and it became a bishopric in the fourth. Over the centuries, four important Benedictine abbeys were established there, plus numerous convents. It is one of the few cities in France to have a Catholic university. The outstanding reminder of this religious devotion remains, however, the imposing Cathédrale Saint-Maurice, to which a monumental staircase leads from the banks of the river. It was built in the twelfth and thirteenth centuries, a very early example of the Plantagenet Gothic style. Its stained glass is from the twelfth to the sixteenth centuries. Several other churches from the medieval period, and imposing townhouses from the medieval and Renaissance periods dot the town.

Many famous figures were born here. They include the political theorist and humanist Jean Bodin (1530–1596); the grammarian Gilles Ménage (1613–1692); the sculptor Pierre-Jean David d'Angers (1788–1856), whose work is celebrated in a gallery devoted to him; the chemists Joseph-Louis

Proust (1754–1826) and Michel-Eugène Chevreul (1786–1889); and the politician Frédéric Falloux (1811–1886).

There are numerous festivals and events throughout the year. The most significant, however, are the Festival d'Anjou in June/July, devoted to artistic and theatrical performances, the Festival Angers l'Eté in July and August (music from round the world, classical music, humour and dance), and the Foire aux vins, in January, with its famous rituals involving the Confrérie des Sacavins.

Tourist information

Office de Tourisme, 7 place Kennedy, BP 15157, 49051 Cedex 02. Tel: 02 41 23 50 00. www.angers-tourisme.com

Hotels
- Hôtel Continental, 12–14 rue Louis de Romain, 49100. Tel: 02 41 86 94 94 (cheerful, near town centre, relatively inexpensive)
- Hôtel du Mail, 8–10 rue des Ursules, 49100. Tel: 02 41 25 05 25 (centrally located, but quiet; quaint)
- Centre d'Accueil du Lac de Maine (UCRIF), 49 av. du Lac de Maine, 49000 Angers. Tel: 02 41 22 32 10 (hostel-style accommodation, a short ride out of town, but near sports facilities)

Youth hostel
Auberge de Jeunesse Darwin, 3 rue Darwin, 49045 Angers Cedex 01. Tel: 02 41 22 61 20

Restaurants
- Le Grandgousier, 7 rue St Laud (regional dishes). Tel: 02 41 87 81 47
- Le Connétable, 13 rue des Deux Haies (good, inexpensive *crêperie*). Tel: 02 41 88 57 04
- Les Templiers, 5 rue des Deux Haies (good lunch menu; open on Sundays). Tel: 02 41 88 33 11

Leisure facilities

Maison des Etudiants: 2 bd Victor Beaussier, 49000. Tel: 02 41 48 27 45

Museums and art galleries
- Château d'Angers, promenade du Bout du Monde
- Musée Jean Lurçat, 4 bd Arago

- Musée de la Tapisserie Contemporaine, bd Arago
- Musée des Beaux-Arts, 10 rue du Musée
- Musée Pincé, 32 bis rue Lenepveu
- Museum d'Histoire Naturelle, 43 rue J Guitton
- Galerie David d'Angers, 37 bis rue Toussaint
- Musée Cointreau, 21 Saint-Barthélemy d'Anjou

Theatre

- Théâtre Municipal, place du Ralliement. Tel: 02 41 24 15 40
- Théâtre Chanzy, 30 av. de Chanzy. Tel: 02 41 88 89 29
- Chambada, 56 bd du Doyenné. Tel: 02 41 96 13 40
- Centre Jean Vilar, place Jean Vilar. Tel: 02 41 68 92 50
- La Comédie, rue Cordelle. Tel: 02 41 87 24 24
- Amphigouri, 4 allée François Mitterrand. Tel: 02 41 96 23 96

Cinema

- Gaumont Variétés, 34 bd Foch. Tel: 08 36 68 75 55
- Multiplexe St-Serge, 1 av. des Droits de l'Homme. Tel: 08 92 69 66 96
- Les 400 Coups, 12 rue Claveau. Tel: 08 92 68 00 72

Sport

SUAPS: 6 bd Beaussier, BP 82022, 49016 Cedex 01. Tel: 02 41 73 50 49
Comité Régional du Sport Universitaire, CU Couffon, rue Léon Pavot.
    Tel: 02 41 87 52 33
Directions Départementales Jeunesse et Sports, 26 ter rue Brissac, 49047
    Cedex. Tel: 02 41 24 35 35:

- Salle Omnisports Jacques Millot
- Parc des Sports de La Baumette
- Complexe Sportif J. Bouin

Swimming pool: Piscine J. Bouin
Skating rink: Patinoire d'Angers, 6 allée du Haras, 49100. Tel: 02 41 88
    28 45

Useful addresses

Main post office: 1 rue Franklin Roosevelt. Tel: 02 41 20 81 81
Bookshop: FNAC, rue Lenepveu. Tel: 02 41 24 33 33
ANPE: 6 square La Fayette, 49000. Tel: 02 41 24 17 20
CIJ: 5 allée du Haras. Tel: 02 41 87 74 47
CAF: 32 rue Louis Gain, 49100. Tel: 02 41 88 30 30
Internet access: Ambiances Multimédia, 10 rue Bodinier. Tel: 02 41 18 26
    24

Préfecture: 1 place Michel Debré, 49100. Tel: 02 41 81 81 81

Health care

CHU: 4 rue Larrey. Tel: 02 41 35 36 37
SUMPPS: Maison des Etudiants, 2 bd Beaussier, 49045 Cedex 01. Tel: 02 41 22 69 10
Local student insurance offices:
- LMDE, 55 bd du Roi René, 49100. Tel: 02 41 87 50 37
- SMEBA, 50 bis bd du Roi René, BP 705, 49100. Tel: 02 41 20 82 82
CPAM: 32 rue Louis Gain, 49000. Tel: 02 41 81 76 76

Travel

Railway station
rue de la Gare. Information: Tel: 08 36 35 35 35

Coach station
place de la République. Tel: 02 41 88 59 25

Taxis
Allo Anjou Taxi, 5 rue St Martin. Tel: 02 41 87 65 00

Buses
(COTRA), BP 90032, 49180 St Barthélemy Cedex. Tel: 02 41 33 64 64.
Tickets and information can also be obtained from the office in place
Lorraine.

Emergencies

Commissariat: 15 rue Dupetit Thouars. Tel: 02 41 57 52 00 **or** 17
Centre Anti-poison: 4 rue Larrey. Tel: 02 41 48 21 21
Late-night chemist: (until 22.00) Pharmacie Galland-Placais, 3 bd Gaston-Ramon. (After 22.00 call the Commissariat central, Tel: 02 41 57 52 00)

4 Besançon

Institutions of higher education and their disciplines

Académie de Besançon
Université de Franche-Comté
1 rue Claude Goudimel, Besançon. Tel: 03 81 66 66 66. www.univ-fcomte.
   fr
SCUIO/SRI: 1 rue Goudimel 25030 Besançon Cedex. Tel: 03 81 66 50 65
Droit, sciences économiques, politiques et gestion, sciences et techniques,
   santé, sport, lettres, langues et sciences humaines
IUT:
- Besançon-Vesoul, 30 av. de l'Observatoire, BP 1559, 25009 Besançon
   Cedex. Tel: 03 81 66 68 20
- Belfort-Montbéliard, 11 rue Engel Gros, BP 527, 90016 Belfort Cedex.
   Tel: 03 84 58 77 00

Courses for foreign students

The CLA organises summer courses, year-long courses and short courses
   in term-time for foreign students.
Centre de linguistique appliquée de Besançon (CLA), 6 rue G. Plançon,
   Besançon. Tel: 03 81 66 52 63 (section langues étrangères); tel: 03 81 66
   52 00 (section français langue étrangère). http://cla.univ-fcomte.fr

CROUS

38 av. de l'Observatoire, 25030 Cedex. Tel: 03 81 48 46 30. http://sjepg.
   univ-fcomte.fr/Services_univ/services.htm
Division vie étudiante: 40 av. de l'Observatoire. Tel: 03 81 48 46 98
OTU: 40 rue Mégevand, 25000. Tel: 03 81 83 03 03

CROUS-controlled accommodation
CROUS offers rooms in halls of residence and in flats (2 to 4 students
sharing) and in studios (T1, T1 bis, T2, T3, T4). Accommodation is also
available for couples. CROUS accommodation is, in the main, furnished
and exempt from the *taxe d'habitation*.
La Bouloie:
- Cité Colette (983 rooms and 199 flats)
- Cité Fourier (757 rooms and 270 flats)

Town centre:
- Cité Canot, 73 quai Vieil Picard (179 rooms and 76 flats)
- Résidence Mégevand, 36 rue Mégevand (27 flats)

Planoise:
- Résidence Planoise, 7 and 11 rue de Cologne (61 flats)

For *logement chez les particuliers* contact the CROUS on 03 81 48 46 95

CROUS restaurants

Tickets-repas are available in all restaurants during opening hours at lunchtime.

- RU du Grand Bouloie (adjacent to the UFR Droit et Sciences Economiques and the UFR Sciences et Techniques)
- RU du Petit Bouloie (close to the library of the UFR Droit)
- RU Canot (town centre), Cité Universitaire (entrance rue Antide Janvier)
- Brasserie Mégevand, 36 rue Mégevand (next to the UFR SLHS)
- 'Le Caveau' (in Mégevand) is open every day until 22.00

Private-sector accommodation

- Le Lauréat 1, 2–4–6 rue Rubens, 25000 Besançon
- Les Jardins de la City, Besançon
- Le Lauréat 2, 6 rue Picasso, 25000 Besançon

The town and its surrounding area

Besançon, with a population of 120,000, is the regional capital of Franche-Comté, which is composed of several *départements*: Doubs, Jura, Haute-Saône and the *territoire de Belfort*. Situated some 390 kilometres south-east of Paris, the town can be reached easily by rail (there is a direct TGV link to Paris), by motorway or by air (Lyon, Mulhouse and Geneva airports are not too far away).

The town is both small and beautiful and is rich in history: dominated by *la boucle*, a lyre shape formed by the meandering of the river Doubs, Besançon boasts an ancient Hôtel de Ville (1573), a Palais de Justice (1585) and the Palais Granvelle (1534–40), which houses the Musée Historique de la Franche-Comté. Victor Hugo and the Lumière brothers were born in Besançon. Other places of interest include the theatre and the Citadelle, which stands over a hundred metres above the river Doubs and which houses a folk museum, a museum of the Resistance, a zoo and an aquarium. The Horloge Astronomique is well worth a visit (Besançon is famous for its major contributions to the watch and clock industry).

Those interested in outdoor pursuits will particularly enjoy Besançon and the surrounding area, which offers beautiful scenery: hiking and skiing are activities which are especially favoured in the region.

There is a good selection of bars, nightclubs and restaurants for a town of Besançon's size, and one factor particularly appreciated by students is the local bus service, which continues to run until about midnight. As Besançon is a small and friendly town, contact with fellow students and with local inhabitants tends to be easier than in many other provincial French towns.

Tourist information

Office de Tourisme, 2 place de la 1ère Armée Française, 25000 Besançon. Tel: 03 81 80 92 55. Minitel: 32 65. www.besancon-tourisme.com

Hotels
For short stays or for visiting parents etc., there are two hotels within walking distance of the railway station:
● Hôtel Florel, 6 rue de la Viotte. Tel: 03 81 80 41 08 (inexpensive)
● Hôtel Foch, 7 bis av. Foch. Tel: 03 81 80 30 41
Nearer to the town centre, there are:
● Hôtel Granvelle, 13 rue Lecourbe. Tel: 03 81 81 33 92
● Hôtel Gambetta, 12 rue Gambetta. Tel: 03 81 82 02 33

Youth hostel
6 rue Madeleine. Tel: 03 81 25 24 00

Restaurants
● Brasserie Granvelle, place Granvelle. Tel: 03 81 81 05 60
● Le Poker d'As, 14 square St-Amour. Tel: 03 81 81 42 49
● Les 4 Saisons, 22 rue Mégevand. Tel: 03 81 82 30 46
● La Tour de la Pelote, 41 quai de Strasbourg. Tel: 03 81 82 14 58 (for special occasions)

Leisure facilities

Museums and art galleries
● Musée Historique de la Franche-Comté, Palais Granvelle, 96 Grande Rue

- Musée des Beaux Arts, place de la Révolution
- Citadelle, rue des Fusillés de la Résistance
- Horloge Astronomique, Cathédrale Saint-Jean, rue de la Convention

Theatre
Rue Mégevand (opposite the Arts Faculty)

Cinema
- Plaza Victor Hugo (3 screens, including 1 *art et essai*), 6–8 rue Gambetta. Tel: 03 81 82 09 44
- Plaza Lumière (5 screens), 59 rue des Granges. Tel: 03 81 83 17 67
- Vox (4 screens), 62 Grande Rue. Tel: 03 81 81 36 18

Sport
FFSU: Gymnase Universitaire de la Bouloie, 25000. Tel: 03 81 50 57 67
Stade Léo-Lagrange, av. Léo-Lagrange. Tel: 03 81 50 37 56
Palais des Sports, av. Léo Lagrange. Tel (conciergerie) 03 81 50 48 17
Swimming pool: 13 rue Mallarmé

Useful addresses

Main post office: 4 rue Robert Demangel. Tel: 03 81 53 98 36
Bookshop: Sandales d'Empédocle, 95 Grande Rue. Tel: 03 81 82 00 88
Municipal library: rue de la Bibliothèque
Mairie de Besançon, 2 rue Mégevand. Tel: 03 81 61 50 50
Chambre de Commerce et d'Industrie, 46 av. Villarceau, 25000 Besançon. Tel: 03 81 25 25 25
ANPE:
- (Besançon République) 27 rue Suard, 25000 Besançon. Tel: 03 81 82 02 89
- (Besançon Planoise) 3 rue Louis Garnier, 25000 Besançon. Tel: 03 81 52 75 10
CAF: 2 rue Denis Papin, 25037 Besançon. Tel: 08 20 25 25 10
CPAM: 2 rue Denis Papin, 25036 Besançon Cedex. Tel: 08 20 90 41 55
CRIJ: 27 rue de la République. Tel: 03 81 21 16 16. www.crijfc.com
Internet café: ID PC, 28 rue de la République. Tel: 03 81 81 26 25

Health care

SUMP: av. de l'Observatoire, BP 1535.

MST-SIDA: free minitel for students in the reception area of SUMPPS
for advice on sexually transmitted diseases/AIDS: 3615 code ms

Hospitals:

- Centre Hospitalier Régional et Universitaire Saint-Jacques, place
  Saint-Jacques. Tel: 03 81 66 81 66
- Centre Hospitalier Régional et Universitaire Jean Minjoz, bd Alex-
  ander Fleming. Tel: 03 81 66 81 66

Local student insurance offices:

- LMDE, 38 rue des Granges. Tel: 32 60 LMDE
- SMEREB, 22–24 rue Ronchaux. Tel: 03 81 81 36 38

Travel

- Compagnie des Transports Bisontins (CTB), 46 rue de Trey. Tel: 08 25
  00 22 44
- Monts-Jura Autocars, 4 rue Berthelot. Tel: 03 81 63 44 44

Railway station
rue Viotte. Tel (information): 08 92 35 35 35

Bus/coach station
9 rue Proudhon

Emergencies

AUMB (Urgence Médicale et Médecine de Nuit). Tel: 03 81 52 11 11
SOS Médecins (24-hour service). Tel: 03 81 41 20 20

5 Bordeaux

Institutions of higher education and their disciplines

Académie de Bordeaux
Université Bordeaux I: Sciences et Technologies
351 cours de la Libération, 33405 Talence Cedex. Tel: 05 40 00 60 00.
    www.u-bordeaux1.fr
SUIO: Domaine Universitaire, Bât 1er Cycle, same address. Tel: 05 40 00
    63 71/72
SRI: Direction des Affaires Internationales, Château Bonnefont, same
    address. Tel: 05 40 00 60 40

Mathématiques et informatiques, sciences et technologies
Antennes at Agen, Gazinet, Gradignan, Mérignac Floirac and Pessac
IUT: Domaine Universitaire, 33405 Talence Cedex. Tel: 05 56 84 57 02

Université Victor Segalen (Bordeaux II)
146 rue Léo Saignat, 33076 Bordeaux Cedex. Tel: 05 57 57 10 10. www.
  u-bordeaux2.fr
SUIO:
- Site Carreire, same address. Tel: 05 57 57 13 81
- Site Victoire, place de la Victoire, Bât F. Tel: 05 57 57 18 04
SRI: Département des Relations Européennes et Internationales, same
  address and telephone number
Santé, sciences, sciences humaines et sociales
Antennes at Dax and Pessac
Some teaching in sport and oenology at Talence

Université Michel de Montaigne (Bordeaux III)
Domaine Universitaire, esplanade Michel de Montaigne, 33607 Pessac
  Cedex. Tel: 05 57 12 44 44. www.u-bordeaux3.fr
SUIO: Domaine Universitaire, Bât Accueil des Etudiants, 33607 Pessac
  Cedex. Tel: 05 57 12 45 00
SRI: same address. Tel: 05 57 12 47 47
Antennes at Agen and Gradignan
IUT: 1 rue Jacques Ellul, BP 204, 33080 Bordeaux Cedex. Tel: 05 57 12
  20 44

Université Montesquieu (Bordeaux IV)
Domaine Universitaire, av. Léon Duguit, 33608 Pessac Cedex. Tel: 05 56
  84 85 86. www.montesquieu.u-bordeaux.fr
SCUIO: Domaine Universitaire, R.-de-C., same address. Tel: 05 56 84
  85 49
SRI: Direction des Relations Internationales, same address. Tel: 05 56 84
  29 02
Antennes at Agen, Bordeaux, Périgueux and Talence
IUT: av. d'Aquitaine, BP 205, 33175 Gradignan Cedex. Tel: 05 57 35 85
  85

Other institutions

Institut d'Etudes Politiques
Domaine Universitaire, 11 allée Ausone, 33607 Pessac Cedex. Tel: 05 56

84 42 52. www.iep.u-bordeaux.fr

Quatre sections au choix à partir du deuxième cycle: administration et gestion publique; gestion des entreprises et des organisations; société et communication; relations internationales

Bordeaux Ecole de Management
Domaine de Raba, 680 cours de la Libération, 33405 Talence Cedex. Tel: 05 56 84 55 55. www.bordeaux-bs.edu

Spécialisations: audit, droit et contrôle de gestion; finance; affaires et développement international; marketing-vente; management général (en anglais); e-management; management industriel

University libraries

- Bordeaux I, allée Baudrimont, 33405 Talence Cedex. Tel: 05 40 00 89 89
- Bordeaux II: Sciences de la Vie et de la Santé, 146 rue Léo Saignat, 33076 Bordeaux Cedex. Tel: 05 57 57 14 52; Sciences de l'Homme et Odontologie, 3 place de la Victoire, 33076 Bordeaux Cedex. Tel: 05 57 57 19 30; Sciences du Sport, Domaine Universitaire, av. Camille Jullian, 33405 Talence Cedex. Tel: 05 56 84 52 07
- SDC Bordeaux III, 4 av. des Arts, 33607 Pessac Cedex. Tel: 05 57 12 47 43
- SDC Bordeaux IV, 4 av. des Arts, 33607 Pessac Cedex. Tel: 05 56 84 86 56
- SICOD (Service Inter-établissements de Documentation et de coopération Documentaire), 4 av. des Arts, 33607 Pessac Cedex. Tel: 05 56 84 86 86

Courses for foreign students

Département d'Etudes de Français-Langue Etrangère (DEFLE), Université Michel de Montaigne, Bordeaux III, Domaine Universitaire, 33405 Talence Cedex. Tel: 05 57 12 44 82

Throughout the university year (mid-October to mid-June) courses in language and culture are run on three bases: accelerated courses for beginners, intermediate-level short courses, and courses leading to university diplomas in French as a foreign language with specialist options.

CROUS

18 rue du Hamel, BP 63 Bordeaux-Midi, 33033 Bordeaux Cedex. Tel: 05 56 33 92 00. www.crous-bordeaux.fr
SAEE: same address and telephone
OTU: 65 cours d'Alsace Lorraine, 33000. Tel: 05 56 44 51 04

CROUS-controlled accommodation

There are traditional rooms available in halls of residence, and flatlets in the more recently constructed blocks. Most of the traditional residences are in the six so-called *villages* on the campus at Talence/Pessac/Gradignan.

- Village 1, Domaine Universitaire, av. de Prévost/av. de Collégno, 33405 Talence (715 traditional rooms, 3 *studios*)
- Village 2, Domaine Universitaire, av. Pey Berland, 33608 Pessac (437 traditional rooms)
- Village 3, Domaine Universitaire, av. Maine de Biran, 33608 Pessac Cedex (888 traditional rooms, 3 *studios*)
- Village 4, Domaine Universitaire, av. Jean Babin, 33608 Pessac Cedex (614 traditional rooms)
- Village 5, Domaine Universitaire, av. de Bardanac et voie romaine, 33608 Pessac Cedex (909 traditional rooms, 16 *studios*)
- Village 6, Domaine Universitaire, rue de Naudet, 33175 Gradignan Cedex (294 traditional rooms)

In town:

- Maison des Etudiants, 50 rue Ligier, 33000 (50 traditional rooms, 5 T1)
- Résidence Budos, 17 rue de Budos, 33000 (219 T1, 12 T1 bis)
- Résidence Tauzin, 32 chemin de Pommerol, 33000 (162 T1, 39 T1 bis)
- Résidence La Boétie, 57 rue Saint James, 33000 (122 T1, 9 T1 bis)
- Résidence de la Marne, 99 cours de la Marne, 33000 (145 T1, 16 T1 bis)

At Mérignac:

- Résidence Clairefontaine, 13 rue F. Ferrer, 33700 Mérignac (138 T1, 38 T1 bis)

At Pessac:

- Résidence Montaigne, 3 rue du 19 mars 1962, 33600 Pessac (61 T1)

At Talence:

- Maison des Scientifiques, Domaine Universitaire, av. des Facultés, 33400 Talence (140 T1, 10 T1 bis)
- Maison des Arts et Métiers, av. P. de Coubertin, 33400 Talence (150 T1 bis)

CROUS restaurants

Of the main student restaurants in Bordeaux, three are on the campus at Talence and three are in the centre. All serve the *menu traditionnel* in addition to a wide range of snacks, pizzas, grills, sandwiches etc.

- Restaurant 1 (near to Bordeaux I and the science establishments), Domaine Universitaire, 33405 (includes a cafeteria)
- Restaurant 2 (near to Village 2), same address (includes a cafeteria and a dining room, where special meals can be served at table if reserved in advance)
- Restaurant 3 (near to Villages 5 and 6), same address (includes its own cafeteria, and also provides cafeteria service for the IUT and the sports facilities of the BEC)
- Cafétéria Le Forum (near the Lecture Theatres for Law, Politics and Economics). Tel: 05 56 37 26 00. Open 7.30–18.30
- Cafétéria Vera Cruz (in Village 3). Tel: 05 57 96 94 18. Open from 7.30 to 18.00, and provides brasserie meals at lunchtime
- Restaurant ABC, place de la Victoire, 33000 (incorporates a cafeteria and brasserie, and has a sandwich point, the Epsilon, in the courtyard of Bordeaux II)

In addition, the CROUS runs a *briocherie-sandwicherie* in Bordeaux II-Médecine, Domaine de Carreire, 146 rue Léo Saignat.

Privately run hostels

For details, write to the *Directeur/Directrice*:

- Foyer Doctrine Chrétienne, 9 rue Bigot, 33000 Bordeaux. Tel: 05 56 33 63 80 (50 places for females)
- Foyer d'Accueil Soeurs Franciscaines AGDAL, 40 rue Kyrie, 33000 Bordeaux. Tel: 05 56 91 78 09 (12 places)
- Foyer l'Eveil, 19 rue des Etuves, 33000 Bordeaux. Tel: 05 56 44 37 55 (100 places for females, with APL)
- Foyer Le Levain, 33 rue P. L. Lande, 33000 Bordeaux. Tel: 05 56 33 66 66 (68 places for females, incl. 25 for students, with APL)
- Foyer Les Acacias, 194 ter bd Albert 1er, 33800 Bordeaux. Tel: 05 56 33 19 96 (140 rooms, mixed)
- Foyer pour tous, 10 rue Voltaire, 33000 Bordeaux. Tel: 05 56 48 10 64
- Sonancotra, Agence de Gironde, 6 quai de Bacalan, 33000 Bordeaux. Tel: 05 56 69 45 70

Private-sector residences

- Les Lauréades de Bordeaux, 35 rue Pauline Kergomard, 33000 Bordeaux. Tel: 0825 332 332
- Les Lauréades de Talence, 340 av. de la Libération, 33400 Talence. Same telephone number.
- Stud'otel, angles rue C. Thomas/Blumerel/F. Sévène, 33400 Talence Tel: 05 56 84 59 59

The town and its surrounding area

Bordeaux, formerly capital of the old province of Guyenne, is today the *préfecture* of the Gironde. It stands on the left bank of the Garonne some 100 kilometres from the point at which it flows into the Atlantic, and about 25 kilometres south of the confluence with the River Dordogne. Good motorway links and fast trains (including a TGV service) link it with Paris, some 565 kilometres away to the north east. There are direct flights to London.

The modern city developed from the prosperous Gallo-Roman town of Burdigala. It is steeped in history. Occupied by the English from the twelfth century to the fifteenth century, it had its heyday in the eighteenth century by virtue of its trade with the Indies. In more recent times, it has been on several occasions the seat of the French government, when the latter has been obliged to leave Paris (1870–71, 1914 and 1940). Famous names connected with the town include the Latin poet Ausonius (c. 310–395); the sixteenth-century *moraliste* Michel de Montaigne, who served two terms as Mayor (1581–85); the painter Francisco de Goya (1746–1828), who died in the town after spending his last four years there; the musician Eugène Goossens (1867–1958); and modern writers like François Mauriac (1885–1970) and Jean Anouilh (1910–1987).

There are many relics of this glorious past. The ruins of a third-century amphitheatre, the Palais Gallien, are a reminder of centuries gone by. The Middle Ages and the Renaissance are represented by churches: Cathédrale St André (twelfth–fifteenth century), St-Seurnin (mainly twelfth–fourteenth century), Ste-Croix (twelfth–thirteenth cenutry), St-Pierre (fifteenth–sixteenth century), St-Michel (fifteenth–sixteenth century); and by monuments such as the Porte de la 'Grosse Cloche' and the Porte Cailhu. The 'Golden Age' of the eighteenth century lives on in the architecture of the place de la Bourse, the place Gambetta, the Grand Théâtre, the impressive *portes* that rear up at various points in the town, in buildings like the Hôtels de Poissac, de Pierlot and de Lalande, and the waterfront façades. A great deal of work has been done to restore buildings in the historical central area, which was made a 'protected sector' (*secteur sauvegarde*) in 1967.

Everyone associates Bordeaux with the wine trade, and it is still its most important commercial activity. However, in recent times it has expanded into new areas, such as the space and aeronautics industries, and other sectors of high technology (bio-technological, bio-medical and so on). If the port is not what it was two centuries ago, the river is still host to plea-sure boats and race craft of all shapes and sizes.

Within easy reach lie the vineyards, the fine sandy beaches of the Atlantic coast, and the pine forests of the Landes.

Tourist information

Maison du Tourisme: 12 cours du XXX Juillet, 33080 Bordeaux Cedex. Tel: 05 56 00 66 00 (With outposts at the main railway station, Cour des Arrivées [Tel: 05 56 91 64 70])

Hotels
- Hôtel Bristol, 14 ter place Gambetta. Tel: 05 56 81 85 01 (centrally situ-ated; well appointed)
- Hôtel des Quatre Soeurs, 7 rue de Sèze. Tel: 05 57 81 19 20 (near the tourist office and the Grand Théâtre; comfortable)
- Hôtel Studio, 26 rue Huguerie. Tel: 05 56 48 00 14 (cheap and good value)

Youth hostel
22 cours Barbey, 33800. Tel: 05 56 33 00 71

Restaurants
- Cassolette Café, 20 place de la Victoire. Tel: 05 56 92 94 96 (popular and good value)
- Bistrot d'Edouard, 16 place du Parlement. Tel: 05 56 81 48 87 (inex-pensive menus)
- Le Port de la Lune, 58 quai de la Paludate. Tel: 05 56 49 15 55 (bistrot which also hosts jazz)
- La Petite Brasserie, 43 rue du Pas St Georges. Tel: 05 56 52 19 79 (traditional cooking)

Leisure facilities

Maison d'Activités Culturelles, Domaine Universitaire (across from Village 4). Tel: 05 56 80 78 28

Museums and art galleries

- Musée d'Aquitaine, 20 cours Pasteur
- Musée d'Art Contemporain, 7 rue Ferrère
- Musée des Arts Décoratifs, 39 rue Bouffard
- Musée des Beaux-Arts, Jardin de la Mairie, 20 cours d'Albret
- Musée des Douanes, 1 place de la Bourse
- Muséum d'Histoire Naturelle, 5 place Bardineau
- Musée Goupil, 20 cours Pasteur
- Centre National Jean Moulin, place Jean Moulin
- Galerie des Beaux-Arts, place Colonel Raynal
- Galerie Condillac, 24 rue Condillac.

Theatre

- Grand Théâtre de Bordeaux, place de la Comédie. Tel: 05 56 00 85 95 (also home of the Opéra National de Bordeaux)
- Théâtre du Port de la Lune, 3 place Renaudel, BP 7, square Jean Vauthier. Tel: 05 56 91 01 81 (also home of the Centre Dramatique National)
- Théâtre Fémina, 20 rue de Grassi. Tel: 05 56 52 45 19
- Théâtre l'Oeil à la Lucarne, 49 rue Carpentyre. Tel: 05 56 92 25 06
- L'Onyx, 11 rue Fernand Philippart. Tel: 05 56 44 26 12
- Centre André Malraux-Conservatoire National de Région, 22 quai Sainte-Croix. Tel: 05 56 92 96 96
- Palais des Sports de Bordeaux, place de la Ferme Richemont. Tel: 05 56 79 39 61

Cinema

- UGC Ciné Cité, 13–15 rue Bonnac, 33000. Tel: 08 92 70 00 00
- Complexe CGR Français, 6 rue Fenelon/rond point de l'Intendance, 33000. Tel: 0892 688 588
- Jean Vigo, 6 rue Franklin. Tel: 05 54 70 01 92
- Utopia, 5 place Camille Jullian. Tel: 05 56 52 00 03
- Megarama, 7 quai de Queyries. Tel: 08 92 69 33 17
- L'Aquitain, 229 cours de la Marne. Tel: 08 92 68 69 29

Sport

FFSU: 18 rue Jean Babin, 33600 Pessac. Tel: 05 57 36 60 51
Palais des Sports, place de la Ferme Richemont. Tel: 05 56 79 39 61

Skating: Patinoire Bordeaux-Mériadek, 95 cours du Maréchal Juin. Tel: 05 57 81 43 75

Swimming:
- Piscine Galin, allée P de Coubertin. Tel: 05 56 86 25 01
- Stéhelin, 217 av. Mar. de Lattre de Tassigny. Tel: 05 56 08 38 03
- Piscine Judaïque, 166 rue Judaïque. Tel: 05 56 51 48 31

Tennis: Antennes Sportives du Lac, cours Jules Ladoumègue. Tel: 05 56 50 92 40

As regards student sport, the SIUAPS is based on the main campus at 16 rue Jean Babin, 33600 Pessac. Tel: 05 56 80 17 49. Well known, too, is the Bordeaux-Etudiants-Club (BEC), same address, tel: 05 56 37 48 48, which enters teams in non-university sports competitions.

Useful addresses

Main post office: 52 rue Georges Bonnac. Tel: 05 57 78 88 88

Municipal library: 85 cours du Maréchal Juin, 33075 Cedex. Tel: 05 56 24 32 51

ANPE: 1 terrasse du Front du Médoc, 33000. Tel: 05 56 90 85 20

Bookshops:
- Chez Mollat, 15 rue Vital Carles. Tel: 05 56 56 40 40
- FNAC, 50 rue Ste Catherine. Tel: 05 56 00 21 30

CIJA: 5 rue Duffour Dubergier and 125 cours Alsace Lorraine, 33000. Tel: 05 56 56 00 56

CAF: rue du Docteur Gabriel Péry, 33078 Cedex. Tel: 05 56 11 15 15

Administrative offices:
- Préfecture de la Gironde, esplanade Charles de Gaulle, 33077 Cedex. Tel: 05 56 90 60 60
- Mairie, place Pey Berland, 33000. Tel: 05 56 10 20 30

Health care

The main hospitals for emergency treatment are:
- CHU Hôpital Pellegrin, place Amélie Raba Léon. Tel: 05 56 79 56 79
- Hôpital Saint-André, 1 rue Jean Burguet. Tel: 05 56 79 56 79
- Hôpital Charles Perrens, 1 rue de la Bèchade. Tel: 05 56 96 84 50
- Hôpital du Haut Lévèque. Tel: 05 56 55 65 55

SIUMPPS: Domaine Universitaire, av. Pey Berland, 33600 Pessac Cedex (by appointment). Tel: 05 56 04 06 06

SSU: Service de Santé Universitaire, 3 ter place de la Victoire, Bât. F. Tel: 05 57 57 19 07

Local student insurance offices:
- LMDE, 24 cours de l'Argonne, 33086 Cedex. Tel: 0810 600 601
- Vittavi (SMESO), 21 place de la Victoire, 33000. Tel: 0803 803 233

CPAM: place de l'Europe, 33085. Tel: 05 56 11 54 54

Travel

Railway station
Gare St-Jean, cours de la Marne, 33000. Tel: 08 92 35 35 35

Coach station
Halte Routière, allées de Chartres. Info CITRAM: Tel: 05 56 43 68 43

Eurolines
32 rue Charles Domercq. Tel: 05 56 92 50 42

Airport
Bordeaux-Mérignac, 33700 Mérignac. Tel: 05 56 34 50 50

Buses and trams
Connex-CGFTE, 25 rue du Commandant Marchand, 33082 Cedex
Allo Bus Tel: 05 57 57 88 88

Emergencies

Médecins du Monde, 6 rue de Turenne. Tel: 05 56 48 52 52
SAMU. Tel: 05 56 96 70 70
SOS Amitiés. Tel: 05 56 44 22 22
All-night chemist. Tel: 05 56 01 02 03
Centre Anti-poison. Tel: 05 56 96 40 80
Duty doctor. Tel: 05 56 99 77 77
Drug addiction: Centre Montesquieu. Tel: 05 56 51 12 22

6 Caen

Institutions of higher education and their disciplines

Académie de Caen
Université de Caen Basse-Normandie
Esplanade de la Paix, 14032 Caen Cedex. Tel: 02 31 56 55 00. www.unicaen.
    fr/unicaen/ufr/index.shtml
SRI: Campus 1 Bâtiment Sciences 1er Cycle, Esplanade de la Paix, 14032
    Caen Cedex 05
SUIO: Esplanade de la Paix, 14032 Caen Cedex. Tel: 02 31 56 55 12. www.
    unicaen.fr/unicaen/service/suio
SUEE: same address
Santé, sciences, sciences économiques et de gestion, sport, sciences
    humaines, langues, droit et sciences politiques
University library: Esplanade de la Paix, 14032 Cedex
● Section Droit-Lettres, Esplanade de la Paix
● Section Sciences, av. de Lausanne
● Section Médecine-Pharmacie, CHU, Côte de Nacre
IUT: 2 bd Maréchal Juin, 14032 Caen Cedex. Tel: 02 31 56 70 00

Courses for foreign students

Centre d'Enseignement du Français pour Etrangers, Université de Caen
    Basse-Normandie, Annexe Vissol, av. de Bruxelles, BP 5186, 14032
    Caen. Tel ('accueil des étudiants'): 02 31 56 59 61. www.unicaen.fr/
    unicaen/service/ceuie/Menu.htm

Other institutions

Ecole de Management de Normandie
9 rue Claude Bloch, 14052 Caen Cedex 04. Tel: 02 31 43 78 78. www.cge.
    asso.fr/ecoles/ECOLE112
30 rue de Richelieu, 76087 Le Havre Cedex. Tel: 02 32 92 59 99. www.
    ecole-management-normandie.fr

CROUS

23 av. de Bruxelles, BP 5153, 14070 Cedex. Tel: 02 31 56 63 00. www.
    unicaen.fr/unicaen/crous/logement.html

OTU: Agence du Campus (same address). Tel: 02 31 56 60 94
SAEE: same address. Tel: 02 31 56 63 36

Crous-controlled accommodation

- La Cité des Peupliers, Campus 1, 23 av. de Bruxelles, BP 5153, 14040 Caen Cedex 5
- La Cité des Tilleuls, Campus 1, 23 av. de Bruxelles, BP 5153, 14040 Caen Cedex 5
- La Cité de Lebisey, 114–116 rue de Lebisey, BP 5153, 14070 Cedex 5
- La Cité de la Côte de Nacre, Campus 2, 2 bd du Maréchal Juin, BP 5153, 14070 Cedex 5
- La Résidence Edmond Bacot, Campus 2, 10 bd du Maréchal Juin, 14000 Caen (*studios* which attract APL)
- La Résidence Jean Grémillon, BP 54, 14202 Hérouville Saint Clair Cedex, Caen
- La Résidence André Breton, av. de la Valeuse, 14200 Hérouville Saint Clair
- La Résidence Flora Tristan av. de la Grande Cavée, 14200, Hérouville Saint Clair
- La Résidence Erik Satie 7/9/10 rue du recteur Daure, 14000 Caen

CROUS-controlled HLM flats are available in Caen and Hérouville Saint Clair, for families with one or more children.

Service de logement en ville, Tel: 02 31 56 63 33

CROUS restaurants

- Restaurant A, Campus 1, 23 av. de Bruxelles
- La Croisée: ground floor of Restaurant A; cafeteria open from 07.30 to 15.00
- L'Intermède: *cafétéria brasserie* close to the Vissol annexe, to the north of the campus, open from 08.30 to 17.45
- La Parenthèse: cafétéria situated in the centre of the campus
- Les Kiosques 'La Parenthèse'; situated in the hallway of the *bâtiment Lettres*, offering sandwiches, salads and drinks
- Restaurant B, same address
- L'Oxygène B: *cafétéria, piano-bar*, open from 11.00 to midnight, seven days a week; sound system, large-screen television, video recorder, newspapers and magazines, concerts
- Le Restaurant de la Côte de Nacre, Campus 2, bd Maréchal Juin. Tickets sold from 11.30 to 13.00 and 18.45 to 19.45
- Le Highland's Bar: *cafétéria, piano bar*; situated on the ground floor of the restaurant; open from 7.30 to 24.00 Monday to Thursday, 15.00 on

Friday; fast food
- Le Bacot: *brasserie*, open from 08.00 to 15.00 Monday to Friday
- Restaurant C, 114 rue de Lebisey. Open 11.30–13.30 Monday to Friday; tickets on sale from 11.30 to 13.00
- Le Mambo: *resto rapide* open 18.00–21.00; *bar* open from 22.00

La Maison de l'étudiant (situated behind the *bibliothèque scientifique*): concert hall, cafeteria (open 10.00–16.00), exhibition area, CROUS services (including temporary work), postal service, cash point, fax-minitel, bus tickets, telephone cards, *tickets de restaurant*, computers with Internet access. Tel: 02 31 56 60 96

Private-sector accommodation

- Résidence Les Doges, 22 rue du Petit Clos St Marc, 14000 Caen
- Résidence Top Campus, 9 av. De Tsukuba, 14200 Caen
- Résidence Tempologis Mémorial, 26 av. du Maréchal Montgomery, 14000 Caen

The town and its surrounding area

Situated 14 kilometres from the coast, and some 230 kilometres west of Paris, Caen is the *préfecture* of the Calvados and the capital of its region (Basse-Normandie), a prosperous agricultural area. It is easily reached by rail from Paris or by boat direct from Portsmouth (Brittany Ferries to Ouistreham). The town suffered massive destruction during World War Two, but has been tastefully rebuilt around gardens in the French style.

Miraculously, some of its architectural heritage survived and has been restored, in particular the huge *château*, still almost surrounded by its twelfth-century walls, the Abbaye-aux-Dames and the Abbaye-aux-Hommes. The *abbayes* were built according to the wishes of Queen Matilde and William the Conqueror respectively and house their remains. The Abbaye-aux-Dames is now the seat of the Conseil Régional, while the Abbaye-aux-Hommes, with its fine Romanesque architecture, has become the Hôtel de Ville. There are a number of interesting churches: Saint-Pierre (fourteenth–sixteenth century), Saint-Nicolas (built in 1083) and Saint-Jean. Buildings such as the Hôtel d'Escoville (1540), the Maison des Quatrans and the half-timbered sixteenth-century houses in the rue Saint-Pierre are but some of the fine examples of civil architecture from the medieval period onwards to be found around the town.

Among personages of note connected with the town are numbered the poet François de Malherbe (1555–1628), the printer Christophe Plantin (1520–1589), the artists Jean Restout le Vieux (1663–1702) and Robert Tournières (1667–1752), and George Bryan ('Beau') Brummell (1778–1840), who was appointed Consul in 1830.

Since World War Two, Caen has seen major expansion, and now has some 120,000 inhabitants. It has developed into a major commercial and industrial centre, and a thriving port, thanks to the long canal which links it to the coast. It also has the reputation of being a lively 'young' town, for about 45 per cent of the population is under twenty-five. It enjoys an active cultural life, with its theatres, cinemas and concert halls. There are ample recreational facilities catering for some sixty sports.

It is at the heart of a region which has much to offer. Bayeux and the Mont Saint-Michel are within easy reach, while for those with interests in more modern 'history' there are the nearby D-Day landing beaches, and the Musée du Débarquement at Arromanches. Inland lies the rural peace of the Normandy countryside or the Gorges de la Vire, ideal territory for exploration on foot, by bicycle or on horseback. There are organizations to promote all these activities: details available from the *Office de Tourisme* (address and telephone below). Pre-planned circuits introduce explorers to the delights of local produce, activities and landmarks: *la route du fromage*, *la route du cidre*, *la route des traditions*, *la route des moulins* and so on.

Tourist information

Office de Tourisme, 12 place Saint-Pierre. Tel: 02 31 27 14 14. www.ville-caen.fr/tourisme/OfficeTourisme/index.asp

Hotels
- Au Départ, 28 place de la Gare. Tel: 02 31 82 44 44 (inexpensive and convenient for the station)
- Hôtel Ibis Centre Paul Doumer, 33 rue de Bras. Tel: 02 31 50 00 00
- Hôtel Formule 1, rue des Frères Lumières, 14120 Mondeville (further out). Tel: 08 91 70 52 03

Youth hostel
Auberge de Jeunesse de Caen, 68 rue Eustache Restout. Tel: 02 31 52 19 96

Restaurants
- Pizza du Château, 28 rue Vaugueux. Tel: 02 31 94 35 70
- Restaurant la Petite Marmite, 43 rue Jacobins. Tel: 02 31 86 15 20

- Restaurant la Taverne du Maître Kanter (brasserie/restaurant, open every day, noon to midnight). Tel: 02 31 50 02 22

Leisure facilities

A useful source of information are the monthly magazine, *Le Mois à Caen* (available from October to June), and *Caen Loisirs* (fortnightly), which are available free in various outlets in town.

Museums and art galleries
- Musée des Beaux-Arts (enceinte du château)
- Musée de Normandie (enceinte du château)
- Musée de la Poste et des Techniques de Communication, 52 rue Saint-Pierre
- Mémorial, un Musée pour la Paix, esplanade Eisenhower

Theatre
- Théâtre de Caen, 135 bd Maréchal Leclerc
- Association Création Théâtre Education Artistique, 32 rue des Cordes
- Centre Choréographique National de Caen-Basse-Normandie, 10 rue Pasteur
- Espace Puzzle, 28 rue de Bretagne
- Théâtre d'Hérouville, square du Théâtre, Hérouville
- Conservatoire National de Région de Caen (Petit Auditorium and Grand Auditorium), 1 rue du Carel, 14027 Caen Cedex

Maisons des Jeunes et de la Culture
- Chemin-Vert, 1 rue d'Isigny
- La Prairie, 11 av. Albert Sorel
- Tandem Centre d'Animation Beaulieu Maladrerie, 8 rue Nicolas Oresme
- La Guerinière, 6 rue des Bouviers
- Centre d'Animation Calvaire Saint-Pierre, 7 rue de la Défense-Passive
- Venoix, 19 bis rue du Maréchal Gallieni

Cinema
- Pathé-Cinémas, 17 bd Maréchal Leclerc. Tel: 02 31 86 36 33
- Lux, Studio du 7ème Art, av. Sainte-Thérèse. Tel: 02 31 82 29 87
- Pathé-Cinémas, 57 rue des Jacobins. Tel: 02 31 85 53 05

Sport
FFSU: esplanade de la Paix. Tel: 02 31 56 55 54

Football: Stade Malherbe de Caen (the professional club), bd Georges Pompidou. Tel: 02 31 29 16 00

Ice hockey: Hockey Club de Caen (the professional side), Patinoire Municipale, rue de la Varende. Tel: 02 31 38 86 42

Skating: Patinage A.C.S.E.L., av. Albert Sorel. Tel: 02 31 85 60 46

Swimming: Stade Nautique, av. Albert Sorel. Tel: 02 31 85 60 46

Rugby: rue d'Alsace. Tel: 02 31 74 44 32

The SUAPS offers facilities in some thirty types of activity. Details of times and places may be obtained from the Secrétariat, 1er étage, Centre sportif. Tel: 02 31 56 64 61

Useful addresses

Main post office: place Gambetta. Tel: 02 31 39 35 78

Municipal library: place Guillouard. Tel: 02 31 30 47 00

Bookshops:

- FNAC, Centre Commercial Paul Doumer, rue Demolombe. Tel: 02 31 39 41 12
- Maxi-Livres, rue Paul Doumier. Tel: 02 31 85 68 74
- Librairie Universitaire Au Brouillon de Culture, 29 rue St Sauveur. Tel: 02 31 50 12 76

Mairie de Caen, Esplanade Jean-Marie Louvel, 14027 Caen Cedex 9. Tel: 02 31 30 45 55

Chambre de Commerce et d'Industrie, 1 rue Cassin Saint Contest, 14911 Caen Cedex 9. Tel: 02 31 54 54 54

ANPE: 42 rue Fred Scamaroni. Tel: 02 31 15 27 27

CPAM: bd du Général Weygand, BP 6048, 14031 Caen Cedex. Tel: 02 31 45 79 00

CAF: 8 av. du 6 Juin. Tel: 02 31 30 90 90

CRIJ: 16 rue Neuve St Jean. Tel: 02 31 27 80 80

Internet café: Systenium, 130 rue Saint Jean. Tel: 02 31 86 78 06

Préfecture: rue Saint Laurent. Tel: 02 31 30 64 00

Caen-Accueil (an organization catering specifically for newcomers): 2 av. 6 Juin. Tel: 02 31 86 02 60

Health care

CHU: av. de la Côte de Nacre, 14032 Cedex. Tel: 02 31 06 31 06

Nearest chemist to halls on Campus I is in the rue du Gaillon. Tel: 02 31 86 09 12

Local student insurance offices:

- LMDE: 23 av. de Bruxelles, Cité Universitaire les Tilleuls, Bâtiment D, BP 5119, 14079 Caen Cedex 5. Tel: 32 60 LMDE
- SMENO, 40 av. de la Libération, 14000, BP 20, 14005 Caen. Tel: 0821 423 423

Travel

OTU Voyage, l'Agence du Campus. Tel: 02 31 56 60 94. Maison de l'Etudiant, Campus 1; open 9.30–17.00

Railway station
Place de la Gare, 14300. Tel: 02 31 34 11 67

Coach station
Next to the Gare SNCF

Airport
Caen-Carpiquet, route Caumont, 14650 Carpiquet. Tel: 02 31 71 20 10 (information, reservations)

Taxis
Abbeilles, 52 place de la Gare (24-hour service). Tel: 02 31 52 17 89

Buses
Syndicat Mixte des Transports en Commun de l'Agglomération Caennaise (CTAC), 15 rue Geôle 14000. Tel: 02 31 15 55 55.

Emergencies

Service des urgences adultes. Tel: 02 31 06 48 25
SAMU: centre 15. Tel: 02 31 06 88 88
Details of the duty chemist and of the roster of night chemists are published in the monthly bulletin of the municipal tourist office.
Gendarmerie. Tel: 02 31 38 41 30

7 Clermont-Ferrand

Institutions of higher education and their disciplines

Académie de Clermont-Ferrand
Université d'Auvergne: Clermont-Ferrand I
49 bd François Mitterrand, BP 32, 63001 Clermont-Ferrand Cedex 1. Tel: 04 73 17 79 79. www.u-clermont1.fr
SCUIO: same address. Tel: 04 73 17 72 74
SRI: same address. Tel: 04 73 17 72 71
- **Clermont-Ferrand**: droit et science politique, sciences économiques et gestion, santé
- **Aurillac**: droit, science politique, administration
Antennes at Aubière, Le Puy-en-Velay
IUT Clermont-Ferrand: Ensemble Unversitaire des Céseaux, BP 86, 63172 Aubière Cédex. Tel: 04 73 40 75 75

Université Blaise Pascal: Clermont-Ferrand II
34 av. Carnot, BP 185, 63006 Clermont-Ferrand Cedex 1. Tel: 04 73 40 63 63. www.univ-bpclermont.fr
SCUIO: 34 av. Carnot, BP 185, 63000 Clermont-Ferrand Cedex 1. Tel: 04 73 40 62 75
SUEE: (same address). Tel: 04 73 40 64 97
- **Clermont-Ferrand**: lettres, langues, sciences humaines, commerce et communication, documentation
- **Aubière**: sciences et techniques, documentation, sport
Antennes at Montluçon, Moulins, Vichy
IUT Montluçon: av. Aristide Briand, BP 408, 03107 Montluçon Cedex. Tel: 04 70 02 20 00.

Other institutions

ESC Clermont-Ferrand: Ecole Supérieure de Commerce
4 bd Trudaine, 63037 Clermont-Ferrand Cedex 1. Tel: 04 73 98 24 24. www.esc-clermont.fr
Préparations possibles pendant le cursus: MSTCF en collaboration avec l'université d'Auvergne, le Diplôme de l'Institut technique de banque, GMAT, TOEFL et TOEIC pour entrer dans les universités américaines, examens de chambres de commerce allemande, britannique, espagnole, italienne et l'université de Cambridge.

University libraries

- Section Lettres, 29 bd Gergovia. Tel: 04 73 34 65 92
- Section Droit et Sciences Economiques, 41 bd Gergovia. Tel: 04 73 43 42 90
- Section Médecine, Pharmacie, Odontologie, 28 place H. Dunant. Tel: 04 73 26 60 54
- Section Sciences et Techniques, Campus des Cézeaux, Aubière. Tel: 04 73 40 74 90

Courses for foreign students

CAVILAM (Centre d'Approches Vivantes des Langues et des Médias): 1 av. des Célestins, BP 2678, 03206 Vichy Cedex. Tel: 04 70 30 83 83. www.cavilam.com

CROUS

25 rue Etienne-Dolet, 63037 Clermont-Ferrand Cedex. Tel: 04 73 34 44 00. www.crous-clermont.fr
SLV (Service du Logement en Ville): same address. Tel: 04 73 34 44 11
SAEE: same address. Tel: 04 73 34 44 15

CROUS-controlled accommodation
There are some 2,400 rooms available in halls, with additional accommodation in HLM for married couples.
- Résidence Amboise, 11 rue d'Amboise. Tel: 04 73 43 72 72
- Résidence des Cézeaux, rue Roche-Genès, 63173 Aubière. Tel: 04 73 28 29 00
- Résidence du Clos St-Jacques, 25 rue Etienne-Dolet. Tel: 04 73 34 44 01
- Résidence Philippe Lebon, 28 bd Côte Blatin. Tel: 04 73 43 72 72
More expensive accommodation in student flats is available:
- Résidence la Châtaignerie, 17 av. de la Châtaignerie, 63122 Ceyrat. Tel: 04 73 28 89 00
- Résidence Paul Collomp, 77 rue Paul Collomp. Tel: 04 72 28 89 00

CROUS-controlled restaurants
- Restaurant du Clos-St Jacques, 25 rue Etienne-Dolet
- Restaurant Philippe Lebon, 28 bd Côte Blatin
- Restaurant la Rotonde, rue de la Rotonde, UFR de Droit
- Restaurant les Céseaux, Campus des Céseaux

Cafétérias

- La Terrasse, 25 rue Etienne Dolet
- Le Cratère, 26 av. Léon Blum
- La Serre, 8 bd Gergovia
- Chez Lily, 28 bd Côte Blatin
- Le Manège, 11 rue Amboise
- Le Campus, Campus des Céseaux, Place Vazarely

Private-sector accommodation

- Foyer Notre Dame, 8 rue de Lezoux, 63000. Tel: 04 73 91 41 10 (females)
- Foyer Home Dôme, 12 place de Regensburg, 68038. Tel: 04 73 29 40 70 (mixed)
- Foyer Ste Marguerite, 15 rue Gaultier-de-Biazat, 63000. Tel: 04 73 37 23 62 (females)

The town and its surrounding area

Though once bitter rivals, the towns of Clermont and Montferrand were merged under Louis XIII in 1630 to become Clermont-Ferrand, now the thriving industrial capital of the Auvergne with a population of 150,000. Perhaps most readily associated with the home of Michelin tyres, the town is also a centre for a variety of chemical and metallurgical industries, as well as factories producing such varied goods as jam, chocolate and polished precious stones. Clermont-Ferrand's rich past is reflected in its old districts, with notable buildings such as the Cathedral Notre-Dame de l'Assomption, the romanesque church Notre-Dame du Port, and several fine town-houses which date from the Middle Ages. The Musée des Beaux-Arts has works from the Middle Ages to the twentieth century, the Musée Bargoin important Gallo-Roman collections, while the Musée Lecocq houses the region's geological and natural history exhibits. The city enjoys an active cultural life and its universities, *grandes ecoles* and other institutions of higher education attract some 30,000 students, including 1,500 foreign students. Standing at the foot of the Puys mountain range, with, to the west, the famous Puy de Dôme, Clermont-Ferrand is a good tourist base for hiking in the Parc des Volcans or for enjoying the many forests, rivers and lakes of the Massif Central. Among the famous people associated with Clermont-Ferrand are the troubadour Peire d'Auvergne (who flourished around the middle of the twelfth century), the scholar Jean

Savaron (1550–1622), the philosopher Blaise Pascal (1623–1662), Chamfort the moralist (1741–1794) and Pierre Teilhard de Chardin (1881–1955). The town is twinned with Aberdeen and Salford. Good transport links are provided by the A71 motorway and regular trains to Paris and to Lyon.

Tourist information

Tourist office: place de la Victoire. Tel: 04 73 98 65 00. www.ot-clermont-ferrand.fr

Hotels
- Hôtel Foch, 22 rue Maréchal Foch. Tel: 04 73 93 48 40
- Hôtel Zurich, 65 av. de l'Union Soviétique. Tel: 04 73 61 30 73

Youth hostel
Auberge du Cheval Blanc, 55 av. de l'Union Soviétique. Tel: 04 73 92 26 39

Restaurants
- Le Dôme, Centre Jaude. Tel: 04 73 93 31 38
- Les Commerçants, 51 av. de l'Union Soviétique. Tel: 04 73 92 37 19
- Le Marché de Natalie, 6 rue des Petits Gras. Tel: 04 73 19 12 12

Leisure facilities

Consult *Le Guide de l'Etudiant Clermont-Ferrand* for regular listings.

Museums and art galleries
- Musée des Beaux Arts, Place Louis Deteix
- Musée Bargoin, 45 rue Ballainvilliers
- Musée du Ranquet, 1 rue Saint-Pierre
- Musée Lecocq, 15 rue Bardoux

Theatre and concert halls
- Comédia, 17 rue Gaultier de Biauzat. Tel: 04 73 31 57 03
- La Coopérative de Mai, rue Serge Gainsbourg. Tel: 04 73 14 48 08
- Le Petit Vélo, 10 rue Fontgiève. Tel: 04 73 36 36 36
- EtcArt, 10 rue Bien Assis. Tel: 04 73 92 55 31
- Théâtre Municipal, rue Nestor Perret. Tel: 04 73 37 56 55
- Orchestre d'Auvergne, 2 rue Urbain II. Tel: 04 73 47 47 47
- Orchestre Municipal d'Harmonie, 3 rue Maréchal Joffre. Tel: 04 73 91 31 50

Cinema

- Pathé Capitole, 32 place de Jaude. Tel: 04 73 93 55 75
- Pathé Jaude, Centre Commercial Jaude. Tel: 04 73 93 27 15
- Paris, 8 place de la Résistance. Tel: 04 73 34 19 39
- Cinémonde, place de la Résistance. Tel: 04 73 93 54 98

Sport

FFSU: 30 rue Etienne Dolet. Tel: 04 73 29 39 40
Office Municipal des Sports: 121 av. de la Libération. Tel: 04 73 35 15 35
SIUAPS, 15 bis rue Poncillon. Tel: 04 73 29 32 00
Maison des Sports, place des Bughes. Tel: 04 73 92 17 05
Bowling: 88 av. du Brézet. Tel: 04 73 92 17 66
Gymnasium: André Autun, rue Torpilleur Sirocco. Tel: 04 73 23 07 15
Ice Skating: 155 rue Gustave Flaubert. Tel: 04 73 26 31 49
Swimming pools:
- Stade Nautique, rue Pierre de Coubertin. Tel: 04 73 17 60 70
- Piscine Jacques Magnier, rue Flamina. Tel: 04 73 24 64 50
Tennis: Stade Marcel Michelin, 35 rue Clos-Four. Tel: 04 73 30 20 11

Useful addresses

Main post office: 1 rue Busset. Tel: 04 73 30 63 00
Municipal library: 9 place Louis Aragon. Tel: 04 73 29 32 50
Bookshops:
- FNAC, Centre Jaude. Tel: 04 73 34 92 00
- Librairie Gibert, 42 av. des Etats-Unis. Tel: 04 73 37 31 88
- Librairie les Volcans, 80 bd François Mitterrand. Tel: 04 73 43 66 75
- Librairie Universitaire les Volcans, 80 bd Gergovia. Tel: 04 73 43 66 60
ANPE: 70 rue Blatin. Tel: 04 73 37 34 34
CAF: rue Pélissier. Tel: 04 73 14 67 00
CRIJ: 5 rue Sat. Genès. Tel: 04 73 92 30 50
CPAM: Cité Administrative, rue Pélissier. Tel: 0820 904 145
Commissariat: 2 rue Pélissier. Tel: 04 73 98 42 42
EDF-GDF: 34 av. de la République. Tel: 0810 633 633
Mairie: 10 rue Philippe-Marcombes. Tel: 04 73 42 63 63
Préfecture: 18 bd Desaix. Tel: 04 73 98 63 63
Internet cafés:
- Internet@café, 34 rue Ballainvilliers. Tel: 04 73 92 42 80
- Visio II, 11 av. Carnot. Tel: 04 73 91 89 36

Health care

Hospital: CHU de Clermont-Ferrand, 58 rue Montalembert. Tel: 04 73
   75 07 50
Chemists:
- Pharmacie Ducher, 1 place Delille. Tel: 04 73 91 31 77 (24-hour
  service)
- Pharmacie Sarret, 13 place Delille. Tel: 04 73 92 60 55
- SIUMPPS: 25 rue Etienne-Dolet, Pavillon B. Tel: 04 73 34 97 20
Local student insurance offices:
- LMDE: 57 bd François Mitterrand. Tel: 0810 600 601
- SMERRA, 63 bd Côte Blatin. Tel: 04 73 35 16 95

Travel

Railway station
Av. de l'Union Soviétique. Tel: 36 35

Bus/coach station
69 bd François Mitterrand. Tel: 04 73 35 05 62

Airport
(Aulnat) Tel: 04 73 62 71 00 (mainly internal flights)

Buses
Transports en Commun de l'Agglomération Clermontoise (T2C), 15–17
   bd Robert Schuman. Tel: 04 73 28 56 56

Taxis
Allô Taxi Radio, 26 av. Puy de Dôme. Tel: 04 73 19 53 53
A.T.A. Taxis, 158 av. Léon Blum. Tel: 04 73 29 99 99

Student travel
OTU: 25 rue Etienne Dolet. Tel: 04 73 34 44 14
Wasteels: 11 av. des Etats-Unis. Tel: 08 25 88 70 34

Emergencies

Hospital. Tel: 04 73 75 07 50
SOS Médecins. Tel: 04 73 42 22 22
SOS Amitié. Tel: 04 73 37 37 37
SOS Femmes. Tel: 04 73 29 32 20

8 Dijon

Institutions of higher education and their disciplines

Académie de Dijon
Université de Bourgogne Dijon
Maison de l'Université, Esplanade Erasme, BP 27877, 21078 Dijon Cedex.
   Tel: 03 80 39 50 00.www.u–bourgogne.fr/Enseignement/index.html
SRI: bureau R24, Maison de l'Université
SCUIO: Maison de l'Université, 21078 Dijon. Tel: 03 80 39 52 40
Sciences économiques et gestion, droit et sciences politiques, langues,
   lettres, sciences humaines, communication, santé, sciences et tech-
   niques, sport, vigne et vin
IUT: bd Docteur Petitjean, BP 17867, 21078 Dijon Cedex. Tel: 03 80 39
   64 01

University libraries

Bibliothèque Universitaire, rue de Sully (main campus, next to Pavillon
   Lamartine)
(Town centre) Ancienne Faculté, 36 rue Chabot-Charny

Courses for foreign students

Centre International d'Etudes Françaises (CIEF), Maison de l'Université,
   BP 87874, 21078 Dijon Cedex. Tel: 03 80 39 35 60

Other institutions

Ecole Supérieure de Commerce de Dijon-Bourgogne
29 rue Sambin, 21000 Dijon. Tel: 03 80 72 59 00. www.escdijon.com
Marketing-consommateur, trade marketing, banque et marchés financiers,
   audit et management financier, management de business unit, conseil,
   ressources humaines, commerce international des vins et spiritueux,
   management des entreprises culturelles

CROUS

Accueil-Logement-Bourse: 3 rue Docteur Maret, 21012 Dijon Cedex.
   Tel: 03 80 40 40 23. www.u–bourgogne.fr/Vie/logement.html

SAEE: same address and telephone
OTU: Antenne Montmuzard, 6B Marcel Bouchard, Campus Universitaire Montmuzard, 21000 Dijon.

Crous-controlled accommodation
- Résidence Maret, 3 rue du Docteur Maret, 21000, Dijon (134 rooms; eligible for APL)
- Résidence Montmuzard, 8 av. Alain Savary, 21000, Dijon (1,227 rooms)
- Résidence Mansart, 94 bd Mansart, 21000 Dijon (907 rooms)
- Résidence Beaune, 37 rue du Recteur Marcel Bouchard, 21000 Dijon (346 rooms; music room available to students)
- Résidence Antipodes, 24–32 rue Alain Savary, 21000 Dijon (307 T1 (hip bath, sink; kitchen: fridge, 2 hotplates, sink and worktop; electric heating; telephone); 4 T1 bis; 32 T2; 4 T3)
- Résidence Jean Zay, 12 rue Edgar Faure, 21000 Dijon (130 T1: shower, sink, WC; kitchen: fridge, 2 hotplates, sink; bedroom: 1 bed (90 cm), stool, desk, table)
- Résidence Arthur Rimbaud, av. du 21ème siècle, 21000 Dijon (165 T1: shower, sink, WC; kitchen: fridge, 2 hotplates, sink; TV socket; telephone socket)
- Résidence Latitude, Hameau de Mirande, 17 rue Pierre de Coubertin, 21000 Dijon (82 T1 (shower, sink, WC; kitchen: fridge, 2 hotplates, sink, kitchen table, chair, cupboard; bedroom: 1 bed (90cm), bedside stool, desk); 8 T1 bis

CROUS restaurants
Town centre:
- Maret (restaurant and *brasserie*), 3 rue Docteur Maret
- Brasserie de l'Ecole Supérieure de Commerce

Campus:
- Montmuzard (restaurant and *brasserie*). Open 7.15–10.00, 11.20–14.00 and 15.00–20.00. *Service express* from 13.15 to 14.00 and 18.15 to 20.00
- La Cafétéria de l'ENSBANA
- La Cafétéria Lamartine
- La Brasserie de l'IUT
- Le Club INTERNET aux Antipodes
- Le Dépanneur, résidence Antipodes. Open 11.30–14.00 and 17.30–21.00

Private-sector accommodation

- Les Estudines Champollion, 2 av. Champollion, 21000 Dijon
- Le Clos Morlot, 4 rue du Docteur J.B. Morlot, 21000 Dijon
- Pythagore Campus, 217 rue d'Auxonne, 21000 Dijon

The town and its surrounding area

Dijon, capital city of the old province of Burgundy, is the *chef-lieu* of the Côte-d'Or. Situated some 310 kilometres south-east of Paris, the town is easily accessible by rail (there is a direct TGV link to Paris) and by road.

The town is noted for its high gastronomic standards, and contains countless buildings of outstanding architectural merit. Of particular interest are the Palais des Ducs de Bourgogne (which is now the Hôtel de Ville and houses one of France's finest provincial museums, the Musée des Beaux-Arts), the Palais de Justice and the Cour de Bar (with its Tour de Bar and Tour de Philippe le Bon). There are many churches ranging from the medieval to the modern; the cathedral is that of St-Bénigne. In the summer there is a music festival, a theatre festival and the Fêtes de la Vigne. Wine-tasting in the vineyards of Burgundy is a popular leisure activity amongst tourists and foreign students. The town boasts a theatre and a number of cinemas, which offer a wide choice of films. There is a good bus service. Restaurants vary greatly in price, but it is possible to eat quite cheaply in a self-service restaurant in the centre of town. The shopping centre is good (shops range from department stores to specialist boutiques). The shop which specializes in mustard is well worth a visit.

Tourist information

Tourist office: 29 place Darcy, 21000 Dijon. Tel: 03 80 44 11 44. Also 34 rue des Forges (same telephone number). www.ot-dijon.fr

Hotels
- Continental Hôtel, 7 rue Docteur Albert Rémy. Tel: 03 80 53 10 11 (very close to the railway station)
- Hôtel de Paris, 9 av. Foch. Tel: 03 80 43 50 23
- Hôtel Ibis Central, 3 place Grangier. Tel: 03 80 30 44 00

Youth hostel
Centre de Rencontres Internationales, 1 bd Champollion. Tel: 03 80 72 95 20

Restaurants

Pizzerias offer the cheapest meals in Dijon and the only real possibility for vegetarians.

- Version Latine, 16 rue Odebert
- Pizzeria Paolo, 18 bis av. du Maréchal Foch
- Taverne de Maître Kanter, 18 bis rue Odebert

Leisure facilities

Museum

Musée d'Histoire Naturelle, rue Jehan de Marville

Theatre

- Théâtre National Dijon Bourgogne, rue Monge
- Théâtre Municipal, 2 rue Longepierre

Cinema

- Cinéma ABC, 7 rue Chapeau Rouge. Tel: 03 80 30 55 66
- Cinéma Gaumont, 16 av. Maréchal Foch. Tel: (special rate) 08 92 69 66 96
- Olympia, same address. Tel: 03 80 43 55 99
- Cinéma Eldorado, 21 rue Alfred de Musset. Tel: 03 80 66 12 34
- Cinéma le Darcy, 8 place Darcy. Tel: 03 80 30 25 13

Sport

FFSU: Maison des Sports, Campus universitaire, BP 27877–21078, Dijon Cedex. Tel: 03 80 39 67 91

Palais des Sports, rue Léon Mauris

Swimming pool: Cours du Parc, next to parc de la Colombière (access via cours Général de Gaulle)

Useful addresses

Post office: rue de l'Arguebuse

Bookshops:

- Librairie de l'Université, 17 rue de la Liberté
- FNAC, 24 rue de Bourg (in town centre)

Mairie de Dijon, place de la Libération, 21000 Dijon. Tel: 03 80 74 51 51

Chambre de Commerce et d'Industrie, 1 place du Théâtre, 21000 Dijon. Tel: 03 80 69 91 00

ANPE: Dijon Toison d'or, 4 rue de Bruges, 21000 Dijon. Tel: 03 80 78 85
10
CIO: 10 rue Colonel Victor Marchand
CAF: 8 bd Georges Clémenceau. Tel: (tarif spécial) 0820 252110
CPAM: 8 rue du Docteur Maret, BP 1548, 21045 Dijon. Tel: 0820 90 31 39
CRIJ: 18 rue Audra, 21026 Dijon Cedex. Tel: 03 80 44 18 44. www.crij-
bourgogne.fr.st
Internet café: Cybercafé Multi-Rezo, 21 cours de la Gare. Tel: 03 80 42
13 89

Health care

Hospital: CHU SAMU, 3 rue Faubourg Raines. Tel: 03 80 40 28 29
SUMP: SMPPS, 6a rue du Recteur Marcel Bouchard, 21000. Tel: 03 80
39 51 53
The nearest chemist to the campus is on the corner of bd Gabriel/bd de
l'Université (about 5 minutes' walk from the halls of residence).
• Pharmacie Bruant, 22 rue de la Liberté. Tel: 03 80 50 19 50
• Pharmacie Centrale, 1 rue Berbisey. Tel: 03 80 30 10 12
Local student insurance offices:
• LMDE: 33 rue Nicolas Bornier. Tel: (tarif spécial) 0810 600 601
• SMEREB: 11 ter bd Voltaire

Travel

Railway station
Gare Foch, av. Foch.
SNCF Voyageurs. Tel: (tarif spécial) 36 35

Coach station
Adjacent to the railway station.
Gare routière SNCF. Tel: 03 80 42 11 00

Taxis
Taxi Radio Dijon, cour Gare. Tel: 03 80 41 41 12

Local travel
STRD, place Grangier. Tel: 03 80 30 60 90

Emergencies

SOS Amitié. Tel: 03 80 67 15 15
Police: 2 place Suquet. Tel: 03 80 44 55 00

9   Grenoble

Institutions of higher education and their disciplines

Académie de Grenoble
Université Joseph Fourier: Grenoble I
621 av. Centrale, Domaine Universitaire, 34000 Saint-Martin d'Hères.
   Tel: 04 76 51 46 00. www.ujf-grenoble.fr
SCUIO: same address. Bibliothèque des Sciences. Tel: 04 76 51 46 21
SRI: same address. Bâtiment administratif. Tel: 04 76 51 42 52
Mathématiques, informatique, sciences et technologies, santé, sport
Antennes at La Tronche, Saint-Martin-d'Hères, Valence, L'Isle-d'Abeau
IUT Grenoble 1: Domaine Universitaire, BP 67, 38402 Saint-Martin
   d'Hères Cedex. Tel: 04 76 82 53 00

Université Pierre Mendès France: Grenoble II
151 rue des Universités, Domaine Universitaire, 38040 Saint-Martin
   d'Hères. Tel: 04 76 82 54 00. www.upmf-grenoble.fr
SCUIO: same address. Tel: 04 76 82 55 45
SRI: same address. Tel: 04 76 82 55 89
● **Grenoble:** sciences économiques, gestion, droit, sciences humaines,
   sciences de l'homme et de la société
● **Saint-Martin d'Hères:** études politiques, administration, commerce
● **Valence:** sciences économiques, droit
Antenne at Vienne
IUT Grenoble 2: place du Doyen Gosse, 38041 Grenoble Cedex. Tel: 04
   76 28 45 09

Université Stendhal: Grenoble III
1180 av. centrale, Domaine Universitaire, 38400 Saint-Martin d'Hères.
   Tel: 04 76 82 43 00. www.u-grenoble3.fr
SCUIO: same address. Tel: 04 76 82 43 11
SRI: same address, bureau Z002. Tel: 04 76 82 41 11
● **Grenoble:** anglais, information et communication
● **Saint-Martin d'Hères:** lettres et langues (sauf anglais)
● **Echirolles:** information, communication

Courses for foreign students

CUEF: Centre Universitaire d'Etudes Françaises
BP 25, 38040 Grenoble Cedex 9. Tel: 04 76 82 43 70. Email: cuef@u-grenoble3.fr

Other institutions

Polytech' Grenoble/ISTG: Ecole Polytechnique de l'Université de Grenoble I
BP 31, 38041 Genoble Cedex 9. Tel: 04 76 82 79 02. www.istg.ujf.grenoble.fr
Spécialités: géotechnique; informatique industrielle et instrumentation; prévention des risques industriels (hygiène, sécurité, environnement); réseaux informatiques et communication multimédia; sciences et génie des matériaux; technologies d'information pour la santé

University libraries

Bibliothèque Interuniversitaire de Grenoble, Domaine universitaire. Tel: 04 76 44 82 18
Bibliothèque universitaire de Droit et Lettres, 1130 av. Centrale. Tel: 04 76 82 61 61
Bibliothèque universitaire des Sciences, Domaine universitaire. Tel: 04 76 51 42 84
Centre National de la Fonction Publique Territoriale, 440 rue des Universités. Tel: 04 76 15 01 03

CROUS

5 rue d'Arsonval, BP 187, 38019 Grenoble Cedex. Tel: 04 76 57 44 00. www.crous-grenoble.fr
BLEU (Bureau de logement d'échanges universitaires): same address. Tel: 04 76 57 44 43
SAEE: same address. Tel: 04 76 57 44 41

CROUS-controlled accommodation
In Grenoble:
• Résidence d'Arsonval, 16 rue Casimir Brenier. Tel: 04 76 87 18 14 (females)

- Le Home d'Etudiantes, 2 av. Général Champon. Tel: 04 76 47 13 54 (females)
- Maison des Etudiants, 6 place Pasteur. Tel: 04 76 47 13 54
- Résidence Le Rabot, 11 rue Maurice Gignoux. Tel: 04 76 87 44 65
- Résidence Olympique, av. Edmond-Esmonin. Tel: 04 76 23 08 63
- Résidence La Tronche, 12 rue du Vercors. Tel: 04 76 42 44 45
- Résidence Beethoven, 9 rue Beethoven. Tel: 04 76 54 90 26
- Résidence Hermite, 31 rue Hermite. Tel: 04 76 54 90 26

On the campus (St Martin d'Hères):

- Résidence Berlioz, 361 allée Hector Berlioz. Tel: 04 76 54 90 00
- Résidence Ouest, 2 rue de la Houille Blanche. Tel: 04 76 82 76 50
- Résidence Condillac, 1220 rue des Résidences. Tel: 04 76 82 76 30/31
- Résidence Faure, 341 rue des Résidences. Tel: 04 76 54 40 54

Accommodation in T1–T1 bis:

- Résidence Les Taillées, 271, 291, 293 rue de la Houille Blanche. Tel: 04 76 54 90 26
- Résidence Les Nocturnes de Faure, 420 rue de la Physique. Tel: 04 76 54 40 54
- Résidence La Halle Brun, 7, 13, 19 place du 24 avril 1915. Tel: 04 76 54 90 26
- Résidence Le Chamandier, 11 rue du Bois-Taillis. Tel: 04 76 54 90 26
- Résidence Carmagnolle-Liberté, 10 rue Pierre Courtade. Tel: 04 76 54 90 00

CROUS restaurants

On the campus:

- Restaurant de Barnave
- Restaurant Diderot
- Restaurant d'Arsonval

Others:

- Home d'Etudiantes, 2 rue du Général Champon
- Maison des Etudiants, 6 place Pasteur
- Restaurant du Rabot, rue Maurice Gignoux

All provide the *menu traditionnel* as well as a *cafétéria* service.

Private-sector accommodation

The free local newspapers *38* and *Info Grenoble* carry accommodation offers. Also try:

- OSE Logement: 11 rue Anthoard. Tel: 04 76 70 99 00

- Le 38 immobilier: 2 rue Narvik. Tel: 04 76 87 26 27
- Les Estudines Europole, 2–4 rue P. Sémard. Tel: 04 76 48 60 97
- Les Estudines Marie Curie, 38–62 rue F. Esclangon. Tel: 04 76 84 16 71
- Les Studélites Gauguin, 2 allée de Béthléem, Tel: 04 76 01 12 84 (campus)
- Les Studélites Klee, 3 allée de Certèze. Tel: 04 76 89 35 55 (campus)
- Les Studélites Matisse, 3 rue du Tour de l'Eau. Tel: 04 76 51 22 78 (campus)

The town and its surrounding area

Capital of the French Alps, Grenoble stands close by the confluence of the Isère and the Drac and is surrounded by mountain ranges: to the north the Grande-Chartreuse massif, to the south-west the Vercors and to the east the Belledonne range. The town has a population of 158,000, with over 56,000 students attending its academic institutions. The university was founded in 1389 and is one of the oldest in Europe. The modern campus at St Martin d'Hères includes halls of residence and is linked to the town centre by regular tram and bus services. Among the famous historical figures associated with Grenoble are the philosophers Etienne Bonnot de Condillac (1715–80) and Jean-Jacques Rousseau (1712–1778), the author Marie Henri Beyle (Stendhal) (1783–1842), the painter Henri Fantin-Latour (1836–1904), the mechanical engineer Jacques de Vaucanson (1709–1782) and Napoleon Bonaparte (1769–1821). There are several buildings worthy of note: the Palais de Justice (sixteenth to nineteenth century), the modern plate-glass Town Hall (1967) by Maurice Noravina, the Musée des Beaux Arts, the Musée Dauphinois and, overlooking the town, the Fort de la Bastille, which is accessible on foot or by cable-car. A former host to the Winter Olympics, Grenoble has a long tradition as a centre for skiing and there are some twenty resorts in the region. Other sporting activities are encouraged with over 250 tennis courts, 20 swimming pools and a covered ice-rink. The mountains provide good walking, rock-climbing and pot-holing. Grenoble is served by two international airports: Lyon-St Exupéry and Grenoble-St-Geoirs. Mountain cheeses such as Emmental, Beaufort or Reblochon are to be enjoyed, as are Grenoble walnuts. To complement meals there are Savoy wines, Chartreuse liqueurs, Evian mineral water or the many *sirops* which are manufactured in the region. There is a TGV service to Paris and *autoroutes* give rapid access to the French capital as well as to Geneva.

Tourist information

Tourist office, 14 rue de la République, 38019 Grenoble. Tel: 04 76 42 41 41. www.grenoble-isere.info

Hotels
The following are near the station.
- Hôtel Suisse et Bordeaux, 6 place de la Gare. Tel: 04 76 47 55 87
- Hôtel de l'Institut Logis de France, 10 rue Barbillon. Tel: 04 76 46 36 44
- Hôtel Gallia, 7 bd Maréchal Joffre. Tel: 04 76 87 39 21

Youth hostel
3 av. Victor Hugo, Echirolles. Tel: 04 76 09 33 52

Restaurants
There are several popular pizzerias along the *quais*; however, it would be foolish to miss the many traditional restaurants offering good-value meals.
- Brasserie le Sporting, 12 place Grenette. Tel: 04 76 44 22 58
- Restaurant la Panse, 7 rue de la Paix. Tel: 04 76 54 09 54
- Restaurant la Petite Ferme, 3 rue Jean-Jacques Rousseau. Tel: 04 76 54 21 90

Leisure facilities

Listings of films, plays and cultural events are found in *Lumières sur la Ville*, which is free from the tourist office.

Museums and art galleries
- Centre National d'Art Contemporain, 155 cours Berriat
- Musée Stendhal, 1 rue Hector Berlioz
- Musée de la Résistance et de la Déportation, 14 rue Jean-Jacques Rousseau
- Musée de Peinture et de Sculpture, place Verdun
- Musée Dauphinois, 30 rue Maurice Gignoux

Theatre
- Théâtre de Grenoble, 4 rue Hector Berlioz. Tel: 04 76 44 03 44
- Le Cargo, 4 rue Paul Claudel. Tel: 04 76 60 79 79
- Théâtre 145, 145 cours Berriat. Tel: 04 76 49 53 39
- Comédie du Dauphiné, 1 rue Président Carnot. Tel: 04 38 37 28 93

Cinema

- Le Club, 9 bis rue du Phalanstère. Tel: 04 76 46 13 38
- Le Rex, 13 rue Saint-Jacques. Tel: 04 76 51 72 00
- Le Méliès, 3 rue de Strasbourg. Tel: 04 76 47 99 31
- Le Vox, 15 rue Thiers. Tel: 04 76 46 43 46
- La 6 Nef, 18 bd Edouard Rey. Tel: 08 92 68 00 31
- La Nef, 1 rue Emile Augier. Tel: 04 76 46 53 25
- Les Nefs Chavant, 21 bd Maréchal Lyautey. Tel: 04 76 12 28 30

Sport

FFSU: CSU, allée de la Passerelle, Domaine universitaire. Tel: 04 76 82 44 10

Office Municipal des Sports, 3 passage du Palais de Justice. Tel: 04 76 44 75 61

Palais des Sports, 14 bd Clemenceau. Tel: 04 76 54 27 27 (includes ice-skating rink)

Centre sportif Berthe de Boissieux, 4 rue Berthe de Boissieux. Tel: 04 76 46 22 11

Mountain sports:

- ANCEF (Association Nationale des Centres de Ski Fond et Montagne): 10 av. Général Champon. Tel: 04 76 87 81 47
- GUC Ski: rue Barbillon. Tel 04 76 57 47 72

Ice skating: Patinoire Pôle Sud, av. Innsbruck. Tel: 04 76 39 25 00

Swimming pools:

- Chorier-Berriat, 12 rue Henri le Chatelier. Tel: 04 76 21 05 91
- Municipale Jean Bron, rue Lazare Carnot. Tel: 04 76 46 13 87

Tennis: Grenoble tennis, 124 cours Libération Général de Gaulle. Tel: 04 76 49 15 53

Useful addresses

Main post office: 7 bd Maréchal Lyautey. Tel: 04 76 43 51 39

Mairie: 11 bd Jean Pain. Tel: 04 76 76 36 36

Municipal libraries:

- Bibliothèque d'Etude et d'Information, 12 bd Mar. Lyautey. Tel: 04 76 86 21 00
- Bibliothèque Municipale Internationale, 6 place Sfax. Tel: 04 38 12 25 41

Maisons des Jeunes et de la Culture:

- 1 place Commune de 1871. Tel: 04 76 51 12 51
- 40 av. Grand Châtelet. Tel: 04 76 54 56 24

Bookshops:
- FNAC, Grand'Place, 119 Centre Commercial Grand'Place. Tel: 04 76 20 40 20
- FNAC Victor Hugo, 4 rue Félix-Poulat. Tel: 04 76 85 85 85
- Librairie Arthaud, 23 Grande Rue. Tel: 04 76 42 49 81
- Librairie Gibert, 4 rue Béranger. Tel: 04 76 43 04 30
- Librairie Decitre: 9 Grande Rue. Tel: 04 76 03 36 34
- Le Square Librairie de l'Université, 2 square du Dr Martin. Tel: 04 76 46 61 63
- La Bouquinerie, 9 bd Agutte Sembat. Tel: 04 76 46 15 32

ANPE: 17 rue Denfert Rocherau. Tel: 04 76 87 61 43
CAF: 3 rue des Alliés. Tel: 04 76 20 61 61
CPAM: 2 rue des Alliés. Tel: 0820 90 41 26
CIO: 10 rue de Belgrade. Tel: 04 76 87 45 63
CRIJ: 16 bd Agutte Sembat. Tel: 04 76 86 56 00
OSE: 7 rue Saint Joseph. Tel: 04 76 87 69 85
Préfecture de l'Isère, 12 place de Verdun. Tel: 04 76 60 34 00
Internet cafés:
- L'Autre Monde, 4 rue Jean-Jacques Rousseau. Tel: 04 76 01 00 20
- E-Toile, 15 rue Jean-Jacques Rousseau. Tel: 04 76 00 13 60

Health care

SUMP:
- 5 rue d'Arsonval. Tel: 04 76 57 50 90
- 180 rue de la Piscine, Domaine Universitaire. Tel: 04 76 82 40 70

BAPU: same addresses and telephone numbers
Hospitals:
- Hôpital Nord, 38700 La Tronche. Tel: 04 76 76 75 75
- Hôpital Sud, av. Grugliasco, 38130 Echirolles. Tel: 04 76 76 75 75

Chemists:
- Pharmacie Berriat, 43 cours Berriat. Tel: 04 76 46 18 09
- Pharmacie Foch, 33 bd Foch. Tel: 04 76 87 36 33
- Pharmacie Centrale, 10 rue Lafayette. Tel: 04 76 44 14 66

Local student insurance offices:
- LMDE, 28 cours Jean Jaurès. Tel: 0 825 000 601
- SMERRA, 15 rue St Joseph. Tel: 04 76 87 88 33

Travel information

Railway station
Gare Europole, 1 place de la Gare. Tel: 04 36 35 35 35

Coach station
11 place de la Gare. Tel: 04 76 87 90 31

Airport
- Grenoble St Geoirs, St-Etienne de St-Geoirs. Tel: 04 76 65 48 48
- Lyon-St Exupéry. Tel: 04 72 22 72 21

Taxis
Taxis grenoblois. Tel: 04 76 54 42 54

Buses and trams
Transportation de l'Agglomération Grenobloise (TAG). Tel: 04 76 20 66
    66
(Unlimited bus and tram travel with the AVANTAG Campus card)

Student travel
OTU:
- 5 rue d'Arsonval (3ème étage). Tel: 04 76 46 98 92
- 432 av. de la Bibliothèque, Domaine Universitaire. Tel: 04 76 51 27 25
Voyages Wasteels: 7 rue Thiers. Tel: 0825 88 70 39. www.wasteels.fr

Emergencies

Hospital. Tel: 04 76 76 75 75
SOS Dentiste. Tel: 0899 650 690
SOS Médecins: 5 chemin Couvent. Tel: 04 38 701 701
SOS Amitié. Tel: 04 76 87 22 22
Police: 36 bd Maréchal Leclerc. Tel: 04 76 60 40 40
Centre Anti-poison (Lyon). Tel: 04 72 11 69 11

10 **Lille**

Institutions of higher education and their disciplines

Académie de Lille
Université des sciences et technologie de Lille: Lille I
Cité scientifique, 59655 Villeneuve d'Ascq Cedex. Tel: 03 20 43 43 43. www.univ-lille1.fr
SCUIO (SCUAIO): av. Carl Gauss, 59655 Villeneuve d'Ascq. Tel: 03 20 05 87 39
SRI: Bât. A3 Cité scientifique, Villeneuve d'Ascq Cedex. Tel: 03 20 43 43 40
Sciences, mathématiques, technologies, informatique, sciences économiques et sociales, sciences de la terre, géographie

Université du Droit et de la Santé: Lille II
42 rue Paul Duez, 59800 Lille Cedex. Tel: 03 20 96 43 43. www.univ-lille2.fr
SCUIO:
● 1 place Déliot, 59024 Lille Cedex. Tel: 03 20 90 74 07
● Fac de médecine Henri Warembourg, 59045 Lille Cedex. Tel: 03 20 62 76 95
SRI: 44 rue Paul Duez. Tel: 03 20 96 43 43
Santé, sciences juridiques, politiques et sociales, environnement urbanisme, techniques économiques et comptables
Antennes at Cambrai et Roubaix

Université Charles de Gaulle: Lille III
Domaine universitaire littéraire de Villeneuve d'Ascq, Pont de Bois, BP 149, 59653 Villeneuve d'Ascq Cedex. Tel: 03 20 41 60 00.www.univ-lille3.fr
SCUIO: same address. Tel: 03 20 41 62 46
SRI: same address, Bâtiment Extension, Tour, Bureau T 402. Tel: 03 20 41 63 90
Mathématiques, sciences économiques et sociales, information documentation, sciences humaines, lettres, langues, arts, sciences de l'éducation
Antennes at Roubaix, Lille, Tourcoing
IUT:
● Lille A: Cité Scientifique, bd Paul Langevin BP 179, 59653 Villeneuve d'Ascq Cedex. Tel: 03 20 43 41 65.
● Lille B: 35 rue Sainte Barbe, BP 460, 59208 Tourcoing Cédex 01. Tel: 03 20 76 25 12
● Lille C: Rond-Point de l'Europe BP557, 59060 Roubaix Cédex 01. Tel: 03 28 33 36 20

Other institutions

EC Lille: Ecole Centrale de Lille
Domaine universitaire scientifique, BP 48, 59651 Villeneuve d'Ascq
Cedex. Tel: 03 20 33 53 53. www.ec.lille.fr
Formation d'ingénieurs généralistes

HEI: Ecole des Hautes Etudes Industrielles
13 rue de Toul, 59046 Lille. Tel: 03 28 38 48 58. www.hei.fr
Formation d'ingénieurs généralistes

ISA: Institut Supérieur d'Agriculture
41 rue du Port, 59048 Lille. Tel: 03 28 38 48 48. www.isa-lille.fr
Agriculture, agro-industrie, agroalimentaire et environnement

Polytech'Lille: Université des Sciences et Technologies de Lille I
Cité scientifique, av. Paul Langevin, 59655 Villeneuve d'Ascq Cedex. Tel:
03 28 76 73 00. www.ploytech-lille.fr
Formation d'ingénieurs avec sept spécialités: génie informatique et statis-
tique; géotechnique, génie civil; industries agroalimentaires; infor-
matique-micro-électronique automatique; science des matériaux;
instrumentation scientifique; mécanique

EDHEC Business School: Ecole des Hautes Etudes Commerciales
58 rue du Port 59046 Lille Cedex. Tel: 03 20 15 45 00. www.edhec.com
Majeures en troisième année: finance, conseil, audit-contrôle de gestion,
marketing, ingénierie juridique et fiscale, management et technologie
de l'information et de la communication, management culturel et
humanitaire

ESC Lille: Ecole Supérieure de Commerce Lille-Paris
Campus de Lille, av. Willy Brandt, 59777 Euralille. Tel: 03 20 21 59 62.
www.esc-lille.fr
Spécialisations de troisième année: audit-ressources humaines, audit et
ruptures d'information, stratégie et management de la communication,
contrôle de gestion et systèmes d'information, approvisionnement
et logistique, finance d'entreprise et de marché, international finance,
management stratégique et entrepreneurial, création d'entreprise,
International Marketing, marketing opérationnel, management de
projets, négociation vente, marketing direct et commerce électronique
e-business

IESEG: Institut d'Economie Scientifique et de Gestion
3 rue de la Digue, 59800 Lille. Tel: 03 20 54 58 92. www.iseg.fr
Spécialisations en: marketing, finance, RH, management des systèmes d'information, gestion des opérations, audit et contrôle, management général. (Courses taught in English)

CROUS

74, rue de Cambrai, 59043 Lille Cedex. Tel: 03 20 88 66 00. www.crous-lille.fr
SAEE: same address and telephone
SCLE (Service Central du Logement Etudiant): same address. Tel: 03 20 52 84 00
Branch office at Villeneuve d'Ascq in the Hall de la Faculté de Droit. Tel: 03 20 91 83 18

CROUS-controlled accommodation
The following halls are on the Villeneuve d'Ascq campus and have a common address: Domaine universitaire scientifique, 59650 Villeneuve d'Ascq.
● Résidence Gaston Bachelard. Tel: 03 20 43 48 71
● Résidence Albert Camus. Tel: 03 20 43 44 60
● Résidence Evariste Gallois. Tel: 03 20 43 43 64
● Résidence Hélène Boucher. Tel: 03 20 43 43 77
● Résidence Gustave Eiffel. Tel: 03 20 47 07 99
● Résidence Pythagore. Tel: 03 20 43 48 71
The following halls are also at Villeneuve d'Ascq:
● Résidence Quartier du Triolo, 8 rue Trémière. Tel: 03 20 91 46 19
● Résidence Quartier du Pont de Bois, 25–27 rue de Fives. Tel: 03 20 04 91 91
The following halls are in Lille:
● Résidence Bas-Liévin, 48–50 rue du Bas-Liévin. Tel: 03 20 53 49 63
● Résidence A. Châtelet, rue F. Combemale. Tel: 03 20 53 62 37
● Résidence G. Lefèvre, 2 bd du Dr Calmette. Tel: 03 20 52 59 58
● Résidence Maupassant, 10 rue de Maupassant. Tel: 03 20 52 98 66

CROUS restaurants
Traditional three-course meal, fast-food and snacks
In Lille:
● RU Cambrai, 74 rue de Cambrai (*métro* Porte de Valenciennes)

- RU Charles Debierre, 171 rue Ch. Debierre (*métro* Mairie de Lille)
- RU Châtillon, 24 rue Gauthier de Châtillon (*métro* République)
- RU Châtelet, rue F. Combemale (*métro* CHR)
- Brasserie 'La Basoche', rue Fontenoy (*métro* Porte de Douai)

In Villeneuve d'Ascq:

- RU Pariselle, Domaine Universitaire Scientifique (*métro* Cité Scientifique)
- RU Sully, Domaine Universitaire Scientifique (*métro* 4 Cantons)
- RU Flers, Domaine Littéraire et Juridique (*métro* Pont de Bois)
- RU Flers 2000 (as above)

Private-sector accommodation

Try the following agencies:

- Agence Capitales: 5–7 place des Patiniers. Tel: 03 28 36 20 00
- Agence Gestrim de Rycker: 39 rue d'Isly. Tel: 03 20 00 16 16
- Agence Les Estudines. Tel: 03 20 63 90 94
- Agence Eurostudiomes. Tel: 0803 332 332

Accommodation addresses:

- Les Estudines d'Artois et Flandre, 87 et 92 rue de Flandre. Tel: 03 20 63 90 94
- Les Lauréades, 51 rue de Tounai. Tel: 03 20 31 42 00
- Appart'City Lille, 30 place Vauban. Tel: 03 20 06 04 70
- Montebello, 140 rue d'Iéna. Tel: 0820 830 820
- Central Fac, 11–13 rue du Machéchal de Lattre de Tassigny. Tel: 0820 830 820

The town and its surrounding area

The second largest town in France, Lille (including the conurbation) has a population of almost 1.7 million, of which some 100,000 are students. Originally a trading post on the River Deûle, the town has retained its lively, commercial atmosphere in its modern transformation while keeping the Flemish character of its old quarters. With Paris just over 200 kilometres away, Lille has long provided an important link between the capital and the Channel ports of Calais and Boulogne and its historical importance as a garrison town is evident from the imposing citadelle. During both world wars, the town was at the centre of fierce fighting and suffered considerable damage. An important manufacturing base, Lille is perhaps best known as the centre for the French textile industry. Among the famous people associated with the city are Charles de Gaulle (1890–1970), Général Faidherbe (1818–1889) and the composer Eduard Lalo (1823–1892).

The town's architecture is eclectic: there are fine historic buildings such as the fifteenth-century Palais Rihour, the seventeenth-century Bourse, Gothic churches, and several merchants' houses dating from the seventeenth and eighteenth centuries, which coexist with more recent constructions such as the unfinished neo-Gothic Cathédrale de Notre Dame de la Treille, the Opera, the Hôtel de Ville and 'Euralille', a futuristic development which includes a new TGV station. As befits a thriving, youthful city there are numerous cultural activities with music, theatre and cinema to the fore. The Palais des Beaux Arts houses one of France's finest collections of artworks while The Piscine, a converted Art Deco swimming pool, is the home of the Musée d'Art et d'Industrie. Cubist masterpieces and an outstanding collection of Modigliani works are housed in the Musée d'Art moderne. The Lillois enjoy sea-food and there are numerous fish restaurants, where *moules*, in particular, are to be enjoyed. The town boasts good transport links with major destinations. The TGV service puts Paris and Calais an hour away and the Eurostar service links the town with London. For international travellers there is the Lille-Lesquin airport and Lille's favoured position in the motorway network ensures rapid travel between France and her north-eastern neighbours. However, the pride of every Lillois is the fully automated *métro* system, which symbolizes the city's innovative, pioneering spirit and determination to be in the vanguard of modern industrial developments.

Tourist information

Office du Tourisme, place Rihour, BP 205, 59002 Lille. Tel: 03 20 30 81 00.
www.lilletourism.com

Hotels
- Hôtel du Coq-Hardi, 34 place de la Gare. Tel: 03 20 06 08 89
- Hôtel Faidherbe, 42 place de la Gare. Tel: 03 20 06 27 93
- Mister Bed Lille, 57 rue de Bethune. Tel: 03 20 12 96 96
- Hôtel Le Globe, 1 bd Vauban. Tel: 03 20 57 29 58

Other short-term accommodation
- Youth Hostel, 12 rue Malpart. Tel: 03 20 57 08 94
- Association des Beds & Breakfast de Lille, 76 rue Caumartin. Tel: 03 20 13 76 57
- Bed & Breakfast de Lille: 51 rue Négrier. Tel: 03 20 51 39 09

Restaurants

Good-value restaurants abound in the pedestrianized area of the *rue de Béthune*, for example:

- Aux Moules, 34 rue de Béthune. Tel: 03 20 57 12 46
- Pizza Pai, 57 rue de Béthune. Tel: 03 20 54 54 11

Also worth trying, are:

- La Pâte Brisée, 65 rue de la Monnaie. Tel: 03 20 74 29 00
- Les 3 Brasseurs, 22 place de la Gare. Tel: 03 20 06 46 25

Leisure facilities

For listings see the magazine *Sortir* published every Wednesday.

Museums and art galleries

Museums are usually closed on either Monday or Tuesday and free on the first Sunday in the month.

- Musée d'Art moderne, 1 allée du Musée, Villeneuve d'Ascq
- Musée des Beaux Arts, place de la République
- Musée de l'Hospice Comtesse, 32 rue de la Monnaie
- Musée des Canonniers, 44 rue des Canonniers
- Musée de la Piscine, 23, rue de l'Espérance (modern art)
- Musée d'Histoire Naturelle et de Géologie, 19 rue de Bruxelles
- Musée de Charles de Gaulle, 9 rue Princesse

Theatre and concert halls

- Opéra de Lille, 2 rue Bons Enfants. Tel: 03 28 38 40 50
- Auditorium Edouard Lalo, place du Concert, Lille. Tel: 03 20 74 57 50
- Orchestre National de Lille, 30 place Mendès France. Tel: 03 20 12 82 40
- Théâtre Le Grand Bleu, 36 av. Max-Dormoy. Tel: 03 20 09 88 44
- La Métaphore, 4 place du Général de Gaulle. Tel: 03 20 14 24 24
- Le Prato, 62 rue Buffon. Tel: 03 20 57 15 42
- Théâtre Sébastopol, place Sébastopol. Tel: 03 20 54 44 50
- Théâtre de la Verrière, 28 rue Alphonse Mercier. Tel: 03 20 64 96 75
- Théâtre de la Rose des Vents, bd Van Gogh, 59650 Villeneuve d'Ascq. Tel: 03 20 61 96 96

Cinema

Special rates apply on Mondays and early in the day.
The following are in Lille:

- Le Majestic, 54 rue de Béthune. Tel: 03 28 52 40 40
- Le Métropole, 25 rue des Ponts-de-Comines. Tel: 08 36 68 00 73
- UGC Cinémas, 40–46 rue de Béthune. Tel: 08 92 68 85 32

The following are in Villeneuve d'Ascq:

- Cinéma 5 Lumières, Centre Commercial V2. Tel: 03 20 91 19 73
- Kinepolis, ZAC Grand But-Lomme. Tel: 08 92 68 03 03
- Le Méliès, bd Van Gogh. Tel: 03 20 61 96 92

Sport

FFSU: CSU, G Berger, 180 av. Gaston Berger. Tel: 03 20 52 59 91
SUAPS: Salle Debeyre, 156 rue Charles Debierre. Tel: 03 20 52 55 81
Complexe Sportif Gaston Berger, rue G. Berger. Tel: 03 20 58 91 60
Association Sportive: Salle des Sports Châtelet, rue F. Combemale. Tel: 03 20 53 50 89

Useful addresses

Main post office: 8 place de la République. Tel: 03 28 36 10 20
Municipal libraries:

- Médiathèque Jean Lévy, 32–34 rue Edouard Delesalle. Tel: 03 20 15 97 20
- Médiathèque du Faubourg de Béthune, square F. Chopin. Tel: 03 20 30 42 00

Bookshops:

- FNAC: 20 rue St Nicolas, 59800 Lille. Tel: 03 20 15 58 15
- Le Furet du Nord, 15 place du Général de Gaulle. Tel: 03 20 78 43 43
- Librairie Meura Hugues 25 rue de Valmy. Tel: 03 20 57 36 44
- Libraire Internationale, 36 rue Tournai. Tel: 03 20 06 81 00

ANPE: 64 rue Buffon, 59000. Tel: 03 20 58 13 60
CAF: 82 rue Brûle Maison. Tel: 03 20 15 57 57
CPAM: 2 rue d'Iéna. Tel: 03 20 42 34 00
CRIJ: 2 rue Nicholas Leblanc. Tel: 03 20 12 87 30
Centre Culturel Britannique: 4 place du Temple. Tel: 03 20 54 22 79
EDF-GDF: 2 rue St Martin. Tel: 03 20 42 55 55
France Télécom: 13 bd de la Liberté. Tel: 03 20 42 33 33
ONISEP: 2 bis place de la République. Tel: 03 20 15 81 61
Gendarmerie: 49 bd Louis XIV. Tel: 03 20 43 56 56
Hôtel de Ville: place R. Salengro. Tel: 03 20 49 50 00
Préfecture du Nord: 171 bis bd de la Liberté (*carte de séjour*)
Internet café: Agence France Télécom, place Général de Gaulle. Tel: 03 20 57 40 00

Health care

Student Health Service:
SIUMPS (CUPS: Centre Universitaire de Promotion de la Santé):
- Lille I: av. H. Poincarré, 59650 Villeneuve d'Ascq. Tel: 03 20 43 65 50 (*métro* Cité Scientifique)
- Lille II (Santé): 24 rue Jeanne d'Arc. Tel: 03 20 54 74 59 (*métro* République).
- Lille II (Droit) and Lille III: rue de Fives, Parking P3, 59560 Villeneuve d'Ascq. Tel: 03 20 91 16 08 (*métro* Pont de Bois)

BAPU: 153 bd de la Liberté, 59800. Tel: 03 20 54 85 26 (*métro* République)
Hospital: Cité Hospitalière, 2 av. Oscar Lambret. Tel: 03 20 44 59 62
Chemists:
- Pharmacie de l'Hôtel de Ville, 9 rue St Sauveur. Tel: 03 20 52 74 80
- Pharmacie Casetta, 35 rue Faidherbe. Tel: 03 20 06 16 31
- Grande Pharmacie de Paris, 1 place de la Gare. Tel: 03 20 06 20 64

Local student insurance offices:
- LMDE: 96–98 rue Hôpital Militaire. Tel: 0 810 600 601
- SMENO: 43 bd Vauban. Tel: 0 825 316 316

Travel

Railway station
- Gare Lille Europe, av. le Corbusier. Tel: 08 36 35 35 35
- Gare Lille Flandres, place de la Gare. Tel: 03 20 12 45 20
- SNCF information: Tel: 03 20 78 50 50

Coach station
23 Parvis St Maurice. Tel: 03 20 78 18 88

Métro
Place des Buisses. Tel: 03 20 98 50 50

Airport
Aéroport de Lille-Lesquin. Tel: 03 20 49 68 68

Taxis
- Taxis Gare de Lille, 11–13 rue de Tournai. Tel: 03 20 06 64 00
- Taxi Union, 359 av. Willy Brandt. Tel: 03 20 06 06 06
- Navarro Taxi, place Buisses. Tel: 06 85 07 27 16

Buses
TCC, rue le Corbusier. Tel: 08 20 42 40 40

Student travel
OTU: 309 rue Gambetta, 59000 Lille. Tel: 03 28 04 76 22
Wasteels, 25 place des Reignaux. Tel: 08 03 88 70 41

Emergencies

Police: 10 rue Ovigneur. Tel: 03 20 62 47 47
Centre Anti-poison. Tel: 0 825 81 28 22
Hospital: CHR Lille, Tel: 03 20 44 59 62
Duty doctor. Tel: 03 20 67 47 47
SOS Médecin, 3 rue Louise Michel. Tel: 03 20 29 91 91
SOS Amitié, bd Carnot. Tel: 03 20 55 77 77

11 Limoges

The institutions of higher education and their disciplines

Académie de Limoges
Université de Limoges
Hôtel de l'Université, 33 rue F. Mitterrand, BP 23204, 87032 Limoges
    Cedex 1. Tel: 05 55 14 91 00. www.unilim.fr
SCUIO: 88 rue du Pont St Martial, 87000. Tel: 05 55 14 90 70
SRI: 33 rue F. Mitterrand, 87032 Cedex 1. Tel: 05 55 14 91 33
Droit, sciences économiques, lettres, langues, sciences humaines, sciences
    et technologies, santé
Antennes at Egleton and Tulle
Some teaching in law and sport at Brive-la-Gaillarde
IUT: allée André Maurois, 87065 Limoges Cedex. Tel: 05 55 43 43 55

University libraries

Service Commun de la Documentation, 39C rue Camille Guérin, 87031
    Cedex. Tel: 05 55 43 57 00
Lettres et Sciences Humaines, same address, 87031 Cedex. Tel: 05 55 45
    57 10
Droit et Sciences Economiques, 5 rue Félix Eboué, 87032 Cedex. Tel: 05

55 14 90 50

Santé, 2 rue du Dr Marchand, 87025 Cedex. Tel: 05 55 43 59 00

Sciences et Tech. du Sport, 123 av. Albert Thomas, 87060 Cedex. Tel: 05 55 45 72 90

Courses for foreign students

Institut de Français Langue Etrangère, Faculté des Lettres et des Sciences Humaines, Campus Universitaire Limoges-Vanteaux, 39 E rue Camille Guérin, 87036 Limoges Cedex. Tel: 05 55 01 26 19

Term-time courses

Courses, which are organized on a semester basis, are offered at Beginners', Intermediate and Advanced levels. There is an intensive Beginners' and post-Beginners' course during the first semester (October–January) based on ten hours of teaching per week. The Intermediate course prepares for the DELF, whilst the Advanced course leads to a *Diplôme d'Université* (DU). There are also specialist options in the language of science, law and economics and in the methodology of teaching French as a foreign language.

Summer course

An intensive three-week refresher course is run in September (27 hours a week).

CROUS

39 G rue Camille Guérin, 87036 Cedex. Tel: 05 55 43 17 00. www.crous-limoges.fr

SAEE: same address and telephone number

CROUS-controlled accommodation

Accommodation is available in both traditional rooms and flatlets.

- Résidence La Guérin, 30 A rue Camille Guérin, 87038 Cedex (353 traditional, ALS possible)
- Résidence de l'Aurence, 24 av. du Prés. Vincent Auriol, 87065 Cedex (247 T1, 30 T1 bis, APL available)
- Résidence Hauts de Vanteaux, 39 A rue Camille Guérin, 87038 Cedex (194 T1, 12 T1 bis, APL available)
- Résidence Beaublanc, 18 bd de la Borie, 87100 (4 T1, 51 T1 bis, ALS possible)

- Résidence La Borie, 185 av. Albert Thomas, 87065 Cedex (605 traditional rooms, ALS possible)
- Résidence Saint Martial, 1 rue Eugène Jamet, 87000 (207 T1, 4 T1 bis, APL available)
- Résidence Emile Zola, 8–12 rue Emile Zola, 87000 (39 T1, APL available)
- Résidence Ester, parc de la Technopole, 87069 Cedex (90 T1, 7 T1 bis, APL available)

CROUS restaurants

The restaurants all offer the *menu traditionnel*, plus a range of pizzas, grills, dishes of the day, sandwiches, salads and pastries. Camille Guérin and La Borie also have *restaurants médico-diététiques* open to students who are referred on medical advice. Les Pyramides, IUFM and ENSIL are closed in the evening.

- Restaurant La Borie, 185 av. Albert Thomas, 87065 Cedex
- Restaurant Les Pyramides, 88 av. St Martial, 87000
- Restaurant Camille Guérin, 39 B rue Camille Guérin, 87000
- Restaurant La Croustadine, rue de la Cornue, 87000
- Restaurant de L'IUFM, 209 bd de Vanteaux, 87000
- Restaurant ENSIL, Ester Technopole, 87000

Privately run hostels

For details, write to the *Directeur/Directrice*:
- Foyer Municipal de Jeunes Travailleurs, 44 rue Emile Montégut, 87000. Tel: 05 55 32 42 36 (males only, aged 16–25)
- Foyer Varlin Pont Neuf, 332 rue de Fontbonne, 87000. Tel: 05 55 30 39 79 (mixed, aged 15–25)
- Accueil FJT 2000, 20 rue Encombe Vineuse, 87100. Tel: 05 55 77 63 97 (mixed, aged 18–35)
- Foyer de l'Institut d'Economie Sociale et Familiale, 5 rue de la Cité, 87000. Tel: 05 55 34 41 25 (rooms must be taken for the full university year; mixed, aged 17–25)
- Résidence Industrie (Sonacotra), 16 rue de l'Industrie, 87000. Tel: 05 55 10 20 93 (mixed; studios with APL available; no age limit)
- Résidence Auguste Renoir (Sonocotra), 10 rue Ernest Mallard, 87000. Tel: 05 55 31 80 20 (mixed, no age limit, APL available)

Private-sector residences

University Meissonnier, 27 chemin d'Antony, 87000. Tel: 05 55 79 33 82
City Club Mauvendière, 7 rue de la Mauvendière, 87000. Same telephone
number

The town and its surrounding area

Situated some 375 kilometres south-south-west of Paris, Limoges is the
préfecture of the Haute-Vienne. It is a medium-sized, pleasant, fairly quiet
town which stands at the heart of Le Limousin, a region renowned for its
woods, rivers and lakes. It is about three hours from Paris by train on the
fast line which serves the south-west, and constitutes a major junction for
the north–south and east–west routes in the region.

There are many remnants of its historic past still in evidence. An
impressive Gothic Cathedral, begun in the thirteenth century, heads the
list of the churches, which includes St-Michel-des-Lions (fourteenth to
sixteenth century), so named because of the two ancient stone lions which
stand guard, and with a 65-metre tower dating from 1373, and St-Pierre-
du-Queyroix, largely rebuilt in the sixteenth century, but sporting an older
bell-tower typical of the region. The eighteenth-century Bishop's Palace,
with its terraced gardens overlooking the River Vienne, is now the home of
the municipal museum. A good deal of restoration work has been put into
the 'Village de la Boucherie', the territory of the influential corporation of
the butchers, which goes back many centuries. Their chapel, St-Aurélien
(fifteenth century, but with a later tower and façade), stands near to the
stalls which still line the rue de la Boucherie. The Thursday market well
deserves a visit.

Eminent sons of the town include the humanist Jean Dorat (c. 1510–1588),
the soldier Maréchal Jourdan (1762–1833), and the painters Auguste Renoir
(1841–1919) and Suzanne Valadon (1867–1938). The well-known playwright
and novelist Jean Giraudoux (1882–1944) was born at nearby Bellac.

The town has known considerable expansion in recent times, and its
industrial base has diversified, in part due to the discovery of uranium
in the area. However, it is most famous for its enamels and its porcelain.
The manufacture of Limoges enamels was already at its height in the
sixteenth century; it died out before the end of the eighteenth century,
but was revived in 1875. The discovery of kaolin in the neighbourhood
in the 1760s led to the establishment of the porcelain industry. Many fine
examples of its wares, along with exhibits of chinaware from much further
afield, can be seen in the Musée National Adrien Dubouché.

Tourist information

Tourist office: 12 bd de Fleurus, 87000. Tel: 05 55 34 46 87.
www.tourismelimoges.com

Hotels
- Hôtel de France, 23 cours Bugeaud, 87000. Tel: 05 55 77 28 34 (near the station)
- Familia, 18 rue du Général du Bessol 87000. Tel: 05 55 77 51 40 (in the town centre; inexpensive)
- Hôtel Royal Limousin, place de la République, 87007. Tel: 05 55 34 65 30 (a three-star hotel which has the reputation of being among the best in town, and good value for the upper end of the market. For those extra-special visitors!)

Restaurants
- Chez François, Halles Centrales. Tel: 05 55 32 32 79 (inexpensive lunches)
- Le Bistrot Gourmand, 5–7 place Winston Churchill. Tel: 05 55 10 29 29 (good food in a popular setting)
- La Marmite, 1 place Fontaine des Barres. Tel: 05 55 33 38 34 (more up-market; traditional Périgord specialities)

Leisure facilities

Museums and art galleries
- Musée Municipal de l'Email, place de la Cathédrale, 87000
- Musée National Adrien Dubouché, place Winston Churchill
- Musée de la Résistance, place de l'Evêché
- Musée des Distilleries Limougeaudes, 52 rue de Belfort
- Musée Haviland, Pavillon de la Porcelaine, av. John Kennedy

Centres culturels et sociaux municipaux
- Jean Gagnant, 7 av. Jean Gagnant. Tel: 05 55 45 94 00
- Jean Le Bail, 9 rue Jean Le Bail. Tel: 05 55 45 61 68
- John Lennon, 41 ter rue de Feytiat. Tel: 05 55 45 61 69
- Jean Macé, rue de New York. Tel: 05 55 45 61 67
- Jean Moulin, 76 av. des Sagnes. Tel: 05 55 35 04 10

Theatre
- Grand Théâtre Municipal, 48 rue Jean-Jaures. Tel: 05 55 45 95 00

- Théâtre de l'Union, 20 rue des Coopérateurs. Tel: 05 55 79 90 00
- Théâtre de la Passerelle, 5 rue du Général du Bessol. Tel: 05 55 72 26 49
- Théâtre Expression 7, 20 rue de la Réforme. Tel: 05 55 77 37 50
- Espace Noriac, rue Jules Noriac. Tel: 05 55 45 10 05
- Conservatoire National de Région, 9 rue Fitz James. Tel: 05 55 45 95 50
- Café Théâtre Universitaire 'Au Cafteur', 105 rue A. Thomas (on campus). Tel: 05 55 79 99 30

CROUS sells a student *passeport culturel* for the year, which entitles holders to reductions of at least 40 per cent in a range of 40 establishments listed on the back.

Cinema

- Le Lido (*d'art et d'essai*), 3 av. du Général de Gaulle. Tel: 08 36 68 20 15
- Les Ecrans, 11 place Denis Dussoubs. Tel: 08 36 68 20 15

Sport

Parc Municipal des Sports (swimming, tennis), bd de Beaublanc. Tel: 05 55 38 50 50

Palais des Sports de Beaublanc, same address. Tel: 05 55 38 50 45

Centre Sportif Municipal de Saint-Lazare (golf, swimming, tennis), 25 av. du Golf. Tel: 05 55 30 21 02

Municipal swimming pools:

- Les Casseaux, bd des Petits Carmes. Tel: 05 55 32 24 12
- Beaubreuil, ZAC de Beaubreuil. Tel: 05 55 35 44 55

Skating: Patinoire des Casseaux, bd des Petits Carmes. Tel: 05 55 34 13 85

FFSU: Gymnase Universitaire de la Borie, 185 av. Albert Thomas, 87000. Tel: 05 55 77 43 20

The SUAPS (Centre Sportif Universitaire, same address. Tel: 05 55 77 22 84) organizes a wide range of activities. Equally, the Association Sportive de l'Université de Limoges enters teams in university competitions in a range of sports. Details may be had from its office at the Centre Sportif Universitaire, same address, same telephone number.

Useful addresses

Main post office: 29 av. de la Libération. Tel: 05 55 44 44 13

Municipal library: Bibliothèque Francophone Multimédia, 2 rue Louis Longequeue. Tel: 05 55 45 96 00

Bookshops:
- Anecdotes, 19 rue Consulat. Tel: 05 55 33 07 61
- Société de Promotion de la Culture et des Loisirs (SPCL), 3 av. du Midi, 87000. Tel: 05 55 32 32 01

ANPE: 36 rue Emile Laboussière. Tel: 05 55 79 23 22
CAF: 25 rue Firmin Delage, 87000. Tel: 05 55 43 40 00
CRIJ: 27 bd de la Corderie, 87031 Cedex. Tel: 05 55 45 18 70
Administrative offices:
- Commissariat de Police, 84 av. Emile Labussière. Tel: 05 55 14 30 00
- Préfecture de Région, rue de la Préfecture. Tel: 05 55 44 18 00
- Mairie, place Léon Betoulle, 87031 Cedex. Tel: 05 55 32 11 87

Health care

Centre Hospitalier Régional Universitaire (CHRU), 2 av. Martin Luther King. Tel: 05 55 05 61 23
SUMPPS, Campus Universitaire, 39 J rue Camille Guérin, 87036 Cedex. Tel: 05 55 43 57 70
CPAM, 22 av. Jean Gagnant. Tel: 05 55 45 87 87
Local student insurance offices:
- LMDE, 8 bis rue A. Dubouché, BP 75, 87002 Cedex. Tel: 05 55 34 61 35
- Vittavi (SMESO), 41 rue des Tanneries, BP 396, 87010 Cedex. Tel: 05 55 32 50 60

Local chemists:
- Pharmacie du Palais, 1 bis place Aine, 87000. Tel: 05 55 34 16 65
- Pharmacie du Vigenal, 2 bd Vigenal, 87100. Tel: 05 55 37 32 88

Travel

Railway station
Gare des Bénédictins, place Maison Dieu (information, tel: 05 55 11 12 00; reservations, tel: 08 36 35 35 35)

Coach station
Le CIEL (Centre International d'Echanges de Limoges) gare des Bénédictins. Tel: 05 55 45 10 10

Airport
Limoges International Airport: Tel: 05 55 43 30 30

Taxis
Tel: 05 55 38 38 38 **or** 05 55 37 81 81

Buses
The local trolley-buses and buses are operated by the Société des Transports en Commun de Limoges (TLC), 10 place Léon Betoulle. Tel: 05 55 32 46 46

Emergencies

SOS Médecins. Tel: 08 03 06 70 00
Drogue Info. Tel: 08 00 13 13 13
Late-night chemist: 56 bd Gambetta. Tel: 05 55 34 61 26
For emergency medical supplies and enquiries, contact the Commissariat de Police, 84 av. Emile Labussière. Tel: 05 55 14 30 00
Centre Anti-poison. Tel: 05 56 96 40 80
SOS Amitié. Tel: 05 55 79 25 25

12 Lyon

Institutions of higher education and their disciplines

Académie de Lyon
Université Claude Bernard:Lyon I
43 bd du 11 Novembre 1918, 69100 Villeurbanne. Tel: 04 72 44 80 00. www.univ-lyon.fr
SCUIO:
● 8 av. Rockfeller, Lyon. Tel: 04 78 77 70 92
● 43 bd du 11 Novembre 1918, Villeurbanne. Tel: 04 72 44 80 59
CELAIO: Campus de la Doua, Tel: 04 72 44 80 59
● **Lyon**: santé
● **Villeurbanne**: sciences et technologie, sport
IUT:
● (A) 43 bd du 11 Novembre 1918, 69622 Villeurbanne. Tel: 04 72 69 20 00
● (B): 17 rue de France, 69627 Villeurbanne. Tel: 04 72 65 53 53

Université Lumière: Lyon II
86 rue Pasteur, 69365 Lyon. Tel: 04 78 69 70 00. www.univ-lyon2.fr
SRI: same address. Tel: 04 78 69 70 00

SCUIO 5 av. Mendès France, Bron. Tel: 04 78 77 23 42
- **Lyon**: études politiques, langues, lettres, sciences du langage, arts, musique
- **Bron**: lettres, langues, sciences du langage, arts, sciences humaines, communication, sciences économiques et de gestion, droit

IUT Bron Lumière: 5 av. Pierre Mendès France, 69676 Bron Cedex. Tel: 04 78 77 23 01

Université Jean Moulin: Lyon III
1 rue de l'Université, 69239 Lyon. Tel: 04 72 72 20 20. www.lyon-univ3.fr
SCUIO: 64 cours Albert Thomas. Tel: 04 78 78 78 40
CELAIO: Université Jean Moulin. Tel: 04 77 42 17 16
Lettres, langues et sciences humaines, droit, administration des entreprises
IUT Lyon 3: 4 cours Albert Thomas, 69372 Lyon Cedex 03. Tel: 04 72 72 44 10

Other institutions

CSI/ITII Lyon: Centre d'Etudes Supérieures Industrielles
19 av. Guy de Collongue, BP 160, 69301 Ecully Cedex. Tel: 04 78 77 07 57. Email: itii.lyon@dial.oleane.com
Ingénieur des techniques de l'industrie

EM Lyon: Ecole de Management
233 av. Guy de Collongue, BP 174, 69132 Ecully Cedex. Tel: 04 78 33 78 00. www.em.lyon.com
Préparation du dipôme ESC/Msc in management. Spécialisation en 3e année: construction du projet professionnel

University libraries

Sciences (Lyon I), 43 bd du 11 Novembre 1918, Villeurbanne. Tel: 04 72 43 12 77
Section Santé (Lyon I), 93 Grande Rue Croix Rousse. Tel: 04 78 39 48 45
Section Lettres et Langues (Lyon II–III), 31 rue Brancel. Tel: 04 37 65 40 20
Droit-Lettres (Lyon I), 5 av. Pierre Mendès France, Bron. Tel 04 78 77 24 87

Droit, AES (Lyon III), 4 rue Rollet
Droit–Gestion (Lyon III) 15, quai Claude Bernard

Courses for foreign students

CIEF (Centre International d'Etudes Françaises): 16 quai Claude Bernard,
69365 Lyon Cedex 07. Tel: 04 78 69 71 36. www.univ-lyon2.fr/cief

CROUS

59 rue de la Madeleine, 69007 Lyon. Tel: 04 72 80 17 70 (*métro* Jean-Macé)

CROUS-controlled accommodation
There are some 3,400 rooms available in mixed halls and a further 100 for
females only in Lirondelle. In addition there are some 800 *studios* which
attract APL.

Résidences universitaires (traditional halls; a nine-month contract is
obligatory from either 1 September or 1 October):

• André Allix, 2 rue Soeur Bouvier, 5e. Tel: 04 78 25 47 13
• Jussieu, 3 av. Albert Einstein, Villeurbanne. Tel: 04 78 93 34 21
• Puvis de Chavannes, 29 rue Marguerite, Villeurbanne. Tel: 04 78 89 62
  02
• André Lirondelle, 6 rue Rachais, 3e. Tel: 04 78 60 13 20 (females only)
• La Madeleine, 4 rue du Sauveur, 7e. Tel: 04 78 72 80 62
• Jacques Cavalier, 8 rue Jeanne Koehler, 3e. Tel: 04 78 54 08 62
• Jean Mermoz, 29 rue Pr J. Nicolas, 8e. Tel: 04 78 74 41 64
• Benjamin Delessert, 145 av. Jean Jaurès, 7e. Tel: 04 78 61 41 41

New-style *studios*/flats (T1):

• Les Antonins, 28–32 rue des Antonins, Villeurbanne. Tel: 04 78 93 34 21
• Le Paradin, 24 rue G. Paradin, 8e. Tel: 04 78 74 41 64
• Einstein, 1 bis av. Albert Einstein, Villeurbanne. Tel: 04 78 93 34 21
• Croix du Sud, 115 av. Général Frère, 8e. Tel: 04 78 74 41 64
• Vieux Fort, 2 rue Soeur Bouvier, 5e. Tel: 04 78 25 47 13
• Arches d'Agrippa, rue du Fort St Irénée, 5e. Tel: 04 78 25 47 13
• Garibaldi, 360 rue Garibaldi, 7e. Tel: 04 78 72 80 62
• Paul Bert, 8 rue Moissonnier, 3e. Tel: 04 78 72 80 62

CROUS restaurants
Restaurants:

• André Allix, 2 rue Soeur Bouvier, 5e
• Bron, av. P. Mendès France, Bron

- La Madeleine, 360 rue Garibaldi, 7e
- La Manu, 1 av. des Frères Lumière, 8e
- Jean Mermoz, 98 av. Mermoz, 8e
- Jussieu, 3 av. Albert Einstein, Villeurbanne
- Puvis de Chavannes, 118 bd du 11 Novembre 1918, Villeurbanne

Cafétérias:

- Café Lumière, av. P. Mendès France, Bron
- Europe, Bâtiment Europe, av. P. Mendès France, Bron
- La Madeleine, 360 rue Garibaldi, 7e
- Le Bistrot de la Manu, 4 cours Albert Thomas, 8e
- Jean Mermoz, 98 av. Mermoz, 8e
- Com'Et, 25 rue Jaboulay, 7e
- Gerland, 14 passage du Vercors, 7e
- Cafétéria la Buire, rue Paradin, 8e
- La Grignote, 3 av. Albert Einstein. Villeurbanne
- Cafétéria des Sports, 14 bd Latarjet, Villeurbanne
- Astrée, av. Gaston Berger, Villeurbanne
- Cybercafé, Campus de la Doua, 24 av. Gaston Berger, Villeurbanne

Private-sector accommodation

There are several privately-run *foyers* and *résidences* in Lyon. A full list can be obtained from the CROUS or OSE. Here is selection:

- Les Estudines Garibaldi, 2 rue du Diapason. Tel: 04 78 60 72 51
- Les Estudines Saxe-Gambetta, 34 Grande Rue de la Guillotière. Tel: 04 72 71 91 92
- Les Studélites Magritte, 98 rue Pasteur. Tel: 04 72 71 42 43
- Les Studélites Limt, 30 bis av. R. Salengro, Villeurbanne. Tel: 04 72 44 00 08
- Résidence Chagall, 96–98 av. R. Salengro, Villeurbanne. Tel: 04 72 44 00 08
- Les Studélites Dufy, 23 rue de Bruxelles. Tel: 04 78 89 98 98

The town and its surrounding area

Standing at the confluence of the Rhône and the Saône, Lyon, with a population of just over 1.5 million, is the third largest town in France. It is a thriving commercial, industrial and academic centre with over 90,000 students. Lyon's rich history is reflected in its varied architecture. Notable features include the stone amphitheatres at Fourvière, testifying to its

Roman origins; the narrow streets and town-houses from the Renaissance period, fine seventeenth-century buildings (the Hôtel de Ville, the Musée des Beaux-Arts, the Musée des Hospices); the civic buildings of the nineteenth century (the Bourse, the Palais de Justice, Théâtre des Célestins and Fourvière Cathedral); and, representing the twentieth century, the Musée de la Civilisation Gallo-Romaine and the cylindrical Tour de la Part-Dieu. Once the undisputed centre of the silk trade, Lyon is now the home of synthetic fibres and chemical products. The town's changing industrial base is recorded in its excellent museums: the Musée Historique des Tissus, the Musée des Arts Décoratifs, the Maison des Canuts and the Musée de la Banque et de l'Imprimerie.

The town is culturally active with several theatres, most notable of which are the Théâtre des Célestins, the Théâtre National Populaire and the Opera House. Lyon's love of the cinema is reflected in its many cinemas and thriving film clubs. Attractive pedestrianized areas, a modern *métro* and a good bus service contribute to the pleasant lifestyle of the town. The two rivers, their bridges, the public squares, notably the tree-lined Place Bellecour, and the magnificent Parc de la Tête d'Or bring beauty to the town. Among the many famous personalities associated with Lyon are the poets Maurice Scève (c.1501–1577) and Louise Labé (c.1524–1566), the novelist Antoine de Saint-Exupéry (1900–1944), and the artist Pierre Puvis de Chavannes (1824–1898). In the sciences there are Joseph Jacquard (1752–1834) inventor of the power loom, the physicist André-Marie Ampère (1775–1836), Auguste Lumière (1862–1954), optical engineer and pioneer of the cinema, and the botanist Bernard de Jussieu (1699–1777).

Lyon and its region is synonymous with good but simple cooking, complemented by the wines of the Rhône valley (Mâcon and Beaujolais). The *charcuterie* of the region is famous, ranging from rolled pig's head with pistachios, *quenelle* (made with fish or chicken), *cervelas* with truffles to the gigantic Lyon Jésus sausage. Desserts include *bugnes*, *matefaims* and walnut gâteaux. The town is twinned with Birmingham in the UK and St Louis in the USA. Lyon enjoys an excellent rail service with several TGV connections, and is served by the motorway network and an international airport, Saint-Exupéry.

Tourist information

Office du Tourisme, place Bellecour, 2e. Tel: 04 72 77 69 69. www.lyon-france.com

Rhône Accueil, 5 place de la Baleine, 5e. Tel: 04 78 42 50 03. www.leprogres.fr/petitpaume or www.mairie-lyon.fr

Hotels

The following are reasonably priced and close to the main stations (Perrache and Part-Dieu) or the town centre:

- Hôtel Dubost, 19 place Carnot. Tel: 04 78 42 00 46 (*métro* Perrache)
- Hôtel des Savoies, 80 rue de la Charité, 2e. Tel: 04 78 37 66 94 (*métro* Perrache)
- Hôtel Columbia, 8 place Aristide-Briand, 3e. Tel: 04 72 84 70 70 (*métro* Saxe-Gambetta)
- Hôtel Bellecordière, 18 rue Bellecordière, 2e. Tel: 04 78 42 27 78 (*métro* Bellecour)

Short-term accommodation

- Auberge de Jeunesse, 51 rue Salengro, Vénissieux. Tel: 04 78 76 39 23
- Bed and Breakfast, 6 rue Joliot-Curie, 5e. Tel: 04 72 57 99 22
- Centre International de Séjour de Lyon (CISL), 101 bd des Etats Unis, 8e. Tel: 04 78 01 23 45
- OSE, 78 rue de Marseille, 7e. Tel: 04 78 69 62 69

Restaurants

Lyon is famous as a gastronomic centre and many restaurants will be beyond a student budget. A number of reasonably priced restaurants with fixed menus are found in rue Mercière and rue Tupin, 2e (*métro* Cordeliers) such as Le P'tit Bouchon, La Traboulerie, Alexandre and Flam's. The following also offer good value, but there are many others to be discovered!

- Aux Trois Tonneaux, 4 rue des Marronniers, 1er. Tel: 04 78 37 34 72
- Le P'tit Comte, 17 rue Auguste Comte, 2e. Tel: 04 72 41 06 09
- Le Caveau, 5 place Antonin Poncet, 2e. Tel: 04 78 37 35 04

English/Irish/Scottish-style pubs

- The Albion, 12 rue Ste-Catherine, 1er. Tel: 04 78 28 33 00
- O'Gorman's, place Ch. Béraudier, 3e. Tel: 04 72 13 13 60
- Les Escossais, 7 rue Charles Dullin, 2e. Tel: 04 78 37 15 54

Leisure facilities

Lyon is second only to Paris in its range of cultural activities. Listings of films, plays, concerts and exhibitions and so on are published in the weekly guide *Lyon Poche*. Students can obtain a range of reductions on presentation of their student card and there is also a special student pass (*le Pass-Culture*). Students from Birmingham (UK), St Louis, Missouri and Montreal should apply to the Hôtel de Ville for a free pass (*le Pass Lyon Cité*) to the city's museums, art galleries, swimming pools and skating rinks.

Museums and art galleries
The following is a selection. Students enjoy considerable reductions.
- Musée des Beaux Arts, 20 place des Terreaux, Lyon 1er
- Musée Saint-Pierre d'Art Contemporain, 16 rue Président Edouard Herriot, 1er
- Musée Historique de Lyon et Musée de la Marionnette, 1 place du Petit-Collège, 5e
- Musée de la Résistance et de la Déportation, 14 av. Berthelot, 7e
- Musée des Arts Décoratifs, 34 rue de la Charité, 2e
- Musée des Tissus, 34 rue de la Charité, 2e
- Institut Lumière, 25 rue du Premier Film, 8e
- Musée de la Banque et de l'Imprimerie, 13 rue de la Poulaillerie, 2e

Theatre
- Théâtre Les Ateliers, 3 rue du Petit David, 2e. Tel: 04 78 37 46 30
- Théâtre des Célestins, 4 rue Charles Dullin, 2e. Tel: 04 72 77 44 00
- Théâtre Guignol, 2 rue Louis Carrand, 5e. Tel: 04 78 28 92 57
- Théâtre de la Croix-Rousse, place Joannès Ambre, 4e. Tel: 04 78 39 52 53
- TNP, 8 place Lazare-Goujon, Villeurbanne. Tel: 04 78 03 30 40
- Théâtre Tête d'Or, 24 rue Dunoir, 3e. Tel: 04 78 95 46 69

Cinemas
Lyon has nearly seventy screens providing a wide choice of programmes. There are multiscreen cinemas showing new releases in rue de la République and the Part-Dieu Commercial Centre as well as several Art cinemas (*les cinémas d'Art et d'Essai*) which screen subtitled foreign films (*en version originale – V.O.*), established classics and second-run popular films. Reductions are available with a student card on specified days. Programmes are published weekly in *Lyon Poche*.
- UGC, 31 cours Vuitton, 6e. Tel: 08 36 68 22 27
- UGC, 13 av. Berthelot, 7e. Tel: 08 36 68 29 31
- UGC Part-Dieu, CC Part-Dieu, 3e. Tel 08 36 65 70 14
- Pathé, 78 rue de la République, 2e. Tel: 08 36 68 20 22
- Les 8 Nefs, 20 rue Thomassin, 2e. Tel: 08 36 68 20 15
- Cinéjournal, 71 rue de la République, 2e. Tel: 08 36 68 20 22

Art cinema:
- CNP Bellecour, 12 rue de la Barre, 2e. Tel: 08 36 68 69 13
- CNP Terreaux, 40 rue E. Herriot, 1er. Tel: 08 36 68 69 13
- Fourmi Lafayette, 68 rue P. Corneille, 3e. Tel: 08 36 68 05 98
- Institut Lumière, rue du Premier Film, 8e. Tel: 04 78 78 18 95

Sport
FFSU, 43 bd du 11 Novembre 1918, Villeurbanne. Tel: 04 72 44 80 89
SIUAPS:
- Lyon I, 43 bd du 11 Novembre 1918, Villeurbanne. Tel: 04 72 44 80 97
- Lyon II, 5 av. Pierre Mendès-France. Tel: 04 78 77 23 16
- Lyon III, 6 cours Albert Thomas. Tel: 04 78 78 78 50
Swimming pools:
- Allo à l'eau: Tel: 04 78 60 18 18 (general information)
- Garibaldi: 221 rue Garibaldi. Tel: 04 78 60 89 66
- Piscine Mermoz, 12 place Latarget. Tel: 04 78 74 33 09
- Piscine Charcal: 102 rue A. Charcal. Tel: 04 78 54 21 97
Skating: SkatePark de Gerland, 24 allée de Caubertin. Tel: 04 78 69 17 86
Tennis:
- Tennis Lyon I, 19 rue Philippe Garrard. Tel: 04 78 27 00 03
- Tennis Lyon III, passage St Marc. Tel: 04 72 34 89 28

Useful addresses

Main post office: place Antonin Poncet, 2e. (*métro* Bellecour). Tel: 04 72
    40 60 50
Municipal libraries:
- 30 bd Vivier-Merle, 3e. Tel: 04 78 62 18 00
- 7 rue St Polycarpe, 1er. Tel: 04 78 27 45 55
- Centre St Irénée, 2 place du Docteur Gailleton, 6e. Tel: 04 78 38 05 07
Bookshops: there are bookshops on each campus (Decitre at la Doua;
Cartillier and Berthezène at Bron-Parilly; ACEML at the Faculté de
Médecine-Rockefeller; Corpo Lyon 3 at La Doua and Quai Bernard).
Branches of the major bookshops are situated around place Bellecour
(*métro* Bellecour). The list is by no means exhaustive.
- Camugli, 6, rue de la Charité, 2e. Tel: 04 78 42 65 50
- Decitre, 6 and 29 place Bellecour, 2e. Tel: 04 72 40 54 54
- Flammarion, 19 place Bellecour, 2e. Tel: 04 72 56 21 21
- FNAC Bellecour, 85 rue de la République, 2e. Tel: 04 72 40 49 49
- FNAC Lyon Part-Dieu, Centre Commercial, 3e. Tel: 04 78 71 87 00
- Gibert, 6 rue de la Barre, 2e. Tel: 04 78 42 22 22

- Eton, 1 rue du Plat, 2e. Tel: 04 78 92 92 36 (specialist English bookshop)

CAF: 67 bd Vivier Merle, 6e. Tel: 0 820 25 69 10

Centre d'Information Municipal, Mairie Annexe, place Louis Pradel, 1er. Tel: 04 78 28 56 26

CIES: 16 av. Berthelot, 7e. Tel: 04 78 69 28 99

CLEF: 8 rue Bourgelat, 2e. Tel: 04 78 38 38 21

CRIJ: 9 quai des Célestins, 2e. Tel: 04 72 77 00 66 (Internet facilities)

EDF-GDF: 14 rue de la République. Tel: 0 810 69 2000

France Télécom: 50 rue de la République. Tel: 10 14 (free)

MJC Monplaisir: 25 av. des Frères Lumière, 8e. Tel: 04 72 78 05 70

OSE: 78 rue de Marseille, 7e. Tel: 04 78 69 62 00

Préfecture du Rhône: 114–116 rue Pierre Corneille, 3e. Tel: 04 72 61 60 60

Lost property: 5 rue Bichat, 2e. Tel: 04 78 42 43 82

Internet cafés:

- Café Berchot, 13 rue Berchot, 8e. Tel: 04 78 74 38 42
- Connecktic: 19 quai St Antoine, 2e. Tel: 04 72 77 98 85
- Médiathèque de Vaize, place Valmy, 9e. Tel: 04 72 85 66 20

Health care

SIUMP (MPU):

- Lyon 1, Campus de la Doua, Tel: 04 72 44 40 80
- Lyon 2, Bron, Bât. L, av. Pierre Mendès France, Bron. Tel: 04 78 77 43 10
- Lyon 3, 6 cours Albert Thomas, 8e. Tel: 04 78 78 78 80

Espace Santé Jeunes, rue St Bonaventure, 2e. Tel: 04 78 37 52 13

Chemists (24-hour service):

- Pharmacie Blanchet, 5 place des Cordeliers, 2e. Tel: 04 78 42 12 42 (*métro* Cordeliers)
- Pharmacie Perret, 30 rue Duquesne, 6e. Tel: 04 78 93 70 96 (*métro* Foch)

Hospitals:

- Centre Hospitalier Lyon-Sud, Pierre Bénite, 6e. Tel: 04 78 86 10 00
- Hôpital Edouard Herriot, 5 place d'Arsonval, 3e. Tel: 04 72 11 73 11
- Hôpital de la Croix Rousse, 93 Grand Rue de la Croix Rousse, 4e. Tel: 04 72 07 10 00
- Hôpital de l'Hôtel Dieu, 1 place de l'Hôpital, 2e. Tel: 04 72 41 30 00

Local student insurance offices:

- LMDE, la Doua, 43 bd du 11 Novembre 1918, Villeurbanne. Tel: 0 810 600 601
- SMERRA, 43 rue Jaboulay. Tel: 04 72 76 70 70

Travel

Railway station
- Gare de la Part-Dieu, bd Vivier Merle, 3e
- Gare de Perrache, 2e

For TGV timetable, telephone 08 36 35 35 35

Coach station
Centre d'Echanges, Perrache. Tel: 04 72 56 95 30 (*métro* Perrache)

Airport
- Lyon-Saint-Exupéry Tel: 04 72 22 72 21 (Satobus from Perrache or Part-Dieu)
- Lyon-Bron. Tel: 04 78 26 81 09

Taxis
- Allo Taxi. Tel: 04 78 28 23 23
- Taxis Lyonnais. Tel: 04 78 26 81 81
- Radio Taxi. Tel: 04 72 10 86 86
- Coopérative Taxis Radio. Tel: 04 78 28 13 14

Bus/métro
Société Lyonnaise de Transports en Commun (TCL). Head office: bd Vivier Merle, Part-Dieu, 69003 Lyon. Tel: 04 78 71 70 00

Student travel
OTU:
- 59 rue de la Madeleine. Tel: 04 72 71 98 07
- 43 bd du 11 novembre, Campus de la Doua, Villeurbanne. Tel: 04 78 93 11 49

Wasteels:
- 24 quai Jean Moulin. Tel: 04 72 61 83 54
- 5 place Ampère. Tel: 04 78 42 09 02

Emergencies

Ambulance. Tel: 04 78 37 19 38
Centre Anti-poison. Tel: 04 72 11 69 11
Chemist (24 hours): Pharmacie Blanchet, 5 place des Cordeliers. Tel: 04 78 42 12 42
SOS Médecins. Tel: 04 78 83 51 51
Urgence dentaire. Tel: 04 72 10 01 01
SOS Amitié. Tel: 04 78 85 33 33

13 Marseille

Institutions of higher education and their disciplines

Académie d'Aix-Marseille
Université de Provence: Aix-Marseille I
3 place Victor Hugo, 13331 Marseille Cedex 3. Tel: 04 91 10 60 00. www.
up.univ-mrs.fr
SCUIO: same address. Tel: 04 91 10 60 58
SRI: 1 allée Bastide des Cyprès, 13100 Aix-en-Provence Cedex 1. Tel: 04
42 17 14 20
• **Aix-en-Provence**: sciences humaines, langues, lettres, arts, communication, musique
• **Marseille**: mathématiques, informatique, technologies, sciences,
lettres, arts, communication

Université de la Méditerrannée: Aix-Marseille II
Jardin du Pharo, 58 bd Charles Livon, 13284 Marseille Cedex 07. Tel: 04
91 39 65 00. www.mediterrannee.univ-mrs.fr
SCUIO:
• St Jérôme, av. Escadrille Normandie Niémen. Tel: 04 91 28 81 18
• 58 bd Charles Livon. Tel: 04 91 39 65 17
• 27 bd Jean Moulin. Tel: 04 91 32 43 57
• 163 av. de Luminy. Tel: 04 91 82 93 89
SRI: 1 allée Bastide des Cyprès, 13100 Aix-en-Provence Cedex 1. Tel: 04
42 17 14 20
• **Aix**: sciences économiques et gestion
• **Marseille**: santé, mécaniques, sport, communication, sciences
économiques et gestion
ACEE: 42 rue du 141e RIA, 13331 Marseille Cedex 3. Tel: 04 91 62 83 85.
acee.marseille@crous-aix-marseille.fr

Université Paul Cézanne: Aix-Marseille III
3 av. Robert Schuman, 13628 Aix-en-Provence Cedex 01. Tel: 04 42 17 28
00. www.univ.u-3mrs.fr
• **Aix**: droit et sciences politiques, études comptables, économie appliquée
• **Marseille**: droit et économie appliquée, sciences et techniques
SCUIO:
• 14 av. Jules Ferry, 13621 Aix-en-Provence Cedex. Tel: 04 42 95 32 23
• 110 la Canebière, Bur. A 1.3, 13001 Marseille. Tel: 04 96 12 61 73
SRI: 1 allée Bastide des Cyprès, 13100 Aix-en-Provence Cedex 1. Tel: 04
42 17 14 20

IUT Marseille: Traverse Charles Susini, 13388 Marseille Cedex 13. Tel: 04 91 28 93 00

Other institution

EUROMED Marseille: Ecole de Management
Domaine de Luminy, BP 921, 13288 Marseille Cedex 09. Tel: 04 91 82 79 53. www.euromed-marseille.com
Affaires internationales; audit; gestion des ressources humaines; finance; marketing, droit, comptabilité, systèmes d'information, logistique, stratégie

University libraries

- Bibliothèque St-Jérôme (Sciences), av. Escadrille Normandie Niémen (Marseille). Tel: 04 91 28 80 42
- Bibliothèque de la Canebière, 110–14 la Canebière (Marseille) Tel: 04 96 12 61 77
- Bibliothèque Droit et Economique, 3 av. R. Schuman (Aix-en-Provence). Tel: 04 42 17 24 40
- Bibliothèque Montperrin, 6 av. de Pigonnet (Aix-en-Provence). Tel: 04 42 95 24 23

Courses for foreign students

IEFEE: Institut d'Etudes Française pour Etudiants Etrangers. Université Paul Cézanne Aix-Marseille III, 25 rue Gaston Saporta, 13265 Aix-en-Provence Cedex 1. Tel: 04 42 21 70 90

CLOUS

42 rue du 141e RIA, 13331. Tel: 04 91 62 83 60. www.crous-aix-marseille. com
ACEE: same address. Tel: 04 91 16 83 85

CROUS-controlled accommodation
- Cité Alice Chatenoud, 10 rue Henri Poincaré. Tel: 04 91 10 11 00
- Cité Claude Delorme, 10 chemin du Bassin. Tel: 04 91 98 32 11
- Cité Gaston Berger, 43 rue du 141e RIA. Tel: 04 91 64 41 73

- Cité Lucien Cornil, 168 rue St Pierre. Tel: 04 91 47 48 76

CROUS restaurants

Restaurants:
- Restaurant de St-Jérôme, av. Henri Poincaré
- Restaurant de Luminy, 171 av. de Luminy
- Restaurant de Galinat, 38 bd Jean Moulin
- Restaurant de l'IMT, Château-Gombert, chemin de la Grave
- Restaurant Gaston Berger, 43 rue du 141e RIA

Cafétérias:
- Cafétéria Saint Charles in the Université de Provence
- Cafétéria de la Canebière in the Faculté de Droit
- Cafétéria de l'IUT, chemin des Géraniums
- Cafétéria de Médecine Nord in the Faculté de Médecine
- Cafétéria Médecine, 27 bd Jean Moulin
- Cafétéria de Pharmacie in the Faculté de Pharmacie

Privately run hostels

All are for male students only.
- Foyer 'Le Phare' 131–133 rue Ferrari, 13005. Tel: 04 91 42 57 70
- Foyer 'Le Home des Etudiants', 35 rue E. Rostand, 13006. Tel: 04 91 37 51 77
- Foyer de la Commanderie, 135 rue de la Commanderie, 13015. Tel: 04 91 60 84 12

Private-sector accommodation

For private-sector accommodation, check the following free local news-papers:
Paru-vendu, Le 13 Marseille, Marseille Hebdo
- Les Estudines Collines de Luminy, rue A. Bourdelle, 13009. Tel: 04 91 82 80 71
- Les Estudines Saint-Jérôme, 40 av. de l'Escadrille Normandie-Niémen, 13013. Tel: 04 95 05 35 05
- La Minoterie, 30 chemin du Bassin, 13014. Tel: 04 91 98 41 61
- Le Quorum, impasse Pindare, 13013. Tel: 04 91 20 30 20
- Résidences J. Vallès et St Sauveur, 59–61 ch. du Marlan, 13014. Tel: 04 91 98 41 61
- Résidence D. Milhaud, traverse Charles Susini, 13013. Tel: 04 91 66 76 07

The town and its surrounding area

Originally a Greek settlement in the seventh century BC, the lively port town of Marseille has accumulated a rich cosmopolitan heritage in becoming France's largest port and second largest town with a population of 1.5 million. For nearly three centuries Marseille's wealth derived not only from its trading port and fishing but also from soap manufacture. This important industry originated in 1660, peaked in 1913 when some 20,000 tons were produced only to decline after World War One. The *vieux port* – once the home to ocean liners and a thriving fishing fleet, and the setting for Pagnol's trilogy *César, Fanny* and *Marius* – is now the centre of a thriving tourist industry with a daily fish market and picturesque cafés and restaurants serving the celebrated local fish stew or *bouillabaisse*. Excursions to Château d'If, the island fortress built to protect Marseille in 1529, are popular amongst tourists perhaps keen to visit the fictional prison of Alexandre Dumas' celebrated Count of Monte Cristo. 'La Marseillaise', originally a march composed by Rouget de l'Isle for the Rhine Army, was adopted as the French national anthem after 600 citizens marching to Paris to join the Revolution popularized the words and music. The town has a number of architectural delights, from early churches (the Abbaye Saint Victor) to the Neo-Byzantine Notre Dame de la Garde, topped by a gilded statue of the Virgin, and the Cathédrale de la Major, which is the largest nineteenth-century church in France. From the port area run narrow, steep streets lined by the elegant façades of eighteenth-century dwellings, which provide a striking contrast to Le Corbusier's enormous housing project, La Cité Radieuse. Of the town's many museums, the Musée des Beaux Arts claims prominence with paintings by Corbet and Rubens. Amongst the famous associated with the city are the caricaturist Honoré Daumier (1808–1879), the dramatist Edmond Rostand (1868–1918) and the influential politicians Emile Ollivier (1825–1913) and Adolphe Thiers (1797–1877), who was also a notable historian. The town has good cultural and sports facilities, including a 60,000-seat arena, and over 45,000 university students. Festivals mark the calendar, in particular Foire aux Santons (last Sunday in November till the end of December) and La Chandeleur (2 February). In the summer months the nearby beaches (la plage du Prado and la plage de la Corniche) are popular among locals. Transport within the town is good with a two-line *métro* supplementing an extensive bus network. For travel further afield, the town enjoys good rail and road links while for air travellers there is the nearby airport of Marseille-Provence.

Tourist information

Tourist office: 4 la Canebière. Tel: 04 91 13 89 00. www.marseille-tourisme.
   com. E-mail: accueil@maresille-tourisme.com

Hotels
The following hotels are reasonably priced and central:
* Hôtel Lutetia, 38 allée Léon Gambetta. Tel: 04 91 50 81 78
* Hôtel Impérial, 87 la Canebière. Tel: 04 91 64 22 22
* Hôtel Alizé, 35 quai des Belges. Tel: 04 91 33 66 97
* Etap Hôtel, 46 rue Sainte. Tel: 0892 680 582

Youth hostel
A.J. Bonneveine, impasse Bonfils, 13008. Tel: 04 91 17 73 30

Restaurants
* L'Ecailler, 10 rue Fortia. Tel: 04 91 54 79 39
* La Manne, 18 bd de la Liberté. Tel: 04 91 50 97 68
* Dar Djerba, 15 cours Julien, Tel: 04 91 48 55 36 (cous-cous)
* O'Provençal Pizzeria, 7 rue de la Palud. Tel: 04 91 54 03 10

Leisure facilities

For listings, see: *In Situ, Le Ventillo, Métro, 20 minutes*

Museums and art galleries
* Musée d'Art Contemporain, 69 bd de Haifa, 8e
* Musée des Beaux Arts. Palais Longchamp, 4e
* Musée d'Histoire Naturelle, Palais Longchamp, 4e
* Musée de la Mode, 11 la Canebière, 1er
* Musée des Docks Romains, place Vivaux, 2e
* Musée Cantini. 19 rue Grignan, 6e
* Musée d'Histoire de Marseille, Centre Bourse, 1er
* Musée Grobelet-Labadié, 140 bd Longchamp, 1er

Theatre
* Théâtre National de Marseille La Criée, 30 quai de Rive Neuve. Tel: 04
   91 54 70 54
* Espace Odéon, 162 la Canebière. Tel: 04 91 92 79 44
* Théâtre du Gymnase, 4 rue du Théâtre Français. Tel: 04 91 24 35 35
* Théâtre les Bernadines, 17 bd Garibaldi. Tel: 04 91 24 30 40

- Théâtre du Merlan, av. Raimu. Tel: 04 91 11 19 20
- Espace Julien, 39 cours Julien. Tel: 04 91 24 34 14
- Théâtre Mazenod, 88 rue Aubagne. Tel: 04 91 54 04 69
- Opéra Municipal, place de l'Opéra. Tel: 04 91 69 08 44
- L'Odéon, 162 la Canebière. Tel: 04 96 12 52 70
- Massalia Théâtre, 41 rue Jobin. Tel: 04 95 04 95 70

Cinema
- Alhambra Cinémarseille, 2 rue du Cinéma. Tel: 04 91 03 84 66
- Le César, 4 place Castellane. Tel: 04 91 37 12 80
- Cinéma Chambord, 283 av. du Prado. Tel: 04 91 25 71 11
- Cinéma de Bonneveine, Centre Commercial Carrefour. Tel: 08 92 62 20 15
- Cinéma les Trois Palmes, 2 bd Léon Bancal. Tel: 08 92 68 20 15
- Cinéma les Variétés, 37 rue Vincent Scotto. Tel: 04 96 11 61 61
- Le Miroir, 2 rue de la Charité. Tel: 04 91 14 58 88
- Pathémadeleine, 36 av. Marechal Foch. Tel: 08 92 68 22 88
- UGC Capitole, 134 la Canebière. Tel: 08 92 68 68 58
- UGC Prado, 36 av. du Prado. Tel: 08 92 68 00 43

Sport
FFSU: 16 rue Bernard du Bois. Tel: 04 91 90 91 38.
CSU/SIUAPS: av. Escadrille de Normandie Nièmen. Tel : 04 91 28 81 05

Useful addresses

Post office: 1 place Hôtel des Postes. Tel: 04 91 15 47 20
Commissariat Central: 2 rue Antoine Berger. Tel: 04 91 39 80 00
Centre des Impôts, 2 rue Borde. Tel : 04 91 17 97 97 (*timbre fiscal*)
Mairie: quai Port. Tel: 04 91 55 11 11
Préfecture des Bouches-du-Rhône, 66 bis rue St Sébastien, 13006. Tel : 04 91 15 68 13 (*carte de séjour*)
Municipal libraries:
- Bibliothèque du Merlan, Centre Commercial du Merlan. Tel: 04 91 12 93 60
- Saint-Charles, 38 rue du 141e RIA. Tel: 04 91 55 36 72
- Panier, 2 rue des Honneurs. Tel: 04 91 91 20 50
Bookshops:
- Librairie des Facultés, 191 bd Baille. Tel: 04 91 47 72 06
- Librairie Maupetit, 142–144 la Canebière. Tel: 04 91 36 50 50
- Librairie Maurel, 95 rue Lodi. Tel: 04 91 42 63 44

- FNAC, Centre Bourse. Tel: 04 91 39 94 00

ANPE:

- 57 rue Brochier. Tel 04 96 12 23 50
- 23 rue Lautard. Tel 04 91 08 25 30

BVE: Faculté des Sciences. Tel: 04 91 28 88 95

CAF: 215 chemin de Gibbes. Tel: 04 91 05 54 54

CPAM: 56 chemin Joseph Aiguier. Tel: 0 820 90 41 86

CRIJ: 96 La Canebière. Tel: 04 91 24 33 50

EDF-GDF: 12 bd National. Tel: 04 91 28 66 29

France Télécom: 11 av. de Luminy. Tel: 04 91 17 24 00

Lost property: 10 rue de la Cathédrale. Tel: 04 91 90 18 21

Internet cafés:

- Cyber-espace CIJPA, 96 la Canebière. Tel: 04 91 24 33 83
- Info-Café, 1 quai Rive, Vieux Port. Tel: 04 91 33 74 98
- Espace Culture Multimédia, 41 rue Jobin. Tel: 04 95 04 95 11

Health care

SUMP:

- 52 av. de l'Escadrille Normandie Niémen. Tel : 04 91 18 95 00
- Jardin de Pharo, 58 bd Charles Livon. Tel : 04 91 39 65 00
- 163 av. Luminy. Tel: 04 91 26 89 08

BAPU: 93 bd Camille Flammarion. Tel: 04 91 50 01 13

Main hospitals:

- Hôpital Laveran, bd Laveran. Tel: 04 91 66 68 11
- Hôpital Ste-Marguerite, 270 bd Ste Marguerite. Tel: 04 91 74 40 80
- Hôpital Timone, bd Jean Moulin. Tel: 04 91 38 50 28

Chemists:

- Pharmacie Centrale, 113 av. Saint-Louis. Tel: 04 91 60 92 92
- Pharmacie de la Gare, Gare St. Charles. Tel: 04 91 05 88 88

Local student insurance offices:

- LMDE : 13 av. Léon Gambetta, 13001. Tel : 0810 600 601
- MEP : 176 bd Baille, 13005. Tel: 0825 081 881

Travel

Railway station
Gare St-Charles, place Victor Hugo. Tel: 08 36 35 35 35

Coach station
place Victor Hugo. Tel: 04 91 08 16 40

Airport
Aéroport Marseille-Provence. Tel: 04 42 14 14 14

Buses and Métro
RTM 6–8 rue des Fabres. Tel: 04 91 91 92 10

Taxis
- Taxi Radio Marseille. Tel : 04 91 02 20 20
- Taxi TUPP. Tel: 04 91 05 80 80
- Taxi du Soleil. Tel : 04 91 44 44 44

Student travel
OTU: 67 la Canebière. Tel: 04 95 09 30 60
Wasteels: 67 la Canebière. Tel: 04 95 09 36 60

Emergencies

All-night chemist: Pharmacie Saint-Louis, 5 cours Saint-Louis. Tel: 04 91 54 04 58
Police: 2 rue du Commissaire Becker. Tel: 04 91 39 80 00
SOS Médecins. Tel: 04 91 52 91 52
Médecins 24/24h. Tel: 04 91 53 24 24
SOS Dentistes. Tel: 04 91 85 39 39
Urgences Dentaires 24/24 h. Tel: 04 91 64 23 23
Centre Anti-poison. Tel: 04 91 75 25 25
SOS Amitié. Tel: 04 91 76 10 10
Le SIDA and MST. Tel: 04 91 78 43 43

14 Metz

Institutions of higher education and their disciplines

Académie de Nancy-Metz
Université Paul Verlaine – Metz
Ile du Saulcy, BP 794, 57012 Metz Cedex 1. Tel: 03 87 31 50 50. www.univ-metz.fr
SRI: Ile du Saulcy, BP 80794, 57012 Metz Cedex 1
SCUIO: Ile du Saulcy, 57012 Metz Cedex. Tel: 03 87 31 50 40
Pôle Universitaire Européen de Lorraine (for practical help): Campus Universitaire, Ile du Saulcy, 57007 Metz. Tel: 03 87 65 81 40

Sciences et techniques, mathématiques, informatique, droit, économie et administration, gestion, lettres, langues, sciences humaines et arts
IUT: Ile du Saucy, BP 794, 57045 Metz Cedex 01. Tel: 03 87 31 51 52

Courses for foreign students

See Nancy (Université de Nancy II)

CLOUS

CLOUS de Metz, 42 Ile du Saulcy, BP 587, 57010 Metz Cedex. Tel: 03 87 31 61 61

CROUS-controlled accommodation
Campus de Saulcy:
• Résidence Saulcy
• Résidence Saint-Quentin
Campus de Technologie:
• Résidence Technopôle
Campus Bridoux:
• Résidence Bridoux

CROUS restaurants
• Campus de Saulcy: Resto'U Baudelaire; Resto'U Rimbaud; Resto'U Verlaine
• Campus du Technopôle: Resto'U Technopôle
• Campus Bridoux: Resto'U Bridoux
• Cafétéria Bridoux, 2 rue Claude Bernard (08.00–14.00)
• Cafétérias Saulcy: RU Rimbaud (09.00–20.00); RU Verlaine (11.30–14.00); Maison de l'Etudiant (10.00–14.00)
• Cafétéria Technopôle, 4 bd Aragon

Private-sector accommodation

• Pythagore Queueleu, 6 rue de Vercly, 57070 Metz
• Amphithéâtre, 76 rue aux Arènes, 57000 Metz
• Pythagore Université, 120–122 route de Thionville, 57050 Metz

The town and its surrounding area

Metz is one of the largest towns in Lorraine with a population of some 130,000 inhabitants. Originally called Divodorum, a prosperous gallo-roman city which was the capital of the 'Mediomatrices', the town was subsequently renamed 'Mettis'. It was converted to Christianity by Saint Clément in the third century, before being sacked by Attila the Hun in 451. Having later become the cradle of the Carolingian dynasty, Metz had a chequered religious and political history which led to its occupation by Henri II in 1552. The siege of the town by Charles Quint was successfully resisted by the Duc de Guise and almost a century later (in 1648), the town was officially attached to France by the Treaty of Westphalia, along with Toul and Verdun. The town was besieged yet again in 1870, this time by the Prussians, and it fell following the Treaty of Frankfurt in 1871. Metz remained in German hands until it was won back from the Kaiser in 1918 by Maréchal Pétain, who relinquished it some twenty years later, when he was head of the Vichy government. It was returned to the French after World War Two. The birthplace of the poet Verlaine (1844–1896), Metz retains architecural vestiges of its mixed Franco-German past and boasts an outstanding Gothic cathedral. Situated some 50 kilometres from Nancy and some 300 kilometres from Paris, it is the administrative capital of Lorraine and boasts a rich cultural life with a whole range of theatrical, musical and festival offerings throughout the year. It is easily reached by plane, being close to both the Aéroport Régional de Metz-Nancy Lorraine and the Aéroport International de Luxembourg. Paris is some three hours away by train.

Tourist information

Office du Tourisme de Metz, 2 place d'Armes, BP 80367, 57007 Metz Cedex. Tel: 03 87 55 53 76 or 78

Hotels
- Hôtel Lafayette, 24 rue des Clercs. Tel: 03 87 75 21 09
- Hôtel Moderne, 1 rue Lafayette. Tel: 03 87 66 57 33
- Hôtel Métropole, 5 place du Général de Gaulle. Tel: 03 87 66 26 22

Youth hostel
Auberge de Jeunesse de Metz, 1 allée de Metz-Plage, 57000 Metz. Tel: 03 87 30 44 02

Restaurants
- Flunch, 17 rue des Clercs. Tel: 03 87 74 44 88
- Brasserie de la Place, 49–51 place Saint Louis. Tel: 03 87 36 52 89

Leisure facilities

Museums and art galleries
- Musées de la Cour d'Or, 2 rue du Haut Poirier. Tel: 03 87 68 25 00
- Galerie D'Art Raymond Schmidt, 17 rue des Jardins. Tel: 03 87 74 01 06
- Galerie Thiam, 30 rue des Clercs. Tel: 03 87 75 28 89
- L'Art du Temps, 25 rue Jardins. Tel: 03 87 74 75 65

Theatre
Opéra Théâtre, place Comédie. Tel: 03 87 75 40 50

Conservatoire
2 rue Paradis. Tel: 03 87 55 54 56

Cinema
- Cinéfil Cinéma Caméo Ariel, 24 rue Palais. Tel: (special rate) 08 92 68 03 89
- Cinéfil Cinéma Palace, 5 rue Fabert. Tel: (special rate) 08 92 68 05 87
- Cinéma Gaumont, 1 place Forum. Tel: 03 87 36 36 36
- Siko, 2 rue Gambetta. Tel: 03 87 18 72 18

Sport
FFSU: Nancy-Metz, Pôle Universitaire Européen, 34 cours Léopold, 54052 Nancy Cedex. Tel: 03 83 17 67 55. www.sport-u-nancy.com
Swimming pools:
- Piscine Belletanche, rue Belletanche. Tel: 03 87 38 00 20
- Piscine de Luxembourg, rue Belle Isle. Tel: 03 87 68 26 50
- Piscine Olympique, 44 rue Lothaire. Tel: 03 87 68 26 40

Useful addresses

ANPE:
- Metz 1, 40 rue Taison. Tel: 03 87 75 12 86
- Metz 2, 2 place Saint Nicholas. Tel: 03 87 75 92 60

CAF: 4 bd Pontiffroy. Tel: 03 87 30 31 31
CPAM: 18–22 rue Haute Selle. Tel: 03 87 39 36 36
Chambre de Commerce et d'Industrie, 10 av. Foch. Tel: 03 87 52 31 00
Espace Multimédia de Metz, 2 rue du Four du Cloître. Tel: 03 87 36 56 56
Mairie de Metz: place d'Armes. Tel: 03 87 55 50 00
Post office: 1 place du Général de Gaulle. Tel: 03 87 56 73 00
CRIJ: 1 rue de Coëtlosquet. Tel: 03 87 69 04 50
Bookshops:

- Hisler-Even, 1 rue Ambroise Thomas. Tel: 03 87 75 07 11
- FNAC, Centre Commercial St Jacques. Tel: 03 87 34 68 68
- Librairie Univers, 51 rue Tanneurs. Tel: 03 87 74 36 11
- Virgin Megastore, 61–63 rue Serpenoise. Tel: 03 87 18 78 38

Internet cafés:

- 11 place de la Cathédrale. Tel: 03 87 76 30 64 (special rate for students)
- Cyber@Plus, 55 bd d'Alsace. Tel: 03 87 74 43 31

Health care

Hôpital Notre-Dame-de-Bon-Secours, 1 place Philippe de Vigneulles. Tel: 03 87 55 31 31
Hôpital Belle-Isle, 2 rue Belle-Isle. Tel: 03 87 34 10 10
LMDE: 8 bd Sérot. Tel: 32 60 LMDE
MGEL: Espace Etudiant MGEL, 11 bd Sérot. Tel: 03 87 30 34 14

Travel

Railway station
Place du Général de Gaulle. Tel: 36 35

Coaches
Les Rapides de Lorraine, 2 rue de Nonnetiers. Tel: 03 87 75 26 62 (coaches to Nancy, etc.)

Buses
TCRM, 1 av. Robert Schuman. Tel: 03 87 76 31 11

Taxis
Tel: 03 87 56 91 92 (at the railway station)

Emergencies

Hôtel de Police: 45 rue Belle-Isle. Tel: 03 87 16 17 17
Gendarmerie: 2 rue Albert Bettannier. Tel: 03 87 56 69 99

15 Montpellier

Institutions of higher education and their disciplines

Académie de Montpellier
Université Montpellier I
5 bd Henri IV, BP 1017, 34006 Montpellier Cedex 1. Tel: 04 67 41 74 00.
 www.univ-montpellier1.fr
SRI: (same address). Tel: 04 67 41 74 32
SCUIO: 3 rue Arc de Morgues, 34006 Montpellier Cedex 01. Tel: 04 67
 61 46 00
Admistration économique et sociale, droit et sciences sociales, sciences
 économiques, santé, sport
Antennes at Nîmes, Le Malzieu-Ville

Université des sciences et des techniques du Languedoc: Montpellier II
Place Eugène Bataillon, 34095 Montpellier Cedex 5. Tel: 04 67 14 30 30.
 www.univ-montp2.fr
SRI: (same address). Tel: 04 67 14 30 26
SCUIO: (same address: Bât. 7). Tel: 04 67 14 30 61
• **Montpellier**: sciences et techniques, administration des entreprises
• **Nîmes**: sciences
Antennes at Bézier, Sète
IUT:
• Montpellier: 99 av. d'Occitanie, 34096 Montpellier Cedex 05. Tel: 04
 67 14 40 40.
• Nîmes: 8 rue Jules Raimu, 30907 Cedex. Tel: 04 66 62 85 00

Université Paul-Valéry: Montpellier III
Route de Mende, 34199 Montpellier Cedex 5. Tel: 04 67 14 20 00. www.
 univ-montp3-fr
SRI: (same address). Tel: 04 67 14 21 31
SCUIO: (same address: Bât. Charles Camproux). Tel: 04 67 14 23 42
• **Montpellier**: lettres, art, sciences humaines, économiques, mathéma-
 tiques et sociales

- **Nîmes**: administration économique, et sociale, arts, sciences humaines et sociales

Antenne at Bézier

Other institutions

ENSAM: Ecole Nationale Supérieure Agronomique de Montpellier
2 place Pierre Viala, 34060 Montpellier Cedex 1. Tel: 04 99 61 22 00. www. agro-montpellier.fr

Formation d'ingénieurs agronomes: agroenvironnement, agrotique, agro-managers, agroalimentaire et agro-industrie, viticulture-oenologie, protection des plantes et de l'environnement, sciences et techniques animales, sciences et techniques des productions végétales, statistiques appliquées

CESI/ITC-BTP: Institut des Techniques de la Construction du BTP
69 impasse MacGaffey-Val de Croze, 34070 Montpellier. Tel: 04 99 51 21 37

Bâtiment et travaux publics

ESC Montpellier: Ecole Supérieure de Commerce
2300 av.des Moulins 34185 Montpellier Cedex 4. Tel: 04 67 10 25 00. www. supdeco-montpellier.com

Spécialisations en quatrième année: audit; contrôle de gestion; crédit management; finance; ingénieur d'affaires en produits et services infor-matiques; international business; marketing; négociation-vente; métiers de la banque; métiers du conseil; négociation en environnement public; management des achats et de la qualité; consultant ERP; commerce international des vins; management des compétences; management des ONG; création d'entreprise; supply chain management; management de projets en net économie, droit des établissements de santé, gestion de projets en technologies émergentes; doing business with Arab and/ or Islamic worlds

University libraries

- Central Services: 60 rue des Etats Généraux. Tel: 04 67 13 43 52
- BU Lettres, route de Mende. Tel: 04 67 14 20 08
- BU Médecine, 2 rue Ecole de Médecine. Tel: 04 67 66 27 77
- BU Pharmacie, 15 av. Charles Flahault. Tel: 04 67 04 30 70
- BU Sciences, place Eugène Bataillon. Tel: 04 67 14 31 28

Courses for foreign students

IEFE: Institut d'Etudes Françaises pour Etrangers: Université Paul Valery, route de Mende, 34199 Montpellier Cedex 5. Tel: 04 67 14 21 01. www.iefe.univ-montp3.fr

CROUS

2 rue Monteil, BP 5053 Montpellier Justice, 34033 Montpellier Cedex. Tel: 04 67 41 50 38. www.crous-montpellier.fr

PUE (Pôle Universitaire Européen): 163 rue A. Broussonnet, 34090. Tel: 04 67 41 67 87 (welcome service for foreign students)

CROUS-controlled accommodation

- Cité Boutonnet, 119 rue du Faubourg Boutonnet, 34053. Tel: 04 67 61 11 31 (767 rooms)
- Cité des Arceaux, 61 bd des Arceaux, 34053. Tel: 04 67 58 17 00 (435 rooms)
- Cité La Colombière, 570 route de Ganges, 34096. Tel: 04 67 04 28 48 (729 rooms)
- Le Triolet, av. Augustin Fliche, 34096. Tel: 04 67 04 10 80 (1,000 rooms)
- Cité Vert-Bois, 192 rue de la Chênaie, 34096. Tel: 04 67 04 02 62 (1,000 rooms)
- Voie Domitienne, 259 voie Domitienne, 34096. Tel: 04 67 04 03 05 (913 rooms)
- Résidence Alain Savary, rue M. et K. Kraft, 34000. Tel: 04 67 63 38 53 (264 *studios*)
- Résidence de Lattes, 4 rue des Jonquilles, 34000 Lattes. Tel: 04 67 58 17 00 (36 *studios*)
- Résidence Colonel Marchand, 6 rue du Colonel Marchand, 34000. Tel: 04 67 61 11 31 (54 *studios*)
- Résidence Minerve, av. de l'abbé Paul Parguel. Tel: 04 67 04 10 80 (196 *studios*)
- Résidence Vert-Bois, 200 av. de Vert-Bois, 34000. Tel: 04 67 04 02 62 (198 *studios*)
- Résidence Alexandrie, 166 rue Messidor, 34000. Tel: 04 67 22 21 05 (128 *studios*)
- Résidence des Arceaux, 61 bd des Arceaux, 34005. Tel: 04 67 58 17 00 (197 *studios*)
- Résidence Agropolis, 98 rue J. François Breton 34000. Tel: 04 67 04 39 14 (204 *studios*)

- Résidence Olympique, allée Pierre Blanchet, 34000. Tel: 04 67 04 39 14 (218 *studios*)

CROUS restaurants

Restaurants:
- RU des Arceaux, rue Gustave
- RU de Boutonnet, 2 rue Emile Duployé
- RU de Vert-Bois, 205 rue de la Chênaie
- RU du Triolet, 1061 rue du Professeur Anglada
- RU Richter, 80 rue Brumaire

Cafeterias:
- Voie Domitienne, 259 rue de la Voie Domitienne
- La Colombière, 570 route de Ganges
- Vert-Bois, 192 rue de la Chênaie
- Odontologie, 55 av. Prof Jean-Louis Vala
- Trioletto, av. Augustin Fiche
- IUFM, place Marcel Godechot

Private-sector accommodation

Addresses of private-sector accommodation can be obtained from the CROUS. Usually two months' rent is payable in advance together with the equivalent of another two months' as a *caution*. Insurance is obligatory.

- Résidence Sun Valley, 400 av. des Moulins. Tel: 04 67 66 02 18
- Résidence Etudiante Observatoire, 1 rue Henri Grunier. Tel: 04 67 58 99 88
- Résidence Etudiante Le Clémenceau, 54 av. Georges Clémenceau
- Résidence Etudiante des Facultés, 71 place Thermidor. Tel: 04 67 15 47 47
- Foyer d'Etudiantes du Carré du Roi, 22 bis Carré du Roi. Tel: 04 67 63 67 09
- Foyer International Theresanium, 6 rue des Carmélites. Tel: 04 67 63 55 49

The town and its surrounding area

In origin a medieval city, Montpellier has been subsequently graced with rich merchants' town houses dating from the seventeenth and eighteenth centuries, and fine public works. It also has several examples of the best of twentieth-century architecture. The Peyrou gardens, the Aqueduc with its magnificent Château d'Eau, the Jardin des Plantes, the Arc de Triomphe, the Place de la Comédie (*l'Oeuf*) with its well-proportioned theatre, all contribute to the beauty of the city. The old quarters with their narrow twisting streets are particularly attractive. Among the more striking modern creations is the imposing Antigone development designed by the Catalonian architect Ricardo Bofill.

Now the prosperous regional *préfecture* of Languedoc-Roussillon with over 230,000 inhabitants, Montpellier is an important administrative, commercial and cultural centre and, with the nearby Mediterranean beaches of Palavas and Carnon, an important tourist area. Inland, the striking Causse region offers several cave systems, including the Grotte de Clamouse, and the picturesque village of Saint Guilhem-le-Désert. The University, founded in 1289, is one of the oldest in Europe and counts among its former students François Rabelais. Montpellier now has three universities, which attract some 55,000 students, and the town is geared to cultural activities, with many theatrical groups, over thirty cinema screens, regular concerts and several good bookshops.

Among the famous associated with Montpellier are Auguste Comte (1798–1857), the founder of Positivism; Pierre Magnol (1638–1715), the botanist credited with plant classification; the artists Sébastien Bourdon (1616–1671), Jean Ranc (1674–1735), F.-X. Fabre (1766–1837) and Frédéric Bazille (1841–1870); and the organ builder Aristide Cavaillé-Coll (1811–1899).

The wines of Languedoc-Roussillon are enjoying increasing esteem and the nearby *bassin de Thau* provides oysters and mussels. The region is known for its fresh fruit and confectionery made from honey and liquorice. A state-of-the-art tramway system is being developed with the second line scheduled for 2006. There are good travel connections with the rest of France and Spain. A TGV service links Montpellier to Paris and the A9 gives access to the motorway system. There are regular flights serving London and New York from the international airport.

Tourist information

Tourist office: 30 allée Jean de Lattre de Tassigny. Tel: 04 67 60 60 60. www.ot-montpellier.fr

Hotels
The following are near the station and convenient for the town centre.

- Hôtel Angleterre, 7 rue Maguelone. Tel: 04 67 58 59 50
- Hôtel Mistral, 25 rue Boussairolles. Tel: 04 67 58 45 25
- Hôtel Colisée-Verdun, 33 rue de Verdun. Tel: 04 67 58 42 63

Youth hostel
Rue des Ecoles Laïques. Tel: 04 67 60 32 22

Restaurants
- Le Feu Follet, 10 rue du petit St-Jean. Tel: 04 67 60 95 04
- La Tomate, 6 rue du Four des Flammes. Tel: 04 67 60 49 38
- Cornélius, 9 rue Puits du Temple. Tel: 04 67 52 82 84

Leisure facilities

Details of cinema, concert and theatre programmes are published in the free listings magazine *Sortir à Montpellier.*

Museums and art galleries
- Musée Fabre, 39 bd Bonne Nouvelle
- Musée Atger, 2 rue Ecole de Médecine
- Musée du Vieux Montpellier, Hôtel de Varenne, 2 place Pétrarque
- Musée Languedocien, 7 rue J. Coeur
- Jardin des Plantes, 163 rue A. Broussonnet

Theatre
- Opéra Berlioz, le Corum. Tel: 04 67 61 66 16
- Opéra Comédie. Tel: 04 67 60 19 99
- Théâtre Gérard Philipe, 7 rue Pagès. Tel: 04 67 58 71 96
- Théâtre du Hangar, 3 rue Nozeran. Tel: 04 67 41 32 71
- Théâtre Iséion, 18 rue Fouques. Tel: 04 67 58 90 78
- Théâtre Lakanal, 17 rue Ferdinand Fabre. Tel: 04 67 64 15 96
- Théâtre Jean Vilar, 155 rue de Bologne. Tel: 04 67 40 41 39
- Théâtre des Treize Vents, domaine de Grammont. Tel: 04 67 99 25 25

Cinema
- Gaumont-Multiplexe, 235 rue Georges Méliès. Tel: 04 99 52 33 00
- Gaumont Comédie, place de la Comédie. Tel: 04 67 60 66 60
- Diagonal-Capitole, 5 rue de Verdun. Tel: 04 67 52 72 00
- Le Royal, 13 rue Boussairolles. Tel: 08 92 68 00 29
- Diagonal Centre, 18 place Saint-Denis. Tel: 08 92 68 00 29

- Diagonal Celleneuve, rue Marcellin Albert. Tel: 04 67 75 41 90
- Diagonal-Campus, 5 av. Docteur-Pezet. Tel: 04 67 52 32 00

Concert halls
- Le Corum, Esplanade Charles de Gaulle. Tel: 04 67 61 67 61
- Conservatoire National, 14 rue Eugène Lisbonne. Tel: 04 67 66 88 40

Sport
FFSU: CSU, 532 rue du Professeur Emile Jeambreau. Tel: 04 67 48 39 18
SUAPS:
- Montpellier I: 15 av. Charles Flahault. Tel: 04 67 54 54 29
- Montpellier II: place Eugène Bataillon. Tel: 04 67 14 30 77
- Montpellier III: route de Mende. Tel: 04 67 14 26 29
Sports centres:
- Salle des Sports Jules Ladoumèque, 419 av. Dr Jacques Forcade. Tel: 04 67 65 30 82
- Complexe Sportif de Grammont, av. A. Einstein. Tel: 04 67 22 29 41
Swimming pools:
- ASPTT, route de Vauguière. Tel: 04 99 52 60 80
- Piscine Pitot, 40 allée Jean Raymond. Tel: 04 67 52 58 59
Ice-skating: Patinoire Végapolis, place de France. Tel: 04 99 52 26 00
Tennis: Complexe Sportif de Grammont, av. A. Einstein. Tel: 04 67 22 29 41
Zoo: parc de Lunaret, 50 av. d'Agropolis, Grammont

Useful addresses

Main post office: place Rondelet. Tel: 04 67 34 50 00
Mairie: 1 place Francis Ponge. Tel: 04 87 34 70 00
Préfecture: 34 place des Martyrs de la Résistance. Tel: 04 67 61 61 61
Commissariat Central: 13 av. Professeur Grasset. Tel: 04 67 22 78 22 (*carte de séjour*)
Lost property: rue des Etuves. Tel: 04 67 60 97 69
Main public library: 240 rue de l'Acropole. Tel: 04 67 34 87 00
Bookshops:
- Book Shop, 6 rue de l'Université. Tel: 04 66 67 09 08 (English books and periodicals)
- FNAC, Centre Commercial Le Polygone, Niveau 1. Tel: 04 67 99 73 00
- Gibert, 3 place des Martyrs de la Résistance. Tel: 04 67 58 63 24

- Sauramps, Le Triangle. Tel: 04 67 06 78 78
- Virgin Megastore, rue de la Loge. Tel: 04 67 63 60 30

ANPE: quai Louis Le Vau, Zac de la Fontaine, Celleneuve. Tel: 04 67 84 78 70

CAF: 8 rue Chaptal. Tel: 0 820 25 34 20

CPAM: 29 rue Gambetta. Tel: 04 99 52 53 54

CRDP: allée de la Citadelle. Tel: 04 67 60 04 50

CRIJ: 3 av. Charles Flahault. Tel: 04 67 04 36 66

DDTE: 615 bd d'Antigone. Tel: 04 67 22 88 67 (temporary work)

EDF-GDF: 17 rue Pont de Lattes. Tel: 0 801 00 34 34

France Télécom: Espace Montpellier Jeunesse. 6 rue Maguelone. Tel: 04 67 92 30 50

Internet cafés:
- Cyberbase, 50 place Zeus. Tel: 04 67 99 61 37
- Le Nautilus, 23 quai des Tanneurs. Tel: 04 67 60 57 57

Health care

SUMPPS:
- Montpellier 1: 15 av. Charles Flahault. Tel: 04 67 54 80 55
- Montpellier 2: Sciences, bât 20, place Eugène Bataillon. Tel: 04 67 14 31 48
- Montpellier 3: Maison de l'Etudiant, 2 route de Mende. Tel: 04 67 14 22 40

Hospitals:
- Hôpital Saint-Eloi, 2 av. Bertin Sans. Tel: 04 67 33 76 52
- Hôpital Saint-Charles, 300 rue A. Broussonnet. Tel: 04 67 33 67 33
- Hôpital Lapeyronie, 191 av. du Doyen Gaston Guiraud. Tel: 04 67 33 67 33

Chemists:
- Pharmacie Blaise-Roques, 1444 route de Mende. Tel: 04 67 52 62 58
- Pharmacie des Facultés, 320 av. Justice de Castelnau. Tel: 04 67 63 80 80
- Pharmacie Gambetta. 30 cours Gambetta. Tel: 04 67 92 05 04

Local student insurance offices:
- LMDE: 22 av. Emile Diacon. Tel: 0 810 600 601
- MEP: 3 place de la Canourgue. Tel: 04 67 66 06 50

Travel

Railway station
Place Auguste Gilbert. Tel: 08 36 35 35 35

Coach station
Place du Bicentenaire. Tel: 04 67 92 01 43

Airport
Aéroport Montpellier-Méditerrannée. Tel: 04 67 20 85 00

Bus and tram
Transports de l'Agglomération de Montpellier (TAM), 6 rue Jules Ferry.
   Tel: 04 67 22 87 87

Taxis
TRDM. Tel: 04 67 10 00 00
Taxis Radio Artisans Montpellier (TRAM). Tel: 04 67 58 10 10

Student travel
OTU: 43 rue de l'Université. Tel: 04 67 66 74 20
Voyages Wasteels: 1 rue Combacérès. Tel: 08 25 88 70 70

Emergencies

Hospital: CHU Lapeyronie, av. Charles Flahault. Tel: 04 67 33 81 67
Police. Tel: 04 67 34 71 00
SOS Médecins, 148 rue Marius Carrieu. Tel: 04 67 03 30 30
SOS Amitié. Tel: 04 67 63 00 63

16 Nancy

Institutions of higher education and their disciplines

Académie de Nancy-Metz
Université Henri Poincaré Nancy I
24–30 rue Lionnais, BP 60120, 54003 Nancy Cedex. Tel: 03 83 68 20 00.
   www.uhp-nancy.fr
SRI: 24–28 rue Lionnais, 54000 Nancy. Tel. 03 83 68 21 40
SCUIO: bd des Aiguillettes, 54506 Vandoeuvre-lès-Nancy Cedex. Tel: 03
   83 68 40 84

Sciences et techniques, mathématiques, informatique, santé
IUT: Nancy-Brabois, Le Montet, 54601 Villers-lès-Nancy Cedex. Tel: 03
   83 68 25 00

Université Nancy II
Rue Baron Louis, BP 454, 54001 Nancy Cedex. Tel: 03 83 34 46 00 www.
   univ-nancy2.fr
SRI: Présidence de l'Université Nancy II, Bureaux 102 et 103, 25 rue
   Baron Louis, BP 254, 54001 Nancy Cedex
SCUIO: 4 rue de la Ravinelle, 54035 Nancy Cedex. Tel: 03 83 36 72 30
Administration économique et sociale, cinéma audiovisuel, mathéma-
   tiques, informatique, gestion, lettres, langues, sciences humaines, droit,
   sciences économiques, commerce
IUT: Nancy-Charlemagne, 2 bis bd Charlemagne, 54000 Nancy. Tel: 03
   83 91 31 31

Courses for foreign students

Département de Français Langue Etrangère, Université de Nancy II, 23
   bd Albert 1er, BP 3397, 54015 Nancy Cedex. Tel: 03 83 96 70 05

Other institutions

Ecole Nationale Supérieure des Mines de Nancy
Formation d'Ingénieurs des Techniques de l'Industrie (FITI), Parc de
   Saurupt, 54042 Nancy Cedex. Tel: 03 83 58 42 32. www.mines.inpl-
   nancy.fr

ICN Ecole de Management
13 rue Michel Ney, 54000 Nancy. Tel: 03 83 39 64 50. www.icn-nancy.
   com
Possibilité de suivre un enseignement entièrement en anglais pour
   l'obtention du BBA (Bachelor in Business Administration); marketing
   et e-commerce, finance et audit, management des organisations, international business (en anglais), expertise comptable, entrepreneuriat,
   SIO, l'entreprise e-business, management des hommes, modélisation
   financière, intelligence économique, audit, décisions; cultures anglo-
   saxonnes (en anglais), médias interactifs

Ecole Nationale Supérieure d'Agronomie et des Industries Alimentaires
2 av. de la Fôret de Haye, BP 172, 54505 Vandoeuvre-lès-Nancy Cedex.
   Tel: 03 83 59 59 59. www.ensaia.inpl-nancy.fr
Formation d'ingénieurs agronomes

Institut National Polytechnique de Lorraine
2 av. de la Forêt de Haye, ZAC de Brabois, BP 3, 54501 Vandoeuvre-lès-
   Nancy Cedex. Tel: 03 83 59 59 59. www.inpl-nancy.fr
Agronomie, électricité, énergétique, métallurgie, géologie

CROUS

75 rue de Laxou, 54042 Nancy Cedex. Tel: 03 83 91 88 29. www.crous-
   nancy-metz.fr
OTU: Tel: 08 25 88 70 70. www.routard.com/guide_agence_detail/id/185.
   htm

Crous-controlled accommodation

• Résidence de Boudonville, 61 rue de Boudonville, CS 5207, 54052
  Nancy Cedex (684 rooms)
• Résidence Monbois, 2 rue Ludovic Beauchet, CS 5208, 54052 Nancy
  Cedex (148 rooms plus 340 refurbished rooms, of which 150 have their
  own toilet; 350 T1)
• Résidence La Batelière, 7–15 route de Metz, 54320 Maxéville (201 T1;
  26 T1 bis, 26 T1 bis for two people)

CROUS restaurants

• Campus de l'Ecole des Mines: Resto'U Saurupt
• Campus Sciences et Médecine: Resto'U Vandoeuvre, Resto'U Brabois
• Campus de l'IUT Charlemagne (Nancy II): Resto'U Médreville
• Campus de l'Ecole d'Architecture: Resto'U Stanislas Meurthe, Resto'U
  Cours Léopold
• Campus Droit: Resto'U Cours Léopold
• Campus Droit: Resto'U Monbois, Resto'U IFRAS

Private-sector accommodation

• Les Estudines Saint Dizier, 11 rue Saint Jean, 54000 Nancy
• Les Estudines Stanislas, 48 av. du XXe Corps, 54000 Nancy
• Les Lauréades de Nancy, 203–205 av. du Général Leclerc, 54500
  Vandoeuvre-Lès-Nancy

The town and its surrounding area

Nancy is situated some 310 kilometres to the east of Paris and is easily accessible by road and rail from the capital. There is a small local airport with flights to Paris, but flights from the UK to Luxembourg offer the best service for British students. Nancy is the historical capital of the Duché de Lorraine. The *vieille ville* is what remains of the town which was developed in the Middle Ages by the Dukes of Lorraine. Charles le Téméraire, Duke of Burgundy, met his death there in 1477 when he was defeated by René II, Duke of Lorraine, in an unsuccessful attack on the refortified town. In 1725, ex-king Stanislas of Poland married his daughter to Louis XV of France and received the Duchy of Lorraine in 1737. He was the last Duke and Lorraine became French on his death in 1766. Le Palais Ducal (only one part of the original façade still stands) now houses the Musée Historique Lorrain which has an outstanding collection. L'Eglise des Cordeliers, adjacent to the Palais, was consecrated in 1487 and contains the tombs of several of the Ducs de Lorraine. The *ville neuve* goes back to the end of the sixteenth century and Charles III; there still remains the Porte de la Graffe, the Porte Notre Dame, the Porte Saint Georges and the Porte Saint Nicholas. The most outstanding architectural feature of the town is undoubtedly the magnificent Place Stanislas (formerly Place Royal), which dates from 1750 to 1755 and is the work of the local architect Emmanuel Héré (1705–1763) and of the famous iron-master Jean Lamour (1698–1771). The shopping centre is excellent and contains a wide range of shops from boutiques to department stores. The local buses and trolley-buses offer a good service. The cultural life of the town has a lot to offer: cinemas, theatre, opera, ballet, jazz clubs, dance, classical concerts and a whole range of sporting activities. A most useful Internet site for current cultural activities is www.spectacles-publications.com/spectacles-nancy. php

Tourist information

Office de Tourisme de Nancy, 14 place Stanislas, 54000. Tel: 03 83 35 22 41

Hotels
- Hôtel Foch, 8 av. Foch. Tel: 03 83 32 88 50 (near town centre and railway station)
- Hôtel Ibis, 3 rue Crampel. Tel: 03 83 32 90 16
- Hôtel Les Portes d'Or, 21 rue Stanislas. Tel: 03 83 35 42 34

Restaurants

- La Bolée, 47 rue des Ponts. Tel: 03 83 37 17 53. www.chez.com/labolée (a *crêperie* popular with students)
- Les Césars, 8 place Stanislas. Tel: 03 83 32 08 86. www.lescesarsnancy. fr (inexpensive; seats 200 people; open every day)
- Excelsior, 50 rue Henri Poincaré. Tel: 03 83 35 24 57. www.brasserie-excelsior.com (inexpensive; seats 160 people; open every day)
- Le Bouchon Lyonnais, 15 rue des Maréchaux. Tel: 03 83 37 55 77. www.bouchon-lyonnais.com (seats 70 people; open every day)
- Chez Marie-Pierre, Marché Couvert, place Henri-Mengin. Tel: 03 83 35 31 49. www.poissonnerieschaller.com (seats 32 people; closed Sunday evening and Monday evening)
- Le Vivier, 13 rue des Maréchaux. Tel: 03 83 30 05 05. www.le-vivier. com (seats 70 people; closed Saturday lunchtime and Sunday)

Leisure facilities

Museums, art galleries and churches

- Palais Ducal et Musée Lorrain, 64 Grande Rue (reduction for students)
- Musée des Arts et Traditions Populaires, Couvent des Cordeliers, 66 Grande Rue
- Eglise des Cordeliers et Chapelle Ducale, 66 Grande Rue (visits leave daily from the Musée Lorrain)
- Musée de l'Ecole de Nancy, 36–38 rue Sergent Blandan (contains works which are characteristic of the French contribution to Art Nouveau [Daum, Gallé, Majorelle, etc.]; reduction for students)
- Musée des Beaux-Arts, 3 place Stanislas (free to students on Wednesdays)

Cinema

- UGC Nancy Saint Jean, 3 rue Bénit, and 54 rue Saint Jean. General number: 08 92 70 00 00
- UGC Saint Sebastien, 6 rue Léopold Lallement
- Caméo Art et Essai, 16 rue de la Commanderie

Opera

Opéra de Nancy et de Lorraine, 1 rue Sainte Catherine, 54000 Nancy. Tel: 03 83 85 33 20

Sport

FFSU: Nancy-Metz, Pôle Universitaire Européen, 34 cours Léopold, 54052 Nancy Cedex. Tel: 03 83 17 67 55. www.sport-u-nancy.com

Swimming pools:

- Piscines de Nancy-Thermal, 43 rue du Sergent Blandan. Tel: 03 83 41 53 53
- Piscine Olympique de Gentilly, av. Raymond Pinchard. Tel: 03 83 96 15 46
- Piscine et Gymnase Pierre de Coubertin, av. Raymond Pinchard. Tel: 03 83 98 39 17

Useful addresses

Préfecture: 1 rue Préfet Claude Erignac. Tel: 03 83 34 26 26

Mairie de Nancy: 1 place Stanislas, 54000. Tel: 03 83 85 30 00

Commissariat Police: 38 bd Lobau. Tel: 03 83 17 27 37

Chamber of Commerce: 53 rue Stanislas. Tel: 03 83 85 54 54

ANPE: Nancy Stanislas, 6 bd du 21e RA. Tel: 03 83 91 66 66

CAF: 21 rue Saint Lambert. Tel: 08 20 25 25 10

CPAM: 9 bd Joffre, 54047 Nancy Cedex. Tel: 03 83 85 50 00

CRIJ: 20 quai Claude Le Lorrain, 54000 Nancy. Tel: 03 83 37 04 46

Post office: 10 rue Saint Dizier, 54000 Nancy. Tel: 03 83 39 75 20

Internet café: E-Café, 11 rue des Quatre Eglises. Tel: 03 83 35 47 34

Médiathèque: 10 rue Baron Louis. Tel: 03 83 39 00 63

Municipal library: 43 rue Stanislas, 54000. Tel: 03 83 37 38 83

Bookshops:

- Hall du Livre, 38 rue Saint-Dizier. Tel: 03 83 35 53 01
- Librairie Didier, 6 rue Gambetta. Tel: 08 83 32 00 63 (student reduction available)
- FNAC, 2 av. Foch. Tel: 03 83 17 37 37

CIO: 15 rue Lyautey. Tel: 03 83 36 73 58

Health care

Hôpital Central, 29 av. du Maréchal de Lattre de Tassigny. Tel: 03 83 85 85 85

LMDE, 55 ter, rue Stanislas, CS 5234. Tel: 32 60 LMDE

MGEL, 44 cours Léopold. Tel: 03 83 300 300

Travel

Railway station
3 place Thiers. Tel: (information and bookings) 36 35

Coach station (for airport)
35 bis rue Malzéville. Tel: 03 83 30 97 17

Local buses and trolley-buses
CGFTE, 59 rue Marcel Brot, 54000 Nancy. Tel: 03 83 30 86 00; (information) 03 83 30 08 08

Taxis
Taxi Nancy, 2 bd Joffre. Tel: 03 83 37 65 37

Emergencies

Centre Anti-poison (Hôpital Central). Tel: 03 83 32 36 36
SOS Amitié Lorraine. Tel: 03 83 35 35 35
Drogues alcool tabac info service. Tel: (free phone) 0 800 23 13 13
Ecoute canabis. Tel: (special rate) 0 811 91 20 20
Ecoute alcool. Tel: (special rate) 0 811 91 30 30

17 Nantes

The institutions of higher education and their disciplines

Académie de Nantes
Université de Nantes
1 quai de Tourville, BP 1026, 44035 Nantes Cedex 01. Tel: 02 40 99 83 83.
    www.univ-nantes.fr
SCUIO: chemin de la Censive du Tertre, 44072 Cedex 03. Tel: 02 40 14
    12 12
SRI: Division des Relations Internationales, 1 quai de Tourville, BP 13522,
    44035. Tel: 02 40 99 84 32
Sciences et techniques, santé, lettres, sciences humaines, langues, droit et
    sciences politiques, sciences économiques et de gestion
Antennes at St Nazaire and La Roche-sur-Yon
IUT: 3 rue du Maréchal Joffre, BP 34103, 44041 Cedex 1. Tel: 02 40 30
    60 90

Other institutions

Polytech' Nantes
Site de la Chantrerie, rue Christian Pauc, BP 50609, 44306 Cedex 3. Tel: 02 40 68 32 00. www.polytech.univ-nantes.fr
Ingénieurs en cinq spécialités: génie électrique; sciences des matériaux; systèmes électroniques et informatique industrielle; systèmes informatiques (logiciels et réseaux); thermique et énergétique

Audencia–Nantes Ecole de Management. Ecole Supérieure de Commerce
8 route de la Jonelière, BP 31222, 44312 Cedex 3. Tel: 02 40 37 34 34. www.audencia.com
Huit majeurs ou spécialisations: dirigeants et entrepreneurs; management des nouvelles technologies; management des institutions culturelles et industries multimédias; marketing-vente chef de produit; marketing-vente responsable commercial; finance; contrôle de gestion-audit; gestion des ressources humaines

Ecole centrale de Nantes (ECN)
1 rue de la Noë, BP 92101, 44321 Cedex 03. Tel: 02 40 37 16 00. www.ec-nantes.fr
Formation d'ingénieurs généralistes associant la mécanique, l'électronique et les matériaux

Ecole Nationale Supérieure des Techniques Industrielles et des Mines des Nantes
4 rue A. Kastler, la Chantrerie, BP 20722, 44307 Cedex 3. Tel: 02 51 85 81 00. www.emn.fr
Ingénieur pluridisciplinaire en génie des systèmes industriels (conception, étude, développement, fabrication, contrôle et service après-vente d'un produit ou processus industriel). Trois domaines majeurs: informatique, automatique-productique, sciences de l'homme et de la société

University library

Chemin de la Censive du Tertre, BP 32211, 44000. Tel: 02 40 14 12 30

Courses for foreign students

Institut de Recherche et de Formation en Français Langue Etrangère (IRFFLE)

Chemin de la Censive du Tertre, BP 81227, 44312 Cedex 3. Tel: 02 40 14 10 39

Term-time courses: courses are offered from beginners onwards, on the basis of 18 hours per week (216 per semester) in language and civilization, plus support courses of 4 to 6 hours a week for those already versed in the language, and special courses for students on ERASMUS exchanges.

CROUS

2 bd Guy Mollet, BP 52213, 44322 Cedex 3. Tel: 02 40 37 13 13. www. crous-nantes.fr

OTU: 14 rue Santeuil, 44000. Tel: 02 40 73 99 17

CROUS-controlled accommodation

Town centre:

- Cité Chanzy, 1 rue Henri Lasne, 44042 Cedex 1 (250 rooms with shower and fridge)
- Cité Casterneau, 1 rue André Baugé, 44042 Cedex 1 (302 traditional rooms)
- Cité Santeuil, 14 rue Santeuil, 44000 (40 traditional rooms)
- Cité Berlioz, 81 rue de la Gaudinière, 44322 Cedex 3 (330 traditional rooms)
- Résidence J. Tusques, 3 rue des Epinettes, 44100 (61 T1, 11 T1 bis, 4 T2)

On campus:

- La Bourgeonnière, 5 rue des Renards, 44072 Cedex 3 (495 traditional rooms)
- Cité Launay Violette, chemin de Launay Violette, BP 12218, 44322 Cedex 3 (300 traditional rooms)
- Fresche Blanc, 51 rue de la Bourgeonnière, 44322 Cedex 3 (412 traditional rooms)
- Les Landes, 36 rue des Landes, 44300 (203 T1, 31 T1 bis, 2 T2)
- Résidence J. Tymen, esplanade de la Pierre Percée, 44300 (180 T1, 26 T1 bis)

There is also some accommodation available in HLM: Service HLM, 81 rue de la Gaudinière, BP 62205, 44100. Tel: 02 40 16 02 60

CROUS restaurants

In town:

- Grill Chanzy (incorporates the cafeteria Le Square) (traditional meals and snacks)

- Cafétéria de l'IUT, 3 rue du Maréchal Joffre (sandwiches, quiches, pastries)
- Ricordeau, 1 place A. Ricordeau, 44000 (traditional meals plus grills, pizzas and snacks; the only restaurant open on Friday evening and Saturday lunchtime)
- Catétéria UFR Médecine (fast food and snacks)

On campus:

- Le Rubis, 2 route de la Jonelière (traditional meals, midday weekdays only)
- Le Tertre, 4 route de la Jonelière (traditional meals and other options)
- La Lombarderie, 30 rue de la Haute Forêt (traditional meals and other options)
- Cafétérias des UFR Droit et Lettres (sandwiches, salads, pastries)
- Cafétéria UFR Sciences (sandwiches, salads, pastries)

At Atlantech:

- La Chantrerie, 4 rue Christine Pauc (traditional meals and other options)
- Ecole Vétérinaire (within the establishment; traditional meals)

Private-sector residences

- Stud'Inn, 50 rue de l'Ouche Buron, 44300 La Beaujoire. Tel: 02 40 50 04 05
- Top Campus, 6 av. du Petit Port. Tel: 02 51 81 75 75
- Les Lauréades de Nantes, 13–15 rue Pitre Chevalier, 44000. Tel: 0825 332 332
- Résidence La Brunellière, 6 rue Mathurin Brissonneau, 44100. Tel: 02 51 84 84 84

Privately run hostels

For details, write to the *Directeur/Directrice*:

- Résidence Sonocotra, Ile de Beaulieu, 3 bd des Martyrs Nantais, 44200. Tel: 02 40 47 84 12
- Foyer de l'Edit de Nantes (FJT), 1 rue de Gigant, 44100. Tel: 02 40 73 41 46
- FJT Port Beaulieu, 2 bd Vincent Gache 44200. Tel: 02 40 12 24 00
- FJT Porte Neuve, 1 place Ste Elisabeth, 44000. Tel: 02 40 20 63 63
- FFJT les Hauts St Aignan, 1 place Pilleux, 44100. Tel: 02 40 12 24 00
- Résidence Sanitat, 18 rue d'Alger. Tel: 02 40 35 32 66

- Résidence Brunellière, 6 rue Mathurin Brissonneau. Tel: 02 51 84 84 84
- Le Caprice, 3 rue du Marais. Tel: 02 40 89 60 60

The town and its surrounding area

Situated some 390 kilometres to the south-west of Paris, Nantes can be reached easily by rail (a TGV service was introduced in late 1989), by air, or indeed by road, via Le Mans and the A11, or along the picturesque route north of the Loire. It is the *préfecture* of the Loire-Atlantique, a bustling modern town of 280,000 or so inhabitants. It has long been one of France's principal ports: its position at the eastern end of the Loire estuary meant that it was prominent in trade with the colonies across the Atlantic Ocean, especially in sugar and slaves. Today the Port Autonome de Nantes Saint-Nazaire is the biggest such development on the Atlantic coast, and the fourth most important in France.

In recent times, the town has diversified and extended its industrial base. To traditional activities such as shipbuilding, smelting and food processing, themselves transformed and revitalized, have been added the aeronautics, electronics and nuclear industries. It has developed into an important financial and administrative centre, too. Yet it remains a very pleasant, if somewhat congested, town, with interesting parks and gardens, and a marked cultural heritage. The Cathédrale Saint-Pierre et Saint-Paul (begun in 1434), the Château des Ducs de Bretagne (late fifteenth century and early sixteenth century) and the architecture of the Ile Feydeau, for example, attract a constant flow of tourists. Distinguished figures connected with the town's past include Pierre Abélard (1079–1142), theologian and philosopher, the politician Aristide Briand (1862–1932), the Napoleonic general Pierre Cambronne (1770–1842), and the writer Jules Verne (1828–1905). The Duchesse Anne, twice Queen of France, was crowned for the second time in the Château in Nantes, and bequeathed her heart to her birthplace.

Nantes is well situated for access to both *château* country to the east, and to the South Brittany coast. La Baule, with its excellent sandy beaches, is only a good hour's drive away, while in the hinterland there is Guérande and the Parc National de Brière.

Cultural and sports facilities are good. There are special opportunities for water and marine sports in the area. The local Association France-Grande-Bretagne welcomes students to its meetings; though it caters for a rather different age-group, it can prove a useful initial point of contact. Equally, the Accueil Familial (see notices in the halls and elsewhere in late

September or early October) is very efficient at putting foreign students in touch with local families. Keen musicians should find no difficulty in joining one of the local bands or orchestras.

Tourist information

Office de Tourisme de Nantes Atlantique, place du Commerce, BP 64106, 44041 Nantes Cedex 1. Tel: 02 40 20 60 00. www.nantes-tourisme.com

Hotels

There are a number of convenient two- and three-star hotels near to the station, including:

- Hôtel de Bourgogne, 9 allée du Commandant Charcot, 44000. Tel: 02 40 74 03 34

Also well situated are:

- Hôtel des Trois Marchands, 26 rue Armand Brossard, 44000. Tel: 03 40 47 62 00 (quiet, near the cathedral)
- Hôtel St Daniel, 4 rue du Bouffay, 44000. Tel: 02 40 47 41 25

Youth hostel

La Manu, 2 place de la Manu, 44000. Tel: 02 40 29 29 20 (a student residence which becomes a youth hostel over the summer months)

Restaurants

- La Ciboulette, 9 rue Saint Pierre. Tel: 02 40 47 88 71 (inexpensive lunchtime meals)
- Chez le Gaulois, 8 rue de la Paix. Tel: 02 40 08 22 98 (demanding meat restaurant!)
- La Cigale, 4 place Graslin. Tel: 02 51 84 94 94 (famous brasserie, Art Nouveau décor)

The combination of an abundant range of local sea-food and local Muscadet (or Gros Plant, if you prefer it) offers real gastronomic delights in the restaurants that line the pedestrian streets around place du Bouffay.

Leisure facilities

Museums and art galleries

- Musée des Beaux-Arts, 10 rue Georges Clémenceau
- Musée du Château des Ducs de Bretagne, 1 place Marc Elder
- Musée Thomas Dobrée, place Jean V/rue Voltaire

- Muséum d'Histoire Naturelle, 12 rue Voltaire
- Musée Jules Verne, 3 rue de l'Hermitage
- Musée de l'Imprimerie, 24 quai de la Fosse
- Musée des Compagnons du Devoir, 14 rue C. Guillon Verne
- Musée de la Poste, 2 bis rue Président Herriot
- Musée Naval Maillé Brézé, quai de la Fosse

Theatre

- Théâtre Graslin Opéra de Nantes, 1 rue Molière, 44000. Tel: 02 40 41 90 77
- Maison de la Culture de Loire-Atlantique, 10 passage Pommeraye, 44000. Tel: 02 51 88 25 25
- Le Lieu Unique, quai Ferdinand Favre, BP 21304, 44013 Cedex 1. Tel: 02 40 12 14 34
- Le Terrain Neutre, 11 allée Maison Rouge, 44000. Tel: 02 40 12 12 28
- Théâtre du Sphinx, 9 rue Monteil, 44000. Tel: 02 40 89 19 09
- Théâtre Universitaire, Petit chemin de la Censive du Tertre, BP 2222, 44322 Cedex 3. Tel: 02 40 14 12 79
- Cité des Congrès, 5 rue Valmy, BP 2410, 44041 Cedex 1. Tel: 02 51 88 20 00
- Espace 44, 10 passage Pommeraye, 44000. Tel: 02 51 88 25 25

In addition, there are a number of *cafés-concerts*, *cafés-théâtres* and *centres sociaux et culturels*. Full details are available from the Office de Tourisme.

Cinema

- Allkom, 1 bis rue Paul Claudel, 44300. Tel: 02 51 77 12 70
- Cinématographe, 12 bis rue des Carmélites. Tel: 02 40 47 94 80
- Concorde, 79 bd de l'Egalité. Tel: 02 40 46 25 29
- Gaumont, 12 place du Commerce. Tel: 02 40 48 24 72
- Katorza, 3 rue Corneille. Tel: 02 51 84 90 60
- Bonne Garde, 20 rue du Frère Louis. Tel: 02 40 75 11 08

Sport

Directions Départementales Jeunesse et Sports: av. François Boussais, 44300. Tel: 02 40 52 44 44

SUAPS: 3 bd Guy Mollet, 43000. Tel: 02 40 76 00 84

The SUAPS organizes a comprehensive programme of activities at various levels covering a wide range of sports. The Association Sportive de l'Université de Nantes facilitates entry into the various championships organised by the FFSU.

Comité Régional du Sport Universitaire: 1 rue Douarnenez, 44300. Tel: 02 40 94 49 50

FFSU: same address and telephone number.

Office Municipal des Sports, 17 rue du Moulin, 44000. Tel: 02 40 47 75 54

Halle des Sports SUAPS, 3 bd Guy Mollet, 44300. Tel: 02 40 76 00 84

Stade de Beaulieu/Michel Lecointre, rue André Tardieu, 44200. Tel: 02 40 47 86 59

Football: Stade de la Beaujoire, bd de la Beaujoire, 44300 (the home pitch of the professional club, FCN). Tel: 0892 707 937

Skating: chemin de la Censive du Tertre. Tel: 02 40 74 01 77

Swimming:
- Piscine Léo-Lagrange, allée de l'Ile Gloriette. Tel: 02 40 99 26 50
- La Durantière, 11 rue de la Durantière. Tel: 02 40 58 24 90
- Jules Verne, rue Grandjouan. Tel: 02 51 89 16 20
- Petit Port, bd du Petit Port. Tel: 02 51 84 94 51

A local directory of sports clubs may be consulted at the Office Municipal des Sports (see above).

Useful addresses

Main post office: place de Bretagne, 44000. Tel: 02 51 82 57 00

Municipal library: rue Gambetta, 44041 Cedex. Tel: 02 40 41 95 95

Bookshops:
- FNAC, place du Commerce, BP 63215, 44032. Tel: 02 51 72 47 24
- Forum du Livre, rue Feltre, 44000. Tel: 02 40 12 13 94

ANPE: Agence Viarme, 4 rue Erlon, 44000. Tel: 02 51 88 64 64

CRIJ, 28 rue du Calvaire, BP 80214, 44002. Tel: 02 51 72 94 50

CAF, 22 rue de Malville Viarme, 44044. Tel: 02 51 83 33 33

Mairie de Nantes, rue de l'Hôtel de Ville. Tel: 02 40 41 90 00

Préfecture, 6 quai Ceinery, BP 33515, 44035 Cedex 1. Tel: 02 40 41 20 20

Internet access: Cyber City, 14 rue Strasbourg. Tel: 02 40 89 57 92

Health care

Hospitals (CHU):
- Hôtel-Dieu, place Alexis Ricordeau, 44093. Tel: 02 40 08 33 33
- Saint-Jacques, 85 rue Saint-Jacques, 44093 Cedex 1. Tel: 02 40 08 33 33
- Hôpital Nord Laënnec, bd Jacques Monod, 44093 Saint-Herblain. Tel: 02 40 08 33 33

CPAM: 9 rue Gaëton Rondeau, 44958 Cedex 9. Tel: 0820 904 187

SUMPPS: 5 rue du Maréchal Joffre, 44000. Tel: 02 40 74 62 38. Free medical treatment is available by appointment, as well as the usual range of specialist consultation and counselling services.

Local student insurance offices:

- LMDE, 1 rue Pierre Chéreau, 44000. Tel: 02 40 48 66 63
- SMEBA, 7 allée Duguay Trouin, 44000. Tel: 02 40 35 90 90

Travel

Railway station
27 bd de Stalingrad. Tel: 08 36 35 35 35. Tickets and information are also available from the SNCF ticket office in the town centre: La Bourse, 12 place de la Bourse.

Coach stations
Allée Baco; Champ de Mars; allée Duquesne. Tel: 02 40 47 62 70 **or** 0825 087 156

Eurolines has an office in allée de la Maison Rouge. Tel: 02 51 72 02 03

Airport
Nantes-Atlantique. Tel: 02 40 84 80 00

Taxis
Tel: 02 40 63 66 66 **or** 02 40 69 22 22

Buses and trams
SEMITAN, 3 rue Bellier, BP 64605, 44046 Cedex 1. Tel: 0810 444 444

Emergencies

Duty doctor or chemist. Tel: 02 40 37 21 21
Nantes Permanence Médicale. Tel: 02 40 35 26 26
SAMU. Tel: 02 40 08 22 22
SOS Médecins. Tel: 02 40 50 30 30
Centre Anti-poison. Tel: 02 41 48 21 21
SOS Amitié. Tel: 02 40 04 04 04
Sida Info Service (free and anonymous). Tel: 0 800 840 800
Hôtel de Police: 6 place Waldeck Rousseau. Tel: 02 40 37 21 21

18 Nice

Institutions of higher education and their disciplines

Académie de Nice
Université de Nice-Sophia Antipolis
Parc Valrose, 28 av. de Valrose, 06108 Nice Cedex 2. Tel: 04 92 07 60 60.
www.unice.fr
SCUIO: bd Edouard Herriot, Bât. H 06204 Nice Cedex. Tel: 04 93 37 54
83
Lettres, arts, sciences humaines, droit, économie, gestion, sciences, santé,
sport, administration des entreprises
Antenne at Cannes
IUT Nice: 41 bd Napoléon III, 06041 Cedex. Tel: 04 97 25 82 00

Other institution

CERAM Sophia Antipolis: Ecole Supérieure de Commerce
BP 085. 06092 Sophia Antiplolis Cedex. Tel: 08 20 42 44 44. www.ceram.
edu
Majeures de troisième année: marketing grande consommation; management du service; marketing B to B; conseil en systèmes d'information;
audit et conseil; finance de marché; finance d'entreprise; entreprises
innovantes; e-business; ressources humaines et management de change-
ment

Courses for foreign students

CUEFLE: Centre Universitaire d'Enseignement en Français Langue
Etrangère
UFR Lettres, Arts et Sciences Humaines, 98 bd E. Herriot, BP 3209,
06204 Nice Cedex 3. Tel: 04 93 37 53 83

CROUS

18 av. des Fleurs, 06050 Nice Cedex 1. Tel: 04 92 15 50 50. www.crous-
nice.fr

CROUS-controlled accommodation

• Résidence Baie des Anges, 55 route St Antoine de Ginestière, 06200.

Tel: 04 92 15 81 00 (mixed; 461 rooms)
- Résidence St Antoine, 69 route de St Antoine de Ginestière, 06200. Tel: 04 93 86 37 19 (mixed; 352 rooms)
- Résidence Collinettes, 3 av. Robert Schuman, 06000. Tel: 04 93 97 06 64 (females; 247 rooms)
- Résidence Montebello, 96 av. Valrose, 06100. Tel: 04 93 84 19 81 (mixed; 408 rooms)
- Résidence Jean Médecin, 25 rue Robert Latouche, 06200. Tel: 04 93 83 34 61 (mixed; 898 rooms)
- Résidence La Madeleine, 150 bd de la Madeleine (196 rooms)
- Résidence les Dolines, 2255 route des Dolines Valbonne (222 rooms)

CROUS restaurants
Five self-service restaurants with fixed opening hours are backed by cafeterias open all day. The full choices of *la restauration diversifiée* exist alongside the *menu traditionnel*.
- Restaurant Nice Carlone, 80 bd Edouard Herriot
- Restaurant Nice Centre, 5 av. Robert Schuman
- Restaurant Montebello, 96 av. Valrose
- Restaurant de la CU Jean Médecin, 25 av. Robert Latouche
- Cafétéria de l'IUT, 41 bd Napoléon III

Private-sector accommodation

Les Estudines Méditerranée, 37 av. de la Bornala. Tel: 04 93 37 64 44
Résidence Régency, 2 rue Sanint-Siagre. Tel: 04 93 62 17 44
Einstein Valley 8, 143 bis rue de France. Tel: 04 93 44 00 36

The town and its surrounding area

With over three miles of beaches, the beautiful Baie des Anges and an exceptional climate, Nice is well known as an attractive holiday centre. However, it is also a town with an interesting history, a rapidly expanding university and a commitment to adding new business ventures to the horticultural and tourist industries in which it has long been pre-eminent. The local roses, in particular, have a world-wide reputation. The town of Nice only became definitively French by the treaty of 1860 which ceded the territories previously held by the Dukes of Savoy. The first settlers were Greek traders and though little of their influence remains there are several vestiges of their Roman successors such as the Arènes de Cimiez. Now among the largest of French towns with a population approaching

350,000, Nice, prosperous and cosmopolitan, has over 24,000 students contributing to its lively atmosphere. There are several museums of note as well as an opera house, theatres and cinemas, not to mention the various cultural activities which take place throughout the year. No visitor should miss the renowned Jazz Festival in July, nor the colourful Carnival in February with its spectacular *Bataille des Fleurs*. The architecture of the town reflects its fashionable past with elegant Belle Epoque buildings, the Opera, landscaped parks and gardens such as the Espace Masséna, the Jardin Albert 1er or the Place Ile de Beauté. Amongst the town's famous sons are the two military geniuses Garibaldi (1807–1882) and Masséna (1758–1817), the artist Carle Vanloo (1705–1765), and celebrated economist Auguste Blanqui (1805–1881). The food and wine of the region are particularly distinctive: the Bellet wines are increasingly appreciated while amongst other regional delights for the palate are to be found *salade niçoise, pissaladière, pan bagnat, socca, soupe au pistou, estocaficada* and *gnocchis*. The town is well served by rail, road and air with a TGV service, the A7 motorway, and the international airport, Nice-Côte d'Azur.

Tourist information

Office du Tourisme: 5 promenade des Anglais, Nice 06302. Tel: 08 92 70
    74 07. www.nice-coteazur.org
Accueil de France, Gare SNCF, av. Thiers. Tel: 04 93 87 07 07

Hotels
Nice has a rich assortment of hotels. The following are among the more modestly priced in the central area:
- Hôtel Darcy, 24 rue d'Angleterre. Tel: 04 93 88 67 06
- Hôtel Lyonnais, 20 rue de Russie. Tel: 04 93 88 70 74
- Hôtel Mono, 47 av. Thiers. Tel: 04 93 88 75 84

Youth hostel
Route Forestière du Mont Alban. Tel: 04 93 98 23 64

Restaurants
Cheap restaurants are around the station; more expensive ones by the *vieux port*.
Here is a selection:
- Le Colbert, 4 rue de Belgique. Tel: 04 93 88 91 40
- La Coupole, 4 rue de France. Tel: 04 93 87 14 15
- Nissa Socca, 5 rue Sainte-Réparate. Tel: 04 93 80 18 35

Leisure facilities

For listings, see *Le Mois à Nice*.

Museums and art galleries
- Musée des Beaux Arts, 33 av. des Baumettes
- Musée Masséna, 65 rue de France
- Musée Naval, Tour Bellanda, parc du Château
- Musée Matisse, 164 av. des Arènes de Cimiez
- Musée Archéologique, 160 av. des Arènes de Cimiez
- Musée Aléxis et Gustav-Adolf Mossa, 59 quai des Etats Unis
- Musée d'Art Moderne et d'Art Contemporain, promenade des Arts
- Musée National Marc Chagall, av. du Docteur Ménard

Theatre
- Théâtre de la Cité, 3 rue Paganini. Tel: 04 93 16 82 69
- Théâtre de Nice, Esplanade des Victoires. Tel: 04 93 13 90 90
- Nice Opéra, 4 rue St François de Paule. Tel: 04 92 17 40 40
- Théâtre Francis Gag, 4 rue St Joseph. Tel: 04 93 62 00 03
- Théâtre de Traverse, 2 rue Francis Guisol. Tel: 04 93 55 67 46
- Théâtre Lino Ventura, 168 bd de l'Ariane. Tel: 04 97 00 16 70

Cinema
- Le Mercury, 16 place Garibaldi. Tel: 04 93 55 37 81
- Pathé Lingostière, 604 route de Grenoble. Tel: 0 892 696 696
- Pathé Masséna, 31 av. Jean Médecin. Tel: 0 892 696 696
- Pathé Paris, 54 av. Jean Médecin. Tel: 0 892 696 696
- Le Rialto, 4 rue de Rivoli. Tel: 04 93 88 08 41
- Les Variétés, 5 bd Victor Hugo. Tel: 04 93 87 74 97

Sport
FFSU: CSU Valrose, 65 av. de Valrose. Tel: 04 93 84 99 17
Swimming pools:
- Jean Bouin, Palais des Sports, Esplanade de Lattre de Tassigny. Tel: 04 93 80 80 80
- Ariane, rue Guiglionda de Ste Agathe. Tel: 04 93 54 94 30
Skating rink: Palais des Sports, Esplanade de Lattre de Tassigny. Tel: 04 93 80 80 80
Tennis:
- Ligue de la Côte d'Azur, 66 route de Grenoble. Tel: 04 93 18 00 95
- Centre Sportif et Loisirs (CSL). Tel: 04 92 29 08 40

Useful addresses

Main post office: 23 av. Thiers. Tel: 04 97 03 82 00
Municipal library: Bibliothèque de Cimiez, 47 av. de Marne. Tel: 04 93 54 55 41
Bookshops:
- La Biblio, 32 av. Honoré d'Estienne d'Orves. Tel: 04 93 97 03 27
- FNAC, La Rivera, 44–46 av. Jean Médecin. Tel: 04 92 17 77 77
- Librairie Campus, 73 bd Edouard Herriot. Tel: 04 93 86 44 56
- Nouvelle Librairie Française, 111 rue de France. Tel: 04 93 44 67 47
- Librairie Privat Sorbonne, 23 rue de l' Hotel des Postes. Tel: 04 93 13 77 88
- Virgin Megastore, 15 av. Jean Médecin. Tel: 04 97 03 09 00

Commissariat Central de Police: 1 av. Maréchal Foch. Tel: 04 92 17 22 22
Préfecture des Alpes-Maritimes: 147 route de Grenoble. Tel: 04 93 72 20 00
Mairie: 5 rue l'Hôtel de Ville. Tel: 04 93 13 20 00
ANPE: 10 rue Oscar II. Tel: 04 93 97 90 00
CAF: 47 av. de la Marne. Tel: 04 93 53 80 00
CPAM: 48 av. Roi Robert Comte-de-Provence. Tel: 0 820 904 130
CRIJ: 19 rue Gioffredo. Tel: 04 93 80 93 93
EDF-GDF: 88 bis av. des Diables bleus. Tel: 0 810 06 06 00
France Télécom: 22 ter rue de France. Tel: 0 800 06 10 14
Lost property: Police Municipale, 5 rue Hôtel de Ville. Tel: 04 97 13 44 10

Health care

Hôpital de Nice (CHU): 30 voie Romaine. Tel: 04 92 03 77 77
SUMPPS: 24 av. des Diables bleus. Tel: 04 92 00 12 30
Chemists:
- Pharmacie de Nuit, 7 rue Masséna. Tel: 04 93 87 78 94
- Pharmacie des Arts, 16 av. St Jean Baptiste. Tel: 04 93 80 21 04
Local student insurance offices:
- LMDE, 18 av. Thiers. Tel: 0810 600 601
- MEP, 36 rue Buffra. Tel: 0 825 081 081

Travel

Railway station
Nice Ville, av. Thiers. Tel: 08 36 35 35 35

Coach station
5 bd Jean Jaurès. Tel: 04 93 85 64 44

Airport
Nice-Côte d'Azur. Tel : 08 92 69 55 55

Taxis
- Allo Taxi Riviéra, 14 av. Mirabeau. Tel: 04 93 13 78 78
- Taxis Niçois Indépendants, av. Thiers. Tel: 04 93 88 25 82

Buses
SUNBUS, 10 av. Félix Faure. Tel : 04 93 16 52 10

Student travel
OTU Voyages:
- Restaurant Nice-Carlone, 80 bd Edouard Herriot. Tel: 04 03 96 85 43
- 48 rue de France. Tel: 04 97 03 60 90
Wasteels, 32 rue de l'Hôtel des Postes. Tel: 04 93 92 06 92

Emergencies

Hôpital de Nice (CHU): 30 voie Romaine. Tel: 04 92 03 77 77
All-night chemist: 7 rue Masséna. Tel: 04 93 87 78 94
SOS Médecins: 49 rue Gioffrédo. Tel: 08 01 85 01 01 (numéro azur)
Centre Anti-poison (Marseille). Tel: 04 91 75 25 25
SIDA info. (numéro vert). Tel: 04 05 36 66 36
SOS Amitié. Tel: 04 93 26 26 26

19 Orléans

Institutions of higher education and their disciplines

Académie d'Orléans-Tours
Université d'Orléans
Château de la Source, BP 6749, 45067 Orléans Cedex 02. Tel: 02 38 41 71 71. www.univ-orleans.fr
SUIO: rue de Tours, BP 6749, 45067 Cedex 02. Tel: 02 38 41 71 72
SRI: Service des Affaires Internationales, 8 rue Léonard de Vinci, 45067 Orléans La Source Cedex 02. Tel: 02 38 49 47 95

Droit, écomonie, gestion, lettres, langues, sciences humaines, administration des entreprises, sciences et techniques, sport
Antennes at Bourges, Chartres, Châteauroux and Issoudun
IUT: rue d'Issoudun, BP 6729, 45067 Cedex 02. Tel: 02 38 41 75 75

Other institution

Polytech' Orléans (ESEM)
8 rue Léonard de Vinci, 45072 Cedex. Tel: 02 38 41 70 50. www.univ-orleans.fr/polytech
Trois spécialités: mécanique, énergétique, matériaux; électronique, optique; génie civil, environnement

University libraries

Droit/Economie/Gestion, 7 rue de Blois, 45072 Cedex 02. Tel: 02 36 49 45 30
Lettres/Langues/Sciences Humaines, 6 rue de Tours, 45072 Cedex 02. Tel: 02 38 41 71 84
Sciences/Technologies/STAF, 9 rue St Amand, 45072 Cedex 02. Tel: 02 38 49 40 66

Courses for foreign students

Centre de Langue et de Civilisation Française (within the Arts Faculty), 10 rue de Tours, 45072. Tel: 02 38 41 71 05
Courses for post-*baccalauréat*-level students only, at a variety of levels aimed at the DEF, DAF, DSF, DELF and DALF. Courses are semester-based, to the tune of 18 hours per week.

CROUS

17 av. Dauphine, 45072 Orléans Cedex. Tel: 02 38 22 61 61. Fax: 02 38 56 42 02. www.crous-orleans-tours.fr
BEE: Maison de l'Etudiant, rue de Tours. Tel: 02 38 49 45 07

CROUS-controlled accommodation
Orléans has a full range of accommodation, from traditional halls, partly refurbished, to well-appointed new *résidences universitaires*.

Traditional halls:

- Résidence de l'Indien, rue de Tours (533 traditional rooms, 376 refurbished rooms and 71 furnished studios)
- Résidence Les Châtaigniers, 3 rue de Vendôme, 45100 Orléans La Source (332 traditional rooms)

New residences:

- Résidence Jacquard, 40 rue de la Bourrie Rouge, 45000 (31 T1, 8 T2)
- Résidence Aristote, 1/5/7 Esplanade de l'Université, 45100 Orléans La Source (233 T1, 19 T1 bis, 4 T2)
- Résidence Les Magnolias, 1 rue de Vendôme, 45100 Orléans La Source (160 T1, 15 T1 bis, 10 T2)
- Résidence Les Charmes, 6 rue d'Issoudun, 45100 Orléans La Source (160 T1, 14 T1 bis, 16 T2)
- Résidence Dessaux, 2 rue de la Folie, 45000 (102 T1, 16 T2)

CROUS restaurants

Traditional meals are served in all restaurants, but there are also cafeterias, pizzerias and *brasseries* for alternative meals and snacks.

- RU Le Lac, 15 rue de Blois, 45072 Cedex 2 (seats 330)
- RU Le Forum, rue de St Amand, 45072 (seats 324)
- Restaurant Le New Orléans, rue de Blois, 45072 Cedex 2 (seats 100)
- RU Dessaux, 3 rue des Africains/Restaurant Le Guignebaud, 2 rue de la Folie, 45000 (seats 130) – also incorporates La Cave de la Folie
- l'Anatidé, rue de St Amand, 45072 Cedex 2 (seats 250) – also has a cafeteria on the first floor
- Pizzéria de Borsalino, rue de Blois, 45072 Cedex 2 (seats 90)
- Cafétéria de la Fac de Sciences, rue de Chartres, 45072 Cedex 2
- Cafétéria Le Bistrot de l'Etudiant, rue de St Amand, 45072 Cedex 2
- Cafétéria de la Fac de Droit, rue de Dundee, rue de Blois, 45072 Cedex 2
- Cafétéria Pub Le Dundee, rue de Blois, 45072 Cedex 2

Private-sector residences

- Les Estudines Jeanne d'Arc, 11 place du 6 juin 1944, 45000. Tel: 02 38 62 93 00
- Les Lauréades, 6 rue Condorcet, 45100 Orléans La Source. Tel: 0825 332 332
- Résidence Pythagore, 21 av. Alain Savary, 45100. Tel: 02 38 25 80 00

Privately run hostels

For details write to the *Directeur/Directrice*:
- FJT Espace Colombier, 25 rue Colombier, 45000. Tel: 02 38 42 23 30
- FJT, 45 ter rue des Montées, 45100. Tel: 02 38 49 15 32
- Résidence de l'Ecu St Laurent, 6 rue de l'Ecu St Laurent, 45000. Tel: 02 38 52 14 71

The town and its surrounding area

Standing at the most northerly point on the river Loire, some 110 kilometres south of Paris, which can be reached in just an hour by train, Orléans is a historic town, *chef-lieu* of the *département* of the Loiret, and capital of the Centre region. The inhabitants of the greater conurbation number some 120,000. It forms the gateway to the Loire valley, a UNESCO World Heritage site, with its many fine and architecturally diverse *châteaux*.

It is a busy industrial and market town, made famous above all by its connection with Jeanne d'Arc, the Maid of Orleans, who, in 1429, rescued the town from the English army beseiging it, which she helped defeat before persuading Charles VII to march north to Reims to be crowned King of France. But its history did not begin there. As a town under the Gauls (Genabum) it formed a centre of revolt against Julius Caesar in 52 BC (for which it suffered being burnt down). Rebuilt, it changed its name to Aurelianis in the third century, was beseiged by Attila the Hun in the middle of the fifth, and became briefly the capital of the Frankish kingdom in 498. When Pope Honorius banned the teaching of law in Paris (but not in Orleans) in 1219 the city grew in reputation as a centre of learning. It was traditionally the point at which goods and passsengers travelling up the Loire, the major economic artery, disembarked for onward staging to Paris, so that its relative decline in the late nineteenth century coincided with the slowing of river traffic.

Today it is a town with a reputation for innovation. With new cosmetics factories set up in the suburbs, and the redevelopment of the riverside quays, the city has recovered some of its economic power. It is also the focus of vinegar-making, which owes its origins, it is said, to the fact that in former times wine, being transported up the river, was delayed by falling water levels and started to turn to vinegar. A new ultra-modern tram line has been built to run from the railway station through the town out to the main university campus at La Source, some 12 kilometres away.

Famous sons of the town include the Renaissance humanist Etienne Dolet (1509–1546), the lawyer Robert-Joseph Pothier (1699–1772), the poet and writer Charles Péguy (1873–1914), and the famous literary historian Gustave Lanson (1857–1934). A museum, the Centre Charles Péguy, is devoted to the writer's life and works.

Not surprisingly, the memory of Jeanne d'Arc is everywhere. The rue Jeanne d'Arc runs through the historic quarter of the city, which miraculously survived bombardments during World War Two. The fifteenth-century house in which she was accommodated during her stay in the town was destroyed during the war, but was lovingly rebuilt in the 1960s, using materials from houses of the same period, and stands as testimony to her actions and her myth. There are statues in the place du Martroi and in the place d'Etape, across from the cathedral, and the stained glass windows in the cathedral nave tell the story of her life and her victory over perfidious Albion, *l'Anglois perfide*, while passing quietly over both the role of the Burgundians in her capture, and the French clergy's betrayal at her trial. An altar in the same church, where she celebrated her victory, commemorates her canonization in 1920.

Other notable sights include the Hôtel Groslot, a Renaissance mansion built in the early 1550s for the city bailiff, whose family lived there until, at the Revolution, it was turned into the town hall, and thereafter given a lavish interior. It is famous for housing the Estates General in 1560, shortly after which François II died in the same house, in a room which is now used for weddings. But, of course, it would be impossible not to mention the magnificent flamboyant Gothic Cathédrale Sainte-Croix, whose dimensions are approximately the same as those of Notre Dame de Paris, but whose modern striking appearance is due to centuries of restoration and rebuilding. Begun in the thirteenth century, the cathedral suffered massively at the hands of Huguenot iconoclasts in 1568, but Henri IV began a reconstruction programme which lasted for three centuries. The stained glass is nineteenth century.

In terms of festivals, the major annual event takes place around 8 May, and since 1430 commemorates the liberation of the town by Jeanne d'Arc. The *fêtes Johanniques* are about a week of street parties, medieval costume parades and concerts, climaxing in mass at the Cathedral. In addition, every other year, the city holds the Fête de la Loire, when a hundred or so boats gather to celebrate the history of the river traffic.

Tourist information

Office de Tourisme, 2 place de l'Etape, BP 95632, 45056 Cedex 1. Tel: 02 38 24 05 05. www.tourisme-orléans.com

Hotels

- Hôtel de l'Abeille, 64 rue Alsace-Lorraine, 45000. Tel: 02 38 53 54 87
- Hôtel St Martin, 52 bd Alexandre Martin, 45000. Tel: 02 38 62 47 47 (near the station)

Youth hostel
Auberge de Jeunesse, 7 bd de la Motte-Sanguin. Tel: 02 38 53 60 06

Restaurants
- Café Estaminet, 4 rue du Maréchal Foch. Tel: 02 38 54 23 11
- La Petite Marmite, 178 rue de Bourges. Tel: 02 38 54 23 83

Leisure facilities

Museums and art galleries
- Musée des Beaux-Arts, place Sainte Croix, 45000
- Muséum, 6 rue Marcel Proust, 45000
- Musée Historique et Archéologique de l'Orléanais, square Abbé Desnoyes, 45000
- Maison de Jeanne d'Arc, 3 place Charles de Gaulle
- Centre Charles Péguy, Hôtel Euverte Hatte, 11 rue du Tabour, 45000
- Galerie d'Art les Alizés, 288 rue de Bourgogne, 45000
- L'Art'y Show, 197 rue de Bourgogne, 45000

Theatre
- Centre Dramatique National d'Orléans (CDN). Tel: 02 38 62 15 55
- Centre d'Art Dramatique d'Orléans (CADO). Tel: 02 38 54 29 29
- Carré St Vincent, bd Aristide Briand, BP 21269, 45002 Cedex 1. Tel: 02 38 62 75 30
- La Tortue Magique, Théâtre Parc Pasteur, rue Eugène Vignat, 45000. Tel: 02 38 81 12 75
- Théâtre Gérard Philipe, 1 av. du Président John Kennedy, 45100. Tel: 02 38 63 22 95
- Ecole Nationale de Musique, Danse et Art Dramatique, 1 place de la République/4 place Ste Croix, 45000. Tel: 02 38 79 21 23
- L'Astrolabe, 1 rue Alexandre Avisse, 45000. Tel: 02 38 54 20 06
- Salle des Spectacles St Jean de la Ruelle. Tel: 02 38 43 97 43

Cinema
- UGC Ciné-Cité, Centre Commercial Place d'Arc, 2 place Nicholas Copernic, 45000. Tel: 08 92 70 00 00

- NovoCiné Les Carmes, 7 rue des Carmes, 45000. Tel: 02 38 62 94 79
- Select Studios, 45 rue Jeanne d'Arc, 45000. Tel: 08 92 68 69 25
- Cinéfil Multiplex Pathé, 45 rue des Halles, 45000. Tel: 02 38 77 70 70
- Artistic, bd Alexandre Martin, 45000. Tel: 08 92 68 69 25

Sport

FFSU: Maison des Sports, 1240 rue de la Bergeresse, 45160 Olivet. Tel: 02 38 49 88 88

ASUO: Point info-sport et association sportive, Maison de l'Etudiant, rue de Tours, BP 6749 Cedex 2. Tel: 02 38 41 71 71

Sports facilities:

- Palais des Sports, rue Eugène Vignat, 45000. Tel: 02 38 53 97 27
- Stade Municipal, 10 rue Gaston Couté, 45000. Tel: 02 38 42 26 91
- Gymnase de la Gare, 3 rue Eloi d'Amerval, 45000. Tel: 02 38 62 36 32

Swimming pool: rue Eugène Vignat, 45000. Tel: 02 38 62 62 52

Skating rink: 1 rue Alexandre Avisse, 45000. Tel: 02 38 24 22 24

Useful addresses

Main post office: place du Général de Gaulle. Tel: 02 38 77 35 35

Municipal libraries:

- (Argonne) place Mozart, 45000. Tel: 02 38 62 21 29
- (Blossières) 28 rue Charles le Chauve, 45000. Tel: 02 38 43 49 47
- (La Source) place Sainte Beuve, 45100. Tel: 02 38 69 37 52

ANPE: 165 bd de Châteaudun, 45000. Tel: 02 38 78 86 80

CAF: (du Loiret) place St Charles, 45946 Cedex 9. Tel: 0820 0820 45

CRIDJ: 3–5 bd de Verdun, 45000. Tel: 02 38 78 91 78

CPAM: place du Général de Gaulle, 45021 Cedex 1. Tel: 0 820 904 103

ANPE: 1 place du Martoi, 45038 Cedex 1. Tel: 02 38 79 85 00

Bookshops:

- Librairie Paes Langues Etrangères, 184 rue de Bourgogne, 45000. Tel: 02 38 54 04 50
- FNAC, 16 rue de la République. Tel: 02 38 79 99 99

Internet access: BSP Infos, 125 rue Bannier. Tel: 02 38 77 02 28

Health care

CHR. Tel: 02 38 51 44 44

SUMPPS 'Jean Zay': 9 rue de Tours, 45072 Cedex 2. Tel: 02 38 41 71 79

Local student insurance offices:

- LMDE, 12 place Louis XI, 45057 Cedex 1. Tel: 32 60 LMDE
- SMECO, 2 rue St Paul, 45000. Tel: 02 38 53 10 11

Travel

Railway station
1 rue Pierre Ségelle. Tel: 08 92 35 35 35

Coach station
1 rue Marcel Proust. Tel: 02 38 53 94 75

Taxis
Taxi Radio d'Orléans. Tel: 02 38 53 11 11

Buses
SEMTAO, 64 rue Pierre Louguet, St Jean de Braye. Tel: 02 38 71 98 00

Emergencies

SOS Amitié. Tel: 02 38 62 22 22
SOS Médecins. Tel: 02 48 23 33 33
Centre Anti-poison (Paris). Tel: 01 40 05 48 48
Drugs/Alcohol/Tobacco Info Service (24-hour). Tel: 113 (confidential)
Aids Info Service (24-hour). Tel: 0800 840 800

20   Paris and *la région parisienne*

Institutions of higher education and their disciplines

Académie de Paris
Université Panthéon-Sorbonne: Paris I
12 place du Panthéon, 75231 Paris Cedex 05. Tel: 01 46 34 97 00. www.
   univ-paris1.fr
SRI: La Maison Internationale, 58 bd Arago, 75013 Paris. Tel: 01 44 07
   76 70
SCUIO: 90 rue de Tolbiac, 75013 Paris. Tel: 01 40 77 18 36
Langues, économie, gestion et économie d'entreprise, droit, science politique, sciences sociales, sciences humaines, arts, mathématiques et
   informatique

Université Panthéon-Assas: Paris II
12 place du Panthéon, 75231 Paris Cedex 05. Tel: 01 44 41 57 00. www.
u-paris2.fr
SRI: 12 place du Panthéon, 75005 Paris
SCUIO: 92 rue d'Assas, 75006 Paris Cedex 06. Tel: 01 44 41 58 75
Droit et sciences politiques, sciences économiques, gestion, administration économique et sociale

Université de la Sorbonne Nouvelle: Paris III
17 rue de la Sorbonne, 75230 Paris Cedex 05. Tel: 01 40 46 28 97. www.
univ-paris3.fr
SRI: Centre Censier, 13 rue de Santeuil, 75231 Paris Cedex 05
SCUIO: 13 rue de Santeuil, 75005 Paris Cedex 05. Tel: 01 45 87 40 01
Langues, lettres, communication, cinéma et audiovisuel, études théâtrales

Université Paris-Sorbonne: Paris IV
1 rue Victor Cousin, 75230 Paris Cedex 05. Tel: 01 40 46 22 11. www.
paris4.sorbonne.fr
SRI: Pôle des Relations Internationales. Accueil des étudiants individuels:
Bureau F364, 1 rue Victor Cousin, 75230 Paris Cedex 05
SCUIO: 1 rue Victor Cousin, 75005 Paris Cedex 05. Tel: 01 40 46 26 14
Lettres, langues, sciences humaines, information, communication, musique

Université René Descartes: Paris V
12 rue de l'Ecole de Médecine, 75270 Paris Cedex 06. Tel: 01 40 46 16 16.
www.univ-paris5.fr
SCUIO: same address, 75006 Paris Cedex 06. Tel: 01 40 46 16 50
SRI: Droit: Centre Universitaire de la Porte de Vanves. Mathématiques et
Informatique: Centre Universitaire des Saints-Pères
Santé, sciences sociales, sciences de l'éducation, mathématiques et informatique, sport, linguistique
IUT: 143 av. de Versailles, 75016 Paris. Tel: 01 44 14 44 00

Université Pierre et Marie Curie: Paris VI
4 place Jussieu, 75252 Paris Cedex 05. Tel: 01 44 27 44 27. www.upmc.fr
SRI: Tour 34, couloir 32–24, 4e étage, porte 413 bis. Tel: 01 44 27 27 49
SCUIO: same address, 75005 Paris Cedex 05. Tel: 01 44 27 33 66 **or** 01 44
27 39 70
Santé, sciences et techniques, informatique, mathématiques, statistiques

Université Denis Diderot: Paris VII
2 place Jussieu, 75251 Paris Cedex 05. Tel: 01 44 27 44 27. www.sigu7.
jussieu.fr
SRI: Bât. RFF, 92 av. de France, 75013. Postal address: Case 7130, 2 place
Jussieu, 75251 Paris Cedex 5
SCUIO: same address, 75005 Cedex 05. Tel: 01 44 27 52 08
Santé, sciences, sciences humaines, sciences sociales, mathématiques,
informatique, lettres, langues, cinéma, communication, information
IUT: same address. Tel: 01 44 27 46 90

Académie de Créteil
Université Vincennes-Saint-Denis: Paris VIII
2 rue de la Liberté, 93526 Saint-Denis Cedex. Tel: 01 49 40 67 89. www.
univ-paris8.fr
SCUIO: same address. Tel: 01 49 40 67 14
SRI: same address. Bât. G, salle 220. Tel: 01 49 40 65 26
Lettres, langues, sciences humaines, informatique, communication et sciences
de l'éducation, arts, administration économique et sociale, droit
IUT:
• 140, rue de la Nouvelle France, 93100 Montreuil-sous-Bois. Tel: 01 48
70 37 01
• Rue de la Râperie, 93290 Tremblay en France. Tel: 01 41 51 12 20/22

Académie de Paris
Université Paris Dauphine: Paris IX
Place du Maréchal de Lattre de Tassigny, 75775 Paris Cedex 16. Tel: 01 44
05 44 05. www.dauphine.fr
SRI: same address
SCUIO: same address. Tel: 01 44 05 44 75
Gestion et économie appliquée, sciences des organisations, mathématiques
de la décision.

Académie de Versailles
Université de Nanterre: Paris X
200 av. de la République, 92001 Nanterre Cedex 01. Tel: 01 40 97 72 00.
www.u-paris10.fr
SRI: 200 av. de la République, Bât A, Bureau 107, 92001 Nanterre
SCUIO: same address. Tel: 01 40 97 75 34
Lettres, langues, sciences humaines, sciences sociales, sciences économi-
ques, gestion, mathématiques et informatique, sport
IUT: 1 chemin Desvallières, 92410 Ville d'Avray. Tel: 01 47 09 70 00

Université Paris-Sud: Paris XI
15 rue Georges Clemenceau, 91405 Orsay Cedex. Tel: 01 69 15 67 50.
www.u-psud.fr
SRI: DR1, Bâtiment 225, 91405 Orsay Cedex
SCUIO:
- 15 rue G. Clemenceau, 91405 Orsay Cedex. Tel: 01 69 15 72 77
- (santé) 63 rue Gabriel Péri, 94276 Le Kremlin-Bicêtre. Tel: 01 49 59 66 25
- (pharmacie) rue J.-B. Clément, 92290 Châtenay-Malabry. Tel: 01 48 83
  53 29
- (droit, économie) 54 bd Desgranges, 92330 Sceaux. Tel: 01 40 91 18 38

- **Orsay**: santé, sciences et technologies, musique
- **Châtenay-Malabry**: pharmacie
- **Sceaux**: droit, sciences économiques, gestion, administration
IUT:
- 9 av. de la Division Leclerc, BP 140, 94234 Cachan Cedex. Tel: 01 41 24
  11 00
- plateau du Moulin, 91400 Orsay. Tel: 01 69 33 60 00
- 8 av. Cauchy, 92330 Sceaux. Tel: 01 40 91 24 99

Académie de Créteil
Université de Paris Val-de-Marne: Paris XII
61 av. du Général de Gaulle, 94010 Créteil Cedex. Tel: 01 45 17 10 00.
www.univ-paris12.fr
SRI: same address
SCUIO: same address. Tel: 01 45 17 12 14
Santé, lettres, sciences humaines et sociales, communication, sciences
économiques et de gestion, administration économique et sociale,
sciences et technologie
IUT:
- same address, Bât. L1. Tel: 01 45 17 17 01
- Sénart-Fontainebleau, 4 av. Pierre Point, 77127 Lieusaint. Tel: 01 64 13
  44 88

Université Paris-Nord: Paris XIII
Av. Jean-Baptiste Clément, 93430 Villetaneuse. Tel: 01 49 40 30 00. www.
univ-paris13.fr
SRI: 99 av. Jean-Baptiste Clément
SCUIO: (Villetaneuse) same address. Tel: 01 49 40 30 30
SCUIO: (Bobigny) 1 rue de Chablis, 93000 Bobigny. Tel: 01 48 38 88 38
- **Villetaneuse**: droit, sciences politiques et sociales, sciences économi-
  ques et de gestion, lettres, sciences humaines, communication

- **Bobigny**: santé

IUT:
- Av. Jean-Baptiste Clément, 93430 Villetaneuse. Tel: 01 49 40 31 28
- 1 rue de Chablis, 93017 Bobigny. Tel: 01 48 38 88 36
- Place du 8 mai 1945, 93206 Saint-Denis Cedex 01. Tel: 01 49 40 61 00

Université de Marne-la-Vallée
5 bd Descartes, Champs-sur-Marne, 77454 Marne-La-Vallée Cedex 2.
    Tel: 01 60 95 75 00. www.univ-mlv.fr
SRI: Bât. Bois de l'Etang, Bureau A 210
SCUIO: same address. Tel: 01 60 95 74 74
Lettres, langues, arts et communication, sciences et technologies, sciences
    humaines et sociales, sciences économiques et gestion, mathématiques,
    sciences et technologies, sport

Académie de Versailles
Université de Versailles-Saint-Quentin-en-Yvelines
23 rue du Refuge, 78035 Versailles Cedex. Tel: 01 39 25 40 00. www.uvsq.fr
SRI: UVSQ, Bâtiment d'Alembert, 5–7 bd d'Alembert, 78047 Guyan-
    court Cedex
SCUIO:
- 47 bd Vauban, 78047 Guyancourt Cedex. Tel: 01 39 25 56 10
- 45 av. des Etats-Unis, 78000 Versailles. Tel: 01 39 25 46 10
Administration économique et sociale, lettres, langues, sciences humaines
    et sociales, économie, gestion
IUT:
- 7 rue Jean Hoêt, 78200 Mantes-la-Jolie. Tel: 01 30 98 13 62
- 10–12 av. de l'Europe, 78140 Vélizy. Tel: 01 39 25 48 33

Université de Cergy-Pontoise
33 bd du Port, 95011 Cergy-Pontoise Cedex. Tel: 01 34 25 60 00. www.
    u-cergy.fr
SRI: Tour des Chênes, Bureau 713. Tel: 01 34 25 67 43
SCUIO: Tour des Chênes, 95011 Cergy-Pontoise Cedex. Tel: 01 34 25 61
    54
Sciences et techniques, langues, lettres et sciences humaines, droit, écon-
    omie et gestion
IUT: Rue d'Eragny, Neuville sur Oise, 95031 Cergy-Pontoise Cedex. Tel:
    01 34 25 68 05

Université d'Evry-Val d'Essonne
Bd François Mitterrand, 91025 Evry Cedex. Tel: 01 69 47 70 00. www.
    univ-evry.fr
SCUIO: same address. Tel: 01 69 47 76 76
Sciences et technologies, droit, sciences économiques, sciences sociales,
    gestion, mathématiques et informatique
IUT: 'Les Passages', 22, allée Jean Rostand, 91025 Evry Cedex. Tel: 01 69
    47 72 00

Courses for foreign students

In addition to the courses run by the former Institut Britannique (see
below), there are summer and term-time courses available that are so
numerous that we do not have room to list them all here. Amongst the
most well-known are the Cours de langue et de civilisation françaises de la
Sorbonne pour étudiants étrangers, 47 rue des Ecoles 75005 Paris. Tel: 01
40 46 22 11, exts: 2664 to 2675.

*The University of London Institute in Paris (formerly Institut Britannique
    de Paris)*
9–11 rue de Constantine, 75340 Paris Cedex 07. Tel: 01 44 11 73 73. www.
    bip.lon.ac.uk
The Institute is divided into the Département d'Etudes Françaises and
the Département d'Etudes Anglaises. The former (Tel: 01 44 11 73 83)
offers a variety of courses for native English-speakers in French language,
literature and civilisation; it is the only department of a British university
where English-speaking students can study French language, etc, entirely
in French and in France. The three-year undergraduate programme caters
for some ninety students and leads to the award of the BA in French
Studies of the University of London. Other courses available include
the University of London MA in Translation, Diploma in Translation
and Certificate in Translation. Part-time courses are available in French
language and translation and/or literature and civilisation. Courses take
full advantage of the cultural facilities on offer in Paris.

The Institute has well-appointed classrooms, a projection room, two
language laboratories, two libraries and a snack bar in the basement where
students can relax in a most friendly atmosphere. One relative disadvantage for some students is the large 'English' presence and the amount of
English spoken outside the classroom.

Other institutions

Ecole Centrale d'Electronique
53 rue de Grenelle, 75007 Paris. Tel: 01 44 39 06 00. www.ece.fr
Trois dominantes: systèmes d'information et de réseaux, systèmes
  embarqués, telecommunications et réseaux

EPF-Ecole d'Ingénieurs
3 bis rue Lakanal, 92330 Sceaux. Tel: 01 41 13 01 51. www.epf.fr
Aéronautique et espace, énergétique et environnement, ingénierie
  d'affaires et de projets, management des systèmes d'information, mécanique des matériaux et des structures, ingénierie industrielle et logistique, systèmes et réseaux informatiques, télécommunications

European School of Management (ESCP-EAP)
79 av. de la République, 75543 Paris Cedex 11. Tel: 01 49 23 20 00. www.
  escp-eap.net
Audit financier et comptabilité, dynamiques d'internationalisation, économie, finance, ingénierie juridique et financière, international business and projects, management général et stratégie, management des
  hommes et des organisations, management public, marketing, organi-
  sation et conseil

Ecole des Hautes Etudes Commerciales (HEC)
1 rue de la Libération, 78351 Jouy-en-Josas Cedex. Tel: 01 39 67 70 00.
  www.hec.fr
Economie, entrepreneurs, Europe, finance, ifac (information, finance,
  audit et conseil), management des arts et de la culture, management
  public, marketing, strategic management, stratégie fiscale et juridique
  internationale, management des nouvelles technologies

Institut National Agronomique Paris-Grignon (INA-PG)
16 rue Claude Bernard, 75231 Paris Cedex 05. Tel: 01 44 08 16 61. www.
  inapg.fr
Agronomie, environnement, productions végétales, industries biologiques
  et alimentaires, protection des plantes et environnement, développement agricole, sciences et technologie de la biologie, la nutrition,
  l'alimentation humaine, sciences animales, gestion du vivant et straté-
  gies patrimoniales, économie et gestion de l'entreprise, informatique

Institut National des Télécommunications (INT Management)
9 rue Charles Fourier, 91011 Evry Cedex. Tel: 01 60 76 46 21. www.int-
  evry.fr/intmanagement

Ingénierie des systèmes d'information, audit et conseil en systèmes d'information, comptabilité-finances, marketing appliqué aux technologies de l'information et de la communication, projets audiovisuel et multimédia, e-business

Ecole Polytechnique ('X')
Route de Saclay, 91128 Palaiseau Cedex. Tel: 01 69 33 33 33.
    www.polytechnique.fr
Formation générale, approfondissement

Ecole Normale Supérieure (ENS Ulm)
45 rue d'Ulm, 75230 Paris Cedex 05. Tel: 01 44 32 30 00. www.ens.fr

Ecole Normale Supérieure Cachan
61 av. Président Wilson, 94235 Cachan Cedex. Tel: 01 47 40 20 00. www.
    ens-cachan.fr

Ecole Nationale Supérieure des Mines de Paris (EMP)
60 bd Saint-Michel, 75272 Paris Cedex 06. Tel: 01 40 51 90 00. www.
    ensmp.fr
BP 87, 91003 Evry Cedex
35 rue Saint-Honoré, 77305 Fontainebleau Cedex
Rue Claude Daunesse, BP 207, 06565 Sophia Antipolis Cedex
Formation d'ingénieurs fonctionnaires, ingénieurs civils généralistes

Ecole Nationale des Ponts et Chaussées (ENPC)
• 28 rue des Saints-Pères, 75007 Paris. Tel: 01 44 58 27 00. www.enpc.fr
• 6 et 8 av. Blaise Pascal, Cité Descartes, 77455 Champs-sur-Marne. Tel:
    01 64 15 30 00. www.enpc.fr
Formation d'ingénieurs à double compétence: technique et management;
    génie civil et construction, génie mécanique et matériaux, ingénierie
    mathématique et informatique, management industriel, sciences
    humaines, économie, gestion, finance, ville, environnement, transport

Ecole Centrale des Arts et Manufactures (ECP ou 'Centrale')
Grande Voie des Vignes, 92295 Châtenay-Malabry Cedex. Tel: 01 41 13 10
    00. www.ecp.fr
Aménagement et construction, génie industriel, informatique et télécom-
    munication, mathématiques appliquées, mécanique, aéronautique,
    énergie, physique appliquée, procédés et environnement, systèmes
    technologiques intelligents; conception, développement, recherche,
    management de projets, management de production et logistique,
    stratégie, marketing, finances

Institut d'Etudes Politiques (IEP Sciences PO)
Sciences Po, 27 rue St Guillaume, 75337 Paris Cedex 7. Tel: 01 45 49 50
  50. www.sciences-po.fr

CROUS

39 av. Georges Bernanos, 75005 Paris.
Cellule d'accueil international: 2e étage. Tel: 01 40 51 37 65 or 67
SAEE: same address and telephone
OTU:
- 39 av. Georges Bernanos, 75005. Tel: 01 44 41 38 51
- 119 rue Saint Martin 75004. Tel: 01 40 29 12 28 or 27
- (Paris IX) 1 place de Lattre de Tassigny, 75016. Tel: 01 47 55 03 01

CROUS-controlled accommodation and restaurants
CROUS-controlled halls and restaurants in Paris are too numerous to list
here; we have included only the establisments that are on the site of the
Cité Internationale. The Latin Quarter continues to offer a wide variety
of menus and of prices in the cosmopolitan, narrow streets close to the bd
Saint Michel. For recommended restaurants, see below.

Cité Internationale Universitaire de Paris
- Fondation Nationale (Pavillon Administratif) 19 bd Jourdan, 75690
  Paris. Tel: 01 44 16 64 00
- Collège Franco-Britannique (Fondation E. and H. Nathan), 9B bd
  Jourdan. Tel: 01 58 10 40 00
- Fondation des Etats-Unis, 15 bd Jourdan. Tel: 01 53 80 68 80
- Maison des Etudiants Canadiens, 31 bd Jourdan. Tel: 01 40 78 67 00
Composed of 39 *maisons*, the Cité Internationale is situated in a park of
some 40 hectares close to the Porte d'Orléans *métro* station and the Cité
Universitaire RER station. Created in 1925, the Cité is a truly international
community for which the participating countries built a hall of residence
in a style which typifies national architectural characteristics. It is popular
with English-speaking students in Paris. Even though rooms there cost
more than double the price of a CROUS-controlled room in the provinces,
they are cheaper by far than comparable private accommodation in the
capital. The Collège Franco-Britannique offers spacious accommodation;
security and discipline are much tighter than in provincial residences.
Facilities include microwaves, fridges and telephones in rooms. Other
halls not mentioned above of particular interest to Modern Languages
students include the Maison Heinrich Heine, the Collège d'Espagne and

the Maison de l'Italie. The Cité has its own library, Service des Activitiés Culturelles and hospital. It has its own CROUS-controlled restaurants and 'fast-food' cafeteria.

Tourist information

Office de Tourisme et des Congrès de Paris, Bureau d'accueil principal, 25 rue des Pyramides, 75001. Tel: (special rate) 08 92 68 3000

Hotels
- Hôtel Parc Montsouris, 4 rue Parc Montsouris, 75014. Tel: 01 45 89 09 72 (adjacent to the Cité Internationale)
- Grand Hôtel de l'Europe, 74 bd de Strasbourg, 75010 Paris. Tel: 01 46 07 76 27 (close to the Gare de l'Est)
- Viator Hôtel, 1 rue Parrot, 75012 Paris. Tel: 01 43 43 11 00 (very close to the Gare de Lyon)
- Hôtel Kuntz, 2 rue des Deux Gares, 75010 Paris. Tel: 01 40 35 77 26 and 01 40 37 75 29 (*métro* Gare du Nord or Gare de l'Est)

Youth hostel
Auberge de Jeunesse Jules Ferry, 8 bd Jules Ferry, 75011. Tel: 01 43 57 55 60 (*métro* République)

Restaurants
- Flunch, Fontaine Innocents, 5 rue Pierre Lescot, 75001. Tel: 01 42 33 50 00
- Restaurant Végétarien Bioart, 1 quai François Mauriac, 75013. Tel: 01 45 85 66 88
- Le Tramway de Lyon, 6 rue Michel Chasles. Tel: 01 43 46 80 38 (very close to the Gare de Lyon)

For more information on Paris restaurants visit www.parisinfo.com/paris_restaurants

Leisure facilities

Museums and art galleries
These are too numerous to list here. Visit www.parisinfo.com/museum_monuments (it is worth checking when there is free entry and also what student reductions are currently available).

Theatre

Again, theatres are too numerous to list. Visit www.parisinfo.com/show_exhibition

Cinema

Check for student reductions.

Sport

Sporting facilities in Paris are, of course, excellent and stadia include the Stade de France (football, rugby and pop concerts), the Parc des Princes (football [Paris Saint-Germain] and rugby) and the Bercy (multisport) complex.

Useful addresses

For students residing at the Cité Internationale, there is a post office at Parc Montsouris and at the Cité itself.

A whole range of bookshops (including the very large Gibert shops) are to be found in the Latin Quarter of Paris, along the bd Saint-Michel; FNAC has some nine branches in Paris (www.fnac.com).

Libraries

- Bibliothèque Nationale de France: Site François Mitterrand, Quai François Mauriac, 75706 Paris Cedex 13. Tel: 01 53 79 59 59; Site Richelieu, 58 rue de Richelieu, 75084 Paris Cedex 02. Tel: 01 53 79 59 59; Arsenal, 1 rue Sully, 75004 Paris. Tel: 01 53 01 25 25
- Centre Culturel Britannique – British Council, 9–11 rue de Constantine, 75007. Tel: 01 49 55 73 00. www.britishcouncil.fr
- Centre Georges Pompidou, 75191 Paris Cedex 04. Tel: 01 44 78 12 33 (*métro*: Rambuteau or Châtelet/Les Halles)
- There are many other libraries listed in the various tourist guides.

FFSU: CIUP, Espace Sud, 9F bd Jourdan, 75014 Paris. Tel: 01 43 13 13 60 or 61. www.sport-u-idf.com

CPAM: (Head office) 21 rue Georges Auric, 75948 Paris Cedex 19. Tel: 01 53 38 70 00. www.cpam-paris.fr

For offices by *arrondissement* visit www.geresco.fr/actualites/AdressesUtiles/SECadrescpam.html

CAF: 18 quai Austerlitz. Tel: 01 45 82 29 65

CIDJ: 101 quai Branly, 75740 Paris Cedex 15. Tel: (switchboard) 01 44 49 12 00

CIDJ Informations Jeunes: 101 quai Branly, 75015 Paris. Tel: 0825 090 630 (Mon–Fri 09.00–12.00 and 13.00–18.00)

Internet cafés:
- Actuel Bureaucratique, 14 rue Santeuil. Tel: 01 43 36 56 67
- Cyberbase, rue de Vaugirard. Tel: 01 40 56 06 27

Chambre de Commerce et d'Industrie de Paris, Délégation de Paris: 2 rue de Viarmes, Paris 1er. Tel: (09.00–18.00) 01 53 40 46 00

Association Nationale pour l'Information sur le Logement (ANIL). Tel: 01 42 02 65 95

ANPE:
- 17 rue Juge, 75015 Paris. Tel: 01 58 01 07 20
- 20 rue Miollis, 75015 Paris. Tel: 01 53 69 99 60
- 123 rue Oberkampf, 75011 Paris. Tel: 01 49 23 33 50

Health care

The Cité Internationale offers good health-care provision centred around the Hôpital Institut Mutualiste Montsouris, 42 bd Jourdan, 75014. Tel: 01 56 61 62 63
- Hôpital Franco-Britannique, 3 rue Barbès, 92300 Levallois Perret. Tel: 01 46 39 22 22
- Hôpital Américain de Paris, 63 bd Victor Hugo, Neuilly sur Seine. Tel: 01 46 41 25 25

LMDE: Tel: 32 60 LMDE
- 6 rue des Fossés Saint Jacques (RER B Luxembourg)
- 10 rue Linné (*métro* Jussieu)
- Centre PMF Tolbiac, 90 rue de Tolbiac

Travel

Rail
- Eurostar: Paris Gare du Nord. Tel: (special rate) 08 92 35 35 39 (*métro/* RER Gare du Nord)
- Train information. Tel: (special rate) 36 35

Coach
Eurolines Travel BSA, 55 rue St. Jacques, 75005. Tel: 01 43 54 11 99

Local travel in Paris
Métro tickets can be bought in *carnets* of 10 tickets to make a saving; the *Carte Orange* (*métro*/buses/RER) offers significant savings for regular travellers and is charged by 'zones'.

International flights
Aéroport de Paris Roissy-Charles-de-Gaulle. Tel: 01 48 62 12 12

Taxis
- Appel taxi, place André Malraux, 75001. Tel: 01 42 60 61 40
- Appel taxi, place Châtelet, 75001. Tel: 01 42 33 20 99
- Taxis at the Cité Internationale: Appel taxi, 1 place 25 Août, 75014. Tel: 01 45 40 52 05

Emergencies

SOS Amitié. Tel: 01 42 96 26 26
SOS Help. Tel: 01 46 21 46 46
SAMU de Paris. Tel: (switchboard) 01 44 49 23 23

21 Pau

The institutions of higher education and their disciplines

Académie de Bordeaux
Université de Pau et des Pays de l'Adour
Domaine Universitaire, BP 576, 64012 Pau Université Cedex. Tel: 05 59
    40 70 00. www.univ-pau.fr
SCUIO: av. de l'Université, 64012 Cedex. Tel: 05 59 40 70 90
SRI: same address as the university. Tel: 05 59 40 70 59
Lettres, langues et sciences humaines, sciences et techniques, droit, écon-
    omie, gestion
Antennes at Anglet, Talence and Ustaritz
IUT: 1 av. de l'Université, 64100. Tel: 05 59 40 71 20

Other institution

Ecole Supérieure de Commerce (ESC)
3 rue St John Perse, 64000. Tel: 05 59 92 64 64. www.esc-pau.fr
Mastère spécialisé: audit et expertise

Courses for foreign students

Institut d'Etudes Françaises pour Etudiants Etrangers (IEFE), Faculté

des Lettres, BP 1160. Tel: 05 59 40 73 85
Semester and term-based courses at various levels, with a variety of diplomas available, on offer to students over 18 years of age.

University libraries

Service Commun de la Documentation: Campus Universitaire, 64000.
  Tel: 05 59 92 33 60
Droit-Lettres: Campus Universitaire, 64000. Tel: 05 59 40 72 00
Sciences: Campus Universitaire, 64000. Tel: 05 59 40 72 22

CLOUS

(Comes under the CROUS in Bordeaux)
7 rue St John Perse, BP 1161, 64011 Cedex. Tel: 05 59 30 89 00. www.
  crous-bordeaux.fr

CROUS-controlled accommodation
The offer ranges from traditional furnished rooms to flatlets in new or renovated blocks.
Principal halls of residence:
- Cité Gaston Pheobus, av. Poplawski (517 traditional rooms on campus)
- Cité Corisande d'Andoins, 3 av. de Saragosse (457 traditional rooms, near town centre and campus)
- Résidence Clé de Sol, 39 av. du Loup (64 T1, 15 T1 bis and 4 T2, 20 mins walk away)
- Résidence Ronsard, rue Ronsard (147 T1 and 16 T1 bis, near campus)
- Résidence Clé des Champs, 7 rue St John Perse (90 T1, 27 T1 bis, 8 T2 and 8 T3, on campus)
- Résidence le Thélème, rue des Frères Camors (149 T1, near campus)

CROUS restaurants
- RU Cap Sud, Maison de l'Etudiant, av. Poplawski (wide variety of full meals and snacks)
- Cafétéria Arlequin (within the Law Faculty) (dish of the day, pizzas, quiches and snacks)
- Brasserie Universitaire La Vague (on campus, between the Arts and Science Faculties; set meals, pizzas and home-made snacks)

Privately run hostels

- Association Logis des Jeunes, 30 ter rue Michel Hounau, 64000. Tel: 05 59 11 05 05
- Foyer d'Hébergement Bon Pasteur, 33 rue Dévéria, 64000. Tel: 05 59 30 64 33
- Foyer d'Amitié, 25 av. Gaston Phoebus, 64000. Tel: 05 59 40 26 67

Private-sector residences

- Victoria Pau Université, 1 rue Ronsard, 64000. Tel: 0820 830 830
- Résidence Pierre et Etudes I et II, 28 rue Ronsard, 64000. Tel: 0820 830 830

The town and its surrounding area

Lying some 760 kilometres south-west of Paris, in the foothills of the Pyrenees, *chef-lieu* of the *département des Pyrénées Atlantiques*, Pau is a medium-sized town of some 140,000 inhabitants, known for its mild and sunny climate, with its reputed curative powers, its profuse greenery and its spectacular location.

From its humble beginnings as a fortified crossing on the River Gave, it rose to become, successively, the fortress capital of the Viscounts of Béarn, the home of the Kings of French Navarre, and birthplace of a great French king, Henri IV. And its royal connections do not stop there: one of its sons, Jean-Baptiste Bernadotte, after first fighting for France – as a senior commander in Napoleon's army, and later an Imperial Marshall – went on to be elected Crown Prince of Sweden in 1810, and King in 1818. His dynasty reigns there to this day. Another *palois*, Henri de Laborde de Monpezat, was a fourth-generation Crown Prince of Denmark.

In the early nineteenth century, the town's mild and clement climate and stunning location attracted the attention of Wellington's troops and officers after their defeat of the French at Orthez in 1814. As a result, for the century from the Romantic era to the Belle Epoque, the place became an 'English city' to which flocked the aristocracy from throughout Europe, especially the English, who brought with them their love of grand houses and gardens and their sporting pastimes, rugby and golf.

It was at this period that Pau developed its 750 hectares of public parks and gardens, so that its ratio of green open space per head of population remains today the highest in Europe, and it has twice been the winner of the Grand Prix National de Fleurissement (in 1990 and 1996).

The town's coat of arms bears witness to its glorious past; but there are many other vestiges too. The *château* that dominates one end of the bd des Pyrénées, with its spectacular views of snow-clad mountain peaks, is perhaps the most obvious – even if its imposing modern aspect owes much to extensive nineteenth-century renovation. A walk through the streets of the *vieille ville*, with its fascinating townhouses that span the years from the medieval period to the eighteenth century, or the later avenues lined with grand nineteenth- and twentieth-century villas and their gardens, demonstrates the continuity of this heritage.

However, its inhabitants insist that, whatever importance may be attached to the past, their eyes remain firmly turned to the future. Today the town has a thriving economy, based upon a high-tech industrial base. Its university, given independent status only in 1972, after existing for years as an outpost of the University of Bordeaux, welcomes some 15,000 students, and their presence gives the town a youthful buzz. Moreover, the university is committed to a policy of interaction with local industry and its research facilities, to push back scientific and technological frontiers. The Centre des Métiers Pétroliers, with its 2,000 researchers and engineers, is one of the most important in the world.

Though remote from the hub of French government and administration, it has good communications with the outside world. Its well-equipped international airport boasts direct scheduled flights to Madrid, London, Geneva and various destinations in northern Italy, as well as nine round trips a day to Paris, and links with other important centres throught France. TGV rolling stock will take the traveller via Toulouse north to Paris, west to the Côte d'Azur, and north-east to Bordeaux and on to Nantes.

Among the important festivals, celebrations and sporting events that are held annually in the town should be included the Carnaval, which is always marked in traditional *béarnais* manner; but the cultural high-point of the year is the Festival de Pau, established in 1977, which takes place from mid-June to mid-July, and is an extravaganza of theatre, music and dance. It attracts performers from throughout France and abroad. Whitsuntide sees the Grand Prix Automobile, a formula 3000 race in the streets of the town, and October brings the Concours Complet International, a gruelling three-day event for some of the world's best horses and riders, and a reminder of Pau's great equestrian tradition.

Tourist information

Office Municipal de Tourisme, place Royale, 64000. Tel: 05 59 27 03 21.
www.pau.fr

Hotels

- Hôtel de la Pomme d'Or, 11 rue Maréchal Foch. Tel: 05 59 11 23 23 (cheerful, relatively inexpensive)
- Hôtel Central, 15 rue Léon Daran. Tel: 05 59 27 33 28 (centrally located, good value)

Youth hostel
30 rue Michel Hounau. Tel: 05 59 11 05 05

Restaurants

- La Brochetterie, 16 rue Henri IV (grills and fish). Tel: 05 59 27 40 33
- Le Berry, 4 rue Gachet (good atmosphere, inexpensive). Tel: 05 59 27 42 95

Leisure facilities

Museums and art galleries
- Château de Pau – Musée National (also contains the Musée Béarnais)
- Musée Bernadotte, rue Tran
- Musée des Beaux-Arts, rue Mathieu Lalanne
- Musée des Parachutistes, Ecole des Troupes Aéroportées

Theatre
- Théâtre Monte Charge, 7 rue Rivarès. Tel: 05 59 27 74 91
- Théâtre Saint Louis, rue St Louis. Tel: 05 59 27 85 80
- Espaces Plurielles, 17 av. Saragosse. Tel: 05 59 84 11 93
- Zénith, bd Cami Salié. Tel: 05 59 80 77 66
- Le Palais Beaumont, Parc Beaumont. Tel: 05 59 11 20 00
- La Scène, 70 rue d'Etigny. Tel: 05 59 72 58 65

Cinema
- Le Méliès, Cinéma d'art et d'essai, 6 rue Bargoin, 64000. Tel: 05 59 27 60 52
- CGR Saint Louis, 11 rue du Maréchal Joffre, 64000. Tel: 08 92 68 04 45
- Méga CGR, place du 7ème Art, 64000. Tel: 05 59 02 93 80

Sport
SUAPS: Bureau des Sports, Présidence de l'UPPA. Tel: 05 59 92 34 70
Direction Départementale de la Jeunesse et des Sports, 8 rue de l'Enfant Jésus, 64000. Tel: 05 59 27 27 56

Swimming pool: Complexe Nautique Louis Péghuilan, bd du Cami Salié.
 Tel: 05 59 84 52 88
Palais des Sports: BP 1163, bd du Cami-Salié, 64011. Tel: 05 59 80 01 22
Skittles: Plantier Municipal de Pau, 5 allée du Grand Tour. Tel: 05 59 62
 37 96
Equestrian sports: Hippodrome de Pau. Tel: 05 59 13 07 07
Pelote basque: Le Jaï Alaï de Pau, Hippodrome de Pau

Useful addresses

Main post office: 21 cours Bosquet. Tel: 05 59 98 54 74
Municipal library: square Paul Lafon. Tel: 05 59 27 15 72
ANPE: 45 rue Emile Guichenné, 64000. Tel: 05 59 83 71 58
Bookshops:
- FNAC, Centre Bosquet, 64000. Tel: 05 59 98 90 00
- Librairie Tonnet, place Marguérite Laborde. Tel: 05 59 30 77 33
CIJ: Bureau d'Information Jeunesse, Complexe de la République, rue
 Carnot, 64000. Tel: 05 59 98 90 40
CAF: 5 rue Louis Barthou, 64000. Tel: 05 59 98 55 00
Internet access: CyberSeventies, 7 rue Léon Duran
Préfecture: 2 rue Mal Joffre, 64000

Health care

Centre Hospitalier de Pau, 4 bd Hauterive, BP 1156, 64046 Pau Univer-
 sité Cedex: Tel: 05 59 92 48 48
SUMPPS: 4 rue Audrey Benghasi. Tel: 05 59 92 32 30
Local student insurance offices:
- LMDE, 53 rue Carnot, 64000. Tel: (N° Indigo) 3620 LMDE
- VITTAVI (SMESO), 4 rue Pasteur, 64000. Tel: 0 825 825 715
CPAM: 26 bis av. des Lilas, 64022 Cedex 9. Tel 05 59 90 30 00

Travel

Railway station
Av. Gaston Lacoste: Tel: 08 36 35 35 35

Coach office
Rue Gachet, Palais des Pyrénées. Tel: 05 59 27 22 22

Buses
STAP: rue Gachet, Palais des Pyrénées. Tel: 05 59 27 69 78

Taxis
Taxis Palois. Tel: 05 59 02 22 22

Emergencies

Commissariat: Hôtel de Police, 5 rue O'Quin, 64000. Tel: 05 59 98 22 22
Centre Anti-poison (Bordeaux). Tel: 05 56 96 40 80
SOS Amitié. Tel: 05 59 02 02 52
Drogues alcool tabac info service (free line). Tel: 0800 23 13 13

22 Poitiers

The institutions of higher education and their disciplines

Académie de Poitiers
Université de Poitiers
Hôtel Pinet, 15 rue de l'Hôtel Dieu, 86022 Poitiers Cedex. Tel: 05 49 45 30
    44. www.univ-poitiers.fr
SCUIO: Planète Info, Maison de l'Etudiant, 101 av. du Recteur Pineau,
    86000 Poitiers. Tel: 05 49 45 33 81
SRI: 40 av. du Recteur Pineau, 86022 Poitiers Cedex. Tel: 05 49 45 42 65
Droit, sciences sociales, sciences économiques, administration des entre-
    prises, sport, santé, sciences fondamentales et appliquées, lettres,
    langues
Antennes at Angoulême, Châtellerault, La Couronne, Jaunay-Clan
    (Futuroscope), Mignalou, Niort and Royan
IUT: 6 allée Jean Monnet, BP 389, 86010 Cedex. Tel: 05 49 45 34 00

Other institution

Ecole Supérieure de Commerce et de Management (ESCEM) (see also Tours)
Campus de Poitiers, 11 rue de l'Ancienne Comédie, BP 5, 86001 Cedex.
    Tel: 05 49 60 58 00
Campus du Futuroscope, Téléport 2, av. Recteur Cassin, BP 10204, 86962
    Futuroscope Cedex. Tel: 05 49 49 48 48. www.escem.fr

University libraries

Service Commun de la Documentation, Section Droit et Lettres, 93 av. du
   Recteur Pineau, BP 608, 86022. Tel: 05 49 45 33 11
Section Médecine-Pharmacie, 34 rue du Jardin des Plantes, BP 605,
   86022. Tel: 05 49 45 43 71
Section Sciences, Bât B 40, 40 av. du Recteur Pineau, BP 605, 86022. Tel:
   05 49 45 33 60

Courses for foreign students

Centre de Français Langue Etrangère (CFLE)
Université de Poitiers, 95 av. du Recteur Pineau, 86022 Poitiers Cedex.
   Tel: 05 49 45 32 94. http://cfle.univ-poitiers.fr
Full-year and semester-based courses

CAREL
48 bd Frank Lamy, BP 219C, Royan Cedex (attached to the University
of Poitiers). Courses of all levels and for all age groups are organized
throughout the year, in response to demand.

CROUS

15 rue Guillaume VII le Troubadour, BP 629, 86022 Cedex. Tel: 05 49 60
   88 00. www.crous-poitiers.fr
OTU: 35 rue Cloche Perse, place Charles VII, 86000. Tel: 05 49 37 25 55
SAEE: 40 av. du Recteur Pineau – Bâtiment I-Médias, 86022 Cedex
Division Vie Etudiant (DVE), 117 av. du Recteur Pineau, 86000 Cedex

CROUS-controlled accommodation
On offer are traditional study bedrooms, some of which have been refur-
bished and enlarged, and larger self-contained flatlets and *studios*.
Traditional halls of residence on campus:
- Cité Rabelais, 38 av. du Recteur Pineau. Tel: 05 49 44 53 35 (411 indi-
   vidual rooms, including 45 en-suite, plus 4 double rooms)
- Cité Descartes, 42 av. du Recteur Pineau (906 individual rooms)
Traditional hall between the campus and the town centre:
- Cité Marie Curie, 21 rue Jean-Richard Bloc (568 individual rooms,
   including 136 en suite, plus 4 *studios*)
Traditional halls in the town:

- Résidence Roche d'Argent, 1 rue Roche d'Argent, BP 607, 86022 Cedex (73 rooms, 19 *studios*)
- Cité Jeanne d'Arc, 49 rue de la Cathédrale (42 single rooms en suite and 1 *studio*)

In addition, there are a number of more modern residences, consisting of flatlets and *studios*, including:

- Résidence Canolle, 15 rue Guillaume VII le Troubadour (in town; 92 T1 bis, and 2 T3)
- Résidence St Eloi, 19–21 av. le Pelletier, 86000 (on campus; 68 T1 and 28 T1 bis)

CROUS restaurants

There is a wide choice of meals, ranging, according to the outlet, from the *menu complet* to pizzas, grills, sandwiches, pastries and snacks.

- RU Roche d'Argent (town centre), 1 rue Roche d'Argent
- Pub Silver Rock (town centre), 1 rue Roche d'Argent
- RU Rabelais (campus), 38 av. du Recteur Pineau
- Brasserie Themis (campus), 93 av. du Recteur Pineau
- Champlain (campus), 117 av. du Recteur Pineau
- Cafétéria des Lettres (campus), 95 av. du Recteur Pineau
- Le Grand Café (campus), Maison des Etudiants, 101 av. du Recteur Pineau
- Brasserie IUT (near IUT), 1 rue Jean Monnet

Privately run hostels

For further details, write to the *Directeur/Directrice*:

- Foyer des Jeunes Travailleurs Kennedy, 1 av. Kennedy. Tel: 05 49 47 52 00
- Foyer des Feuillants, 9 rue des Feuillants. Tel: 05 49 55 19 87
- Foyer du Travailleur Poitevin, 15 rue Dieudonné Coste. Tel: 05 49 58 36 44

Private-sector accommodation

- Les Lauréades de Poitiers, 1 av. Mozart, 86000. Tel: 0825 332 332
- Top-Campus Poitiers, 3 av. d'Iassy. Tel: 05 49 44 96 94

The town and its surrounding area

Lying some 340 kilometres to the south-west of Paris, to which it is connected by a good rail link (the TGV service puts it about an hour and a half away), Poitiers is the ancient capital of Poitou, and the modern *préfecture* of the Vienne. The original town occupied a naturally strong site on a hill above the rivers Clain and Boivre. Today's much-expanded city has sprawled well beyond this, with industrial suburbs to the south and east in particular. However, the town centre retains something of the atmosphere and charm of the *ancienne ville*.

Its historic past goes back to at least the Bronze Age, as recent excavations have shown. It subsequently became an important outpost of the Roman Empire, before falling to the Visigoths. In 732, it was at the Battle of Poitiers that Charles Martel turned back the Moorish hordes. In the Middle Ages, the town was subject to the powerful Counts of Poitou and Dukes of Aquitaine, and shuttled backwards and forwards between English and French rule. The University was founded by Charles VII in 1431.

Famous names connected with the town's past include Eléonor (or Aliénor) d'Aquitaine (1122–1204), Queen of France and then of England; Jean Bouchet (1476–c.1557), the *rhétoriqueur* poet and friend of Rabelais; Guillaume Bouchet (c1513–1593), author and bookseller; and Michel Foucault (1926–1984), the structuralist philosopher.

Important vestiges of the town's history remain. The Hypogée Martyrium is a seventeenth-century underground chapel built on a site where 72 Christian martyrs were buried by the Romans. The Baptistère St-Jean from the sixth century is one of the oldest Christian monuments in France. The impressive medieval churches include the twelfth-century Cathédrale St-Pierre, the Romanesque jewel Notre-Dame-la-Grande (twelfth-century) and St Hilaire le Grand, which was rebuilt in the eleventh to twelfth century on the site of a Gallo-Roman edifice. At the other end of the scale, and just a little to the north of the town, lies Futuroscope, a science-orientated amusement park which is a show place for new technology, particularly in the field of communications.

Modern Poitiers is a pleasant town, very manageable in terms of size. Its bustle is in no small measure due to the presence of some 26,000 students among its 125,000 inhabitants. It is possible to walk to almost any destination; but, given the nature of the terrain, a love of hills and a strong pair of shoes are absolute necessities.

Tourist information

Office du Tourisme, 45 place Charles de Gaulle. Tel: 05 49 41 21 29

Hotels
- Modern Hôtel, 153 bd du Grand Cerf. Tel: 05 49 58 46 72 (opposite the railway station, a short walk [or rather climb!] to the town centre)
- Hôtel de l'Europe, 39 rue Carnot. Tel: 05 49 88 12 00
- Hôtel Abori – Relais du Stade, 86 av. Jacques Coeur. Tel: 05 49 46 25 12 (near to IUT)

Youth hostel
Auberge de Jeunesse, 1 allée Roger Tagault. Tel: 05 49 30 09 70

Restaurants
- La Périgourdine, 38 rue Magenta. Tel: 05 49 60 70 66
- Bistrot de l'Absynthe, 6 rue Carnot. Tel: 05 46 43 77 52
- Bistrot La Villette, 21 rue Carnot. Tel: 05 49 60 49 49

Leisure facilities

Museums and art galleries
- Musée Sainte Croix, 3 bis rue Jean Jaurès
- Musée de Chièvres, 9 rue Victor Hugo
- Espace Mendès-France, 1 rue de la Cathédrale et du Cardinal

Theatres and performance venues
- Le Carré Bleu, 2 bis rue de Nimègue (music, including jazz). Tel: 05 49 45 88 78
- Le Théâtre-Scène Nationale de Poitiers, Espace Accueil/Expo, 8 rue des Grandes Ecoles. Tel: 05 49 39 29 29
- Le Confort Moderne, 185 faubourg du Pont Neuf (music, mainly modern). Tel: 05 49 46 08 08
- Le Pince Oreille, 11 rue Trois Rois (*café-concert* and *café-théâtre*). Tel: 05 49 60 25 99
- Centre Socioculturel de la Blaiserie, rue des Frères Montgolfier. Tel: 05 49 58 05 52

Cinema
- C.G.R. Rabelais, place Maréchal Leclerc. Tel: 08 92 68 04 45
- C.G.R. Castille, 24 place du Maréchal Leclerc. Tel: 08 92 68 04 45

- Le Théâtre, 1 place du Maréchal Leclerc. Tel: 05 49 88 05 05
- Le Dietrich, 34 bd Chasseigne. Tel: 05 49 01 77 90

Sport

SUAPS, Gymnase Universitaire No. 2, 40 av. du Recteur Pineau. Tel: 05 49 45 31 71 (programmes in some 20 sports)
FFSU: 17 av. R. Schuman. Tel: 05 49 38 35 45
Stadium: Stade Rébeilleau, 53 av. Jacques Coeur. Tel: 05 49 46 23 27
Skating rink: 54 av. Jacques Coeur. Tel: 05 49 46 26 68
Swimming pool: 27 rue de la Ganterie. Tel: 05 49 46 27 28
Salle Omnisports, rue de la Ganterie. Tel: 05 49 41 28 13
Centre Equestre, 1 route de Chauvigny. Tel: 05 49 53 31 02

Useful addresses

Main post office: Hôtel des Postes, 16 rue A. Ranc. Tel: 05 49 55 50 00
Bookshops:
- Librairie de l'Université, 70 rue Gambetta. Tel: 05 49 41 02 05
- FNAC, 4 rue Henri Oudin, BP 50988, 86038. Tel: 05 49 00 59 00
ANPE: 10 rue Camille St Saens, 86000. Tel: 05 49 88 86 90
CRIJ: 64 rue Gambetta, BP 176, 86004. Tel: 05 49 60 68 68
CAF: 41 rue du Touffenet, 86044 Cedex. Tel: 05 49 44 73 94
Internet access: Cybercafé LRM, 171 Grande Rue
Préfecture de la Vienne, 1 place Aristide Briand, 86031 Cedex. Tel: 05 49 55 69 11 (for *carte de séjour*)

Health care

Centre Hospitalier Régional de Poitiers (La Milétrie), 350 av. Jacques Coeur. Tel: 05 49 44 44 44
Drug abuse: Centre du Tourniquet. Tel: 05 49 88 84 95
SUMPPS: 2 av. Jean Monnet. Tel: 05 49 45 33 54
Local student insurance offices:
- LMDE, 16 rue des Vieilles Boucheries, 86000. Tel: 0810 600 601
- SMECO, 73 rue de la Cathédrale, 86036 Cedex 01. Tel: 05 49 88 38 57
CPAM: 41 rue du Touffenet. Tel: 05 49 44 55 08

Travel

Railway station
Bd du Grand Cerf. Tel: 08 36 35 35 35

Coach station
Leave from outside the railway station: Rapides du Poitou. Tel: 05 49 46 27 45

Taxis
Centrale Radio Taxis. Tel: 05 49 88 12 34

Buses
Société des Transports Poitevins (STP), 9 av. de Northampton (next to the Parc des Expositions). Tel: 05 49 44 66 88

Emergencies

Emergency night medical attention. Tel: 05 49 38 50 50
Police. Tel: 05 49 60 60 00
Fire Brigade. Tel: 05 49 03 00 60
SOS Amitié. Tel: 05 49 45 71 71
SOS déprime. Tel: 01 42 59 19 53
Suicide écoute. Tel: 01 45 39 40 00

23 Reims

Institutions of higher education and their disciplines

Académie de Reims
Université de Reims Champagne-Ardenne
Villa Douce, 9 bd de la Paix, 51097 Reims Cedex. Tel: 03 26 91 30 00. www.univ-reims.fr
SRI: 32 rue Ledru Rollin, 51100 Reims
SCUIO: 23 rue Boulard 51100 Reims. Tel: 03 26 86 80 20
Santé, sport, sciences, sciences économiques et gestion, droit et science politique, lettres et sciences humaines
IUT: rue de Crayères, BP 1035, 51687 Reims Cedex 02. Tel: 03 26 05 30 02

Université de Technologie de Troyes
12 rue Marie Curie, BP 206, 10010 Troyes. Tel: 03 25 71 76 00
IUT: 9 rue du Québec, BP 396, 10026 Troyes Cedex

University libraries

- Droit–Lettres, av. François Mauriac, 51095 Reims. Tel: 03 26 91 31 97
- Section Santé, 51 rue Cognacq-Jay, 51097 Reims. Tel: 03 26 91 39 01
- Sciences et Techniques, Moulin de la Housse, BP 1040, rue des Crayères, 51687 Reims Cedex 2. Tel: 03 26 91 32 95

Other institutions

Conservatoire des Arts et Métiers (CNAM/IIT BTP Champagne-Ardenne)
Moulin de la Housse, BP 1034, 51687 Reims Cedex 2. Tel: 03 26 36 80 25.
www.cnam-champagne-ardenne.fr
Ingénieur des techniques du bâtiment et des travaux publics

Ecole Supérieure de Commerce, Reims Management School
59 rue Pierre Taittinger, BP 302, 51061 Reims Cedex. Tel: 03 26 77 47 47.
www.reims-ms.fr
Analyse, gestion et politique financière, banque-finance, international stratégie, comptabilté et fiscalité des sociétés et groupes, communication et publicité

Courses for foreign students

CIEF, 32 rue Ledru Rollin, 51100 Reims. Tel: 03 26 47 04 11

CROUS

34 bd Henri Vasnier, 51100 Reims. Tel: 03 26 50 52 90. www.crous-reims.
fr/hebres04.php3
OTU: Tel: 08 25 88 70 70. www.routard.com/guide_agence_detail/
id/185.htm

CROUS-controlled accommodation
Résidences/*studios*:

- Résidence de l'Europe (near to the *campus sciences* and the IUT)
- Résidence Charbonneaux
- Résidence Berlioz

Cités universitaires:

- Cité universitaire Gérard Philippe (near to the *campus sciences* and the IUT)
- Cité universitaire Teilhard de Chardin-Evariste Galois (on the *campus sciences*)
- Cité universitaire Paul Fort (near to the *campus lettres-droit*)

There are also 800 furnished HLM rooms and 115 furnished HLM flats (T1 bis to F3). Contact Services de gestion des chambres et des appartements HLM (address and telephone as above).

For accommodation in the town (*hébergement en ville*), contact Services centraux. Tel: 03 26 50 59 08

CROUS restaurants

- Campus Croix-Rouge: RU Jean-Charles Prost (wide range of meals and snacks in different outlets). Tel: 03 26 08 04 80
- Cafétéria de l'UFR Droit
- Brasserie Cité Paul Fort
- Campus Science and IUT:
  RU Moulin de la Housse. Tel: 03 26 85 30 18
  Cafétéria UFR Sciences; Cafétéria de l'IUT
- Cafétérias des Cités Teilhard de Chardon et Evariste Galois
- Brasserie Cité St Nicaise

Private-sector accommodation

- Résidence Courteaux, 31–37 rue Colonel Moll, 51100 Reims
- Résidence du Parc, 21 bis à 25 av. Henri Farman, 51100 Reims

The town and its surrounding area

Now synonymous with champagne, Reims was once more widely known as a textile manufacturing centre. With a population of 185,000, of whom some 20,000 are students, the city has good cultural and sports facilities. A university was first established in Reims by Cardinal Charles of Lorraine in 1548 and this prospered until 1793. The modern university campus dates from the 1960s. The town was badly damaged in the two world wars, but many architectural monuments have survived including the Porte de

Mars, a Roman triumphal arch, and the magnificent Gothic Cathedral, perhaps the finest in France. Among the famous coronations which have taken place in Reims is that of Charles VII, who, in 1429, with the help of Jeanne d'Arc, outwitted the occupying English forces. The Musée Saint-Denis houses paintings by Corot, a rich ceramics collection and fifteenth-century tapestries. Among celebrated figures associated with Reims are Louis XIV's minister Jean-Baptiste Colbert (1619–1683), Gilles Gobelin the sixteenth-century tapestry weaver, the artist Jean-Louis Forrain (1852–1931), and the poet Paul Fort (1872–1960). The town will also be remembered as the birthplace of the first French newspaper, the *Gazette de France*, and for the unconditional surrender of the Germans on 7 May 1945. Apart from champagne, Reims is also noted for its biscuits, while the region is associated with bird *pâtés* and bottled vegetables. The town is accessible by the A4, and although it is not on a direct line, it is only about one and a half hours away from Paris by train.

Tourist information

Office de Tourisme de Reims, 2 rue Guillaume de Machault, 51100. Tel: 03 26 77 45 00

Hotels
The first two listed are near the station and the town centre.
- Ardenn'Hôtel, 6 rue Caqué. Tel: 03 26 47 42 38. www.ardennhotel.fr
- Hôtel Touring, 17 ter bd Général Leclerc. Tel: 03 26 47 38 15. www.au-touring-hotel.com
- Au Bon Accueil, 31 rue de Tillois. Tel: 03 26 88 55 74
- IBIS Reims Centre Sephi, 28 bd Joffre. Tel: 03 26 40 03 24

Restaurants
- La Lorraine, 7 place Drouet d'Erlon. Tel: 03 26 47 32 73
- La Taverne de Maître Kanter, 25 place Drouet d'Erlon. Tel: 03 26 47 00 45
- Les Trois Brasseurs, 73 place Drouet d'Erlon. Tel: 03 26 47 86 28
- Aux Bons Amis, 13 rue Gosset. Tel: 03 26 07 39 76

Leisure facilities

Museums and art galleries
- Musée des Beaux-Arts, 8 rue de Chanzy. Tel: 03 26 47 28 44

- Musée Automobile de Reims Champagne, 84 av. Georges Clémenceau. Tel: 03 26 82 83 84
- Palais du Thau, 2 place Cardinal Luçon (collection of tapestries and cathedral treasures). Tel: 03 26 47 81 79
- Musée de la Reddition, 12 rue Franklin Roosevelt (commemorates the German surrender in the Second World War). Tel: 03 26 47 84 19
- Musée Abbaye Saint Rémi, 53 rue Simon. Tel: 03 26 85 23 36

Visits to the famous champagne *caves* take place throughout the year. The following can be recommended:

- Lanson, 66 rue de Courlancy. Tel: 03 26 78 50 50
- Mumm, 34 rue Champ de Mars. Tel: 03 26 49 59 70
- Pommery, 5 place du Général Gouraud. Tel: 03 26 61 62 56
- Taittinger, 9 place St Nicaise. Tel: 03 26 85 45 35
- Veuve Clicquot-Ponsardin, 1 place des Droits de l'Homme. Tel: 03 26 89 54 40

Theatre
- Grand Théâtre de Reims, place Myron-Herrick. Tel: 03 26 50 03 92
- La Comédie de Reims, 3 chaussée Bocquaine. Tel: 03 26 48 49 00

Cinema
- Cinéma Opéra, 3 rue Théodore Dubois. Tel: 03 26 47 29 36
- Cinéma Gaumont, Parc Millésime. Tel: 03 26 08 06 06
- Cinéma Gaumont, 72 place Drouot d'Erlon. Tel: 0892 696 696

Sport
Swimming pools:
- Piscines de Reims, 36 rue Léo Lagrange. Tel: 03 26 77 32 42
- Aqua Attitude, 59 rue Vieux Colombier. Tel: 03 26 86 42 57
- Piscine du Château d'Eau, 12 allée Landais. Tel: 03 26 86 18 38

Useful addresses

MJC:
- 24 rue Marlot. Tel: 03 26 77 67 87
- 1 place Paul Claudel. Tel: 03 26 06 13 75

Service Culturel (CROUS), 20 rue Rilly la Montagne. Tel: 03 26 04 15 50

FFSU: UFR Sciences, Moulin de la Housse, BP 1039, 51697 Reims Cedex 2. Tel: 03 26 91 31 31

Post office: 2 rue Olivier Métra. Tel: 03 26 50 58 22

Municipal libraries:
- Annexe Holden, place Alfred Brouette. Tel: 03 26 02 40 11
- Annexe Laon Zola, 2 rue Neuvillette. Tel: 03 26 47 79 41
- Annexe St Rémi, 19 esplanade Capucins. Tel: 03 26 85 11 34

Bookshops:
- FNAC, Espace Drouet d'Erlon. Tel: 03 26 84 39 39
- Librairie Universitaire Nouvelle, 78 rue Chanzy. Tel: 03 26 47 30 60
- La Procure, 15 rue Carnot. Tel: 03 26 77 58 41

ANPE:
- Agence locale Reims 1, 60 rue Docteur Lemoine. Tel: 03 26 89 52 60
- Agence locale Reims 2, 51 esplanade Fléchambault. Tel: 08 26 84 68 50
- Agence locale Reims 3, 33 bis rue Hincmar. Tel: 03 26 89 52 70

CAF: 202 rue des Capucins. Tel: 08 20 25 51 10

Internet café: Clique et Croque, 27 rue Vesle. Tel: 03 26 86 93 92

Chambre de Commerce et d'Industrie: 5 rue Marmouzets. Tel: 03 26 50 62 50

CPAM: 14 rue du Ruisselet, 51086 Reims Cedex. Tel: 08 20 90 41 47

CIO: 36 rue Boulard. Tel: 03 26 88 22 32

CRIJ: 41 rue de Talleyrand, 51100 Reims. Tel: 03 26 79 84 79. www.crij-ca.fr

Direction Départementale de la Sécurité Publique, 40 bd Louis Roederer. Tel: 03 26 61 44 00

Mairie: place de l'Hôtel de Ville. Tel: 03 26 77 78 79

Health care

Hospital: Centre Hôpitalier Universitaire de Reims, rue Général Koenig. Tel: 03 26 78 78 78

Chemist: Pharmacie d'Erlon, 70 place Drouet d'Erlon. Tel: 03 26 47 26 00

LMDE, 8 rue Jeanne d'Arc, 51100 Reims. Tel: 32 60 LMDE

MGEL, Campus Croix Rouge, 34 rue Rilly la Montagne. Tel: 03 26 87 79 79

Travel

Railway station
Cour de la Gare. Tel: 03 26 88 11 63

Coach station
Routair (for Roissy), 18 bd Joffre. Tel: 03 26 40 38 28

Taxis
- Les Taxis de Reims, cour de la Gare. Tel: 03 26 47 05 05
- Taxis Radio Reims, 24 rue Brazzaville. Tel: 03 26 02 15 02
- Artisan Taxi Reims. Tel: 06 07 08 31 11

Buses
Transports Urbains de Reims (TUR), 6 rue Chanzy. Tel: 03 26 88 25 38

Emergencies

Gendarmerie Nationale. Tel: 03 26 09 18 22
SOS Amitié. Tel: 03 26 05 12 12
Sida Info Service. Tel: (freefone) 0800 840000

24 Rennes

The institutions of higher education and their disciplines

Académie de Rennes
Université de Rennes I
2 rue du Thabor, 35065 Rennes Cedex. Tel: 02 99 25 36 36. www.univ-rennes1.fr
SCUIO: 8 rue Kléber, 35000 Rennes. Tel: 02 23 23 39 79
SRI: Service des Affaires Internationales (SAI), Bât. 12D, Salle 181, Campus Beaulieu, 35042 Cedex. Tel: 02 23 23 36 71
Mathématiques, sciences, santé, sciences économiques, droit
Antennes at Lannion and St Malo. Some courses in law at St Brieuc
IUT: 3 rue du Clos Courtel, BP 90422, 35704 Rennes Cedex 7. Tel: 02 23 23 40 00

Université de Haute Bretagne (Rennes II)
Place Recteur Henri Le Moal, CS 24307, 35043 Rennes. Tel: 02 99 14 10 00. www.uhb.fr
SCUIO: same address. Tel: 02 99 14 13 91
SRI: Services Centraux, Bât. La Présidence, Niveau 4, place Recteur Henri Le Moal, CS24307, 35043. Tel: 02 99 14 10 92
Sciences sociales, arts, lettres et communication, sciences humaines, musiciens intervenants dans les écoles, sport
Some teaching in the humanities, the social sciences and sport in St Brieuc

Other institutions

Institut d'Etudes Politiques (IEP)
104 bd de la Duchesse Anne, 35700. Tel: 02 99 84 39 39. www.rennes.iep.fr
Section service publique; section économique et finance; section politique
    économique et sociale

Ecole Supérieure de Commerce (ESC)
2 rue Robert d'Arbrissel, CS 76522, 35065 Cedex. Tel: 02 99 54 63 63.
    www.esc-rennes.fr
Trois filières en plus du cursus généraliste: restauration-agroalimentaire
    et hôtellerie-tourisme; nouvelles technologies; sports-loisirs-culture

Ecole Nationale Supérieure Agronomique de Rennes (ENSA)
65 rue de Saint-Brieuc, CS 84215, 35042 Cedex. Tel: 02 28 48 50 00. www.
    agrorennes.educagri.fr
Neuf spécialisations: biochimie et technologie des produits animaux;
    économie-gestion; génie de l'environnement; halleutique; physique
    des surfaces naturelles et génie hydrologique; protection des plantes et
    environnement; sciences et techniques animales; sciences et techniques
    des productions végétales; statistiques appliquées

University libraries

Service Commun de Documentation, 4 rue Lesage, BP 90404, 35704
    Cedex 7. Tel: 02 23 23 34 00
Section Sciences Economiques et Gestion, Sciences Juridiques et
    Politiques, same address and telephone number
Section Sciences et Philosophie, 18 av. Charles Foulon, 35700. Tel: 02 23
    23 34 31
Section Santé, Hôpital Sud, 16 bd de Bulgarie, BP 4183, Cedex 2. Tel: 02
    99 26 67 29

Courses for foreign students

Centre International Rennais d'Etudes du Français pour Etrangers
    (CIREFE), Bât. E, Salle E412, place Recteur Henri Le Moal, CS
    24307, 35043. Tel: 02 99 14 13 01
Runs support courses in language and methodology for foreign students
registered in the University (intensive 15 days in September, followed by 4

evening hours per week during the semesters) and FLE courses for a wider international audience throughout both semesters, with a varied range of diplomas as targets. Summer courses are also available.

CROUS

7 place Hoche, CS 26428, 35064 Rennes Cedex. Tel: 02 99 84 31 31. www. crous-rennes.fr
OTU: 10 rue Saint Mélaine, 35000. Tel: 02 23 20 52 05

CROUS-controlled accommodation
Accommodation ranges from cheap rooms in traditional halls of residence to self-contained flatlets and *studios* for higher rents.
Villejean:
- Résidence Villejean Alsace, 2 rue d'Alsace, CS 74303 (930 traditional rooms, 240 T1, 45 T1 bis and 14 T2)
- Résidence Patton, rue du Houx, 35700 (335 traditional rooms)
- Résidence La Harpe, 10 rue du Doyen Denis Leroy, 35043 (108 T1, 8 T1 bis and 3 T2)
- Résidence Villejean Ouest Maine, 5 rue du Maine, 35043 (910 traditional rooms)
- Résidence La Touche, 33 rue Léon Ricottier, 35043 (95 T1, 20 T1 bis and 16 T2)
Town centre:
- Résidence Sévigné, 94 bd de Sévigné, 35700 (140 rooms, males only)
- Résidence Jules Ferry, 28 rue du Doyen Roger Houin, 35700 (51 traditional rooms, 49 *studettes* and 22 T1 bis)
- Résidence St Hélier, 20 rue Saint Hélier, 35000 (112 traditional rooms, females only)
- Résidence de la Gare, 4 bd Solférino, 35000 (68 T1, 6 T1 bis and 3 T2)
Beaulieu:
- Résidence Beaulieu 29, 29 av. du Professeur Charles Foulon, BP 9037, 35701 Cedex 7 (700 traditional rooms)
- Résidence des Buttes de Coësmes, 23 av. du Professeur Charles Foulon, 35700 (105 T1, 11 T1 bis and 2 T1 bis [mini])
- Résidence Beaulieu 33, 33 av. du Professeur Charles Foulon, 35700 (1,004 traditional rooms)
- Résidence Mirabeau, 32 rue Mirabeau, 35700 (558 T1, 40 T1 bis and 20 T2)

The CROUS also administers 93 HLM flats for *jeunes ménages d'étudiants* (enquiries to 32 rue Mirabeau, above).

CROUS restaurants

Town centre:

- RU Le Fougères, 46 rue Jean Guéhenno, 35000 (traditional meal, pizzas, snacks and grills)
- RU du Champ de Mars, 1 bis bd de la Liberté, 35000 (fast food, salads, snacks and pizzas)
- RU Duchesse Anne, 110 bd de la Duchesse Anne, 35000 (cafeteria meals)
- Brasserie Hoche, 2 rue Lesage, 35000 (dish of the day, with starter and dessert, or snacks)

Beaulieu:

- RU L'Etoile I, 37 av. du Professeur Charles Foulon, 35700 (traditional meals, snacks and pasta dishes)
- 'Astrolabe (le p'tit RU), allée Jean d'Alembert, 35700 (dish of the day, pasta dishes, and cafeteria snacks)
- La Cafétéria de l'IUT, rue du Clos Courtel, 35014 (specialities [crêpes, galettes], paninis, dish of the day, etc.)

Villejean:

- RU Le Métronome, av. de la Bataille Flandres-Dunkerque 35000 (fast food area, sandwich area, cafeteria and grill/dish of the day area)
- RU La Harpe, 36 av. Winston Churchill (traditional meal, fast food [pasta, dish of the day, etc.], cafeteria meals, grills and sandwiches)
- RU Le Melenik, 148 bd de Verdun, 35000 (self-service, lunchtime only)

The various formulae are available for standard *tickets de restaurant* or cash: in either case, further dishes may be bought for cash. The snack outlets deal mainly in cash.

Privately run hostels

- FJT Bourg-L'Evêque, 30 rue de Brest, 35000. Tel: 02 99 54 39 33
- Résidence Etudiante, 4 rue Tabor, 35000. Tel: 02 99 87 94 00
- Foyer Robert Rême, 8–11 av. Gros Mahon, 35000. Tel: 02 99 59 30 02

Private-sector residences

- Les Estudiantines de Bretagne, 23 rue de Châtillon, 35000. Tel: 02 99 51 54 95
- Apart' City, 5 allée Marie Berhault, 35000. Tel: 02 23 20 54 24
- Cap Beaulieu, rue Jean Jugan, 35000. Tel: 0820 830 820

The town and its surrounding area

The former capital of Britanny, and seat of the Parlement de Bretagne from 1561 until the end of the *ancien régime*, Rennes is still the administrative centre of the Breton peninsula. It is also the *préfecture* of the Ille-et-Vilaine. The inauguration of the TGV service has meant that it is now just 125 minutes away from Paris, in addition to being easily accessible from Normandy by way of Caen.

Its history stretches back to ancient times when Condate, the capital of the Celtic tribe, the Riedones, stood at the confluence of the R. Ille and the R. Vilaine. It was a stronghold of the Francs before it fell to the Bretons. However, a great fire in 1720 destroyed much of the centre, after which it was rebuilt in grand eighteenth-century style. The picturesque areas around the *ville neuve* offer numerous examples of buildings from medieval times to the seventeenth century, including half-timbered houses. However, pride of place goes to the more formal developments in reddish granite centred upon two former royal squares, now called the *place de la Mairie* and the *place du Palais*. The sector has been restored and partly pedestrianized, and is host to fashionable shops. Equally, the Jardin du Thabor, consisting in part of the gardens of the former Benedictine abbey of Saint-Melaine, is a very attractive park.

Famous sons are not legion. However, they include Admiral La Motte-Piquet (1720–1791) and the reactionary Général Boulanger. It was also in Rennes that, in 1899, Alfred Dreyfus's sentence of deportation was commuted to ten years' imprisonment.

The industrial and commercial activities of the town have much expanded in recent years, including the creation in 1982 of a *zone d'innovation et de recherches scientifiques et techniques*, Rennes Atalante. The construction work which has resulted from this expansion has given the place a distinctly heterogeneous look, which some may find unharmonious. However, it is the administrative and educational sectors which predominate and which establish the tone. A number of important festivals are held in the course of the year: Les Transmusicales (rock music) in December, the Festival des Arts Electroniques in June (every other year) and the Tombées de la Nuit (Breton Arts) in July.

Rennes is about an hour and a half away from the Channel coast and the South Brittany coast. The Mont Saint Michel, Saint Malo, Vannes and La Baule are within easy reach, as also are the great fortresses of the Marches de Bretagne: Châteaugiron, Fougères, Combourg and Vitré.

With its concern for Breton culture, and the impetus provided, in part, by the existence of a large student population, Rennes has proved popular with students who find it a humane and manageable town.

More recent years have seen the introduction of a *métro* system, which has revolutionized travel between the centre of town and the Villejean campus in particular.

Tourist information

Office de Tourisme, 11 rue St Yves, chapelle St Yves. Tel: 02 99 67 11 11. www.tourisme-rennes.com

Hotels
- Hôtel de Bretagne. Tel: 02 99 31 48 48 (near the station)
- Hôtel Kyriad, Rennes Centre, 6 place de la Gare. Tel: 02 99 30 25 80 (convenient for the station)
- Hôtel de Léon, 15 rue de Léon. Tel: 02 99 30 55 28 (near the R. Vilaine, off quai de Richemont)
- Hôtel Maréchal Joffre, 6 rue Maréchal Joffre. Tel: 02 99 79 37 74 (north of the station, inexpensive and cheerful)

Youth hostel
10–12 canal St-Martin. Tel: 02 99 33 22 33

Restaurants
- La Toque Rennaise, 9 rue Emile Souvestre. Tel: 02 99 30 84 25 (in the town centre, near the Champ de Mars; for more special occasions)
- Crêperie des Portes Mordelaises, 6 rue des Portes Mordelaises. Tel: 02 99 30 57 40 (a good cheap *crêperie*, below the old city walls)
- Le Parc à Moules, 8 rue Georges Dottin. Tel: 02 99 31 44 28 (serves mussels from St Michel bay in a large variety of forms)

Leisure facilities

Museums and art galleries
- Musée des Beaux Arts, 20 quai Emile Zola
- Musée de Bretagne, same address
- Ecomusée du Pays de Rennes, La Bintinais, route de Châtillon

Theatres and performance venues
- Théâtre National de Bretagne, 1 rue Saint-Hélier. Tel: 02 99 31 12 31
- L'UBU, 1 rue St Hélier. Tel: 02 99 30 31 68
- Opéra de Rennes, place de la Mairie. Tel: 02 99 78 48 78
- Le Triangle Culture et Congrès, bd de Yougoslavie. Tel: 02 99 22 27 27
- Le Liberté, esplanade Général de Gaulle. Tel: 02 99 85 84 83
- Le Tambour, Université Haute Bretagne Rennes II. Tel: 02 99 14 11 59
- Espace Culturel CROUS, 20 rue St Hélier

Cinema
- Arvor, 29 rue d'Antrain. Tel: 02 99 38 78 04
- Colombier, place du Colombier. Audiotel: 08 36 68 06 66
- Gaumont, 8 quai Duguay-Trouin. Audiophone: 02 31 57 92 92
- Ciné TNB, 1 rue Saint-Hélier. Tel: 02 99 31 12 31

Sport
Maison Départementale des Sports, 13B av. du Cucillé. Tel: 02 99 54 67 67

Office des Sports, Maison de la Vie Associative, cours des Alliés, 35043 Cedex. Tel: 02 23 20 42 90

SIUAPS:
- (Beaulieu) Gymnase Universitaire, av. du professeur Charles Foulon, 35700. Tel: 02 99 28 63 87
- (Villejean) Hall B, Université de Rennes II, 6 av. Gaston Berger, 35043. Tel: 02 99 14 14 70

FFSU: Université Rennes II, La Harpe, 2 rue du Doyen Denis Leroy, 35044 Cedex

Football: Stade Rennais, 111 route de Lorient. Tel: 02 99 14 35 80

Skating rink: Le Blizz, av. des Gayeulles. Tel: 02 99 38 28 10

Swimming pools:
- Piscine de Villejean, square d'Alsace. Tel: 02 99 59 44 83
- Piscine Olympique de Bréquigny, bd Albert ler. Tel: 02 99 35 21 30

Useful addresses

Main post office: 27 bd du Colombier. Tel: 02 99 01 22 11
Préfecture: 3 av. de la Préfecture. Tel: 02 99 02 10 35
ANPE: 22 bd St Conwoïon, 35000. Tel: 02 99 85 71 71
Bookshops:
- FNAC, Centre Colombier. Tel: 02 99 67 10 10
- Forum Privat, 5 quai Lamartine, 35000. Tel: 02 99 79 38 93
CAF: 2 cours des Alliés, 35028 Cedex 9. Tel: 02 99 29 19 99. A permanent
 office is also located at CROUS headquarters.
CRIJ Bretagne, 6 cours des Alliés. Tel: 02 99 31 47 48
Mairie: BP 3126, place de l'Hôtel de Ville. Tel: 02 99 28 55 55
Internet access: CIJB, Champ de Mars, 6 cours des Alliés (free). Tel: 02
 99 31 47 48 **or** France Telecom, place de la République (beside the post
 office). Tel: 10 14

Health care

CHU, Hôpital de Pontchaillon, 2 rue Henri Le Guilloux. Tel: 02 99 28
 43 21
SUMPS:
- (Villejean) La Harpe, av. C. Tillon, 35044. Tel: 02 99 14 14 67
- (Beaulieu) 263 av. Gén. Leclerc, 35042 Cedex. Tel: 02 99 28 26 30
- (Beaulieu) av. du Professeur Charles Foulon, Bât. 33, 35042 Cedex. Tel:
 02 99 36 39 14
Local student insurance offices:
- LMDE, 29 quai Chateaubriand, 35000. Tel: 02 99 86 90 20
- SMEBA, 4 rue Victor Hugo, BP 30814, 35108. Tel: 02 99 78 33 66
CPAM: 1 cours des Alliés, BP 34A, 35024 Cedex. Tel: 02 99 29 44 44

Travel

Railway station
Place de la Gare. Tel: 02 99 29 11 92; SNCF tickets. Tel: 08 92 35 35 35;
 timetable info. Tel: 02 91 67 68 69

Coach station
16 place de la Gare (immediately east of the railway station's north entrance).
 Tel: 02 99 30 87 80

Airport
Rennes St Jacques, 35136 St Jacques de la Lande. Tel: 02 99 26 60 00

Buses
Service de Transports de l'Agglomération Rennaise (STAR), 12 rue du
    Pré Botté. Tel: 02 99 79 37 37

Emergencies

Centre 15 (medical emergencies). Tel: 15
SAMU. Tel: 02 99 59 16 16
SOS Médecins, 19 rue Le Guen de Kerangal. Tel: 02 99 53 06 06
Night chemist. Tel: 02 23 45 04 04
Centre Anti-poisons (CHU). Tel: 02 99 59 22 22
Centre de Dépistage SIDA (CHU). Tel: 02 99 28 43 02
SOS Amitié. Tel: 02 99 59 71 71
SOS Victimes. Tel: 02 99 35 06 07

25 Rouen

Institutions of higher education and their disciplines

Académie de Rouen
Université de Rouen
1 rue Thomas Becket, 76821 Mont Saint Aignan Cedex. Tel: 02 35 14 60
    00. www.univ-rouen.fr
SRI: 17 rue Lavoisier, 76821 Mont Saint Aignan Cedex
SCUIO: rue Lavoisier, 76821 Mont Saint Aignan Cedex. Tel: 02 35 14 63
    06
● **Mont Saint Aignan**: lettres, langues, sciences humaines, sciences
    sociales, sciences et techniques, sport
● **Rouen**: santé, droit, sciences économiques, gestion, administration des
    entreprises
IUT: rue Lavoisier, BP 246, 76821 Mont Saint Aignan Cedex. Tel: 02 35
    14 62 02

Université du Havre
25 rue Philippe Lebon, BP 1123, 76063 Le Havre Cedex. Tel: 02 32 74 40
    00. www.univ-lehavre.fr
SCUIO: 50 rue Jean-Jacques Rousseau, 76000 Le Havre. Tel: 02 32 74 42
    29

Lettres et sciences humaines, langues, sciences et techniques, gestion

Courses for foreign students

Alliance française de Rouen, 29 rue de Buffon, 76000 Rouen. Tel: 02 35 98 55 99. Offers the *Test de connaissance du français* from January to November.

Other institutions

Conservatoire d'Etudes Supérieures Industrielles (CESI Normandie)
1 rue Marconi, Parc de la Vatine, 76130 Mont Saint Aignan. Tel: 02 35 59 66 20. www.cesi.fr
Spécialité: management industriel

Ecole Supérieure de Commerce de Rouen
1 rue Maréchal Juin, BP 215, 76825 Mont Saint Aignan. Tel: 02 32 82 57 00. www.esc.rouen.fr
Audit et expertise comptable, banque, finance, management des organisations, marketing et communication, stratégie juridique de l'entreprise

CROUS

3 rue d'Herbouville, 76042 Rouen Cedex 1. Tel: 02 32 08 50 00. http://crous.crihan.fr
SAEE: same address and telephone
OTU: Maison de l'Université, 2 rue Lavoisier, 76821 Rouen. Tel: 02 35 70 21 65

CROUS-controlled accommodation
- Cités Traditionnelles du Panorama, bd Siegfried, 76130 Mont Saint Aignan. Tel: 02 32 10 09 04
- Résidence Universitaire du Bois, rue du Maréchal Juin, 76130 Mont Saint Aignan. Tel: 02 35 75 83 83
- Résidence Universitaire la Pléiade (1, 2 & 3), rue du Maréchal de Tassigny, 76130 Mont Saint Aignan. Tel: 02 35 75 83 83
- Pavillon d'Herbouville (Rouen Nord), 3 rue d'Herbouville, 76042 Rouen Cedex 1. Tel: 02 32 10 09 04

CROUS restaurants
- Cafétéria de Martinville (Nord)
- Cafétéria Pasteur (Nord)
- Restaurant Universitaire Martainville (Nord), 22 bd Gambetta, 76183 Rouen Cedex
- Restaurant Universitaire Pasteur (Nord), 3 rue Emile Leudet, 76000 Rouen. Tel: 02 32 76 95 00
- Restaurant Universitaire du Panorama, bd Siegfried, 76130 Mont Saint Aignan. Tel: 02 35 70 70 45

Private-sector accommodation

- Les Lauréades de Rouen, 130 bd de l'Europe, 76100 Rouen
- Le Central Fac, 6 bd Gambetta, 76000 Rouen
- Le Facotel, 2 av. Pasteur, 76000 Rouen

The town and its surrounding area

The historical capital of Normandy, Rouen, with a population of 105,000, is the *chef-lieu* of the *département* of Seine-Maritime. Situated some 125 kilometres north-west of Paris on the river Seine, it is a town which suffered greatly in World War Two but which still has many outstanding buildings and monuments: the Cathédrale Notre Dame (which dates from the twelfth to thirteenth centuries and which was painted on a number of occasions by Monet), l'Eglise Saint-Ouen, the Eglise Saint Maclou (the only remaining charnel-house in France), the Gros-Horloge (sixteenth century) and the Palais de Justice. The town, noted for its art as well as its industry, is the birthplace of the dramatists Thomas (1625–1709) and Pierre Corneille (1606–1684), the philosopher Fontenelle (1657–1757), the composer Adrien Boiëldieu (1775–1834), the painter Théodore Géricault (1791–1824) and the celebrated nineteenth-century novelist Gustave Flaubert (1821–1880). The narrow pedestrian streets in the town centre attract large numbers of tourists in summer, as does the place du Vieux Marché where Jeanne d'Arc was martyred and where the modern church which bears her name rises in sharp contrast to the surrounding buildings. The thriving port is situated on the Seine, half-way between Paris and the sea.

The campus is located at Mont Saint Aignan, at the top of a very steep hill and at some distance from the centre of the town. Rouen is only one and a half hours from Paris by train, and is ideally placed for the coastal and inland towns of Normandy.

Tourist information

Office de Tourisme: 25 place de la Cathédrale, 76008 Rouen Cedex. Tel:
03 32 08 32 40

Hotels
- Hôtel Le Morand, 1 rue Morand. Tel: 02 35 71 46 07
- Hôtel du Palais, 12 rue du Tambour. Tel: 02 35 71 41 40
- Hôtel Ibis Rouen Rive Droite, 56 quai Gaston Boulet, 76000 Rouen.
  Tel: 02 35 70 48 18
- Hôtel le Chapeau Rouge, 129 rue Lafayette, 76100 Rouen. Tel: 02 35 72
  23 72

Restaurants
- Brasserie le Départ, 25 rue Verte. Tel: 02 35 71 10 11
- Brasserie Paul, 1 place de la Cathédrale. Tel: 02 35 71 86 07
- Flunch, 60 rue des Carmes. Tel: 02 35 71 81 81
- Brasserie d'Arc, 26 place du Vieux Marché. Tel: 02 35 71 97 06
- Café Leffe, 36 place des Carmes. Tel: 02 35 07 47 17

Leisure facilities

Museums and art galleries
- Musée des Beaux-Arts, esplanade Marcel Duchamp. Tel: 02 35 71 28 40
- Musée de la Céramique, Hôtel d'Hocqueville, 1 rue Faucon. Tel: 02 35
  07 31 74
- Musée le Secq-des-Tournelles (wrought ironwork) 2 rue Jacques
  Villon. Tel: 02 35 88 42 92
- Musée Flaubert et d'Histoire de la Médecine, Hôtel-Dieu, 51 rue de
  Lecat. Tel: 02 35 15 59 95 (former apartment of Achille Flaubert, the
  surgeon and father of Gustave)
- Le Donjon, Tour Jeanne d'Arc, rue du Donjon (closed on Tuesdays)
- Musée de Cire Jeanne d'Arc. www.jeanne-darc.com
- Musée Pierre Corneille, 4 rue de la Pie. Tel: 02 35 71 63 92
- Musée National de l'Education, 185 rue Eau de Robec. Tel: 02 32 82 95
  95
- Musée Maritime, Fluvial et Portuaire, Hangar portuaire no.13, quai
  Emile Duchemin. Tel: 02 32 10 15 51

Theatre
- Opéra de Rouen Haute Normandie, 7 rue du Dr Rambert. Tel: 02 35 98
  50 98

- Théâtre des Deux Rives, 48 rue Louis Ricard. Tel: 02 35 89 63 41
- Théâtre de l'Echarde, 16 rue Flahaut. Tel: 02 35 89 42 13
- Théâtre de la Canaille, 8 rue Blaise Pascal. Tel: 02 35 03 88 60
- Théâtre Duchamp-Villon, Centre Commercial St Sever, 16 place Verrerie. Tel: 02 32 18 28 10

Cinema
- Cinéma UGC Ciné Cité, Centre Commercial Saint Sever (rive gauche). Tel: (special rate) 08 92 70 00 00
- Cinéfil Cinéma le Melville, 75 rue du Général Leclerc. Tel: (special rate) 08 92 68 03 62
- Cinéma Gaumont, 28 rue de la République. Tel: 02 35 07 82 70

Sport
FFSU: Centre Sportif Universitaire (CSU), 33 bd Siegfried, 76821 Mont St Aignan Cedex. Tel: 02 32 10 07 03

Direction Régionale et Départementale de la Jeunesse et des Sports: 55 rue de l'Amiral Cécille. Tel: 02 32 18 15 20

Swimming pools:
- Ile Lacroix, av. Jacques Chastellain. Tel: 02 35 07 94 70
- Piscine Diderot, 112 bd de l'Europe. Tel: 02 35 63 59 14

Useful addresses

Main post office: 45 rue Jeanne d'Arc. Tel: 03 35 15 66 73

Mairie de Rouen: place Général de Gaulle. Tel: 02 35 08 69 00

Préfecture de la Seine Maritime: 7 place de la Madeleine. Tel: 02 32 76 50 00

Municipal library: 3 rue Jacques Villon (near to square Verdrel). Tel: 02 35 15 66 73
- Bibliothèque Roger Parment, Espace du Palais, 8 allée Eugène Delacroix. Tel: 02 35 70 61 06
- Bibliothèque St-Sever, 65 av. de Bretagne. Tel: 02 32 81 50 30

Bookshops:
- Librairie Universitaire Colbert, 1 place Colbert, 76130 Mont Saint Aignan. Tel: 02 32 10 84 84
- FNAC, Espace du Palais, 8 allée Eugène Delacroix. Tel: 02 35 52 70 20
- Virgin Megastore, 14 rue Guillaume le Conquérant. Tel: 02 35 07 84 84
- Arts Diffusion Loisirs, 31 rue du Bac. Tel: 02 32 08 67 29

CRDP: 2 rue Professeur Fleury, 76130 Mont Saint Aignan. Tel: (switchboard) 02 32 82 81 00; (bookshop) 02 32 82 81 02; (médiathèque) 02 32 82 81 03

Centre d'Information et d'Orientation: 16 rue Racine. Tel: 02 35 98 14 61

ANPE: Rouen Cauchoise, 1 place Cauchoise, BP 891, 76007 Rouen Cedex. Tel: 02 32 08 33 00

CPAM: 50 av. de Bretagne, 76039 Rouen Cedex. Tel: 02 35 03 63 63

CAF: 4 rue des Forgettes. Tel: 02 35 52 66 97

CRIJ: 84 rue Beauvoisine, 76000 Rouen. Tel: 02 32 10 49 49. www.crij-haute-normandie.org

Chambre de Commerce et d'Industrie, Palais des Consuls, 7 quai de la Bourse. Tel: 02 35 14 37 37

Internet cafes:
- The Web Café, 14–16 rue du Général Leclerc. Tel: 02 35 71 51 93
- Cyber @ Net, 47 place du Vieux Marché. Tel: 02 35 07 73 02

Maison des Jeunes: 1 place des Faïenciers. Tel: 02 32 81 53 60

Health care

SUMPPS: bd Siegfried, Mont Saint Aignan. Tel: 02 32 76 92 92

Centre Hospitalier Universitaire de Rouen, 1 rue de Germont. Tel: 02 32 88 89 90

Chemist: Pharmacie Taurin Guy, place Colbert, Mont Saint Aignan. Tel: 02 35 70 11 99

LMDE: 15 rue Grand Pont, 76000, Rouen. Tel: 32 60 LMDE

SMENO: 7 place Colbert, BP 86, 76132 Mont Saint Aignan. Tel: 0820 423 423

Travel

Railway station
Rive Droite, place de la gare. Tel: (special rate) 36 35

Coach station
Quai de la Bourse – Quai du Havre. Eurolines – Intercars Wasteels Agent, 111 bis rue Jeanne d'Arc. Tel: 02 35 71 06 77

Taxis
Radio Taxis, 67 rue Jean Lecanuet. Tel: 02 35 88 50 50
Les Taxis Blancs, 18 rue Richard Wagner. Tel: 02 35 61 20 50

Buses
- TCAR (Transports en Commun de l'Agglomération Rouennaise), 15 rue de la Petite Chartreuse, 76002 Rouen Cedex. Tel: 02 35 52 52 52
- CNA (Compagnie Normande d'Autobus): 10 bd Industriel, 76300 Sotteville lès Rouen. Tel: (special rate) 0 825 076 027

Emergencies

Commissariat de Police, 44 bd de l'Yser. Tel: 02 35 07 85 70
Hôtel de Police, 9 rue Brisout de Barneville. Tel: 02 32 81 25 00
Centre Anti-poison, 1 rue de Germont. Tel: 02 35 07 85 70
SOS Amitié. Tel: 02 35 03 20 20

26   Saint-Etienne

Institutions of higher education and their disciplines

Académie de Lyon
Université Jean Monet Saint-Etienne
34 rue Francis Baulier, 42023 Saint-Etienne Cedex 02. Tel: 04 77 42 17 00.
    www.univ-st-etienne.fr
SCUIO: same address. Tel: 04 77 42 17 16
SCRI: same address. Tel: 04 77 42 18 01
- **Saint-Etienne**: arts, lettres et arts, sciences humaines et sociales, administration, économie, gestion, sciences et techniques, santé, sport
- **Roanne**: administration économique et sociale, sciences et techniques
IUT:
- Saint Etienne: 28 av. Léon Jouhaix, 42023 Saint Etienne Cedex 02. Tel: 04 77 46 33 00
- Roanne: Centre Pierre Mendès France, 20 av. de Paris, 42334 Roanne Cedex. Tel: 04 77 44 89 00

Other institution

ENSAM-SE: Ecole Nationale Supérieure des Mines de Saint-Etienne
158 cours Fauriel, 42023 Saint-Etienne Cedex 2. Tel: 04 77 42 01 23. www. emse.fr
Formation d'ingénieur civil de mines. Domaines: ingénierie et conduite de

projet, gestion industrielle, environnement, mathématiques appliquées à l'industrie et à la finance, procédés industriels, matériaux, informatique (réseaux, TIC), microélectronique

University libraries

- Section Droit/Lettres, 1 rue Tréfilerie. Tel: 04 77 42 16 98
- Section Médecine, 15 rue Ambroise Paré. Tel: 04 72 42 14 19
- Section Sciences, 21 rue du Dr Paul Michelon. Tel: 04 77 48 15 90

Courses for foreign students

CILEC (Centre International de Langue et de Civilisation), 21 rue Denis Papin. Tel: 04 77 43 79 70

CLOUS

11 rue Tréfilerie, 42023 St-Etienne Cedex 2. Tel: 04 77 81 85 50. www. crous-lyon.fr

CROUS-controlled accommodation
Traditional hall accommodation:
- La Cotonne, 17 bd Raoul Duval. Tel: 04 77 57 30 14
- La Métare, 25 rue Docteur Paul Michelon. Tel: 04 77 25 14 62
New-style residences:
An obligatory 12-month contract for T1 *studios* runs from 1st September to 31 August. All residences have the same administrative number. Tel: 04 77 81 85 50
- Résidence La Palle, rue Henri Matisse
- Résidence Tréfilerie, 20 rue Richard
- Résidence Le Théâtre, 47 rue Tarentaiz

CROUS restaurants
- La Métare, 25 rue Paule Michelon.
- La Tréfilerie, 31 bis rue du 11 novembre
Cafétérias:
- Bellevue, 15 rue Amboise Paré
- IUT, 28 rue Léon Nautin

- La Métare, 25 rue Paul Michelon
- La Tréfilerie, 31 bis rue du 11 novembre

Private-sector accommodation

Agencies:
- OSE: Tel: 04 77 80 45 09
- Gestrim: 1 rue Edouard Vaillant. Tel: 04 77 49 19 19
- Logêka: 16 rue Charles de Gaulle. Tel: 04 77 339 445
Accommodation:
- Les Studélites Monet, 68 rue Désirée Claude. Tel: 04 77 80 75 18
- Facotel, 47 rue Désirée Claude. Tel: 04 77 49 19 19
- Résidence le Charcot: 66 rue des Docteurs Charcots. Tel: 04 77 33 31 35

The town and surrounding area

Capital of the *département de la Loire*, St-Etienne has a population of some 175,000. The town was established as a major industrial centre in the fifteenth and sixteenth centuries due to its extensive coal deposits and the skill of its inhabitants in manufacturing armaments. Silk manufacture was initiated here and the local museum houses the revolutionary Jacquard loom. The importance of the town's steel-making and coal-mining led, in 1827, to Europe's first railway with trucks drawn by horses and, by 1832, the town was linked by rail to Lyon. The importance of St-Etienne as an industrial base has declined, but the past is celebrated in the impressive Musée d'Art et d'Industrie. A second important museum is the Musée d'Art Moderne with work by Rodin, Matisse and Léger, while the Mémorial de la Résistance et de la Déportation marks the region's role in the Resistance during the Nazi Occupation. The University was created in 1969 and the 15,000-strong student population has brought more dynamism to the town, with the Place des Peuples providing a lively focal point, particularly at weekends. The town is twinned with Coventry in the UK and Des Moines, Iowa in the USA. There are good transport facilities (including a new tramway system), with daily TGVs to Lyon and Paris, and an expanding local airport served, from the UK, by Ryanair.

Tourist information

Tourist office: 16 av. de la Libération. Tel: 04 77 49 39 00. www.tourisme-st-etienne.com

Hotels
- Hôtel Albatros, 67 rue St Simon. Tel: 04 77 41 41 00
- Le Cheval Noir, 11 rue François-Gillet. Tel: 04 77 33 41 72
- Hôtel de la Tour, 1 rue Mercière. Tel: 04 77 32 28 48

Youth hostel
Rue Fontenille, 42300 Roanne. Tel: 04 77 72 52 11

Restaurants
- Corne d'Aurochs, 18 rue Michel Servet. Tel: 04 77 32 27 27
- Les Deux Cageots, 3 place Grenette. Tel: 04 77 32 89 85
- Restaurant La Botticella, 17 place Jean-Jaurès. Tel: 04 77 93 62 21

Leisure facilities

Museums and art galleries
- Musée d'Art Moderne, La Terrasse
- Musée de la Mine, 3 bd F. d'Esperey
- Musée d'Art et d'Industrie, 2 place Louis Comte
- Musée de la Résistance, 9 rue du Théâtre
- Musée de la Manufacture d'Armes, rue J. Pagnon

Theatre
- Comédie de St Etienne, 7 av. E. Loubet. Tel: 04 77 25 01 24
- L'Epalle Théâtre, 11 rue Pierre Ternier. Tel: 04 77 21 93 63
- L'Esplanade, Jardin des Plantes. Tel: 04 77 47 83 47
- Le Palais des Spectacles, bd Jules Janin. Tel: 04 77 49 47 81
- Théâtre de Poche, 44 rue Mulatière. Tel: 04 77 38 09 77

Cinema
- Le Méliès, 38 rue Gambetta. Tel: 04 77 32 32 01
- Le Royal, 31 av. de la Libération. Tel: 08 96 68 05 92
- Le Gaumont, place Jean-Jaurès. Tel: 08 92 68 75 55
- Le France, 8 rue Valse. Tel: 04 77 32 71 71
- La Cinémathèque, 24 rue Jo Gouttebarge. Tel: 04 77 43 09 77

Useful addresses

Main post office: 8 av. de la Libération. Tel: 04 77 43 40 40
ANPE: 12 rue Claude Odde. Tel: 04 77 93 58 25
CAF: 3 av. du President E. Loubet. Tel: 04 77 42 25 00
CPAM: 3 av. du Président E. Loubet. Tel: 08 20 90 41 21
Club Franco–Britannique: 4 rue André Malraux. Tel: 04 77 25 88 50
Commissariat Central: 99 bis cours Fauriel. Tel: 04 77 25 22 21
Centre Informatique: 6 rue Basse des Rives. Tel: 04 77 42 19 00 (Internet access)
France Télécom: 4 place de l'Hôtel de Ville. Tel: 08 00 42 10 14
EDF–GDF: 2 rue Lamartine. Tel: 0 81010 1000
Espace Accueil Jeunes: 4 place St Roch. Tel: 04 77 41 85 58
Mairie: place de l' Hôtel de Ville. Tel: 04 77 48 77 48
Préfecture de Police: 7 rue du Président Wilson. Tel: 04 77 32 15 36 (*carte de séjour*)
Municipal library: 24 rue Jo Gouttebarge. Tel: 04 77 43 09 77 (closed Monday)
St-Etienne Accueil: 11 rue du Président Wilson. Tel: 04 77 25 26 65
Bookshops:
● FNAC Galeries Dorian, 16 rue Louis Braille. Tel: 04 77 43 43 43
● Librairie Forum, 2 rue Général Foy. Tel: 04 77 32 36 59
● Librairie de Paris, 6 rue Michel Rondet. Tel: 04 77 32 89 34
● Librairie Gibert, 18 rue Pierre Bérard. Tel: 04 77 21 07 77

Sport
STAPS: 3 impasse Georges Clemenceau. Tel: 04 77 41 64 10
SUAPS: 34 rue Francis Baulier (2nd floor). Tel: 04 77 42 17 96
FFSU: 3 impasse Georges Clemenceau. Tel: 04 77 47 05 99
Sport Animation Vie Associative: 6 rue de la Résistance. Tel: 04 77 42 89 70
Fédération Sportive et Culturelle de France: 10 cours P. Buisson. Tel: 04 77 38 17 60
Swimming pools:
● Palais des Sports, parc de la Plaine Achille. Tel: 04 77 38 21 21
● Piscine Grouchy: 179 rue Bergson. Tel: 04 77 74 37 13
Ice-skating rink: 45 bd Jules Janin. Tel: 04 77 34 14 11

Health care

Hospital: CHU Hôpital Bellevue, 27 bd Pasteur. Tel: 04 77 12 74 00
Chemists:
● Pharmacie de la Préfecture, 11 rue Ch. de Gaulle. Tel: 04 77 32 26 76

- Pharmacie Cuvelle, 37 rue Palle, Tel: 04 77 25 37 11
- Pharmacie de la République, 38 rue de la République. Tel: 04 77 32 43 99

Local student insurance offices:

- LMDE: 54 rue 11 novembre. Tel: 04 77 32 38 31
- SMERRA: 37 rue 11 novembre. Tel: 04 77 80 02 17

SMPPS: 14 rue de la Charité. Tel: 04 77 32 40 43
BAPU: same address and telephone number

Travel

Train station
Gare de Châteaucreux. Tel: 0892 353 535

Coach station
Gare de Châteaucreux. Satobus to Lyon St-Exupéry airport: Tel: 0826 800 826

Buses
STAS (Société des Transports de l'Agglomération Stéphanoise). 5 place Jean Jaurès. Tel: 04 77 33 31 35

Airport
Aéroport de Saint-Etienne/Bouthéon, 412160 Andrezieux-Bouthéon: Tel: 04 77 55 71 71 (Ryanair service from Stanstead)

Taxis
- Radio–Taxis Saint-Etienne, 4 rue Ronsard. Tel: 04 77 25 42 42
- Taxi C.S., 13 rue R. Khan. Tel: 04 77 74 61 57

Student travel
- OTU: RU Tréfilerie, 31 bis rue du 11 Novembre. Tel: 04 77 36 68 05
- Wasteels: 28 rue Gambetta. Tel: 04 77 32 31 22

Emergencies

Centre Anti-poison (Lyon). Tel: 04 72 11 69 11
Duty doctor. Tel: 04 77 59 10 10
SOS Amitié. Tel: 04 77 74 52 52
SOS Médecins. Tel: 04 77 33 30 30
Police. Tel: 04 77 43 28 28
Gendarmerie. Tel: 04 77 92 81 00

27 **Strasbourg**

Institutions of higher education and their disciplines

Académie de Strasbourg
Université Louis Pasteur (Strasbourg 1)
4 rue Blaise Pascal, 67070 Strasbourg Cedex. Tel: 03 90 24 50 00. www.
ulp.u-strasbg.fr
SRI: same address
SCUIO: same address. Tel: 03 90 24 11 50
Santé, paramédical, sciences et techniques, sciences économiques et
gestion, sciences humaines, sciences de l'éducation, mathématiques et
informatique
IUT:
● 1 allée d'Athènes, 67300 Schiltigheim. Tel: 03 90 24 25 26
● 30 rue du Maire A. Traband, 67500 Hagueneau. Tel: 03 88 05 34 00

Université Marcel Bloch (Strasbourg II)
22 rue René Descartes, 67084 Strasbourg Cedex. Tel: 03 88 41 73 00.
http://umb.u-strasbg.fr
SRI: same address
SCUIO: same address. Tel: 03 88 60 03 25
Lettres, langues, sciences humaines, arts, sciences de l'éducation, sciences
sociales, théologie

Université Robert Schuman (Strasbourg III)
1 place d'Athènes, BP 66, 67045 Strasbourg Cedex. Tel: 03 88 41 42 00.
www.urs.u-strasbg.fr
SRI: Ensemble Saint-Georges, 47 av. de la Forêt Noire, 67082 Strasbourg
Cedex
SCUIO: 1 place d'Athènes. Tel: 03 88 41 42 40
Droit, sciences politiques, gestion, administration des entreprises, jour-
nalisme
IUT: 72 route du Rhin, BP 10315, 67411 Illkirch-Grafenstaden Cedex.
Tel: 03 88 67 63 00

University libraries

Bibliothèque Nationale et Universitaire de Strasbourg, 6 place de la
République
Bibliothèque de Langues, Campus de l'Esplanade
Bibliothèque des Sciences Sociales, Campus de l'Esplanade

Courses for foreign students

Institut International d'Etudes Françaises, Le Pangloss, 2 allée René Capitant, 67084 Strasbourg Cedex. Tel: 03 88 41 59 50 or 51

Other institutions

Institut d'Etudes Politiques
47 av. de la Forêt Noire, 67082 Strasbourg. Tel: 03 88 41 77 63. www.iep. u-strasbg.fr

Ecole Nationale d'Administration (ENA)
1 rue Sainte Marguerite, 67000 Strasbourg. Tel: 03 88 21 44 44. www.ena. fr

Institut Européen d'Etudes Commerciales Supérieures
Pôle Européen de Gestion et d'Economie, 61 av. de la Forêt Noire, 67085 Strasbourg Cedex. Tel: 03 90 41 42 00. www.iecs.edu
Banque-finance, finance-comptabilité-contrôle, supply chain management, entrepreneuriat-organisation-conseil, management des systèmes d'information, marketing-vente

CROUS

1 quai du Maire Dietrich, BP 50168, 67004 Strasbourg Cedex. Tel: 03 88 21 28 00. www.cours-strasbourg.fr
OTU: 3 bd de la Victoire, 67084 Strasbourg. Tel: 03 88 25 53 99

CROUS-controlled accommodation
- Cité Universitaire Paul Appell. 8 rue de Palerme. Tel: 03 88 15 54 00
- Cité Universitaire Alfred Weiss (Neudorf), 7 quai du Bruckhof. Tel: 03 88 34 99 00
- Cité Universitaire de la Robertsau, 14 route de la Wantzenau. Tel: 03 88 45 88 00
- Cité Universitaire de la Somme, 13 rue de la Somme. Tel: 03 88 61 12 45
- Cité Universitaire Gallia, 1 bd de la Victoire. Tel: 03 88 21 28 50
CROUS *studios*:
- Studios les Flamboyants, 8 rue Schnitzler (Esplanade). Tel: 03 88 45 52 40

- Studios les Cattleyas, 2 rue du Vieil Armand (Neudorf). Tel: 03 88 34 99 06
- Studios les Agapanthes, 58 rue Schott (Robertsau). Tel: 03 88 45 88 20
- Studios les Héliotropes, 78 route du Rhin (Illkirch). Tel: 03 88 67 80 18
- Résidence les Houblonnières, 5 rue St-Charles (Schiltigheim). Tel: 03 88 21 28 85
- Résidence Alfred Weiss, 4 rue du Vieil Armand. Tel: 03 88 34 90 00

CROUS restaurants
- RU Esplanade, 32 bd de la Victoire (closed in the evening)
- RU Paul Appell, 10 rue de Palerme
- RU Pasteur, 5 rue du Faubourg National
- RU Cronenbourg, 23 rue du Loess
- RU Illkirch, 76 route du Rhin-Illkirch (closed in the evening)

Other, non-CROUS restaurants popular with students are:
- Foyer de l'Etudiant Catholique (FEC) 17 place Saint Etienne (close to the cathedral)
- Restaurant Gallia, 1 place de l'Université

Private-sector accommodation

- Les Estudines Européennes, 29 rue Déserte, 67000 Strasbourg
- Les Estudines Kléber, 16 rue Hannong, 67000 Strasbourg
- Les Lauréades de Strasbourg, 25–27 rue de Londres, Quartier de l'Esplanade, 67000 Strasbourg

Privately run hostels

- Foyer de l'Etudiant Catholique (FEC), 17 place Saint Etienne. Tel: 03 88 35 36 20
- Foyer Jean Sturm, 2A rue Salzmann. Tel: 03 88 15 76 00
- Foyer Notre Dame, 3 rue des Echasses. Tel: 03 88 32 47 36
- Aumônerie Universitaire Catholique, Centre Bernanos, 30 rue du Maréchal Juin
- Aumônerie Universitaire Protestante, 7 av. de la Fôret-Noire. Tel: 03 88 61 07 28
- Maison de l'Etudiante, 7 bd de la Victoire. Tel: 03 88 35 32 67
- Résidence Universitaire Nideck, 33 rue de la Kurvau. Tel: 03 88 55 93 40

The town and its surrounding area

Strasbourg is the capital of Alsace and the *chef-lieu* of the *département* of the Bas-Rhin, and has a population of some 270,000. Situated on the Rhine some 450 kilometres to the east of Paris and adjacent to the German border, the city is rich in history and has many architectual reminders of its German heritage, particularly those which came in the wake of the Franco-Prussian War (the city was in German hands between 1870 and 1918). Goethe, Metternick and Napoleon are among the more famous graduates of the University. In more recent years Strasbourg has assumed increasing importance at European level (the Council of Europe and the European Parliament) and is now a thriving, cosmopolitan city with easy access to Germany (students often shop in an inexpensive supermarket in Kehl). The town has a busy local airport and good rail connections, including the one to Paris (the journey time is just over 4 hours [*Train Corail*]). A major pedestrianization scheme operates in the city centre and an extensive rapid transit network has been constructed. Cinemas, theatres and music thrive in the city, and there are various festivals throughout the year: film, theatre, music, dance and so on. The city boasts a most unusual cathedral (dating from the eleventh century to the fifteenth century) and a whole range of museums and art galleries. The picturesque suburb known as La Petite France contains some of the most attractive buildings in the local architectural style (*maisons à colombage*) and also a number of the more expensive restaurants. The *Strasbourgeois* are renowned for their ability to consume huge amounts of food and drink. The region has many attractions, from vineyards in the summer to skiing in the winter.

Tourist information

Tourist office: Office du Tourisme de Strasbourg, 17 place de la Cathédrale, 67000 Strasbourg. Tel: 03 88 52 28 28. www.ot-strasbourg.fr

Hotels
There are a number of hotels in the large semi-circle in front of the railway station; booking is advisable in the tourist season and also when the European Parliament is in session.
- Hôtel Vendôme, 19 rue du Maire Kuss/9 place de la Gare, 67000 Strasbourg. Tel: 03 88 32 45 23
- Hôtel Ibis Centre Gare, 10 place de la Gare. Tel: 03 88 23 98 98
- Hôtel Continental, 14 rue du Maire Kuss. Tel: 03 88 22 28 07
- Hôtel Kyriad Centre Gare, 2 place de la Gare. Tel: 03 88 22 30 30

Youth hostels
- Auberge de Jeunesse René Cassin, 9 rue de l'Auberge de Jeunesse. Tel: 03 88 30 26 46
- Auberge de Jeunesse du Parc du Rhin, rue des Cavaliers. Tel: 03 88 45 54 20

Restaurants
- Au Pont St. Martin, 15 rue des Moulins. Tel: 03 88 32 45 13
- Pizzeria chez Matteo, 30 rue des Juifs. Tel: 03 88 36 01 28
- Taverne Kanter, 13 rue des Grandes Arcades. Tel: 03 88 32 15 93

Leisure facilities

Museums, art galleries and buildings of interest
- Le Château des Rohan, completed in 1742 by Robert de Cotte for the *Cardinal-prince-évêque* Armand Gaston de Rohan-Soubise, houses the Musée des Beaux-Arts, the Musée des Arts Décoratifs and the Musée Archéologique: Palais Rohan, 2 place du Château. Tel: 03 88 52 50 00
- Musée Alsacien, 23–25 quai St-Nicolas. Tel: 03 88 52 50 01
- Musée d'Art Moderne et Contemporain, 1 place Hans-Jean Arp. Tel: 03 88 23 31 31
- Musée de l'Oeuvre Notre-Dame, 3 place du Château. Tel: 03 88 52 50 00
- Collection de dessins de la donation Tomi Ungerer, 4 rue de la Haute Montée. Tel: 03 88 32 31 54

Theatre and performance venues
- Opéra National du Rhin, 19 place Broglie. Tel: 03 88 75 48 23
- Théâtre National de Strasbourg, 1 av. de la Marseillaise. Tel: 03 88 24 88 24
- Théâtre de la Choucrouterie, 20 rue Saint Louis. Tel: 03 88 36 07 28
- Jazz d'Or, 12 rue des Juifs. Tel: 03 88 37 17 79
- Le Maillon Théâtre de Strasbourg, 13 place André Maurois. Tel: 03 88 27 61 71
- Orchestre Philarmonique de Strasbourg, Palais de la Musique et des Congrès-Entrée Schweitzer, place de Bordeaux. Tel: 03 88 15 09 09

Cinema
- UGC Ciné Cité Strasbourg-Etoile, 25 route du Rhin. Tel: 08 92 70 00 00

- Pathé Vox, 17 rue des Francs-Bourgeois. Tel: 08 36 68 22 88
- UGC Capitole, 3–5 rue du 22 novembre. Tel: 0892 700 000
- L'Odyssée, 3 rue des Francs-Bourgeois. Tel: 03 88 75 10 47

Sport

FFSU: CSU, rue Gaspard Monge, 67000 Strasbourg. Tel: 03 88 60 55 96
Swimming pools:
- Piscine Couverte Kibitzenau, 1 rue Kibitzenau. Tel: 03 88 55 90 55
- Piscine Robertsau, 210 route de la Wantzenau (Robertsau). Tel: 03 88 31 32 33
- Piscine de Hautepierre, rue Baden Powell. Tel: 03 88 29 01 81
- Piscine Ile du Wacken, 8 rue Pierre de Coubertin. Tel: 03 88 31 49 10
- Nautiland, 8 rue Dominicains (Haguenau). Tel: 03 88 90 56 56

Useful addresses

Main post office: 5 av. de la Marseillaise. Tel: 03 88 52 35 01
Bookshops:
- FNAC, 22 place Kléber, Maison Rouge. Tel: 03 88 52 21 21
- Librairie des Facultés, 12 rue de Rome. Tel: 03 88 60 12 12
- Librairies des Facultés Etrangères, 2 rue de Rome. Tel: 03 88 60 80 35
Municipal library: rue Khun (near to the railway station).
CPAM: 16 rue de Lausanne, 67000 Strasbourg. Tel: 0 820 904 150
ANPE: 20 rue Wodli, 67081 Strasbourg Cedex. Tel: 03 88 21 42 70
CAF: 18 rue de Berne, 67092 Strasbourg Cedex. Tel: 0820 25 67 10
Internet café: Cyber Café l'Utopie, 21 rue du Fossé des Tanneurs. Tel: 03 88 23 89 21
Chambre de Commerce et d'Industrie de Strasbourg et du Bas-Rhin, 10 place Gutenberg. Tel: 03 88 75 24 24
Mairie de Strasbourg, 1 parc Etoile, 67000 Strasbourg. Tel: 03 88 60 90 90
CIJ: 7 rue des Ecrivains. Tel: 03 88 37 33 33. www.cija.org

Health care

Hospitals:
- Hôpitaux universitaires de Strasbourg (Hôpital Civil), 1 place de l'Hôpital. Tel: 03 88 11 67 68
- Clinique de l'Orangerie, 29 allée Robertsau. Tel: 03 88 56 73 00

SUMP: 6 rue de Palerme. Tel: 03 88 36 02 34

Chemist: (adjacent to the halls of residence at Weiss) Pharmacie des Tuileries, 92 av. Jean Jaurès. Tel: 03 88 34 05 79

Local student insurance offices:

- LMDE, 10 rue de l'Abreuvoir, 67084 Strasbourg. Tel: 32 60 LMDE
- MGEL: 4 rue de Londres, 67000 Strasbourg. Tel: 03 88 60 26 26

Travel

Railway station

Place de la Gare. Tel: 0892 35 35 35

Coach station

Eurolines Intercars, 61 place Austerlitz. Tel: 03 90 22 14 60

Airport

Aéroport International de Strasbourg, route de Strasbourg, 67960 Entzheim. Tel: 03 88 64 67 67

Taxis

Association Centrale des Autos Taxis Strasbourg, 30 av. de la Paix. Tel: 03 88 36 13 13

Local transport

Compagnie des Transports Strasbourgeois (CTS). Tel: 03 88 77 70 70 (bus and tram information)

Emergencies

Gendarmerie. Tel: 03 88 37 52 99

Centre Anti-poison. Tel: 03 88 37 37 37

SOS Amitié. Tel: 03 88 22 33 33

SIDA Info Service. Tel: 0800 840 800

28 **Toulouse**

The institutions of higher education and their disciplines

Académie de Toulouse

Université des Sciences Sociales (Toulouse I)

Place Anatole France, 31042 Toulouse Cedex. Tel: 05 61 63 35 00. www.
univ-tlse1.fr

SCUIO: place Anantole France, 31042 Cedex. Tel: 05 61 63 37 28

SRI: Bureau J104, Université des Sciences Sociales, same address and
telephone number

Droit, étude politique, sciences économiques, techniques économiques et
comptables, administration économique et sociale, informatique

Antennes at Albi, Montauban, Rodez and Tarbes

Université de Toulouse-le-Mirail (Toulouse II)

5 allées Antonio Machado, 31058 Cedex. Tel: 05 61 50 42 50. www.univ-
tlse2.fr

SCUIO: same address, Cedex 9. Tel: 05 61 50 45 15

SRI: SEE, Bâtiment 15 (de l'Arche), 31058 Cedex 9. Tel: 05 61 50 45 90

Sciences humaines, sciences sociales, arts, langues, lettres, musique, information, communication tourisme, informatique

Antennes at Albi, Blagnac, Castres, Cahors, Figeac, Foix, Montauban
and Rodez.

IUT: 1, place Georges Brassens, BP 73, 31073 Blagnac Cedex. Tel. 05 62
74 75 75

Université Paul Sabatier (Toulouse III)

118 route de Narbonne, 31062 Cedex. Tel: 05 61 55 66 11. www.ups-tlse.fr

SUIO: same address, Cedex 4. Tel: 05 61 55 61 32

SRI: Bâtiment Administratif, same address. Tel: 05 61 55 66 24

Santé, sport, sciences et technologies, mathématiques, informatique,
gestion

IUT: 115 route de Narbonne, 31077 Toulouse Cedex. Tel: 05 62 25 80 00

Institut National Polytechnique de Toulouse (INP) (Toulouse IV)

6 allée Emile Monso, BP 34038, 31029 Cedex. Tel: 05 62 24 21 00. www.
univ-inpt.fr

Incorporates four institutions:

- Ecole Nationale Supérieure Agronomique de Toulouse (ENSAT):
  av. de l'Agrobiopole, BP 32607 Auzeville Tolosane, 31326 Castanet-
  Tolosan

- Ecole Nationale Supérieure d'Electrotechnique, d'Electronique, d'Informatique, d'Hydraulique et des Télécommunications (ENSEEIHT): 2 rue Charles Camichel, BP 7122, 31071 Cedex 7
- Ecole Nationale Supérieure des Ingénieurs en Arts Chimiques et Technologiques (ENSIACET): 118 route de Narbonne, 31077 Cedex
- Ecole Nationale d'Ingénieurs de Tarbes (ENIT): 47 av. d'Azereix, BP 1629, 65016 Tarbes Cedex

SUIO: 6 allée Emile Monso, 31029 Toulouse Cedex. Tel: 05 62 25 54 32

Formation d'ingénieurs en agronomie, chimie, génie chimique, électrotechnique, électronique, informatique et hydraulique

Other institutions

Institut d'Etudes Politiques (IEP)
2 ter rue des Puits Creusés, 31000. Tel: 05 61 11 02 60. www.univ-tlse1.fr/iep

Ecole Supérieure de Commerce (ESC)
20 bd Lascrosse, BP 7010, 31068 Cedex 7. Tel: 05 61 29 49 49. www.esc-toulouse.fr

Options de troisième année: banques et marchés financiers; Business to Business; gestion des produits de grande consommation; management des entreprises culturelles; métiers de conseil en management; management des ressources humaines, activités de service; contrôle de gestion; corporate finance; International Business; management en environnement hi-tech; Entrepreneur; aerospace management; business immobilier – développement urbain et loisirs; management stratégique des grands groupes; supply chain management; trade marketing et négotiation; programme de recherche en management; audit et consulting

University libraries

Lettres et sciences humaines: 5 allées A. Machado. Tel: 05 61 50 40 64
Droit, économie et sciences sociales, ouvrages anciens: 11 rue des Puits Creusés. Tel: 05 34 45 61 00
Sciences: 118 route de Narbonne. Tel: 05 62 17 37 17
Médecine: 65 chemin du Vallon. Tel: 05 62 17 28 88

Courses for foreign students

Université de Toulouse-le-Mirail, Département d'Enseignement du Français Langue Etrangère (DEFLE), 5 allées Antonio Machado, 31058 Toulouse Cedex. Tel: 05 61 50 46 94. Courses are reserved for students who have obtained the *baccalauréat* or equivalent, and are therefore entitled to register at the university.

A wider range of provision is available at the Institut Universitaire de Langue et de Culture Françaises (IULCF), Institut catholique de Toulouse, 31 rue de la Fonderie, BP 7012, 31068 Cedex 7. Tel: 05 61 36 81 30. Courses at all levels, in two-month bursts, throughout the academic year, and in the summer.

CROUS

58 rue du Taur, 31070 Toulouse Cedex. Tel: 05 61 12 54 00. www.crous-toulouse.fr
SAEE: same address. Tel: 05 61 12 54 33
OTU: same address. Tel: 05 61 12 18 88

CROUS-controlled accommodation
Available in both *cités universitaires* (traditional study bedrooms) and *résidences universitaires* (furnished *studios* and flatlets) in various locations.
- Cité de l'Arsenal, 2 bd Armand Duportal, 31070 Cedex
- Cité Chapou, 1 rue Saunière, 31069 Cedex
- Cité Ponsan Bellevue, rue Maurice Bécanne, 31078 Cedex
- Cité de Rangueil, 118 route de Narbonne, 31077 Cedex
- Cité du Taur, 6 rue Bellegarde, 31070 Cedex (has some T1 *studios*; 164 rooms, females only)

Of these, Arsenal, by virtue of its central location, and Chapou would seem traditionally to have been the most popular with foreign students.

There are also *studios* and flatlets (with the possibility of APL) available for allocation to individual students at the following locations:
- Résidence Daniel Faucher, allées Camille-Soula, 31078 Cedex (T1 and T1 bis)
- Résidence Les Jardins de l'Université, 31 rue Valade, 31070 Cedex (T1 bis and T3)
- Résidence Larrey, rue Larrey, 31000 (T1 and T1 bis)
- Résidences Les Humanités 1, Campus du Mirail, 4 allée Antonio Machado, BP 1276, 31058 Cedex (T1 and T1 bis)
- Résidence Les Intégrales, Campus de Rangueil, 118 route de Narbonne,

31077 Cedex (T1 and T1 bis)
- Résidence Latécoère, 6 av. du Lieutenant Lafay, 31400 (T1)
- Résidence Parc-Bellevue, 3 av. du Professeur Ducuing, 31400 (T1)

CROUS restaurants

There are some 18 restaurants and cafeterias within the conurbation, serving varied fare, as indicated below: The main restaurants also have cafeterias attached:
- Arsenal, Campus des Sciences Sociales, 2 bd Armand Duportal, 31070
- Blagnac, Campus de l'IUT, 5 rue Georges Sand, 31700 Blagnac
- ENSAT, av. de l'Agrobiopôle, 31326 Castanet Tolosan
- Mirail, Campus du Mirail, 31100
- Rangueil 1, Campus Paul Sabatier, 118 route de Narbonne, 31077 Cedex
- Rangueil 2, Campus Paul Sabatier, 118 route de Narbonne, 31077
- Rangueil 3, Campus Médecine, 133 route de Narbonne, 31077
- Chapou, 1 rue Saunière, 31069 (cafeteria)
- ENSEEIHT, 2 rue Carmichel, 31071 (cafeteria)
- IEP, 2 ter rue des Puits Creusés, 31000 (cafeteria)
- Manufacture des Tabacs, allée de Brienne, 31000 (cafeteria)
- Université des Sciences Sociales, place Anantole France, 31000 (cafeteria)

Privately run hostels

For details, write to the *Directeur/Directrice*.
Foyers UNESCO:
- 38 rue Valade. Tel: 05 61 21 12 83
- 79, allées Charles de Fitte. Tel: 05 61 42 90 09 (the general secretariat)
- 5 rue Héliot. Tel: 05 61 62 40 10
- 29 rue de Stalingrad. Tel: 05 61 63 70 47
- 66 rue Bayard

Others:
- Foyer d'Etudiantes-La Présentation, 47 rue des Trente-six Ponts, 31400. Tel: 05 61 52 91 90
- Foyer Familial, 23 rue Joly, 31400. Tel: 05 61 52 93 63 (females only)
- Foyer Garrigou-Desclaux, 13 rue Romiguières. Tel: 05 61 21 53 44 (females only)
- Foyer de la Gravette, 42 rue de la Gravette. Tel: 05 61 42 91 90 (females only)
- Foyer de Jeunes Filles Sahuc-Mazas, 11 rue de la Delbade. Tel: 05 61 52 67 63 (females only)

Private-sector residences

Les Lauréades de Toulouse Brienne, 5 av. de l'Ancien Vélodrome, 31000.
Tel: 0825 332 332

Résidence Castelbou, 22 bis rue Léonce Castelbou, 31000. Tel: 05 61 22
98 45

Compans Avenir, 19 esplanade Compans Caffarelli, 31000. Tel: 0820 830
820

The town and its surrounding area

Préfecture of the Haute-Garonne, Toulouse is the fourth largest city in
France, and is second only to Paris in the number of students it hosts
(more than 100,000). It stands on the Garonne some 680 kilometres south
of the capital, to which it is connected by fast rail links and motorways.

Known as *la ville rose*, because of the brick of which the old nucleus
of the town is built, it has long been a place of great importance. It was
successively the Visigothic capital, capital of the Kingdom of South Aquitaine, capital of the independent *comté* of Toulouse and capital of the royal
province of Languedoc. Today, it is still proud of its Occitan heritage and
its important Spanish connections.

Many relics of its glorious past, both secular and religious, are still to
be seen. The Basilique St-Sernin is the largest Romanesque cathedral in
France, while Les Jacobins is a magnificent example of *gothique du Midi*.
To these should be added the Cathédrale St-Etienne, which was deemed to
be following more northern models. The Hôtel de Ville or Capitole, which
dominates the square of the same name, dates from the early seventeenth
century, though the west front was added in the mid-eighteenth century.
Hôtels commemorating the prosperous commercial history of the town are
dotted throughout Vieux Toulouse. Particular mention should be made
of the Hôtel d'Assézat (1558), which today still houses the Académie des
Jeux Floraux.

Sons of the town who have risen to distinction include: Nicolas Bachelier
(c.1485–1557), the sculptor and architect responsible for the design of
several surviving buildings in Toulouse; Jacques Cujas (1522–1590), the
jurist and consul; Guy du Faur de Pibrac (1529–1584), the moralist; and
the mathematician Pierre de Fermat (c.1595–1665).

In more recent times, the town has seen a series of massive influxes
of immigrants: Spaniards after the Civil War, Jews from Central Europe,
North Africans and Portuguese. It has an engaging atmosphere all of
its own, with its picturesque squares, bustling cafés, lively markets and

inviting parks (Jardin des Plantes, Jardin Royal, etc.). Education has always played a large part in the town since the University was founded in 1299, as part of a campaign to suppress heresy in the area. The presence of so many students, while it might create accommodation problems, helps to promote a lively social and cultural environment. The town was granted the status of *pôle européen* in the early 1990s. Gastronomically, too, there is much on offer: *cassoulet*, cheeses like Roquefort and St-Nectaire, full-bodied regional red wines and sweet white dessert wines.

In recent decades, the town has developed significantly as a centre for research and industry. Electronics and aircraft research and construction lead the way: ARIANE, Concorde and Airbus are names that readily spring to mind in this respect. It is this exciting and successful mixture of the old and the new which gives Toulouse its distinctive stamp. A modern, fully automated *métro* line now runs across the town, linking the railway station to the town centre, and replacing the traditional slow bus journey out to the campus at Le Mirail.

From Toulouse, there is easy access to the Mediterranean coast, or to the Pyrenees for walking, climbing, skiing or even shopping in the duty-free haven of Andorra! Nearby, too, is Albi and Cathar country, with fascinating churches and fortified towns. The Canal du Midi, which links the principal towns of the region, also makes for interesting exploration.

Tourist information

Tourist office: Donjon du Capitole, BP 0801, 31080. Tel: 05 61 11 02 22

Hotels
There are a number of centrally situated cheaper hotels:
- Hôtel des Arts, 1 bis rue Cantegril, 31000. Tel: 05 61 23 36 21
- Hôtel de l'Université, 26 rue Emile Cartailhac, 31000. Tel: 05 61 21 35 69
- Hôtel du Grand Balcon, 8 rue Romiguières, 31000. Tel: 05 61 21 48 08 (interesting because of its association – recalled by the press cuttings on the walls downstairs – with St-Exupéry, and the early days of pioneering mail flights)

Rather more up-market but well placed for the town centre:
- Hôtel Saint Sernin, 2 rue St Bernard, 31000. Tel: 05 61 21 73 08
- Hôtel de Brienne, 20 bd Maréchal Leclerc, 31000. Tel: 05 61 23 60 60

Toulouse no longer has a youth hostel.

Restaurants

Cheap, copious lunches may be had, Tuesday–Sunday, in the restaurants above the stalls in the Halles Victor Hugo, or in the students' outlets along the rue du Taur. Other possibilities include:

- Au Gascon, 9 rue des Jacobins. Tel: 05 61 21 67 16
- Restaurant des Saveurs Bio, 22 rue Maurice Fonvieille, 31000. Tel: 05 61 12 15 15
- Brasserie des Beaux-Arts, 1 quai de la Daurade, 31000. Tel: 05 61 21 12 12 (for more special occasions)

Leisure facilities

For details of what's on in Toulouse, obtain copies of the weekly *Toulouse Hebdo* or *Le Flash*, or the more culturally focused *Toulouse Culture* (available from various outlets including the *mairie* and the tourist office).

Museums and art galleries
- Musée des Augustins, 21 rue de Metz
- Musée Saint Raymond, place St-Sernin
- Musée Paul Dupuy, 13 rue de la Pléau
- Musée Georges Labi., 43 rue des Martyrs de la Libération
- Museum d'Histoire Naturelle, 35 allées Jules Guesde
- Fondation Bemberg (within the Hôtel d'Assézat), 7 place Assézat
- Galerie Municipale du Château d'Eau, 1 rue Laganne
- Centre de l'Affiche, de la Carte Postale et de l'Art Graphique, 58 allées Charles de Fitte
- Cité de l'Espace, av. Jean Gonord (rocade est, sortie 17)

Theatre
- Théâtre du Capitole, place du Capitole. Tel: 05 61 63 13 13
- Théâtre Sorano, 35 allées Jules Guesde. Tel: 05 61 32 17 68
- Théâtre Jules Julien, 6 av. des Ecoles Jules Julien. Tel: 05 61 25 79 92
- Théâtre Garonne, 1 av. du Château d'Eau. Tel: 05 62 48 56 56
- Théâtre de la Digue, 3 rue de la Digue. Tel: 05 61 42 97 79
- Théâtre du Jour, 23 bis rue des Potiers. Tel: 05 61 62 07 64
- Théâtre du Pavé, 34 rue Maran. Tel: 05 62 26 43 66
- Théâtre de la Cité-Théâtre National de Toulouse Midi-Pyrénées, 1 rue Pierre Baudis. Tel: 05 34 45 05 05
- Théâtre des Mazades, 10 av. des Mazades. Tel: 05 61 47 68 04
- Les Abattoirs, 76 allées Charles de Fitte. Tel: 05 62 48 58 00

- Halle aux Grains, place Dupuy. Tel: 05 34 45 05 61
- Centre Culturel Albin Minvelle, 63 allée de Bellefontaine Tel: 05 61 43 60 20
- Centre Culturel des Mazades, 10 av. des Mazades. Tel: 05 61 47 68 04
- Centre Culturel des Minimes, place du Marché aux Cochons. Tel: 05 61 22 51 77
- Espace Croix-Baragnon, 24 rue Croix-Baragnon. Tel: 05 61 52 57 72
- Espace Bonnefoy, 4 rue du Faubourg Bonnefoy. Tel: 05 61 61 82 40
- Espace Saint Cyprien, 56 allées Charles de Fitte. Tel: 05 61 22 27 77
- Le Zénith, 11 av. Raymond Badiou. Tel: 05 62 74 49 49

Cinema

- Cinémathèque de Toulouse, 69 rue du Taur. Tel: 05 62 30 30 10

Commercial cinemas in the town centre include:

- Le Gaumont Wilson, 3 place Wilson. Tel: 0892 696 696
- UGC, 9 allées du Président Roosevelt. Tel: 0892 70 00 00
- ABC, 13 rue St Bernard. Tel: 0892 68 01 43
- Utopia, 24 rue Montardy. Tel: 05 61 23 66 20

This list takes no account of the more adventurous *salles d'art et d'essai*, of suburban cinemas, of the film activities of local MJC and *centres culturels*, or of the numerous ciné-clubs (in student halls of residence or elsewhere). There are also film festivals in the area.

Sport

FFSU: Université Paul Sabatier, Villa FNSU, 118 route de Narbonne, 31062 Cedex. Tel: 05 62 88 91 91

Service Municipal des Sports, Parc Municipal des Sports, 7 allées Gabriel Biénés, 31400 (publishes a very full and useful Guide des Sports, available also from the Hotel de Ville and other outlets)

Football: Le Stadium de Toulouse, Ile du Ramier, allées Gabriel Biénés, 31000 (site of some World Cup matches)

Rugby: Stade Wallon, Sept Deniers (the famous French club, Stade Toulousain), 114 rue des Troènes

Skating: Patinoire de Bellevue, 69 ter route de Narbonne, 31400

Swimming: Piscine Léo-Lagrange, 4 place Riquet

The town has four large sports and leisure complexes: Ponts Jumeaux, Les Argoulets, Gironis and Sésquières, and a host of other facilities. For further information, contact the Service Municipal des Sports.

Useful addresses

Main post office: 9 rue Lafayette. Tel: 05 34 45 70 51
Municipal library: Bibliothèque d'Etude et du Patrimoine, 1 rue de Péri-
    gord, BP 7092, 31070. Tel: 05 62 27 66 66
Bookshop: FNAC Toulouse-Wilson, 16 allées Franklin Roosevelt, 31000.
    Tel: 05 61 11 01 01
Préfecture: 1 place St Etienne, 31000. Tel: 05 34 45 36 66
ANPE: 47 rue de la Balance, 31100. Tel: 08 11 01 31 01
CAF: 24 rue Riquet, 31000. Tel: 05 61 99 77 00
CRIJ: 17 rue de Metz, 31000. Tel: 05 61 21 20 20
Internet access:
- Cyber King, 31 rue Gambetta
- Résomania, 85 rue Pargaminières

Health care

The main hospitals are:
- CHU Rangueil, av. Jean Poulhès. Tel: 05 61 32 25 33
- CHU Purpan, place du Docteur Joseph Baylac. Tel: 05 61 77 22 33
- Hôpital des Enfants, 330 av. de Grande-Bretagne
- Hôpital de la Grave, place Lange. Tel: 05 61 77 78 33
- Hôtel-Dieu Saint-Jacques, 2 rue Viguerie. Tel: 05 61 77 82 33
- Hôpital Joseph Ducuing, 15 rue de Varsovie. Tel: 05 61 77 34 00

There are dispensaries (*infirmeries*) in the main halls (Rangueil, Ponsan-
Bellevue, Chapou and Arsenal).
The SIMPPS offers various forms of treatment, by appointment, at its
    various centres:
- Cour de l'Institut d'Etudes Politiques, Anciennes Facultés, 2 rue Albert
    Lautmann. Tel: 05 61 63 37 49
- Centre du Mirail, Galerie de la Mémoire, Campus du Mirail, 5 allées
    Antonio Machado. Tel: 05 61 50 41 41
- Centre de Rangueil (Université Paul Sabatier, INP), Campus Universi-
    taire, 31062. Tel: 05 61 14 81 50

CPAM: 3 bd du professeur Leopold Escande, 31093 Cedex 9. Tel: 05 62
    73 80 00
Local student insurance offices:
- LMDE, 97 rue Riquet, 31007. Tel: 0825 000 601
- Vittavi, 5 rue des Lois, 31000 Tel: 0825 825 715

Travel

Railway station
Gare Matabiau, bd Pierre Sémard. Tel: 36 35

Coach station
68–70 bd Pierre Sémard, 31000 (next to SNCF). Tel: 05 61 61 67 67

Airport
Toulouse-Blagnac. Tel: 05 61 42 44 00

Taxis
- Radio-Taxi Toulousain, 18 rue Digue. Tel: 05 61 42 38 38
- Capitole Taxi, 2 impasse Alphonse Brémond, 31200. Tel: 05 34 250 250

Local travel
SEMVAT operates the local bus and *métro* services. Tickets and information from: Espace Transport, 7 place Esquirol. Tel: 05 61 41 70 70

Emergencies

SOS Médecins. Tel: 05 61 33 00 00
Centre Anti-poison. Tel: 05 61 77 74 47
All-night chemist: 70–76 allées Jean Jaurès (entrance in rue Arnaud Vidal). Tel: 05 61 62 38 05
Duty doctor. Tel: 15 **or** 05 61 49 66 66 **or** 05 61 22 00 00
Police: Commissariat Central, 23 bd de l'Embouchure. Tel: 05 61 12 77 77
HIV: Sida Info Service (freephone 24-hour number). Tel: 0 800 840 800

29 **Tours**

Institutions of higher education and their disciplines

Académie d'Orléans-Tours
Université François-Rabelais Tours
3 rue des Tanneurs, 37041 Tours Cedex. Tel: 02 47 36 66 00. www.univ-tours.fr
SCUIO: same address. Tel: 02 47 36 64 75

SRI: Bel Air, La Grignière, BP 16. Tel: 02 47 42 71 00
CIO: 64 bis bd Beige. Tel: 02 47 20 57 20
Droit, économie et sciences sociales, administration des entreprises, lettres, langues, arts et sciences humaines, santé, sciences et techniques
Antenne at Blois
IUT Tours: 29 rue du Pont-Volant, 37023 Tours Cedex. Tel: 02 47 36 75 03

Other institution

Ecole Supérieure de Commerce et de Management (ESCEM)
1 rue Léo Délibes, BP 0535, 37205 Tours Cedex 3. Tel: 02 47 71 71 71
Diplôme de l'ESCEM (Tours–Poitiers): treize filières en cursus 'classique' et quatre filières en cursus 'apprentissage'

University libraries

- Section Lettres et Sciences Humaines: 5 rue des Tanneurs. Tel: 02 47 36 64 94
- Section Droit: 50 av. Jean Portalis. Tel: 02 47 36 11 25
- Section Médecine: 2 bis bd Tonnellé. Tel: 02 47 36 61 11
- Section Sciences et Pharmacie: parc de Grandmont. Tel: 02 47 36 70 70

Courses for foreign students

Centre Universitaire d'Enseignement du Français aux Etudiants Etrangers (CUEFEE)
SRI, 8 rue des Tanneurs 37041 Cedex. Tel: 02 47 36 64 53. www.cuefee-tours.fr

CLOUS

Cité Sanitas, bd de Lattre de Tassigny, 37041 Tours Cedex. Tel: 02 47 60 42 42. www.crous-orleans-tours.fr
SAEE: (same address). Tel: 02 47 60 42 43

CLOUS-controlled accommodation
Tours has three well-appointed *résidences universitaires* with a total of 1,871 rooms. For student couples there are flats in HLM. Approved private-

sector accommodation lists are also available through the CLOUS office.
- Résidence de Grandmont, Parc de Grandmont. Tel: 02 47 25 13 43
- Résidence Saint-Symphorien, 25 rue du Pont Volant. Tel: 02 47 42 96 43
- Résidence du Sanitas, bd de Lattre de Tassigny. Tel: 02 47 60 17 60
- Résidence Hélène Boucher, 9 rue Hélène Boucher. Tel: 02 47 60 17 60
- Résidence Croix-Montoire, 8 place Choiseul. Tel: 02 47 54 22 49
- Résidence du Technopôle, 7 allée Guy Charff. Tel: 02 47 25 46 03
- Résidence les Garennes, 6 rue Gaspard Cariolis. Tel: 02 47 25 13 43
- Résidence Europa, allée Rhierry d'Argenlieu. Tel: 02 47 60 17 60
- Résidence Christophe Colomb, 21 rue Christophe Colomb. Tel: 02 47 60 17 60
- Résidence Tonnellé, bd Tonnellé. Tel: 02 47 60 42 42

CLOUS restaurants
Traditional meals are served in all restaurants, but there are also cafeterias and brasseries for alternative meals.
Restaurants universitaires:
- RU le Sanitas, bd de Lattre de Tassigny
- RU Grandmont, parc de Grandmont (also *brasserie*, *cafétéria* and *sandwicherie*)
- RU Saint-Symphorien, 25 rue du Pont Volant (also *cafétéria*)
- RU Les Tanneurs, 40 rue des Tanneurs (also *cafétéria*)
- RU Oury Gatelmand, 40 av. Jean Portalis
- RU Mare Nostrum, Jardin François 1er
- RU Tonnellé, 2 bis bd Tonnellé
Cafétérias:
- Cafétéria Anatole France, place Anatole France
- Cafétéria de l'Université, 2 rue de la Loire
- Cafétéria de la Fac de Médecine, bd Bretonneau
- Cafétéria L'Express-Maison de l'Etudiant, av. Monge

Private-sector accommodation

- Les Estudines Léonard de Vinci, 1 place F. Truffaut . Tel: 02 47 05 19 00
- Foyer Saint Thomas, 17 quai Portillon. Tel : 02 47 62 49 91 (females)
- Foyer Clair Logis, 159 rue Victor Hugo. Tel: 02 47 36 21 50 (females)
- Foyer des Jeunes Travailleurs, 16 rue Bernard Palissy. Tel: 02 47 60 51 51

The town and its surrounding area

Situated between the Loire and Cher rivers, Tours, once the capital of Touraine, is now the thriving *préfecture* of the Indre-et-Loire with a population of 137,000. The town and its region are associated with many celebrated writers, poets and artists, such as the novelists Honoré de Balzac (1799–1850) and Anatole France (1844–1924), the poet Philippe Néricault Destouches (1680–1754), the poet and historian René Rapin (1621–1687), the sculptor François Sicard (1862–1934) and the artists Jean Fouquet (1415–1481), Jean Bourdichon (1457–1521) and François Clouet (1510–1572). Tours has many fine civic buildings: the Hôtel de Ville with its allegorical statuary; the Palais de Justice; the Musée des Beaux-Arts and the Cathedral. The old part of the town is rich in fifteenth-century houses, particularly in the place Plumereau and rue Briçonnet. The University is one of the 67 new institutions created by the 12 November 1968 decree and has some 20,000 students. The region, often known as the Garden of France, has considerable natural beauty and, with its justly famous châteaux at Amboise, Chenonceau, Azay-le-Rideau, Loches, Chinon or Villandry, it attracts many tourists throughout the season. Sports facilities are good and there is a strong theatrical tradition, not to mention the many cinemas which also offer student reductions. The region has many gastronomic delights. Tours is famous for *charcuterie*, especially *rillettes* and game *pâtés*, while local market-garden produce includes such delicacies as asparagus. The Touraine wines are light and fruity, and the *crêpes* and barley sugar associated with Tours are also to be enjoyed. There are good road links with Paris together with fast, regular train connections, including the TGV Atlantique service.

Tourist information

Office de Tourisme, 78–82 rue Bernard Palissy, BP 4201, 37042 Tours Cedex 1. Tel: 02 47 70 37 37. www.ligeris.com

Hotels
- Etap Hôtel, 27 rue Edouard Vaillant. Tel: 0892 680922
- Hôtel Rosny, 19 rue Blaise Pascal. Tel: 02 47 05 23 54
- Hôtel Mondial, 3 place de la Résistance. Tel: 02 47 05 24 60

Youth hostel
5 rue Bretonneau, 37000 Tours. Tel: 02 47 37 81 58

Restaurants

There are several good value restaurants in rue Colbert and place Plumereau, for example:

● Le Petit Patrimoine, 58 rue Colbert. Tel: 02 47 66 05 81
● Le Charolais Chez Jean Michel, 123 rue Colbert. Tel: 02 47 20 80 20
● Au Bureau, place Plumereau. Tel: 02 47 20 57 57

Leisure facilities

Museums and art galleries

● Musée des Beaux-Arts, 18 place François Sicard
● Musée du Gemmail, 7 rue Mûrier
● Musée du Compagnonnage, Cloître St Julien, 8 rue Nationale
● Musée des Vins de Touraine, 16 rue Nationale

Theatres

● Théâtre Municipal, 34 rue de la Scellerie. Tel: 02 47 60 20 00
● Théâtre 'Le Plessis', rue du Plessis. Tel: 02 47 38 29 29
● Théâtre Louis Jouvet, 12 rue Léonard de Vinci. Tel: 02 47 64 50 50
● Compagnie RA, 3 rue des Tanneurs. Tel: 02 47 36 64 19

Cinema

● Cinémathèque de Tours, 7 rue des Tanneurs. Tel: 02 47 39 04 97
● CRG Méga, quartier des 2 Lions. Tel: 0892 680445
● Pathé, 4 place François Truffaut. Tel: 02 47 60 10 60
● Rex, 45 rue Nationale. Tel: 0892 680 445
● Le Studio, 2 rue des Ursulines. Tel: 0892 682 015

Sport

SUAPS: 14 av. Monge. Tel: 02 47 36 70 24

FFSU (Orléans–Tours): Maison des Sports, 1240 rue de la Bergeresse, 45160 Olivet. Tel: 02 38 49 88 88

Centre Municipal des Sports, 1 bd de Lattre de Tassigny. Tel: 02 47 70 86 00 (swimming pool and skating rink)

Useful addresses

Main post office: 1 bd Béranger (place Jean-Jaurès). Tel: 02 47 60 34 20

Municipal libraries:

● 2 bis av. André Malraux. Tel: 02 47 05 47 33

- Sanitas, place Neuve. Tel: 02 47 31 39 01

Bookshops:
- FNAC, Galeries Nationales, 72 rue Nationale. Tel: 02 47 31 27 00
- Le Bouquiniste, 20 rue Gambetta. Tel: 02 47 20 07 38
- Le Livre, 24 place du Grand Marché. Tel: 02 47 66 35 52
- La Boîte à Livres, 19 rue Nationale. Tel: 02 47 05 70 39

ANPE: 9 rue du Docteur Herpin. Tel: 02 47 60 58 58

BIJ: 22 rue Blaise Pascal. Tel: 02 47 64 69 13

CAF: 1 rue Alexandre Flemming. Tel: 02 47 31 55 16

CPAM: 36 rue Edouard Vaillant. Tel: 08 20 90 09 00

EDF-GDF. Tel: 0810 837 837

France Télécom: 31 rue Nationale. Tel: (free) 10 14

Internet café: Cyber Micro Touraine, 2 place de la Victoire. Tel: 02 47 20 89 69

Mairie: 1–3 rue des Minimes. Tel: 02 47 21 60 00

Préfecture: 15 rue Bernard Palissy. Tel: 0821 803 037

Police: 70–72 rue de Marceau. Tel: 02 47 60 70 69

Health care

SUMP: 2 rue du Hallebardier. Tel: 02 47 20 55 55

BAPU: 8 rue de la Pierre. Tel: 02 47 54 18 42

Hospital: CHRU Tours, rue de Loches. Tel: 02 47 47 47 47

Chemists:
- Pharmacie Principale, 53 rue Nationale. Tel: 02 47 05 21 29
- Pharmacie de Sanitas, 3 place Neuve. Tel: 02 47 05 43 05

Local student insurance offices:
- LMDE, 4 bis rue Paul-Louis Courier, BP 5934, 37039 Tours. Tel: 02 47 37 01 01
- SMECO, 4 rue Chanoineau. Tel: 02 47 20 88 17

Travel

Railway station
Place du Général Leclerc. Tel: 08 92 35 35 35

Coach station
Place du Général Leclerc. Tel: 02 47 05 30 49

Airport
Aéroport de Tours, 40 rue de l'Aéroport. Tel: 02 47 49 37 00

Taxis
- Groupement Taxi Radio Tours, 13 rue de Nantes. Tel: 02 47 20 30 40
- Taxis Morin, 3 impasse Rivoli. Tel: 06 80 37 05 36

Buses
Fil Bleu, 5 bis rue Dolve. Tel: 02 47 66 70 70

Student travel
Wasteels, 8 place du Grand Marché. Tel: 02 47 64 04 48

Emergencies

SOS Médecins. Tel: 02 48 23 33 33
Centre Anti-poison. Tel: 02 47 64 64 64
Hospital: CHRU Tours, rue de Loches. Tel: 02 47 47 47 47
SOS Amitié. Tel: 02 38 62 22 22

Glossary and abbreviations

The following glossary contains the most commonly used terms (including acronyms and abbreviations) which you are likely to come across during your period of residence in France. Acronyms in particular need to be mastered so that you can find your way through your preparatory paperwork and complete formalities (including choice of course options where applicable) with the minimum of difficulty. Some terms and abbreviations not contained in this glossary are to be found in the index, as they are explained more fully in the main body of the text.

Académie   Administrative division of France for the purposes of education
Accusé de réception   Acknowledgement of receipt (of letter, document, etc.)
ADP   Aéroports de Paris
ADPF   Association pour la Diffusion de la Pensée Française
AES   *Administration Economique et Sociale:* a *Licence* 'strand' *(filière)*
AFI   Association des Foyers Internationaux
Agréé(e)   Officially approved or contracted (as applied to hostels, restaurants, etc.)
Agrégation (agrèg)   The highest French teaching qualification (for secondary or tertiary education) awarded on the basis of a competitive examination, abbreviated to *agrèg* and held by an *agrégé(e)*
AIESEC   Association Internationale des Etudiants en Sciences Economiques et Commerciales
AJ   *Auberge de jeunesse* (youth hostel)
Ajiste   Youth hosteller
Ajourné(e)   Deferred (of exam results)
ALS   *Allocation de logement à caractère social*
Aménagement d'études   Document granting dispensation from course units, possibly in different years of a given programme
Amphithéâtre (amphi)   (Large) lecture room/theatre
ANIL (ADIL)   Association Nationale (Départementale) pour l'Information sur le Logement
Année scolaire   Academic year, session

ANPE Agence Nationale pour l'Emploi (Job Centre)

APL *Aide personnalisée au logement*: a housing subsidy available to students in certain forms of accommodation

ASU Administration Scolaire et Universitaire

Bac *Baccalauréat* (*qv*)

Baccalauréat (*bac, bachot*) Diploma awarded to a *bachelier* at the end of secondary education studies (in a *lycée*); more broadly based than A level in the UK, grouping a number of complementary subjects into different *filières* (strands), under the general headings *baccalauréat général, baccalauréats technologiques* and *baccalauréat professionnel*. There are some 12 *filières* in total. The diploma gives automatic right of entry to most first-year university courses

BAFA *Brevet d'Aptitude aux Fonctions d'Animateur*: a qualification for intending activity leaders/camp counsellors in a Centre de Vacances ou de Loisirs

BAPU Bureau d'Aide Psychologique Universitaire

BEES *Brevet d'Etat d'Educateur Sportif*

BEP *Brevet d'Etudes Professionnelles*

BEPC *Brevet d'Etudes du Premier Cycle du Second Degré*

BGF *Boursier du gouvernement français* (holder of a French government grant)

BO(EN) *Bulletin Officiel du Ministère de l'Education Nationale*

Boursier/Boursière Holder of a grant (*bourse*)

BP *Boîte postale*

BTS *Brevet de Technicien Supérieur*: a qualification awarded after two years of specialized, post-*baccalauréat* study in a *lycée*; see STS below

BU *Bibliothèque universitaire*

BUIIO Bureau Universitaire d'Information, d'Insertion et d'Orientation

CAF Caisse d'Allocations Familiales: the local or regional state benefits office, through which, for example, housing subsidies are paid

CAIO Centre d'Aide Administrative, Information, Orientation

CPAM Caisse Primaire d'Assurance Maladie: the office from which beneficiaries of *sécurité sociale* reclaim the state contribution towards medical expenses

CAP *Certificat d'Aptitude Professionnelle*: a vocational training certificate

CAPEPS *Certificat d'Aptitude au Professorat d'Education Physique et Sportive*

CAPES *Certificat d'Aptitude à l'Enseignement Secondaire*: a postgraduate teaching qualification (cf PGCE in the UK) awarded on the basis of a competitive examination

CAPET *Certificat d'Aptitude à l'Enseignement Technique* (cf CAPES)

Carnet A 'book' of tickets for local travel/student restaurants, etc.

Carte 12–25 Young Person's Railcard; offers reductions of up to 50 per cent for those under 26

Carte Bleue A system in France which covers the use of most major domestic and foreign credit cards

Carte Orange Travel Card in the Paris region; works by 'zones' and covers buses, *métro*, RER and suburban trains

Caution **Either**: a deposit (equivalent to one or two months' rent) paid by students entering a *résidence universitaire* or private accommodation, to cover breakages, unpaid rent, etc. **or:** a financial guarantor, an individual or an institution acting as security for accommodation, etc.

CDDP Centre Départemental de Documentation Pédagogique

CDIA Centre de Documentation et d'Information de l'Assurance. See also FFSA

CEAM Carte Européenne d'Assurance Maladie. See EHIC

CEDEX Courrier d'Entreprise à Distribution Exceptionnelle. (Where appropriate, this is placed at the end of a postal address; corresponds roughly to PO Box but deliveries are to the actual address)

CEFI Comité d'Etudes sur les Formations d'Ingénieurs

CES **Either:** *collège d'enseignement secondaire* **or:** *Certificat d'Etudes Spéciales*

CFB Collège Franco-Britannique: the British Hall of Residence at the Cité Universitaire Internationale de Paris

Chambre passagère A room in a hall of residence, let to students on a temporary basis, particularly outside term-time, at a special rate – the *tarif passager*

CHR Centre Hospitalier Régional

CHU Centre Hospitalier Universitaire

CIEE Council on International Educational Exchanges

Cité universitaire (A group of) student halls of residence run by the CROUS

CLE *Couverture logement étudiant.* Insurance policy for (private) accommodation

CLEF Centre pour le Logement des Etudiants de France

CLOUS Centre Local des Oeuvres Universitaires et Scolaires (a sub-branch of the Regional Welfare and Accommodation Office; see CROUS)

CM *Cours magistral* (lecture in a large lecture room)

CNAM Conservatoire National des Arts et Métiers

CNESER Conseil National de l'Enseignement Supérieur et de la Recherche

CNDP Centre National de Documentation Pédagogique

CNOUS Centre National des Oeuvres Universitaires et Scolaires (coordinates and oversees the work of the various CROUS – see below – and adminsters French ERASMUS awards, for example)

CNR Conservatoire national de région

CNRS Centre National de la Recherche Scientifique

CNSM Conservatoire national supérieur de musique

Coéfficient The weighting accorded to a given unit within a course structure

Commission pédagogique Validating committee in a university which examines applications by students to be granted the right to enter a course at a level other than the first year (see also *validation d'acquis*)

Conseil de résidence paritaire Joint committee in halls of residence made up of CROUS officials and student representatives

Contrôle continu Continuous assessment based on assignments and class tests

Conventionné(e) (médecin) Recognized practitioner working within the state health system

Courriel *Courrier électronique* (e-mail). See also *Messagerie électronique*

Cours magistral(-aux) (CM) (Formal) lectures as opposed to practical classes (TD)

CP *Cours préparatoire*

CPAM Caisse Primaire d'Assurance Maladie

CPGE *Classes préparatoires aux grandes écoles*

CRAPEL Centre de Recherches et d'Application Pédagogiques en Langues (Nancy)

CRDP Centre Régional de Documentation Pédagogique (teachers' regional resource centre)

CREDIF Centre de Recherches et d'Etudes pour la Diffusion du Français

C(R)IDJ Centre (Régional) d'Information et de Documentation Jeunesse

CRITER Centre de Ressources Informatiques, Télécommunications et Réseaux

CROUS Centre Régional des Oeuvres Universitaires et Scolaires (the regional headquarters of the welfare and accommodation services, dependent on the relevant *rectorat*; responsible for the provision of meals throughout the education system at post-*bac* level and for student accommodation. Also responsible for the promotion of social and cultural activities. Administers arrangements for *boursiers du gouvernement français*)

CSEN *Conseil supérieur de l'éducation nationale*

CSU *Comité Sportif Universitaire*

CU *Cité universitaire*

CV *Curriculum vitae* (in French and English)

CVL Centre de vacances ou de loisirs. The BAFA (*qv*) is the qualification needed to work at one of these centres

Cybercafé Internet café

Cycle One of three tiers in higher education in France: *premier*, *deuxième* and *troisième cycles*. See section 2.1, pp. 21–6

DALF *Diplôme Approfondi de Langue Française*

DAP *Demande d'admission préalable*: screening procedure for foreign students wishing to enter university

DDJS Direction Départementale de la Jeunesse et des Sports. Amongst its many roles, it validates the BAFA (*qv*)

DEEC *Diplôme européen d'études commerciales*

DEEM *Diplôme européen d'études en management*

DELF *Diplôme élémentaire de langue française*

Dérogation Special dispensation to depart from normal university regulations

DES Direction de l'Enseignement Supérieur (Ministère de l'Education Nationale)

DEUG *Diplôme d'études universitaires générales* (a two-year diploma)

DEUST *Diplôme d'études universitaires scientifiques et techniques*

Deuxième session Second examination period for students who missed the first session (*première session*) or who are required to resit

Devoir sur table Class test, written exercise done in class

Doctorat Doctoral thesis or course of study

DOM Département(s) d'Outre-Mer

DPFE *Diplôme de professeur de Français à l'étranger*

DRIC Direction des Relations Internationales et de la Coopération (Ministère)

DRJS Direction Régionale de la Jeunesse et des Sports. Amongst its many functions, it validates the BAFA (qv)

Droits d'inscription Registration fees paid at the beginning of the academic year

DUP *Docteur de l'Université de Paris*

DUT *Diplôme universitaire de technologie.* A two-year diploma awarded in the IUT (*qv*)

ECTS European Credit Transfer Scheme

EDF Electricité de France

EEE Espace Economique Européen

Egide Since 2000, the new name for the former Centre International des Etudiants et Stagiaires (CIES)

EHIC European Health Insurance Card. See CEAM

ENA Ecole Nationale d'Administration, whose students/graduates are known as *énarques*

ENM Ecole Nationale de Musique

ENSAM Ecole Nationale Supérieure des Arts et Métiers

ENSBA Ecole Nationale Supérieure des Beaux-Arts

ENSEPS Ecole Nationale Supérieure d'Education Physique et Sportive

ENSI Ecole Nationale Supérieure d'Ingénieurs

ENSMA Ecole Nationale Supérieure de Mécanique et d'Aérotechnique

Equivalence Recognition of a qualification as being of a sufficient standard to be considered as 'equivalent to' a French diploma or university UV/UE

ERASMUS EuRopean (Community) Action Scheme for the Mobility of University Students; the higher-education sector of the SOCRATES mobility scheme. Students under this scheme are known as *erasmiens*

ES (*bac*) *Economique et Social*

ESC Ecole Supérieure de Commerce

ESIB European Students Information Bureau. This is the 'National Unions of Students in Europe', an information-sharing body that is also a political organization representing the views of students to European institutions

ESSEC Ecole Supérieure des Sciences Economiques et Commerciales

EU European Union

EVS European Voluntary Service. A scheme operated through the British Council

Faculté (Fac) Grouping of academic disciplines, officially superseded. See UFR. *Fac* is a familiar term for 'university'

FFSA Fédération Française des Sociétés d'Assurance. See www.ffsa.fr

FFSU Fédération Française du Sport Universitaire

Fiche pédagogique Academic record card

Filière A 'strand' or programme of studies leading to an academic award

FLE *Français Langue Etrangère*

FNAC Fédération Nationale d'Achat des Cadres (a chain of discount retail outlets specializing in books, CDs, DVDs, photographic supplies, etc.)

FNAIM Fédération Nationale de l'Immobilier. Grouping of housing agencies

Foyer   A hostel

France Télécom   The French telephone system provider

FSU   Fonds de Solidarité Universitaire: offers grants or interest-free loans to students and is administered by the CROUS

GAP   Organization which arranges work placements abroad for UK sixth-formers intercalating a year prior to higher education

Gare routière   Bus/coach station

Gare SNCF   Railway station

GDF   Gaz de France

HEC   (Ecole des) Hautes Etudes Commerciales

HLM   *Habitation à loyer modéré* (corresponds roughly to 'council flat' in the UK. A number of CROUS let HLM to students)

IAESTE   International Association for the Exchange of Students for Technical Experience

IDHEC   Institut des Hautes Etudes Cinématographiques

Inscription   Registration. The first stage is *Inscription administrative* (= *pré-inscription*), usually in July, and the second stage is *Inscription Pédagogique*, usually in September

INSEP   Institut National du Sport et de l'Education Physique

INP   Instituts Nationaux Polytechniques

INSSET   Institut Supérieur des Sciences et Techniques

Internaute   Internet user, surfer

ISIC   International Student Identity Card

IUFM   Institut Universitaire de Formation des Maîtres

IUP   Institut Universitaire Professionnalisé

IUT   Institut Universitaire de Technologie

JYA   Junior Year Abroad

L (*bac*)   *Littéraire*

LEA   *Langues étrangères appliquées*: modern languages courses which include the study of two foreign languages with elements of economics, business studies and law

LIC   *Langages, images, communication*

Licence   Corresponds to the honours degree in Australia and the UK, and to the Master's degree in the USA

LINGUA   An EC programme promoting the exchange of modern languages students – theoretically restricted to those intending to become teachers but in reality open to all languages students; promotes 'minority' languages in particular

LMD   *Licence, Master, Doctorat*. The new structure in French universities, which is being introduced progressively to meet the demands of the Europe-wide credit transfer system. Known originally as '3/5/8'

LMDE   La Mutuelle des Etudiants. Most useful as suppliers of insurance to 'top up' either E111/EHIC or *sécurité sociale étudiante*

LP   **Either:** *Lycée polyvalent* **or:** *Lycée professionnel*

LV   *Langues vivantes*

LVE *Langues vivantes étrangères*

Lycée Secondary education establishment in which pupils (called *lycéens/lycéennes*) prepare their chosen strand of the *baccalauréat*; see also CPGE

Master Replaced the term 'mastaire' in 2002 under the LMD (*qv*) reforms

MCF *Maître de conférences* (university lecturer)

Médecine préventive Corresponds roughly to 'student health' in British universities; see S(I)UMPPS

MEN Ministère de l'Education Nationale

MEP Mutuelle des Etudiants de Provence. See also LMDE/USEM

Messagerie électronique E-mail. See also *Courriel*

MGEL Mutuelle Générale des Etudiants de l'Est. Operated originally in Lorraine only (hence the acronym), but spread to Alsace and Champagne-Ardenne in 1970

Minitel Terminal (private or public) of the French telecommunications system which enables subscribers/users to access information services on a small screen; includes the electronic telephone directory (*annuaire électronique*); available in post offices

Module Course unit; replaced UV. See UV/UE

MPU Médecine Préventive Universitaire. See also S(I)UMPPS

MRH *(Contrat) multirisques habitation*. Insurance policy for (CROUS) accommodation

MSG *Maîtrise de sciences de gestion*

MST **Either**: *maîtrise de sciences et techniques* **or**: *maladies sexuellement transmissibles*

MSTCF *Maîtrise de sciences et techniques comptables et financières*

Mutuelle **Either**: the organization which provides 'top-up' health policies and other insurance for students or employees **or**: (short for) the insurance policy itself

OMI Office des Migrations Internationales. The organization responsible for the recruitment of foreign labour and its integration within French society

ONISEP Office National d'Information sur les Enseignements et les Professions

Option libre A course unit, chosen freely from among the whole range of possibilities on offer, as part of course requirements in a given 'strand'

OSE Office des Services Etudiants: an association dedicated to helping students with practical problems, in particular with accommodation

OTU Voyages Student travel organization in France, which has 27 offices on university campuses and in town centres

Partiel(s) Mid-session examination(s) counting towards the assessment of a course unit

PCEM *Premier cycle d'études médicales*

Pièces justificatives Supporting documentation accompanying application forms, etc.

PMI-PME *Petites et moyennes industries-petites et moyennes entreprises*

PNF *Plan national de formation*

Poste (la)   The French post office (which also offers a banking service)

PRAG   *Professeur agrégé.* See *agrégation*

Première session   The main examination period, usually in May/June

Procès verbal   Academic profile

RATP   Régie Autonome des Transports Parisiens (the Paris transport network)

Recteur/Rectorat   The *rectorat* comprises the administrative offices of the *recteur*, the representative of central authority at the head of an *académie* (*qv*)

REP   *Réseaux d'éducation prioritaire*

RER   Réseau Express Régional: high-speed underground and suburban rail network in the Paris region

Résidence universitaire   Student residence (usually modern blocks) run by the CROUS

Restaurant universtaire (RU), abbreviated as either *Restau-U* or *Resto-U*. Student restaurant run by the CROUS; meals are subsidized and are usually purchased with vouchers (*tickets de restaurant*)

RIB   *Relevé d'identité bancaire* (Bank name, sort code and account number)

Routière   See *gare*

SAEE   Service d'Accueil des Etudiants Etrangers

SAMU   Service d'Aide Médicale d'Urgence (ambulance service, etc.)

SATA   Student Air Travel Association

Scolarité (Bureau de)   Corresponds to the academic registration office in British institutions; registers students with the French university concerned to establish student status and subsequently enrols them for examinations

S(C)RI   Service (Commun) des Relations Internationales

Science po   Abbreviation of *Sciences politiques*

SC(I)UIO   Services Communs (Inter)Universitaires d'Information et d'Orientation et d'Insertion Professionnelles des Etudiants

Sécurité sociale (sécu)   The French health-care scheme which provides cover for up to 70–80 per cent of allowable medical expenses and includes *sécurité sociale étudiante* (that part of the scheme designed specifically for students)

SERNAM   Service National des Messageries: a nationwide delivery service for large parcels, including trunks; it is part of the SNCF (*qv*)

Session   Examination period (see *première* and *deuxième*)

SIAPS   Service Inter-universitaire des Activités Physiques et Sportives. See also SUAPS

S(I)UMPPS   Service (Inter-)Universitaire de Médecine Préventive et de Promotion de la Santé.

SL   *Sciences du langage*

SMEBA   Société Mutualiste des Etudiants de Bretagne Atlantique. See also LMDE/USEM

SMECO   Société Mutualiste des Etudiants du Centre-Ouest. See also LMDE/USEM

SMENO   Société Mutualiste des Etudiants de la Région du Nord-Ouest. See also LMDE/USEM

SMEREB   Société Mutualiste des Etudiants de la Région de Bourgogne. See also

LMDE/USEM

SMEREP   Société Mutualiste des Etudiants de la Région Parisienne. See also LMDE/USEM

SMERRA   Société Mutualiste des Etudiants de la Région Rhône-Alpes. See also LMDE/USEM

SMIC   *Salaire minimum interprofessionnel de croissance*: the national minimum wage in France

SMS   *Sciences medico-sociales* (*filière* and *baccalauréat*)

SNCF   Société Nationale des Chemins de Fer Français. See also *gare*

SNV   *Sciences de la nature et de la vie*

SRI   Service des Relations Internationales

Stage   Work experience placement or training course undertaken by a *stagiaire*

STAPS   *Sciences et techniques des activités physiques et sportives*

STS   *Sections de techniciens supérieurs*

SUAPS   Service Universitaire des Activités Physiques et Sportives

Taxe d'habitation   Local tax, payable on 1 January by residents of houses, flats and so on

TCF   *Test de connaissance du français*: an essential element of the application procedure for foreign students seeking a place in a French university

Télécopie/Télécopieur/Telco   Fax/Fax machine/Fax number

TGV   *Train à grande vitesse*

Ticket(s) de restaurant   Meal voucher(s), purchased in books of ten, for use in CROUS-controlled restaurants

TOM   Territoire(s) d'Outre-Mer

Travaux dirigés (TD)   Classes in which smaller groups do work in support of large lectures; corresponds to British 'seminars' and 'tutorials' but the groups are much larger

Travaux pratiques (TP)   Practical classes (as opposed to *cours magistraux*)

Tutorat   (System of) tutorial guidance; introduced for 'exchange students' in particular; a variation is also being offered to first-year students

U3M   Plan 'Université du Troisième Millénaire'

UC   *Unité de compte*

UE   **Either**: Union Européenne **or**: *unite d'enseignement*

UFR   Unité de Formation et de Recherche; academic school or department; corresponds roughly to the old *facultés*, subject disciplines/groupings for administrative purposes

UFRAPS   Unité de Formation et de Recherche des Activités Physiques et Sportives

UKSEC   UK Socrates-Erasmus Council

UNEF   Union Nationale des Etudiants de France

USEM   Union Nationale des Sociétés Etudiantes Mutualistes Régionales: an umbrella organization for local student health-insurance provision

UV   *Unité de valeur*: a course unit under the *DEUG/Licence/Maîtrise* system. *UV obligatoire* was a 'core course' and *UV optionnelle* or *option libre* was an optional course unit

Validation d'acquis   Process of ratifying qualifications for *équivalence* (*qv*)

VITTAVI   Suppliers of student insurance as a 'top-up' for EHIC in Acquitaine, Limousin and Midi Pyrénées. See also LMDE and USEM

ZEP   *Zone d'éducation prioritaire*

Appendices

The Appendices below provide the information and sample letters which were referred to at various junctures in the text in Part II, where advice was given for job/course applications and registration purposes. In the following letters and CV, intended to serve as models, the fictitious name of Butterworth has been used.

1 Useful addresses (language assistants and work placements)

1.1 *Language assistants*
The British Council (Education and Training):
(England and Wales) 10 Spring Gardens, London SW1A 2BN
(Scotland) The Tun, Holyrood Road, Edinburgh EH8 8PJ
(Northern Ireland) 7 Fountain Street, Belfast BT1 5EG
Internet for all of the above: www.languageassistant.co.uk

1.2 *General employment*
Centre d'Information et de Documentation pour la Jeunesse, 101 quai Branly, 75015 Paris Cedex 15. Tel: 01 44 49 12 00

1.3 *Information on opportunities for vacation work*
This may be obtained from the French Cultural Service, 23 Cromwell Road, London SW7 2JB. Tel: 020 7073 1300

1.4 Au pair *work*
Accueil Familial des Jeunes Etrangers, 23 rue du Cherche-Midi, 75006 Paris. Email: accueil@afje-paris.org
Association Catholique Internationale au Service de la Jeunesse Féminine, 63 rue Monsieur le Prince, 75006 Paris. Tel: 01 44 32 12 90
Alliance Française de Paris, 101 bd Raspail, 75270 Paris Cedex 06. Tel: 01 42 84 90 00

1.5 Au pair contracts (Paris region)

These can be obtained by employers from:

Renseignements Main-d'Oeuvre Etrangère, 210 quai de Jemmapes, 75010 Paris. Tel: 01 44 84 42 86

Direction Départementale du Travail, de l'Emploi et de la Formation Profession-nelle, 109 rue Montmartre, 75084 Paris Cedex 02. Tel: 01 44 76 69 30

In the provinces, contracts may be obtained from the Direction Départementale du Travail.

1.6 Hotel and catering posts

Espace Emploi International, 48 bd de la Bastille, 75012 Paris. Tel: 01 53 02 25 50

EURES (European Employment Service), TGWU Centre, East Sussex, BN21 4DN. Tel: 0132 343 3900

1.7 Information on Social Security arrangements

The Department For Work and Pensions, The Pensions Service, International Pension Centre, Medical Benefits Section, Tyneview Park, Whitley Road, Newcastle-upon-Tyne NE98 1BA. Tel: 01291 218 7547

For general advice on health and welfare abroad, American travellers should contact CIEE, 205 East 42nd Street, New York, NY 10017

1.8 BAFA training courses

Courses have to be validated by the Direction Départementale (or Régionale) de la Jeunesse et des Sports. Paris address: DRJS Paris, 618 rue Eugène Oudiné, 75013 Paris. Tel: 01 40 77 55 00

Participating organizations and associations include:

Association Nationale Sciences et Techniques Jeunesse (ANSTJ), Planète Sciences, 16 place Jacques Brel, 91130 Ris-Orangis. Tel: 01 69 02 76 10

Centre d'Entraînement aux Méthodes d'Education Active (CEMEA): Association Nationale, 24 rue Marc Seguin, 75883 Paris, Cedex 18. Tel: 01 53 26 24 24

Comité Protestant des Centres de Vacances (CPCV): Fédération de l'Entraide Protestante, 47 rue de Clichy, 75009 Paris. Tel: 01 48 74 50 11

Union Française des Centres de Vacances (UFCV): La Délégation Régionale Ufcv, 10 quai de la Charente, 75019 Paris. Tel: 01 44 72 14 14

Union Nationale des Centres Sportifs de Plein Air (UCPA), 104 bd Blanqui, 75013 Paris

2 Job application and CV

BUTTERWORTH, Sophie Jane
23 Brunel Street
Birmingham B27 4JT
Royaume Uni

à

Monsieur le Directeur du Personnel
Société Finesherbes
12, place du Général de Gaulle
59000 Lille
France

Birmingham, le 25 mars 2006

Objet: demande d'emploi de programmeur/-euse

Monsieur,

En réponse à votre annonce parue dans *Les Echos du Nord* du 23 mars, je me permets de poser ma candidature au poste de programmeuse dans votre société (emploi été 2006).

Je vous prie de bien vouloir trouver ci-joint mon curriculum vitae. Je me tiens à votre disposition pour vous communiquer tout renseignement complémentaire que vous pourriez souhaiter.

Dans l'espoir que vous voudrez bien considérer favorablement ma demande, et dans l'attente de votre réponse, je vous prie de croire, Monsieur le Directeur, à l'assurance de mes sentiments respectueux.

Signature,
[followed by your surname (capital letters) and forenames printed in full].
BUTTERWORTH, Sophie Jane (Mlle)

CURRICULUM VITAE

Nom: BUTTERWORTH

Prénoms: Sophie Jane

Adresse: 23 Brunel Street,
Birmingham B27 7JT
Royaume Uni

Téléphone: 00–44–21–414–5966

Date et lieu de naissance: 03.10.86 à Exeter, Angleterre

Situation de famille: célibataire

Nationalité: Britannique

Langues: Anglais (langue maternelle)
          Français (parlé et écrit: niveau supérieur)
          Espagnol (parlé et écrit: niveau élémentaire)

Formation:
2002–2004 GCE A Levels (diplôme de fin d'études secondaires, équivalent du baccalauréat) en français, histoire, biologie, mathématiques.
2004–2005 BA (Licence) en français et informatique, première année. Résultat: reçue.
2005–2006 BA (Licence) en français et informatique, deuxième annee. Résultat: en cours.

Postes occupés: Employée de bureau (poste temporaire), CHP Secretarial Services, Birmingham, décembre 2004–janvier 2005.
                Vendeuse stagiaire, Computerbods plc. Birmingham, été 2005.

Autres renseignements: Permis de conduire.
De nombreux voyages en Europe.

3 Letter of acceptance

BUTTERWORTH, Sophie Jane
23 Brunel Street
Birmingham, B27 4JT
Royaume Uni

à

Monsieur le Directeur du Personnel
Socété Finesherbes
12 place du Général de Gaulle
59000 LILLE
France

Birmingham, le 5 mai 2006

Objet: offre d'emploi de programmeuse

Monsieur le Directeur,
    Je vous accuse réception de votre lettre du 27 avril. Je suis très heureuse d'accepter votre offre d'emploi en tant que programmeuse dans votre société. Comme convenu, j'arriverai à Lille le 4 juillet, 2006, et je me présenterai dans vos bureaux à 8 heures ce matin-là.

Si vous avez besoin de renseignements supplémentaires, vous pourrez me rejoindre à l'adresse citée ci-dessus. Je me permets de vous rappeler aussi mon numéro personnel: (00 44) 21 414 5966.

Dans l'attente de faire votre connaissance, je vous prie, Monsieur le Directeur, de bien vouloir agréer l'expression de mes sentiments les plus dévoués.

Signature
[followed by your surname (capital letters) and forenames printed in full].
BUTTERWORTH, Sophie Jane (Mlle)

4 CROUS application form

The following CROUS form, or similar, will be sent to you following an initial Internet application. It is in your interest to complete the form as fully as possible since the information given will determine your chances of gaining accommodation in your chosen university(ies). You will, of course, be required to substantiate the accuracy of the details provided.

A FOURNIR EN PLUS: 1 enveloppe non timbrée au nom et adresse de l'étudiant(e). En plus, (pour le logement uniquement), une enveloppe 16x22,5 sans adresse.

Pour les réadmissions, joindre obligatoirement la fiche de réadmission.

Un RIB au nom de l'étudiant. OBLIGATOIRE: joindre votre certificat de scolarité 2004–2005 et la fiche de renseignements ci-jointe.

SCOLARITE[1]

NIVEAU D' ETUDE plus haut atteint à ce jour:[1]

VŒUX d' étude et demandes d'aide :
1 – Académie: Clermont-Frnd , UFR Lettres Sc. Humaines (Clermont)
          Cursus licence

2 – Académie:

3 – Académie:

4 – Académie:

5 – Académie:

6 – Académie:

7 – Académie:

SITUATIONS PARTICULIERES[2]

Nombre d'enfants à la charge de vos parents[3] ....

    étudiants dans le supérieur, vous excepté ....

    non étudiants dans le supérieur, vous excepté[4]...................................

Nombre d'enfants à votre charge[3] ....

Votre père ou mère élève seul(e) un ou plusieurs enfants...........................

Vous avez interrompu vos études pour maternité en 2004–2005 ....

Vous êtes atteint d'une incapacité permanente ....

Vous souffrez d' un handicap physique nécessitant l'aide d'une tierce personne

Vous êtes pupille de la nation ou bénéficiaire d'une protection particulière[5] ...

RESSOURCES DE LA FAMILLE

Profession du chef de famille:

REVENU BRUT GLOBAL:

ETAT CIVIL et ADRESSE(S)

Numéro de Dossier:

                            Nom:

Date de naissance: Prénom:

                            Adresse familiale:[7]

Situation de famille:[6]

Adresse personnelle:

NATIONALITE: votre pays d'origine:[8]

                  votre situation:[9]

Numéro national (INE/BEA):[10]

COLOCATION

Si vous avez sollicité un logement à plusieurs, et si vous confirmez cette demande, indiquez pour votre ou vos colocataire(s):[11]

Numéro de dossier social étudiant: Nom et prénom:

Téléphone Code connection: Dossier édité le:

VOTRE CURRICULUM (à compléter ou corriger)[12]

Année d'obtention du Baccalauréat ou titre equivalent: Mention:

Inscriptions Universitaires:	Niveau d'étude: bac+ ?	Etablissement: Discipline ou autre situation:	Etiez-vous? Boursier[13]	Logé en Résidence Universitaire[13]
2001–2002				
2002–2003				
2003–2004				
2004–2005				

Notes:

1 Scolarité: you may apply to up to seven institutions of higher education, though it is more usual to limit your selection to two or three. After NIVEAU D'ETUDE indicate your current year of study in French terms, e.g. Bac+1, Bac+2 etc.

2 Situations particulières: personal circumstances

3 A la charge de: dependent upon

4 Non étudiants dans le supérieur: not qualifying for French 'student' status, i.e. salaried or over 26 years of age

5 Protection particulière: indicate any special status

6 Situation de famille: marital status

7 Adresse familiale: permanent address

8 Pays d'origine: country of birth

9 Votre situation: current status, e.g. étudiant(e) de nationalité britannique

10 Numéro national: attributed in response to request for CROUS application

11 Colocation: French students are being encouraged to share accommodation

12 Votre curriculum: academic profile to date in your country of origin

13 These columns relate only to France.

5 University applications

5.1 Course application form (including L3 and higher)
See pages 334–5 over

Université
Victor Segalen
Bordeaux 2

N° de dossier : 06/   [1]
DAERI-form1

Demande d'admission préalable 2006 – 2007
sauf Médecine Spécialisée(AFS-AFSA-FFI européen)
et 1ᵉ année d'Université

> La délivrance d'une demande d'admission ne constitue pas une autorisation d'inscription.
> L'autorisation d'inscription ne sera délivrée qu'après étude du dossier complet et décision de la Commission Pédagogique.
> L'autorisation d'inscription n'est valable que pour une année universitaire.

Identification du Candidat
(écrire en lettres majuscules)

☐ Mr   ☐ Mle   ☐ Mme *indiquez également votre nom avant mariage (...)*

Nom : ....   Né(e) le : __ / __ /**19**__

Prénom : ....   Nationalité : ....

Adresse du candidat pour toute correspondance :

N°, rue ....

Résidence, Bât, Esc ....

Ville : ....   Pays : ....

Courriel : [2] ....

Nom de l'Etablissement d'origine : ....

Ville : ....   Pays : ....

Site internet : http//www ....   Fax : ( ) ....

La demande d'admission est présentée dans le cadre :

☐ d'une convention   ☐ d'un échange Erasmus   ☐ à titre individuel ou (ECTS)

▶ *Indiquez la formation demandée ((cf site internet de l'Université : www.u-bordeaux2.fr/ formations)*

Discipline : [3] ....
(ex : Sociologie)

Année demandée : .Bac + ...   Diplôme : ....
     (ex Bac +4)   (ex : Master 1)

Durée du séjour : ☐ année universitaire
                 ☐ < à l'année universitaire : du .... au .... = ...mois
                              (ex : du 01/10/2006 au 15/04/2007)

N° de dossier : 06/
DAERI-form1

| Niveau linguistique en Français |
4

❖ Votre niveau en Français est :   ☐ débutant   ☐ faible   ☐ moyen   ☐ courant
❖ Vous êtes titulaire d'un diplôme de la langue française :   ☐ oui   ☐ non
   si oui, précisez :   ☐ DELF 1er Degré   ☐ DELF 2e Degré   ☐ DALF
❖ Vous êtes titulaire du TCF (Test de Connaissance en Français)* :   ☐ oui   ☐ non
   *ce test peut être exigé pour l'acceptation de la candidature (pays francophone excepté)
   si oui : date d'obtention : /___ /___ /___ / niveau obtenu : .... note : ..../

| Moyens financiers durant la formation |
5

Moyens financiers dont disposera le candidat durant sa formation en France :

☐ Bourse : organisme : ....}
☐ Ressources personnelles : ....} montant * : .... €/mois
☐ Autres (précisez) : ....} (* convertir en euros si monnaie différente)

| Logement |

☐ Vous souhaitez un logement universitaire, vous devez **obligatoirement** compléter le formulaire de
   demande de logement universitaire via internet : www.crous-bordeaux.fr [6]

☐ Vous ne souhaitez pas un logement universitaire, consultez le site internet de l'Université Victor
   Segalen Bordeaux 2 : www.sri.u-bordeaux2.fr/international/

Date limite de dépôt de candidature (sauf demandes Erasmus) [7]

31 mars 2006 (cachet de la poste faisant foi)

Erasmus - dates limites de dépôt de candidature -
- **15 mai 2006** pour les mobilités du 1er semestre (sept à février)
- **30 novembre 2006** pour les mobilités du 2e semestre (mars à août)

Partie réservée à l'Université Victor Segalen Bordeaux 2	
Avis de la Commission Pédagogique	
	Date et signature
Pr	

Notes:
Forms should be completed in capital letters. Married women should also give their maiden name, where specified.

1 N° de dossier: supplied in response to initial online registration, and request for the Demande d'admission préalable form

2 Courriel: e-mail address

3 Discipline: this should be chosen from those listed on the website of the university concerned, and the desired year of entry should be specified in terms of the normal year of post-baccalauréate study this represents (for example, in terms of LMD, licence 3 = bac+3, master 1 = bac+4). You should also specify, as indicated, whether your study abroad will be for a full academic year, or from date X to date Y.

4 Niveau linguistique en Français: be frank about your achievement here. If you already have a qualifying certificate, indicate the details. If you have taken the TCF (Test de Connaissance du Français) organized by your embassy, give details; if not, you will in all probability be required to take it.

5 Moyens financiers durant la formation: specify in euros the sums available to you, and their sources (student loan, etc.), bearing in mind that the recommended minimum sums for a student living in France in 2006 was €700 per month.

6 Logement: the form indicates that if you wish to apply for university accommodation you must do so via the website specified; if you do not, you should consult the alternative website for options.

7 Please observe the deadlines specified, and obtain certificates of posting, as the date of posting will be accepted as proof.

A Learning Agreement (*contrat pédagogique* or *contrat d'études* – see Appendix 5.4) should be included by all who are not seeking to register for a French qualification as the outcome of their stay. Each module chosen should be listed with an indication of its orientation (theoretical or practical) and credit value. Some room must be available for subsequent modifications in the light of clashes, or the discontinuation of modules.

The completed Learning Agreement should be signed, dated and stamped by the appropriate accredited representative(s) of the home institution.

All completed applications and their signed summary sheets (*récapitulatif*) should be accompanied by:

● photocopies of your baccalaureate or equivalent qualification giving access to university study;

● photocopies of any university qualification obtained;

● photocopy of some official document verifying nationality (e.g. birth certificate);

● photocopies of documents tracing your university career and marks obtained; and

● the Learning Agreement in duplicate.

Non-ERASMUS candidates should also add:
- certification of your financial resources (e.g. grant statement, or loan agreement, plus bank statements for yourself and your guarantor);
- proof of your competence in French (qualifying certificate, or results of the TCF); and
- any other documents relevant to your application.

5.2 Requesting recognition of qualifications

In order to gain admission to a French university, you will need to establish that you have already achieved an equivalent qualification to the *baccalauréat*, and that the qualification that you hold would entitle you to enter a university in your own country (*titres admis en équivalence du baccalauréat*). Chapter 5.1 has already explained what you will need to take for this purpose. However, it may also be the case, if you are a 'free mover', that you wish to enter the course at a level other than the first or second year. If this is so, you will need to request that your existing qualifications be recognized as sufficient to excuse you from the relevant part of the course (*validation d'acquis*). To obtain such *équivalences*, you will need to apply for the appropriate form from the Bureau de Scolarité. It is advisable to start this process well before you arrive (e.g. at the end of the previous academic year). A normal formula might be as follows.

M/Mlle (your name)

à

Monsieur/Madame le Chef du Service
de la Scolarité
(Full address)

Birmingham, le 12 janvier 2006

Monsieur/Madame le Chef de Service

J'ai l'honneur de vous informer que je voudrais venir étudier l'année prochaine en L3/Master/Doctorat/[1] à l'Université de ... Compte tenu des conseils donnés par le Ministère de l'Education Nationale, je vous écris directement pour demander la validation de mes acquis, afin de pouvoir poser ma candidature. J'ai l'honneur, donc, de vous demander de me faire parvenir le dossier qui me permettra de faire la demande d'équivalence ou d'aménagement d'études en vue de mon inscription.

Je joins sous ce pli deux coupons-réponse internationaux pour faciliter cette démarche.

Je vous prie, Monsieur/Madame, de bien vouloir agréer l'expression de mes sentiments respectueux.

Signature
followed by name and forename in full.

[1] The text should be modified according to individual circumstances.

When you have received and sent back the completed form, with the necessary documents attached, you should append the appropriate version of the letter below.

M/Mlle (your name)

à

Monsieur/Madame le Président
de (name of the University)

Birmingham, le 15 février 2006

Monsieur/Madame le Président,

J'ai l'honneur de solliciter de votre haute bienveillance (1) l'équivalence de mes diplômes or (2) un aménagement d'études en vue de mon inscription à l'UFR de …

Je joins sous ce pli la photocopie, et la traduction, des titres britanniques/américains etc., admis en équivalence du baccalauréat, que j'ai obtenus en 20.. (give year) et qui m'ont permis de m'inscrire à l'Université de … (give name), ainsi qu'une attestation détaillée et traduction, certifiées conformes, des cours déjà suivis à l'Université où je suis inscrit(e) depuis un/deux/trois ans.

Veuillez croire, Monsieur/Madame le Président, à l'expression de ma haute considération.

Signature
followed by your name and forename printed in full.

(1) and (2) It is probable that only one of these will apply. The appropriate form will have made this clear. Modify the text accordingly.

In all cases, ensure that you include all the documentation specified on the *dossier de demande d'équivalence/d'aménagement d'études*.

Whenever your correspondence invites a reply, always enclose a self-addressed envelope and at least one international reply coupon.

5.3 *Confirming your place at a French university*

When you hear that you have been accepted by one of the French universities to which you applied (the *réponse de la première/deuxième université*), you will be required to confirm your acceptance of the offer before 31 July at the latest. Keep this notification as it will be needed when you register at your French university, but return a photocopy with your letter of acceptance (see model below). This letter should be addressed to Monsieur/Madame le Chef du Service de la Scolarité in the UFR in which you are to register.

M/Mlle (your name)
à
Monsieur/Madame le Chef du Service
de la Scolarité/Service des Relations Internationales
UFR de (full address)

Birmingham, le 20 juin 2006

Monsieur/Madame le Chef de Service,

J'ai l'honneur de vous accuser réception de votre lettre du 10 juin dernier qui confirme que ma demande d'inscription à l'UFR/l'Université de ('Faculty' title/ name of University) a été acceptée.

Je suis très heureux/heureuse de vous informer que je m'inscrirai pour l'année 2006–07 et que je me présenterai pendant la période des inscriptions indiquée dans votre communication. Je joins sous ce pli la photocopie de votre réponse à ma demande d'inscription préalable.

Je ne manquerai pas de vous informer de la date précise de mon arrivée à (town).

Je vous prie, Monsieur/Madame, de bien vouloir agréer l'expression de mes sentiments respectueux.

Signature
followed by name and forename printed in full.

5.4 *Learning agreement* (contrat pédagogique *or* contrat d'études)

Université
Victor Segalen
Bordeaux 2

N° de dossier : 06/
DAERI-form1

CONTRAT PEDAGOGIQUE

<u>Document à compléter uniquement par les candidats **en mobilité** (Erasmus, ECTS par ex) **ne s'inscrivant pas à un diplôme** de l'Université Victor Segalen Bordeaux 2, mais venant suivre une période d'étude qui sera validée par son Université d'origine. Il est obligatoire car indispensable à la validation du parcours pédagogique effectué.</u>

✳ Les étudiants en Médecine 2ᵉ cycle doivent compléter un contrat pédagogique spécifique sur le site :
   www.sri.u-bordeaux2.fr/international/médecine 2e cycle

Nom de l'étudiant :

Choix des enseignements	Théoriques	Pratiques ou Stages	Nombre de crédits

Date et signature du candidat

Approbation du contrat pédagogique par l'Etablissement d'origine

L'Université approuve le programme pédagogique de M ....

Avis motivé et recommandations particulières relatives aux objectifs pédagogiques souhaités ou à atteindre :
....
....
....
....

Pr : ....   Pr : ....
   Doyen, Président, Recteur d'Université   Responsable de la Formation
   (rayer les mentions inutiles)   *(rayer les mentions inutiles)*

Date et signature   *Date et signature*

Nom et cachet de l'Etablissement d'origine

Avenant au contrat d'études ECTS
Annex to the ECTS learning agreement

Année académique 20   /20

Nom de l'étudiant
Name of student

Etablissement   Pays
d'accueil

Modifications au programme d'études initial

Changes to the original proposed study programme (to be filled in only if appropriate)

Code du cours *Course unit code*	Titre du cours *Course title*	Quadrimestre *Semester*	Cours supprimé *Deleted course*	Cours ajouté *Added course*	Crédits ECTS *ECTS credits*
			☐	☐	☐
			☐	☐	☐
			☐	☐	☐
			☐	☐	☐
			☐	☐	☐
			☐	☐	☐

Signature de l'étudiant...........................   Date
Student's signature   Date

Institution d'origine *Je confirme que les modifications au programme d'études énumerées ci-dessus sont approuvées.*

Sending institution   I confirm that the above-listed changes to the initially agreed programme of study are approved.

Coordonnateur académique de l'étudiant *Student's academic coordinator*	Nom: *Name*	Signature: .... *Signature*
	Date: *Date*	Cachet *Seal*

Institution d'accueil *Je confirme que les modifications au programme d'études énumerées ci-dessus sont approuvées.*

Receiving institution   I confirm that the above-listed changes to the initially agreed programme of study are approved.

Coordonnateur académique de l'étudiant *Student's academic coordinator*	Nom: *Name*	Signature: .... *Signature*
	Date: *Date*	Cachet *Seal*

6 **Accommodation**

6.1 *Websites*

The following represent a series of well-known websites that may help in the search for accommodation. Some of the commercial sites may require a subscription before they will give up the information you are seeking (addresses, etc.).

For general information on the legislative position for tenants and landlords, see the website of the Association Nationale pour l'Information sur le Logement: www.anil.org

For detailed information and addresses of lets:

- www.123immo.com
- www.fnaim.fr
- www.adele.org
- www.immostreet.com
- www.alouer.fr
- www.leclubetudiant.com
- www.appartager.com
- www.bordeaux.fr (*)
- www.capcampus.com
- www.mapiaule.com
- www.bonjour.fr
- www.pap.fr
- www.explorimmo.com
- www.paruvendu.com
- www.fac-habitat.com
- www.seloger.com
- www.figaroetudiant.com
- www.unmw.asso.com

* Modify with name of relevant town/city

Once accommodation has been secured, the following websites will help with the connection of utilities (gas, electricity, telephone):

- www.edf.fr/1i/Accueil.html
- www.gazdefrance.fr
- http://francetelecom.com/fr

6.2 *Common abbreviations used in advertisements*

The following are the most common abbreviations you are likely to come across in advertisements in French newspapers, when looking for rooms/studios/flats, etc.

à déb.: *à débattre* – negotiable
ag. s'abst: *agences s'abstenir* – no agencies
ap.: *après* – after (6 o'clock)
appart.: *appartement* – apartment, flat

av.: *avec* – with

caut.: *caution* – deposit

cc/tcc: *toutes charges comprises* – all inclusive (NB **cc** or **c.c.** also means *chauffage central* –central heating)

ch.: *chambre* – bedroom

chauff.: *chauffage* – heating

chauff.coll.: *chauffage collectif* – communal heating

chauff.ind.: *chauffage individuel* – separate heating

ch.c.: *chauffage central* – central heating

ch./chge: *charges* – service charges

cuis.: *cuisine* – kitchen

cuis.équip.: *cuisine équipée* – fully fitted kitchen

ds: *dans* – in

écr.jrnl: *écrire au journal* – write to the newspaper

env.: *environ* – about

état nf.: *état neuf* – as new

excel.ét.: *excellent état* – in excellent condition

except.: *exceptionnel* – exceptional

gaz: *chauffage au gaz* – gas central heating

gge/gar.: *garage* – garage

grds: *grand(e)s* – large

HB/hor.bur.: *heures/horaires de bureau* – office hours (normally between 8 and 12, 2 and 5)

HR: *heures des repas* – at meal times (normally between 12 and 2, 7 and 9)

imm./im.: *immeuble* – block (of flats)

imméd.: *immédiatement* – available immediately

ind.: *individuel* – single

kitch.: *kitchenette* – cooking area

kitch.équip.: *kitchenette équipée* – fully fitted kitchen area

lib. de suite: *libre tout de suite* – available immediately

ll: *machine à laver/lave-linge* – washing machine

lv: *machine à laver la vaisselle/lave-vaisselle* – dishwasher

mais.indiv.: *maison individuelle* – detached house

mens.: *mensuel* – per month

ns.: *nous* – we

p.: *pièce* – room

p.350: *poste 350* – extension 350

park.: *parking* – parking space

part.: *particulier* – private individual

part.à part: *particulier à particulier* – private let

poss.cuis.: *possibilité de faire la cuisine* – cooking facilities available

pr./prox.: *près de/à proximité de* – close to

quart./quartier résid./quartier univ.: *quartier/quartier résidential/quartier universitaire* – neighbourhood/ residential area/university area

quinz./sem.: *quinzaine/semaine* – fortnightly/weekly

rés.: *résidence* – apartment block/complex
s'adr.: *s'adresser à* – contact
sdb: *salle de bain* – bathroom
stand.: *de bon standing* – desirable
tt/tout conf./tt cft: *tout confort* – all mod cons
t.b.é: *très bon état* – in very good condition
urgt/URG: *urgent* – urgently

7 Embassies and Consulates General

British Embassy
Ambassade de Grande Bretagne, 35 rue du Faubourg St Honoré, 75383 Paris
    Cedex 08. Tel: 01 44 51 31 00
Consulats-Généraux de Grande Bretagne:
- 18 bis, rue d'Anjou, 75008 Paris. Tel: 01 44 51 31 02
- 353 bd du Président Wilson, 33073 Bordeaux Cedex. Tel: 05 57 22 21 10
- 11 square Dutilleul, 59800 Lille. Tel: 03 20 12 82 72
- 24 rue Childebert, 69002 Lyon. Tel: 04 72 77 81 70
- 24 avenue de Prado, 13006 Marseille. Tel: 04 91 15 72 10

American Embassy
American Embassy, 2 av. Gabriel, 75382 Paris Cedex 08. Tel: 01 43 12 22 22
American Embassy: Office of American Services, 2 rue Saint Florentin, 75001
    Paris 08
US Consulates General:
- 12 place Varian Fry, 13086 Marseille. Tel: 04 91 54 92 00
- (Consular agency) 7 av. Gustave V, 3rd floor, 06000 Nice. Tel: 04 93 88 89 55
- 15 av. d'Alsace, 67082 Strasbourg. Tel: 03 88 35 31 04

Australian Embassy
Ambassade d'Australie, 4 rue Jean Rey, 75724 Paris Cedex 15. Tel: 01 40 59 33 00

Canadian Embassy
Ambassade du Canada, 35 av. Montaigne, 75008 Paris. Tel: 01 44 43 29 00
Consulat de Canada: 30 av. Emile Zola, 59000 Lille. Tel: 03 20 14 05 78

New Zealand Embassy
7 ter rue Léonard de Vinci, 75116 Paris. Tel: 01 45 01 43 44

Republic of Ireland Embassy
2–4 rue Rude, 75116 Paris. Tel: 01 44 17 32 85

Select bibliography and internet addresses

Significant legislation on higher education in France

Loi No 68–978 du 12 novembre 1968 d'orientation de l'enseignement supérieur (Journal Officiel, 13 novembre 1968).

Loi No 84–52 du 26 janvier 1984 (Réforme Savary sur l'enseignement supérieur), Journal officiel, no. 3, 27 janvier 1984.

Loi d'orientation sur l'éducation, Loi No 89–486 du juillet 1989 (B O spécial, no. 4, 31 août 1989).

CNOUS publications

Visit the CNOUS website (www.cnous.fr); under the heading 'Etudiants Etrangers' on the home page, you will find information on all aspects of going to France to study as a foreign student.

CROUS publications

The various CROUS publish their own guides under a variety of titles such as *Guide de l'étudiant*, *CROUS en poche*, *INFOCROUS* or *Labyrinthe*. These can be obtained from the local CROUS offices or can be found on the local CROUS websites. See Part III for the address of the individual CROUS.

Student publications

Some student groups or associations publish their own guides, under titles such as *Le Dahu* (Grenoble), *L'Indic* (Tours) or *Le Petit Paumé* in Lyon. There is normally an associated website.

CIDJ website: courses for foreign students

For information on *Les cours de français pour étrangers*, visit the following website:
www.cidj.asso.fr/contents/309092003165648.pdf

Official (French) ministry websites

For information on language courses for foreign students (*le français langue étrangère*), visit www.culture.gouv.fr/culture/dglf/politique-langue/frcs-lang-etrang.html

For information on the LMD reform, visit the following websites:
- www.education.gouv.fr/sup/lmd/default.htm
- www.education.gouv.fr/sup/lmd/presente/action.htm
- www.onisep.fr

For information on the *universités européennes d'été* (created in 2000) visit the following websites:
- www.education.gouv.fr/sup/appel_univ.htm
- www.education.gouv.fr/sup/lmd/presente/action.htm

For information on the Bologna Process (the full texts of ministerial agreements), visit www.bologna-bergen2005.no

University publications

Each UFR publishes its own handbook under a variety of titles such as *Guide pédagogique*, *Guide de l'étudiant* and so on. University websites (see individual entries in Part III) contain information on courses and have sections devoted to *étudiants étrangers*.

Additionally, many SRI produce a useful handbook specifically aimed at foreign students, under such titles as *Guide d'accueil des étudiants étrangers* and *Guide d'informations générales*.

Background books on France

(a) *Travel and tourist information*

Abram, B., Blackmore, R., Dodd, J., Benson, A., Cathos, B., 2005, *Rough Guide to France (Rough Guides)*, London, Rough Guides Ltd.
Fisher, R.I.C. (ed.), 2004 *Fodor France*, New York, Fodor.
Let's Go: The Budget Guide to France, 2006, New York, St Martin's Press.
Michelin 2004 Red Guide France, 2004, Clermont-Ferrand, Editions des Voyages
Robertson, I., 1997, *Blue Guide France*, New York, W.W. Norton.

Trombetta, M. (ed.), *AA Baedeker's France*, 1997, Baskingstoke, AA Baedeker's Publishing.
Tucker, A., 1994, *The Berlitz Travellers Guide to France*, New York, Hungry Minds Inc.

(b) History, culture and society
Alexander, M. (ed.), 1999, *French History Since Napoleon*, London, Arnold.
Aplin, R. and Montchamp, J. (eds), 1999, *A Dictionary of Contemporary France*, London, Fitzroy Dearborn.
Ardagh, J., 2000, *France in the New Century*, Harmondsworth, Penguin.
Cook, M. (ed.), 1993, *French Culture Since 1945*, London, Longman.
Flower, J. E. (ed.), 1997, *France Today*, London, Hodder Arnold.
Forbes, J., Hewlett, N. and Nectoux, F. (eds), 2001, *Contemporary France. Essays and Texts on Politics, Economics and Society*, 2nd edn, London, Longman.
Frémy D. and M., *Quid 2005*, Paris, Robert Laffont.
Hughes, A. and Reader, K. (eds), 1998, *Encyclopedia of Contemporary French Culture*, London and New York, Routledge.
INSEE, *France, portrait social 2004–2005*, 2004, Paris, INSEE.
Kelly, M., 2001, *French Culture and Society (The Essentials)*, London, Hodder Arnold.
Mermet, G., 2005, *Francoscopie. Pour comprendre les Français*, 2004, Paris, Larousse.
Renaut, A., 1995, *Les Révolutions de l'université. Essai sur la modernisation de la culture*, Paris, Calmann-Lévy.

Articles
Cousins, R., Hallmark, R. and Pickup, I., 'Preparing for the Year Abroad: Savoir-faire or laissez faire?', *French Studies Bulletin*, no.36, autumn 1990, pp. 14–16.
Cousins, R., Hallmark, R. and Pickup, I., 'Evaluating Study Residence Abroad', *Higher Education Quarterly*, vol. 36, no.1, winter 1992, pp. 124–7.
Firth, K., 'French Universities: The Difficult Road to Reform', *Modern Languages*, vol. 70, no. 1, March 1989, pp. 82–97.

French periodicals
L'Etudiant and *Le Monde de l'Education* are monthly publications which provide invaluable information on the French educational system, reforms, new legislation and the courses available in higher education in France. The following is of particular interest:
L'Etudiant. Le guide 2006 des études supérieures (hors série) 2006.

Studying, working and living in France

(a) *Books and articles*

Bariet, A. and Rollot, O. (adapted by Archer, W.), 1993, *Studying in Europe* (Student Helpbooks), Cambridge, CRAC.

Carroll, R., 1987, *Evidences Invisibles*, Paris, Seuil.

CIEE, 1994, *Work, Study, Travel Abroad: The Whole World Handbook*, New York, St Martins Press.

(La) Documentation Française, 2004, *Dossier 'Université, Recherche'* in *Regards sur l'Actualité*, no. 301, mai 2004, Paris, La Documentation Française.

Hallmark, R.E., 1998, 'Universities' (pp. 541–3) and 'Educational elitism: the *grandes écoles*' (pp. 180–1) in Hughes, A. and Reader, K. (eds), *Encyclopedia of Contemporary French Culture*, London and New York, Routledge.

Hempshell, M., 1993, *How to Get a Job in France: Guide to Employment Opportunities and Contacts*, Plymouth, How to Books Ltd.

Jones, R., 1994, *How to Teach Abroad: A Guide to Opportunities Worldwide*, Plymouth, How to Books Ltd.

ONISEP, 2004, *Après le bac: le guide des études supérieures 2004*, Paris, Les Dossiers ONISEP.

ONISEP, 2005, *Université, mode d'emploi*, Paris, ONISEP.

Penrith, D, 2005, *Jobs and Careers Abroad*, Oxford, Vacation Work Publications, 12th edition.

Prevost Logan, N., 1993, *How to Live and Work in France*, Plymouth, How to Books Ltd.

Pybus, V., 2005, *Live and Work in France*, Oxford, Vacation Work Publications (available to purchase online, at a discount, on www.vacationwork.co.uk).

Toulemonde, B. (ed.), 2003, *Le Système éducatif en France*, Paris, Les Notices de la Documentation Française.

Tronquoy, P. (ed.), 1999, *Le Système éducatif*, Paris, Les Cahiers Français, no 285.

Withers, A. and Bingham, D. (eds), 2005, *The Gap-Year Guidebook*, Great Glemham, Peridot Press, 13th edition.

Woodward, D. (ed.), 2005, *Summer Jobs Abroad 1993*, Oxford, Vacation Work Publications.

(b) *Major websites*

EduFrance: www.edufrance.fr (offers foreign students advice on studying, working and finding accommodation in France. Postal address: EduFrance, 173 bd Saint-Germain, 75006, Paris).

Egide: visit the website www.egide.asso.fr/fr/guide to access Egide's *Guide de l'étudiant étranger.*

ONISEP: www.onisep.fr (an invaluable source of information on higher education in France. It has a bookshop at 168 bd du Montparnasse, 75014 Paris).

Resort Jobs: for summer jobs visit www.resortjobs.co.uk

English reference works

Banker, A.K., 2004, *Advanced Learners English Dictionary*, London, Collins Cobuild.

Biber, D., Leech, G., and Conrad, S., 2002, *The Longman Student Grammar of Spoken and Written English*, London, Longman.

Blanchard, M., 2005, *English Grammar*, London, Collins Cobuild.

Burt, A., 2004, *Quick Solutions to Common Errors in English: An A–Z Guide to Spelling, Pronunciation and Grammar*, Plymouth, How to Books.

Leech, G., Cruickshank, R., Ivanic, R., 2001, *An A–Z of English Grammar and Usage*, London, Longman.

Soanes, S., and Stevenson, A., 2003, *Oxford Dictionary of English*, Oxford, Oxford University Press.

Index

Note. As a general rule, headings and sub-headings which appear in the Contents have been excluded from this index; page numbers in italics refer to illustrations.

Index

Note: As a general rule, headings and sub-headings which appear in the **Contents** have been excluded from this Index; page numbers in italics refer to illustrations